PERGAMON INTERNATIONAL LIBRARY
of Science, Technology, Engineering and Social Studies
*The 1000-volume original paperback library in aid of education,
industrial training and the enjoyment of leisure*
Publisher: Robert Maxwell, M.C.

MEAT SCIENCE

GW00401667

THIRD EDITION

THE PERGAMON TEXT BOOK
INSPECTION COPY SERVICE

An inspection copy of any book published in the Pergamon International Library will gladly be
sent to academic staff without obligation for their consideration for course adoption or
recommendation. Copies may be retained for a period of 60 days from receipt and returned if not
suitable. When a particular title is adopted or recommended for adoption for class use and the
recommendation results in a sale of 12 or more copies, the inspection copy may be retained with
our compliments. If after examination the lecturer decides that the book is not suitable for
adoption but would like to retain it for his personal library, then a discount of 10% is allowed on
the invoiced price. The Publishers will be pleased to receive suggestions for revised editions and
new titles to be published in this important International Library.

Other Titles of Interest

BIGWOOD E J
Protein and Amino Acid Functions

BIRCH G G *et al*
Food Science 2nd Edition

DILLON J L
The Analysis of Response in Crop and Livestock Production
2nd Edition

FIENNES R N
The Biology of Nutrition

GAMAN P D & SHERRINGTON K B
The Science of Food
An Introduction to Food Science, Nutrition and Microbiology

MORTON R A
Fat-Soluble Vitamins

NELSON R H
An Introduction to Feeding Farm Livestock 2nd Edition

PARKER W H
Health and Disease in Farm Animals 2nd Edition

PRESTON T R & WILLIS H B
Intensive Beef Production 2nd Edition

RAO K P N & SINCLAIR H M
Food Consumption and Planning

MEAT SCIENCE

by

R. A. LAWRIE

Ph.D., D.Sc., Sc.D., F.R.S.E., F.R.I.C., F.I.F.S.T.

Professor of Food Science, University of Nottingham
Formerly Head, Meat Biochemistry Group,
Low Temperature Research Station, Cambridge

THIRD EDITION

PERGAMON PRESS

OXFORD · NEW YORK · TORONTO · SYDNEY · PARIS · FRANKFURT

U.K.	Pergamon Press Ltd., Headington Hill Hall, Oxford OX3 0BW, England
U.S.A.	Pergamon Press Inc., Maxwell House, Fairview Park, Elmsford, New York 10523, U.S.A.
CANADA	Pergamon of Canada, Suite 104, 150 Consumers Road, Willowdale, Ontario M2 JIP9, Canada
AUSTRALIA	Pergamon Press (Aust.) Pty. Ltd., P.O. Box 544, Potts Point, N.S.W. 2011, Australia
FRANCE	Pergamon Press SARL, 24 rue des Ecoles, 75240 Paris, Cedex 05, France
FEDERAL REPUBLIC OF GERMANY	Pergamon Press GmbH, 6242 Kronberg-Taunus, Pferdstrasse 1, Federal Republic of Germany

Copyright © 1979 R. A. Lawrie

First English edition 1966
Reprinted 1968
Spanish edition 1967
German edition 1969
Japanese edition 1971
Russian edition 1973
Second English edition 1974
Reprinted 1975
Reprinted 1976 with corrections
Second Spanish edition 1977
Third English edition 1979

British Library Cataloguing in Publication Data
Lawrie, Ralston Andrew
Meat science.—3rd ed.— (Pergamon international library).
1. Meat
I. Title   II. Series
641.3′6   TX373   78–40300

ISBN 0-08-023173-X (Hardcover)
ISBN 0-08-023172-1 (Flexicover)

Printed and bound at William Clowes & Sons Limited Beccles and London

CONTENTS

PREFACE TO THE THIRD EDITION

SCIENTIFIC investigations in areas relevant to our understanding of meat quality continue vigorously. Thus, there have been significant discoveries on the nature, arrangement and reactions of the myofibrillar and collagenous proteins of muscular tissue *in vivo* and on their behaviour when muscle becomes meat post-mortem. Concomitantly, means of applying basic findings on muscle to the handling of meat in practice have also been developing. Such have been reflected in new or amended procedures pre-slaughter, during abattoir operations and in subsequent preservation, storage and cooking. Some findings, being particularly unexpected, have made obligatory the abandonment of what seemed firmly-established and widely-accepted views. They have also made it essential to prepare a third edition of *Meat Science* after a considerably shorter period than elapsed between publication of the first and second editions.

Although, technologically, there is ample reason for this development, it might be thought unrealistic in some other respects. Thus, apparent correlations between the incidence of cardiovascular diseases or carcinoma of the digestive tract and the habit of meat-eating are currently prevalent. These may have some validity; but similar correlations can be established between such diseases and numerous other factors which have not the remotest connection with diet. Moreover, the large number of human beings who eat and enjoy meat with apparent impunity into old age, and the not insignificant few who do so as healthy centenarians, can neither be ignored nor simply dismissed. It is evident that much has yet to be learned about the nutritional requirements of the individual and of the various organs of the body whose proper functioning is essential for well-being.

Criticism of meat animals, because they are much less efficient in producing protein than either plants or micro-organisms, is also current; and it is soundly based. But, equally, it should be acknowledged that two-thirds of the world's usable land surface cannot support crops and is too inaccessible for the complex infrastructure needed for microbial fermentation factories. There is no means, other than by the ruminant, of converting the sparse vegetation of these predominating regions into a highly nourishing and organoleptically desirable commodity for human consumption.

Meat animals will—and indeed must—remain a source of food for man far into the future, even if less meat becomes available for the individual. The need to ensure maximum satisfaction in eating and in nutritional benefit from the meat which is produced scarcely requires emphasis; but it makes equally essential continuing scientific study of the commodity

In this volume, and in accordance with policy, the subject has been presented again in the manner adopted in the first and second editions.

I continue to be grateful for the helpful comments of many colleagues both in this country and abroad; and for the opportunity given me to see recent work before publication.

Sutton Bonington   R. A. LAWRIE

PREFACE TO THE FIRST EDITION

THE scientific study of food has emerged as a discipline in its own right since the end of the 1939–45 war. This development reflects an increasing awareness of the fact that the eating quality of food commodities is determined by a logical sequence of circumstances starting at conception of the animal, or at germination of the seed, and culminating in consumption. From this point of view, the food scientist is inevitably involved in various aspects of chemistry and biochemistry, genetics and microbiology, botany and zoology, physiology and anatomy, agriculture and horticulture, nutrition and medicine, public health and psychology.

Apart from the problems of preserving the attributes of eating quality and of nutritive value, it seems likely that food science will become increasingly concerned with enhancing the biological value of traditional foods and with elaborating entirely new sources of nourishment, as the pressure of world population grows. Moreover, a closer association of food science and medicine can be anticipated as another development. This will arise not only in relation to the cause or remedy of already accepted diseases, but also in relation to many subclinical syndromes which are as yet unappreciated. Such may well prevent us as individuals and as a species from attaining the efficiency and length of life of which our present evolutionary form may be capable.

Meat is one of the major commodities with which food science is concerned and is the subject of the present volume. It would not be feasible to consider all aspects of this vast topic. Instead, an attempt has been made to outline the essential basis of meat in a sequence of phases. These comprise, in turn, the origin and development of meat animals, the structural and chemical elaboration of muscular tissue, the conversion of muscle to meat, the nature of the adverse changes to which meat is susceptible before consumption, the discouragement of such spoilage by various means and, finally, the eating quality. The central theme of this approach is the fact that, because muscles have been diversified in the course of evolution to effect specific types of movement, all meat cannot be alike. It follows that the variability, in its keeping and eating qualities, which has become more apparent to the consumer with the growth of prepackaging methods of display and sale, is not capricious. On the contrary, it is predictable and increasingly controllable.

Those aspects of meat which have not been introduced in the present volume have mainly economic implications and do not involve any concept which is incompatible with the basic approach adopted. They have been thoroughly considered by other authors.

In addition to acknowledging my specific indebtedness to various individuals and organizations, as indicated in the following paragraphs, I should like to express my appreciation of the co-operation of many colleagues in Cambridge and Brisbane during the 15 years when I was associated with them in meat research activities.

I am especially grateful to Mr. D. P. Gatherum and Mr. C. A. Voyle for their considerable help in the preparation of the illustrations. I should also like to thank Prof. J. Hawthorn, F.R.S.E., of the Department of Food Science, University of Strathclyde, for useful criticism.

Sutton Bonington   R. A. LAWRIE

ACKNOWLEDGEMENTS

I wish to thank the following individuals for their kindness in permitting me to reproduce the illustrations indicated:

Prof. M. E. Bailey, Dept. Food Science & Nutrition, University of Missouri, Columbia, U.S.A. (Table 5.5); Mr. J. Barlow, A.R.C. Meat Research Institute, Bristol (Fig. 6.1); Dr. E. M. Barnes, A.R.C. Food Research Institute, Norwich (Fig. 6.6); Dr. J. R. Bendall, A.R.C. Meat Research Institute, Bristol (Fig. 4.2); Dr. M. R. Dickson, Meat Industry Research Institute of New Zealand Inc., Hamilton, New Zealand (Fig. 5.2); Prof. T. Dutson, Texas A & M University, Texas, U.S.A. (Table 3.3); Dr. J. B. Fox, Jr., American Meat Institute Foundation, Chicago, Ill., U.S.A. (Fig. 10.1); Prof. J. Gross, Massachusetts General Hospital, Boston, U.S.A. (Fig. 3.3); Mr. K. C. Hales, Director, Shipowners Refrigerated Cargo Research Council, Cambridge (Fig. 7.2); Prof. R. Hamm, Bundesforschungsanstalt für Fleischwirtschaft, Kulmbach, Germany (Figs. 8.1, 8.2, 8.4 and 10.2); the late Sir John Hammond, F.R.S., Emeritus Reader in Animal Physiology, University of Cambridge (Figs. 1.1, 1.2 and 1.3); Dr. H. E. Huxley, F.R.S., M.R.C. Unit for Molecular Biology, Cambridge (Figs. 3.4(f), 3.4(g), 3.5(a) and 3.5(c)); Mr. N. King, A.R.C. Food Research Institute, Norwich (Fig. 3.4(e)); Prof. G. G. Knappeis, Institute of Neurophysiology, University of Copenhagen, Denmark (Fig. 3.5(e)); Dr. Susan Lowey, Harvard Medical School, U.S.A. (Fig. 3.5(d)); Dr. B. B. Marsh, Muscle Biology Laboratory, University of Wisconsin, U.S.A. (Fig. 4.6); Dr. H. Pálsson, Department of Agriculture, Reykjavik, Iceland (Fig. 2.1); Dr. I. F. Penny (Fig. 8.7), Dr. R. W. Pomeroy (Fig. 3.2), Mr. D. J. Restall (Figs. 3.4(d) and (e)) and Dr. R. K. Scopes (Figs. 4.1 and 5.3), A.R.C. Meat Research Institute, Bristol; Dr. W. J. Scott formerly of Meat Investigations Laboratory, Brisbane, Queensland (Fig. 6.4); the late Dr.

J. G. Sharp, formerly of Low Temperature Research Station, Cambridge (Figs. 3.4(a), 5.4 and 8.3); Dr. M. C. Urbin, Swedish Covenant Hospital, Chicago, Ill., U.S.A. (Fig. 10.3); Mr. C. A. Voyle, A.R.C., Meat Research Institute, Bristol (Figs. 3.4(c), 3.6 and 3.7); and Dr. J. Wismer-Pedersen, Royal Veterinary University, Copenhagen, Denmark (Fig. 3.8).

I am similarly indebted to the following publishers and organizations: Academic Press Inc., New York (Figs. 6.6, 8.1, 8.2, 8.4 and 10.2); Butterworths Scientific Publications, London (Figs. 2.1 and 5.1: Table 4.1); Cambridge University Press (Fig. 3.2); Commonwealth Scientific and Industrial Research Organization, Melbourne, Australia (Figs. 6.4, 7.1, 7.4, 10.4 and 10.5); Food Processing and Packaging, London (Fig. 8.7); Garrard Press, Champaign, Ill., U.S.A. (Food Research) (Fig. 10.1); Heinemann Educational Books Ltd., London (Fig. 4.2); The Controller of Her Majesty's Stationery Office, London (Figs. 6.2, 6.3 and 8.3); Journal of Agricultural Science, Cambridge (Figs. 3.2 and 4.8); Journal of Animal Science, Albany, N.Y., U.S.A. (Fig. 10.3); Journal of Cell Biology, New York (Fig. 3.5(e)); Journal of Food Technology, London (Fig. 7.6); Journal of Molecular Biology, Cambridge (Fig. 3.5(d)); Journal of Physiology, Oxford (Fig. 4.7); Journal of Refrigeration, London (Fig. 7.5); Royal Society, London (Fig. 7.3); Meat Industry Research Institute of New Zealand, Inc. (Fig. 5.2); Science and the American Association for the Advancement of Science, Washington (Figs. 3.5(a) and 3.5(c)); Scientific American Inc., New York (Fig. 3.3) and the Society of Chemical Industry, London (Figs. 4.6, 5.4, 8.5 and 8.6).

CHAPTER 1

INTRODUCTION

1.1. MEAT AND MUSCLE

Meat is defined as the flesh of animals used as food. In practice this definition is restricted to a few dozen of the 3000 mammalian species; but it is often widened to include, as well as the musculature, organs such as liver and kidney, brains and other edible tissues. The bulk of the meat consumed in the United Kingdom is derived from sheep, cattle and pigs: rabbit and hare are, generally, considered separately along with poultry. In some European countries (and elsewhere), however, the flesh of the horse, goat and deer is also regularly consumed; and various other mammalian species are eaten in different parts of the world according to their availability or because of local custom. Thus, for example, the seal and polar bear are important in the diet of the Eskimoes, and the rhinoceros, hippopotamus and elephant in that of certain tribes of Central Africa: the kangaroo is eaten by the Australian aborigines and the whale in Norway and Japan; and, indeed, human flesh is still consumed by cannibals in remote areas (Bjerre, 1956).

Very considerable variability in the eating and keeping quality of meat has always been apparent to the consumer; it has been further emphasized in the last few years by the development of prepackaging methods of display and sale. The view that the variability in the properties of meat might, rationally, reflect systematic differences in the composition and condition of the muscular tissue of which it is the post-mortem aspect is gradually being recognized. An understanding of meat should be based on an appreciation of the fact that muscles are developed and differentiated for definite physiological purposes in response to various intrinsic and extrinsic stimuli.

1.2. THE ORIGIN OF MEAT ANIMALS

The ancestors of sheep, cattle and pigs were undifferentiated from those of man prior to 60 million years ago, when the first mammals appeared on Earth. By 1–2 million years ago the species of man to which we belong (*Homo sapiens*) and the wild ancestors of our domesticated species of sheep, cattle and pigs were probably recognizable. Man's ape-like ancestors gradually changed to human beings as they began the planned hunting of these and other animals. There are archaeological indications of such hunting from at least 500,000 B.C. It is *possible* that reindeer have been herded by dogs from the middle of the last Ice Age (about 18,000 B.C.), but it is not until the climatic changes arising from the end of this period (i.e. 10,000–12,000 years ago) that conditions favoured domestication by man. It is from about this time that there is definite evidence for it, as in the cave paintings of Lascaux.

According to Zeuner (1963) the stages of domestication of animals by man involved firstly loose contacts, with free breeding. This phase was followed by the confinement of animals, with breeding in captivity. Finally, there came selected breeding organized by man, planned development of breeds having certain desired properties and extermination of wild ancestors. Domestication was closely linked with the development of agriculture and although sheep were in fact domesticated before 7000 B.C., control of cattle and pigs did not come until there was a settled agriculture, i.e. about 5000 B.C.

Domestication alters many of the physical characteristics of animals and some generalization can be made. Thus, the size of domesticated animals is, usually, smaller than of their wild ancestors. Their colouring alters and there is a tendency for the facial part of the skull to be shortened relative to the cranial portion; and the bones of the limbs tend to be shorter and thicker. This latter feature has been explained as a reflection of the higher plane of nutrition which domestication permits; however, the effect of gravity may also be important, since Tulloh and Romberg (1963) have shown that, on the same plane of nutrition, lambs to whose back a heavy weight has been strapped, develop thicker bones than controls. Many domesticated characteristics are, in reality, juvenile ones persisting to the adult stage. Several of these features of domestication are apparent in Fig. 1.1 (Hammond, 1933–4). It will be noted that the domestic Middle White pig is smaller (100 lb) than the wild boar (300 lb), that its skull is more juvenile, lacking the pointed features of the wild boar, that its legs are shorter and thicker and that its skin lacks hair and pigment.

Apart from changing the form of animals, domestication encouraged an increase in their numbers for various reasons. Thus, for example, sheep, cattle and pigs came to be protected against predatory carnivores (other than man), to have access to regular supplies of nourishing food and to suffer less from neonatal losses. Some idea of the present numbers and distribution of domestic sheep, cattle and pigs is given in Table 1.1 (Anon., 1973).

TABLE 1.1. *Numbers of Sheep, Cattle and Pigs in Various Countries (1973)*

Country	Approx. million head		
	Sheep	Cattle	Pigs
Argentina	42	55	4
Australia	140	29	3
Brazil	26	85	33
Denmark	—	3	8
France	10	22	12
Germany (West)	1	14	20
Italy	8	9	8
Japan	—	4	7
Netherlands	1	5	7
New Zealand	70	9	1
Poland	3	12	20
Turkey	39	13	—
U.K.	28	15	9
U.S.A.	18	122	59
U.S.S.R.	139	104	67
Yugoslavia	8	5	6

The large numbers of sheep in Australia, New Zealand and U.S.S.R., of cattle in Argentina, Brazil, U.S.A. and U.S.S.R., and of pigs in Brazil, West Germany, Poland, U.S.A. and U.S.S.R. are noteworthy.

FIG. 1.1. Middle White Pig (aged 15 weeks, weighing 100 lb), and Wild Boar (adult, weighing about 300 lb), showing difference in physical characteristics. Both to same head size (Hammond, 1933–4). (Courtesy Sir John Hammond.)

1.2.1. *Sheep*

Domesticated sheep belong to the group *Ovis aries* and appear to have originated in western Asia. The sheep was domesticated with the aid of dogs before a settled agriculture was established. Four main types of wild sheep still survive—the Moufflon in Europe and Persia, the Urial in western Asia and Afghanistan, the Argali in central Asia and the Big Horn in northern Asia and North America. In the United Kingdom, the Soay and Shetland breeds represent remnants of wild types.

By 3500–3000 B.C. several breeds of domestic sheep were well established in Mesopotamia and in Egypt: these are depicted in archaeological friezes. Domestication in the sheep is often associated with a long or fat tail and with the weakening of the horn base so that the horns tend to rise much less steeply. The wool colour tends to be less highly pigmented than that of wild sheep.

Nowadays, about forty different breeds of sheep exist in the United Kingdom. Some of these are shown in Table 1.2.

TABLE 1.2. *Some Breeds of Sheep found in the United Kingdom*
(after Gerrard, 1951)

(a) HILL BREEDS			
Scotch Blackface	Cheviot	Welsh Mountain	Lonk
Herdwick	Derbyshire Gritstone	Penistone	Rough Fell
Swaledale	Limestone	Exmoor Horn	Dartmoor
Kerry Hill	Radnor	Soay	Shetland
(b) LONG WOOL BREEDS			
Leicester	Romney Marsh (Kent)	Border Leicester	Lincoln
Devon Longwood	South Devon	Wensleydale	Roscommon Cotswold
(c) DOWN BREEDS			
Southdown	Suffolk	Oxford Down	Hampshire Down
Dorset Down	Shropshire Down	Dorset Horn	Ryeland

The improved breeds, such as the Suffolk, tend to give greater carcase yield than semi-wild breeds such as the Soay or Shetland sheep, largely because of their increased level of fatness (Hammon, 1932a). Again, of the improved breeds, those which are early maturing, such as the Southdown and Suffolk, have a higher percentage of fat in the carcase than later maturing breeds, such as the Lincoln and Welsh; moreover, the subcutaneous fat appears to increase, particularly in the former. The English mutton breeds (e.g. Southdown and Cotswold) have a greater development of subcutaneous connective tissue than wool breeds, e.g. Merino. The coarseness of grain of the meat from the various breeds tends to be directly related to overall size, being severe in the Large Suffolk sheep: the grain of the meat from the smaller sheep is fine. Breed differences manifest themselves in a large number of carcase features— in the actual and relative weights of the different portions of the skeleton, in the length, shape and weight of individual bones, in the relative and actual weights of muscles, in muscle measurements, colour, fibre size and grain and in the relative and actual weights and distribution of fat (Pállson, 1939, 1940).

The shape of the l. dorsi muscle (back fillet) in relation to fat deposition is shown for several breeds of sheep in Fig. 1.2: the relative leanness of the hill sheep (Blackface) will be immediately apparent.

1.2.2. *Cattle*

The two main groups of domesticated cattle, *Bos taurus* (European) and *B. indicus* (India and Africa), are descended from *B. primigenius*, the original wild cattle or aurochs. The last representative of the aurochs died in Poland in 1627 (Zeuner, 1963). Although variation in type was high amongst the aurochs, the bulls frequently had large horns and a dark coat with a white stripe along the back. These characteristics are found in the cave paintings of Lascaux. Certain wild characteristics survive more markedly in some domestic breeds than in others, for example, in West Highland cattle and in the White Park cattle. Some of the latter may be seen at Woburn Abbey in England: similar animals are also represented pictorially at Lascaux.

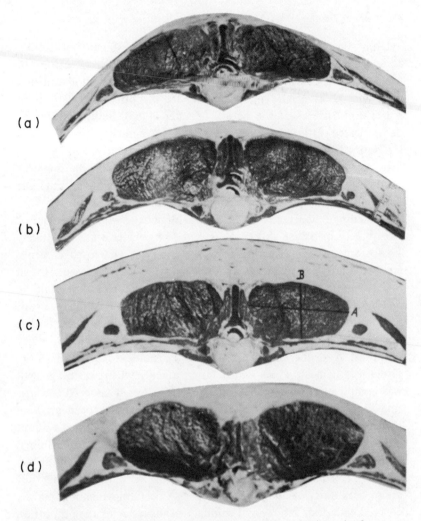

FIG. 1.2. The effect of breed on the shape and fat cover of the l. dorsi muscle of sheep (Hammond, 1936).

	A (mm)	B (mm)	Shape index
(a) Blackface	52	24	46
(b) Suffolk	65	35	54
(c) Hampshire	58	33	57
(d) Southdown	62	43	69

All the photographs have been reduced to the same muscle width (A) in order to show the proportions. (Courtesy Sir John Hammond.)

Domestication of cattle followed the establishment of settled agriculture about 5000 B.C. Domesticated hump-backed cattle (*B. indicus*, "Zebu") existed in Mesopotamia by 4500 B.C. and domesticated large-horned cattle in Egypt by about 4000 B.C.: both of these appear on pottery and friezes of the period (Zeuner, 1963). Several breeds of domesticated cattle were known by 2500 B.C. An interesting frieze from Ur, dating from 3000 B.C., shows that cows were then milked from the rear. According to Zeuner, this is further evidence that the domestication of sheep preceded that of cattle. About this same time the fattening of cattle by forced feeding was practised in Egypt.

According to Garner (1944) the more immediate wild predecessor of most breeds of British cattle was *B. longifrons*, which was of relatively small frame, rather than *B. primigenius*, which is said to have been a massive animal. Indirectly, the development of many present British breeds was due to the early improvements initiated by Bakewell in the middle of the eighteenth century, who introduced in-breeding, the use of proven sires, selection and culling. In the United Kingdom prior to that time cattle had been developed, primarily, for draught or dairy purposes. A deliberate attempt was now made to produce cattle, primarily for meat, which would fatten quickly when skeletal growth was complete. During the last 200 years the trend has been towards smaller, younger and leaner animals; and there has been growing realization that breed potentialities will not be fully manifested without adequate food given at the right time in the growth pattern of the animal (Hammond, 1932a; Garner, 1944). Some of the present breeds of British cattle are listed in Table 1.3; they are grouped according to whether they are of beef, dairy or dual-purpose types. A beef animal should be well covered with flesh, blocky and compact—thus reducing the proportion of bone. Muscle development should be marked over the hind, along the back and down the legs. In a dairy animal, on the other hand, the frame should be angular with relatively little flesh cover, the body should be cylindrical (thus accommodating the large digestive tract necessary for efficient conversion of food into milk) and mammary tissue should be markedly developed.

In terms of numbers, Shorthorns (dairy and beef types) are

predominant, but Aberdeen Angus has been regarded as the premier breed for good-quality meat (Gerrard, 1951). The carcase gives a high proportion of the cuts which are most in demand, there is, usually, a substantial quantity of intramuscular (marbling) fat and the eating quality of the flesh is excellent; on the other hand, the carcase is relatively light. One of the reasons for the good eating quality of the Aberdeen Angus is its tenderness, which is believed to be partly due to the small size of the muscle bundles, smaller animals having smaller bundles.

TABLE 1.3. *Some Breeds of Cattle found in the United Kingdom*

(a) BEEF TYPE		
Aberdeen Angus	Devon	Hereford
West Highland	Galloway	Sussex
(b) DAIRY TYPE		
Ayrshire	Guernsey	Jersey
Kerry	Friesian	
(c) DUAL-PURPOSE TYPE		
Dexter	South Devon	Shorthorn
Red Poll		Welsh Black

Because of the small carcase, however, such meat is relatively expensive. One way of making available large quantities of the relatively tender meat would be to use large-framed animals at an early age when the muscle bundles would still be relatively small (Hammond, 1963a). This is being done by feeding concentrates such as barley to Friesians (Preston *et al.*, 1963). Aberdeen Angus, Herefords and Shorthorns (beef-types) have been extensively used to build up beef herds overseas, as in Argentina and Queensland.

Callow (1961) has suggested that selection for beef qualities has brought about various differences between beef and dairy breeds. Thus, Friesians (a milk breed) have a high proportion of fat in the body cavity, and low proportion in the subcutaneous fatty tissue. In Herefords (a beef breed), on the other hand, the situation is reversed. The distribution of fat in Shorthorns (a dual-purpose breed) is intermediate between that of Herefords and Friesians. In the United Kingdom about 80 per cent of home-killed beef is derived from dairy herds (Hammond, 1963b).

There are, of course, many other modern breeds representative of *B. taurus*, for example the Simmental in Switzerland, the "Wagyu" in Japan, the Charollais in France; and, in warmer areas, *B. indicus* is widely represented. Attempts have been made to cross various breeds of *B. indicus* (Indian Hissar—"Zebu"—cattle have been frequently involved) with British breeds, to combine the heat-resisting properties of the former with the meat-producing characteristics of the latter. Such experiments have been carried out for example in Texas and Queensland. A fairly successful hybrid, the Santa Gertrudis, consists of three-eighths "Zebu" and five-eighths Shorthorn stock.

Usual types of cattle are, occasionally, found within a normal breed. Thus, dwarf "Snorter" cattle occur within various breeds in U.S.A.; and pronounced muscular hypertrophy, which is often more noticeable in the hind quarters and explains the name "doppelender" given to the condition, arises in several breeds—e.g. Charollais and South Devon (McKeller, 1960). Recessive genes are thought to be responsible in both cases.

1.2.3. Pigs

The present species of domesticated pigs are descendants of a species-group of wild pigs, of which the European representative is *Sus scrofa* and the eastern Asiatic representative *S. vittatus*, the banded pig (Zeuner, 1963). As in the case of cattle, pigs were not domesticated before the permanent settlements of Neolithic agriculture. There is definite evidence for their domesticity by about 2500 B.C. in what is now Hungary, and in Troy. Although pigs are represented on pottery found in Jericho and in Egypt, dating from earlier periods, these were wild varieties. The animal had become of considerable importance for meat by Greco–Roman times, when hams were salted and smoked and sausages manufactured.

About 150 years ago European pigs began to change as they were crossed with imported Chinese animals derived from the *S. vittatus* species.

These pigs had short, fine-boned legs and a drooping back. Then in 1830, Neapolitan pigs, which had better backs and hams, were introduced. According to McConnel (1902) it was customary in the past to classify British pigs by their colour—white, brown and black —and the older writers mention thirty breeds. Few of these are now represented. Some of the more important British breeds of pigs are shown in Table 1.4.

TABLE 1.4. *Some Breeds of Pig found in the United Kingdom*
(after Hammond, 1932b)

(a) PIGS USED FOR PORK
   Middle White   Berkshire

(b) PIGS USED FOR BACON OR PORK
   Large White   Essex   Large Black   Gloucester Old Spot
   Wessex Saddle Back

(c) PIGS USED FOR BACON
   Welsh   Landrace   Tamworth

(d) PIGS USED FOR MANUFACTURE
   Lincoln   All breeds if
                overweight

The improvement of pigs has not been continuous in one direction, but has been related to changing requirements at different periods. Of the improved breeds of pig now in use in the world the majority originated in British stock (Davidson, 1953). The first breed to be brought to a high standard was the Berkshire: it is said to produce more desirably shaped and sized 1. dorsi muscles than any other breed. Berkshire pigs, crossed with the Warren County breed of U.S.A., helped to establish the Poland China in that country a century ago. The change of type which can be swiftly effected within a breed is well exemplified by the Poland China, which altered over only 12 years from a heavy, lard type to a bacon pig (Fig. 1.3: Hammond, 1932b). Berkshire pigs have also been employed to upgrade local breeds in Germany, Poland and Japan.

Pigs of the Large White breed are the most numerous in the United Kingdom (Table 1.5).

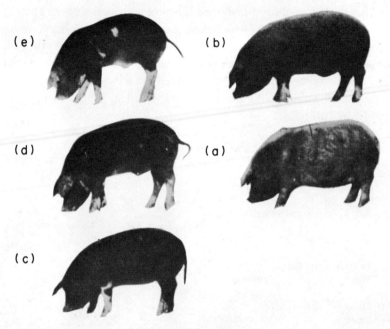

FIG. 1.3. The effect of intensive selection over 12 years on the conformation of the Poland China Pig in changing from a lard to a bacon type (Hammond, 1932b). (a) 1895–1912, (b) 1913, (c) 1915, (d) 1917, (e) 1923. (Courtesy Sir John Hammond.)

In recent years Landrace pigs from Scandinavia have strongly competed with them as bacon producers. The Landrace was the first breed to be improved scientifically. In Denmark, these animals have been intensively selected for leanness, carcase length and food-conversion efficiency with a view to the production of Wiltshire bacon. For pork production in the United Kingdom animals of the Middle White breed are used most frequently (Gerrard, 1951). Pigs of 200 lb live weight, irrespective of breed, have been used for pork, bacon or manufacturing purposes in Denmark, according to the conformation and level of fatness (Hammond, 1963b). In Hungary, there is a meat pig (the Mangalitsa) which is said to be particularly useful for the making of salami, partly because it has a rather highly pigmented flesh.

TABLE 1.5. *Relative Numbers of*
Pigs of Various Breeds in the
United Kingdom (based on number
of boars licensed, 1965–6)

Breed	Per cent
Large White	55·8
Landrace	31·2
Welsh	9·4
Wessex Saddleback	1·9
Essex	0·9
Large Black	0·6
Berkshire	0·05
Gloucester Old Spot	0·1
Tamworth	0·05

1.3. CURRENT TRENDS

The increasing pressure of world population, and the need to raise living standards, has made the production of more and better meat, and its more effective preservation, an important issue. It is sobering to realize that the need for animal protein may have increased by 300 per cent in the year 2000 as compared with 1960 (Wright, 1960).

Thus, progeny testing, based on carcase measurement, is being increasingly recognized as an efficient way of hastening the evolution of animals having those body proportions which are most desirable for the meat consumer. It has been applied especially to pigs (Harrington, 1962); but progeny testing of both cattle and sheep is developing. Artificial insemination has afforded a means of vastly increasing the number of progeny which can be sired by a given animal having desired characteristics. In the future, it may well be that young bulls of under 15 months will increasingly replace steers of this age since they produce the lean flesh which is now in demand in greater quantities—and more economically. The somewhat higher incidence of "dark-cutting" beef in bulls is probably a reflection of their stress susceptibility (cf. §5.1.2.) and can be overcome by careful handling. With the increasing development of prepackaged consumer cuts, the larger continental breeds have certain advantages over traditional British beef animals. Such breeds as Limousin, Charollais and Chianina produce leaner carcases at traditional slaughter weights; and attain these weights faster. There are occasionally reproductive problems; but these can be controlled by improved management (Allen, 1974). There has been a tendency towards the consumption of lamb in recent years, since it is more tender than mutton and produces the small joints now in demand. To some extent the increased costs which this trend entails have been offset by increasing the fertility of the ewe and thus the number of lambs born. The Dorset Horn ewe breeds throughout the year; but ewes of other breeds are being made to breed with increased frequency by hormone injections which make them more responsive to mating with the rams (Hammond, 1963b). The goat, being able to thrive in poor country, may well be developed more intensively. Nevertheless, goat meat tends to be less desirable in flavour and tenderness than beef, pork and lamb when samples of comparable maturity and fatness are considered (Smith, Pike and Carpenter, 1974); but, of course, the overall acceptibility of the species is determined by local custom.

Increasing attention is being directed to the potential of hitherto unexploited animals for meat production. Berg and Butterfield (1975), in studying the muscle/weight distribution in a number of novel species, noted that those which were more *agile* had greater muscle development in the fore limbs: in *mobile* species the musculature of all limbs was highly developed. In the elephant seal, the abdominal muscles are especially involved in locomotion, and their relative development is about three fold that of corresponding muscles in cattle, sheep or pigs.

In large areas, such as Central Africa, where the more familiar European types of domestic animal do not thrive well, there are a number of indigenous species in game reserves, well adapted to the environment, which could be readily used for meat production, e.g. the giraffe, roan antelope and springbok (Bigalke, 1964). Satisfactory canned meats can be prepared from the wildebeest antelope, if it is processed on the day of slaughter (Wismer-Pedersen, 1969a). The meat may become pale and watery if the animals are not killed by the first shot. Of the East African ungulates the meat quality of wildebeest, buffalo and zebra is probably the most acceptable organoleptically. The water buffalo is a species which shows considerable promise. The world population of buffalo is already one ninth of that of cattle; in the Amazon basin they are increasing at 10 per cent per year (Ross Cockrill, 1975). The eating quality of the meat is similar to that of beef (Joksimovic, 1969); and, indeed, may be preferred in some areas. Having less fat, the flesh of the water buffalo conforms to current trends. It thrives in the wet tropics—an extensive area which European cattle find distressing. The eland antelope shows particular promise for development in Africa. For example, they have behavioural and physiological characteristics which enable them to survive even when no drinking water is available and temperatures are high. It feeds mainly at night when the bushes and shrubs have a tenfold higher water content than in daytime (Taylor, 1968). Such species as oryx can withstand body temperatures of 45§C for short periods by a specialized blood flow whereby the brain is kept relatively cool (Taylor, 1969).

Since cattle eat grasses wherein the proportion of lignin in the stem is below a certain maximum and eland prefer to eat the leaves of bushes, there are advantages in mixed stocking (Kyle, 1972). Indeed a surprising number of species can subsist in the same area, without encroaching upon one another's feed requirements, by eating different species of plant, or different parts of the same species of plant, and by feeding at different heights above the ground (Lamprey, 1963).

In Scotland there is interest in the development of the red deer as an alternative meat producer to sheep in areas where cattle rearing or agriculture is not feasible. It has been shown that, when fed on concentrates after weaning, stags can achieve feed conversion efficiencies better than 3 lb feed dry matter per pound of gain (Blaxter, 1971–2). This conversion rate is better than that achieved with cattle or intensive lamb production.

A completely different approach to meat production is exemplified by the efforts which have been made to manufacture artificial meat from spun protein fibres derived from vegetable and microbial sources; and from slaughterhouse waste (cf. § 11.2).

CHAPTER 2

FACTORS INFLUENCING THE GROWTH AND DEVELOPMENT OF MEAT ANIMALS

"As an animal grows up two things happen: (i) it increases in weight until mature size is reached; this we call Growth and (ii) it changes in its body conformation and shape, and its various functions and faculties come into full being; this we call Development" (Hammond, 1940). The curve relating live weight to age has an S-shape and is similar in sheep, cattle and pigs (Brody, 1927). There is a short initial phase when live weight increases little with increasing age: this is followed by a phase of explosive growth; then finally, there is a phase when the rate of growth is very low.

When animals are developing, according to Hammond, a principal wave of growth begins at the head and spreads down the trunk: secondary waves start at the extremities of the limbs and pass upwards: all these waves meet at the junction of the loin and the last rib, this being the latest region to develop.

The establishment of different breeds of sheep, cattle and pigs is partly attributable to artificial selection practised by man under domestication, but the types of pre-existent animals from which such selection could be made have been determined by numerous, long-term extraneous influences, which continue—however much obscured by human intervention. These influences have caused overall alterations in the physiology of the animals concerned, involving the expression, suppression or alteration of physical and chemical characteristics. It must be presumed that such changes have been caused by mutations in the genes in response to the micro or macro environment and that they have been subsequently perpetuated by the genes. In decreasing order of

16

fundamentality, the natural factors influencing the growth and development of meat animals can be considered in three categories— genetic, physiological and nutritional.

2.1. GENETIC ASPECTS

Genetic influences on the growth of animals are detectable early in embryonic life. Thus Gregory and Castle (1931) found that there were already differences in the rate of cell division between the embryos of large and small races of rabbits 48 hr after fertilization. The birth weight of cattle and sheep, but not that of pigs, is influenced to an important extent by the nature of the respective embryos (Table 2.1).

TABLE 2.1. *Estimates of Heritability of Growth Characteristics of Cattle, Sheep and Pigs*

Character	Species	Average heritability (per cent)
Prenatal growth (birth weight)	Cattle	41
	Sheep	32
Weaning weight	Cattle	30
	Sheep	33
	Pigs	17
Post-weaning weight	Cattle	45
	Sheep	71
	Pigs	29
Feed conversion efficiency	Cattle	46
	Sheep	15
	Pigs	31

At birth the pig is by far the most immature physiologically of the three domestic species. Differences in the physiological age at birth mainly depends on how great a part of the total growing period is spent in the uterus. The birth weight is influenced by the age, size and nutritional state of the mother, by sex, by the length of the gestation period (5, 9 and 4 months in sheep, cattle and pigs respectively) and by the numbers of young born (Pállson, 1955). An interesting aspect of this latter influence is the finding that embryos next to the top and bottom of each horn of the uterus develop more rapidly than those in intermediate positions (McLaren and Michie, 1960; McCance, 1970). The supply of nutrients to these embryos is particularly good since the pressure of blood is high at the top through the proximity of the abdominal aorta and at the bottom through the proximity of the iliac artery. Environmental and genetic factors are closely interrelated: favourable environmental conditions are necessary for the full expression of the individual's genetic capacity. Irrespective of the birth weight, however, the rate of weight increase in young pigs is largely determined by the establishment of a suckling order: those piglets feeding from the anterior mammary glands grow fastest, probably because the quantity of milk increases in proceeding from the posterior to the anterior glands of the series on each side of the sow (Barber, Braude and Mitchell, 1955).

In general, the birth weights of the offspring from young mothers are lower than those from mature females and the birth weights of the offspring from large individuals are greater than those from small mothers.

In most species of mammals, although the female matures earlier, the male is heavier and larger than the female in adult life; and since the different parts of the tissues of the body grow at different rates, the difference in size between the sexes results in a difference in the development of body proportions. Castrated female pigs, however, mature later than castrated male pigs, contrary to the situation in sheep and cattle. Castration of either sex tends to reduce sex differences in growth rate and body conformation (Hammond, 1932a).

Certain major growth features in cattle are known to be due to recessive genes. One of these is dwarfism (Baker, Blunn and Plum, 1951), where the gene concerned primarily affects longitudinal bone growth and vertebral development in the lumbar region, and males rather than females (Bovard and Hazel, 1963). Another is doppelender development (McKellar, 1960). Neither has so far proved controllable. Selection of stock for improved performance seems feasible, however, on the basis of the heritability (or predictability) found for birth weight, growth from birth to weaning, post-weaning growth and feed utilization efficiency (Table 2.1, after Kunkel, 1961).

There are indications that there exist genetically determined differences in the requirement for essential nutrients by domestic animals, such as vitamin D (Johnson and Palmer, 1939) and pantothenic acid (Gregory and Dickerson, 1952).

A most important aspect of genetic variability is that determining the balance of endocrine control of growth and development. In this context, Baird, Nalbandov and Norton (1952) showed that the pituitary glands of a group of fast-growing pigs contained significantly greater amounts of growth hormone than those of a corresponding group of slow-growing pigs. In the opinion of Ludvigsen (1954, 1957) the intensive selection of pigs for leanness and carcase length has automatically meant selection of those animals having a high content of growth hormone in the pituitary. There would appear to be a concomitant deficiency of ACTH (i.e. the hormone which controls the outer part of the adrenal gland) and possibly, therefore, an inability to counteract the initial increase in blood-borne potassium which arises during exposure to stress. Whatever the mechanism, such pigs produce a white, exudative musculature postmortem; and, according to Davidson (1953), there is a weakness in the hind limbs. It would seem that the condition represents an undesirable effect of genetic makeup. It will be discussed in greater detail in a subsequent chapter. Singh, Henneman and Reineke (1956) noted that lambs with intrinsically higher rates of thyroid secretion gained weight more rapidly than those with an intrinsically low rate. There is some evidence that the dwarf gene is associated with an increased sensitivity to insulin (Foley, Heidenreich and Lasley, 1960).

Some variations in growth are apparently effected by genetically determined compatibility or incompatibility with the environment. Thus, the resistance of pigs to brucellosis (Cameron, Gregory and Hughes, 1943) and of cattle to ticks (Johnson and Bancroft, 1918) can be inherited.

2.2. PHYSIOLOGICAL ASPECTS

The subject of heat regulation in farm animals has a wide economic significance. Sheep, cattle and pigs attempt to maintain their body temperature at a constant value which is optimum for biological activity. Of the three domestic species, sheep are most able to achieve this, and pigs least able (Findlay and Beakley, 1954): indeed, newborn pigs are particularly susceptible to succumb to heat stress. Even so, adult pigs in a cold environment can maintain their skin temperatures at 9°C when exposed to air at −12°C (Irving, 1956).

The environmental temperatures normally tolerated by living organisms lie in the range 0–40°C, but some animals habitually live below the freezing point or above 50°C. For short periods even more severe conditions are compatible with survival: certain polar animals, for example, will withstand −80°C (Irving, 1951). Under such conditions, body temperatures are maintained. Nevertheless, the body temperature of certain small mammals can be depressed below the freezing point without causing death (Smith, 1958). In an environment of low temperature the development of many animals is prolonged (Pearse, 1939): under high temperatures it is frequently retarded in unadapted stock. A variable temperature has a greater stimulatory effect on metabolism than those which are uniformly low or high (Ogle and Mills, 1933). Prolonged exposure of an animal to heat or cold involves hormonal changes which are specific to these two stresses, whereas acute exposure of an animal to heat, cold, danger or other aspects of stress elicits a typical complex of reactions from the endocrine system, referred to as the general adaptation syndrome (Selye, 1950; Webster, 1975).

In general it would be expected that in a cold environment a large body would be advantageous since its relatively low surface to volume ratio would oppose heat loss; and that in a warm environment a high surface to volume ratio would help to dissipate heat. This generalization appears to apply to animals of similar conformation (Bergmann, 1847). Some of these principles can be seen to operate with domestic stock (Wright, 1954). Among cattle the yak, which inhabits regions of cold climate and rarified atmosphere, possesses a heavy, compact body with short legs and neck: it is also covered with thick, long hair. Cattle of more temperature regions have a somewhat less compact frame; while tropical cattle have an angular frame, larger extremities, a large dewlap (i.e. the fold of skin hanging between the throat and brisket of certain cattle) and a coat of very short hair. Thus among dairy cattle in the U.S.A. it is found that whereas Holsteins predominate in temperate areas, the smaller Jersey and Guernsey cattle predominate in the hotter, more humid environments. In Australia, United Kingdom breeds of sheep thrive in the cooler and wetter areas and Spanish Merino sheep in the vast arid regions. Some of the greater heat tolerance of tropical cattle can be attributed to a diminished emphasis of the subcutaneous region as a storage depot for fat (Ledger, 1959). A thick layer of subcutaneous fat would accentuate the stress caused by a hot, humid environment. On average, Hereford cattle possess 20 per cent greater tissue insulation than Friesians of comparable size and condition, although differences in tissue insulation between individuals, due to differences in body composition, can be as much as 60 per cent (Webster and Young, 1970). In sheltered conditions the growth rate of cattle is likely to be unimpaired until the air temperature falls below $-20°C$. Rapidly growing beef cattle and high-yielding dairy cows produce so much heat that they are unlikely to experience cold severe enough to increase metabolic rate under normal winter conditions in Britain. The zone of thermal neutrality for cattle is that in which metabolic heat production is independent of air temperature (Webster, 1976). Cattle can regulate evaporative heat loss over a wide range at little metabolic cost. Thus, the zone of thermal neutrality for cattle is broad (ca. 20°C). The pig has a much narrower zone of thermal neutrality (Ingram, 1974).

Bearing in mind that radiant energy is absorbed more by dark coloration and reflected more by light, it is not unexpected that many tropical cattle have a lightly coloured coat. Findlay (1950) has shown experimentally that cattle having a white, yellow or red coat, especially if the coat is of smooth, glossy texture, will absorb markedly less heat than those of a darker colour. Moreover, under given conditions of heat stress, the temperate breeds will have a higher body temperature than tropical breeds. The mechanisms for heat disposal (evaporation of water from respiratory passages, transudation of moisture through the skin and depression of metabolic rate) are less efficient and temperate stock tend to seek relief by behavioural mechanisms such as voluntary restriction of food intake, inactivity and seeking shade. This must necessarily restrict their development in relation to tropical breeds. There are many records to show that cattle with "Zebu" blood produce a higher percentage of better-quality carcases in hot, humid conditions (e.g. Queensland) than do animals of entirely temperate blood (Colditz and Kellaway, 1972). This tendency can be offset to some extent by providing pasture for night grazing.

Among sheep it is found that those in temperate areas are generally of moderate size, of compact conformation and with short legs and a thick wool coat. In tropical areas sheep have long bodies, legs, ears and tails, and a coat of short hair rather than wool. In arid areas sheep frequently develop an enlarged tail, where fat is stored: the metabolism of the latter offsets the environmental scarcity of water and food.

In general it is not the degree of heat alone which causes distress to animals in the tropics but its combination with humidity and the duration of these conditions. 70°F (21°C) provides a rough division between temperate amd tropical stock, the latter functioning efficiently above this temperature (Wright, 1954). A useful measure of the bearability of climate is given by the number of months per year when the mean 24-hr wet bulb temperature is above 70°F (Anon., 1950). Few cattle of the class *bos taurus* can maintain appetite and growth rate at air temperatures above 25°C (Colditz and Kellaway, 1972). Normally there are no sudden changes in the form or functions of domestic stock: the characteristics typical of each successive environmental zone will merge with those of its neighbours imperceptibly, this being facilitated by interbreeding at zonal boundaries (Wright, 1954). As witness to this, the number of local breed varieties is very large. Mason (1951) lists 250 breeds of cattle and 200 breeds of sheep.

Intense light has an influence independently of temperature. Radiation in the ultraviolet wavelengths converts the precursor of vitamin D in the skin into the active molecule; and this may explain the rarity of rickets in the tropics. The ultraviolet components of sunlight also elicit the formation of the dark pigment, melanin, in the skin, presumably as a protective mechanism, since they have marked carcinogenic properties when lightly pigmented skin is exposed to them.

The suitability of livestock for introduction into new areas is not limited to physiological reactions: they must meet the economic and social needs of the population. Thus, for example, the excellent draught qualities of Indian cattle should not be sacrificed in an attempt to raise milk yields, and animals introduced into warm areas, because of their heat tolerance, should possess a potential for meat production (Wright, 1954).

An effect on growth, so far unexplained, is the retardation caused by a static magnetic field (Bernothy, 1963).

2.3. NUTRITIONAL ASPECTS

"All cold-blooded animals and a large number of warm-blooded ones spend an unexpectedly large proportion of their time doing nothing at all, or at any rate, nothing in particular . . . when they do begin, they spend the greater part of their lives eating" (Elton, 1927). Finding enough of the right kind of food is the most important general factor determining the development, dominance and survival of all living organisms.

2.3.1. *Plane of Nutrition*

Differences in the plane of nutrition at any age from the late foetal stage to maturity not only alter growth generally but also affect the different regions, the different tissues and the various organs differentially. Thus animals on different planes of nutrition, even if they are of the same breed and weight, will differ greatly in form and composition (Hammond, 1932a; McMeekan, 1940, 1941; Pomeroy, 1941; Wallace, 1945, 1948). These workers showed that, when an animal is kept on a submaintenance diet, the different tissues and body regions are utilized for the supply of energy and protein for life in the reverse order of their maturity. Under such conditions fat is first utilized, followed by muscle and then by bone; and these tissues are first depleted from those regions of the body which are latest to mature. The relationship between plane of nutrition and development of the different tissues of the body has been shown by Hammond (1944): the brain and the nervous system have priority over bone, muscle and fat in that order. Figure 2.1 shows the order in which the different parts of the body develop on high and low planes of nutrition and in early and late maturing animals (Pállson, 1955). There are other views, however, on this topic. Thus Tulloh (1964) contends that carcase composition is weight-dependent and largely uninfluenced by age or nutritional regime. In an assessment of the different hypotheses, Lodge (1970) concludes that, while muscle weight appears to increase in proportion to total weight in a simple fashion, complexities arise from the degree of fat, and to a lesser extent that of bone, associated with the muscle.

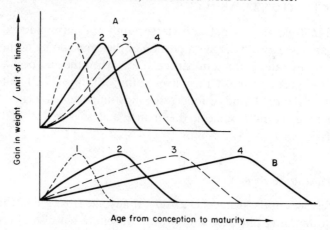

FIG. 2.1. The effect of maturity and plane of nutrition on the rate of increase of different portions of the body (Pállson, 1955). A, early maturity or high plane of nutrition. B, late maturity or low plane of nutrition.

Curves	1	2	3	4
	Head	Neck	Thorax	Loin
	Brain	Bone	Muscle	Femur
	Cannon	Tibia-Fibula	Femur	Pelvis
	Kidney fat	Intermuscular fat	Subcutaneous fat	Intramuscular fat

(Courtesy Dr. H. Pállson.)

In the view of Hammond (1932a) domestication favours the later developing parts of the body by providing a higher plane of nutrition. Selective breeding, if practised in primitive farming conditions, may fail to improve stock. Such characters as good muscle development in the loin would be incapable of expression to their full genetic potential in underfed animals. Nevertheless, the proportion of muscle in the carcase tends to be higher in wild types than in improved breeds, largely because of the relative absence of fat in the former. The greatest effect of breeding on the chemical composition of the musculature is shown in those muscles which have the greatest rate of postnatal development. That cattle, sheep and pigs differ in the partition of fatty tissues between subcutaneous and intermuscular locations may also be an effect of domestication (Callow, 1948). Subcutaneous fat, which is developed later than intermuscular fat, is favoured more in pigs than in sheep and more in sheep than in cattle. Pigs produce more generations in a given period of time than sheep and sheep more than cattle, so that the effects of domestication would be expected to be most marked in the former and least in the latter. Since the subcutaneous depot fats have a greater proportion of unsaturated fatty acids than do internal ones (Duncan and Garton, 1967), this may be a factor contributing to the greater problems of rancidity development in pork. According to Braude (1967) it will not be long before breeding and feeding policy have produced a desirable carcase so soon after birth that nearly half of the pig's effective life will have been spent *in utero*. This will increase the importance of assessing prenatal influences on growth. Clausen (1965) has found evidence that the amino-acid requirements for optimum growth of the carcase in pigs may be different from those for optimum pork quality. A positive correlation between rate of growth (in the pig) and the blood serum cholesterol level has been reported (Heidenreich, Garwood and Harrington, 1964).

2.3.2. *Interaction with Other Species*

Man is the only creature which can catch and destroy animals of any size; and this he has only been able to do in the latter part of his history

(Elton, 1927). In general, there are definite upper and lower limits to the size of animal which a carnivore can utilize. It obviously cannot reach and destroy animals above a certain size; and below a certain size it cannot catch enough to get satisfaction. The development and growth of sheep and cattle, which may be conveniently regarded as herbivores, are not, therefore, influenced directly by the availability of food animals; but their numbers may be depleted by the larger carnivores in tropical areas and by smaller carnivores, such as wolves and dogs, in more temperate regions. Such losses need not represent direct attack, but may result from worrying or harassing activities. Moreover, young stock— lambs or calves—may be destroyed by predatory birds. The most serious effects of other animal species on domestic stock, however, arise indirectly when the rate of natural increase of small species, such as mice, rats and rabbits, is strongly enhanced over a short period because of some sudden environmental change or for other as yet obscure reasons.

Plagues of locusts, mice and rats have long troubled mankind by their widespread destruction of growing crops or stored grain—and hence caused substantial losses of stock by depleting their natural food. Such plagues may arise when a species which is normally not troublesome is introduced into a new environment from which its natural enemies are absent. Thus, the rabbit, when introduced into Australia, increased at a phenomenal rate and denuded vast areas of the vegetation upon which stock had previously subsisted. Again, in New Zealand the introduction of starlings, by causing the spread of thorn bushes, brought about much loss of lambs which became entangled in them.

Some species, of course, are beneficial to domestic stock. Ruminants largely depend on the micro-organisms in their digestive tract to break down the cellulose of plant foods to easily assimilable, energy-yielding molecules such as fatty acids; and, in some cases, for the elaboration of vitamins and other accessory food factors. They are thus equipped to make use of poor-quality diets. On the other hand, the rumen micro-organisms tend to degrade high-quality protein if supplied in excess. The feeding of antibiotics to livestock has a conditioning effect upon the contribution of gut micro-organisms to animal nourishment.

Unfortunately, there are a large number of parasitic organisms belonging to various zoological phyla which cause diseases involving wasting and even death (Thornton, 1939). The nature of these organisms, and hence of the diseases which they cause, depends on the environment.

2.3.3. *Soils and Plant Growth*

Although some animals are carnivores they are ultimately as dependent on plant life for their sustenance as the herbivores. Food represents energy stored in a form assimilable and utilizable by animals and from which it can be released at a rate determined by metabolic needs. On the Earth, the major ultimate source of energy is sunlight; and it is only in the Plant Kingdom that a mechanism exists for its conversion into a stored form—the photosynthesis of carbohydrate from carbon dioxide and water by the green, light-sensitive pigment chlorophyll. In turn the availability of plants depends upon types of soil and the interaction of the latter with climatic conditions. In the last analysis, of course, the remote cosmological events which caused the cooling of the Earth, the primary parting of the elements (Goldschmidt, 1922, 1923), the formation of rocks and the distribution of minerals, and the more recent ones, whereby solar activity and, hence, the Earth's climate, fluctuate cyclically, have been jointly responsible for the types of soils originally formed, eventually produced and currently altered. The fertility of soils depends not only on the chemical nature of the rocks from which they have been formed but also on particle size. The latter determines how much moisture soils will hold and for how long, and the availability of its nutrients to plants. Soil fertility, of course, is also influenced by such extrinsic factors as temperature, rainfall and topography (including the depth of the soil layer above the underlying, unaltered rock). Soil-types range from podsols, from which exposure to rainfall of high intensity has leached out the more soluble alkaline minerals and trace elements, to solonized soils, in which alkali and salts have accumulated because of the absence of rainfall and the existence of conditions favouring evaporation. The acid reaction of podsols tends to favour the growth of rank grasses, which have a relatively low nitrogen content, and to discourage the growth of legumes.

The type of rainfall is important: knowledge of the average number of inches of annual precipitation is of limited usefulness in itself. Thus, the *variability* of the rainfall from the mean annual value is especially high in some parts of the world, causing a succession of droughts and floods: its *effectiveness* is important, since much precipitation may be unavailable if conditions of evaporation are high, as would be the case if all the rainfall occurred in the hot season; and its *intensity* (or the amount of rain at any one precipitation) determines the amount of soil erosion and whether moisture is deficiently, or optimally or excessively available for plant growth.

Many of the interrelations between soil type, climatic conditions and plant growth, on the one hand, and the breeding and fattening of sheep, cattle and pigs, on the other, are well exemplified by the conditions in Australia (Anon., 1959; Beattie, 1956).

Soils and climate affect plant growth qualitatively as well as quantitatively. As already mentioned, rank grasses of low nitrogen content develop on acid soils: the nitrogen content of grasses and legumes diminishes on prolonged exposure to high temperatures. Again, the digestibility of plants may be altered artificially. The increasing use of plant growth substances, such as gibberellic acid, which increases the internode distance in grasses, tends to lower the nitrogen content of grasses and to decrease digestibility (Brown, Blaser and Fontenot, 1963).

2.3.4. *Trace Materials in Soils and Pastures*

It is being increasingly recognized that many animal ailments can be explained on the basis of dietary deficiencies or excesses of biologically potent materials which are present only in minute quantities in soils and pastures. The great importance of traces of certain elements in the nutrition of ruminants was first realized about 40 years ago when workers in western and southern Australia discovered that a deficiency of cobalt in the soils of certain areas was the cause of various wasting and nervous diseases in cattle and sheep which had been known for many years by settlers. Animals, after grazing for several months, would lose their appetite and finally die in the midst of rich pasture (Russell and Duncan, 1956). Spraying land with cobalt sulphate (only 5 oz per acre annually), or the giving of cobalt orally, eliminated the condition. Since then, soil areas in many other countries have been found to be deficient in cobalt. The ingestion of liver was long known to be effective in cases of pernicious anaemia. With the isolation from liver of an active principle, vitamin B_{12}, and the demonstration that its molecule contained 4 per cent of cobalt (Smith, Parker and Fantes, 1948), it appeared that anaemia might be a significant aspect of cobalt deficiency syndromes. This is still in doubt, however. Several of these cobalt-deficiency diseases involve a concomitant deficiency of copper; but there are other ailments affecting stock where the primary deficiency is one of copper, e.g. swayback in lambs, a nervous affliction arising in the United Kingdom. Copper is important for blood formation; but it is also an essential part of enzymes which oxidize phenols in plants. Polymerized phenols (e.g. leuco-anthocyanins) form lignin (Bate-Smith, 1957); and plants having a high lignin content resist attack during digestion by the ruminant micro-organisms. Seasonal changes in the quantities of polyphenols in plants, due to the availability of copper, may thus affect ruminants indirectly (Greene, 1956).

An excess of molybdenum in the soil is said to enhance copper deficiency in animals; conversely, a deficiency of molybdenum may cause toxicity through making excess copper available (Russell and Duncan, 1956). Numerous ailments due to an excess or deficiency of elements in the soil and pasture are known. An excess of selenium interferes with metabolism by displacing sulphur from the essential —SH groups of dehydrogenase enzymes; an excess of potassium, by interfering with the accumulation of sodium, alters the ionic balance of body fluids and may cause hypersensitivity to histamine. Conditions such as grass tetany and milk fever, wherein the magnesium or calcium content of blood serum is especially low, are said to arise in this way. Muscular tissue tends to accumulate caesium-137 from radioactive fallout (Hanson, 1967).

Toxicity in stock may also arise by the excess ingestion of trace organic substances. Thus, lambs in New Zealand suffer from facial eczema if they graze pasture including red clover. Under certain environmental conditions the latter harbours the fungus *Penicillium chartarum* which elaborates a toxin deranging liver metabolism. As a result, haematin compounds are broken down abnormally, producing the photosensitive pigment phyloerythrin which circulates in the blood, causing the skin to react severely to sunlight (Thornton and Ross, 1959). The ingestion of sweet clover may cause haemorrhagic disease because of its content of dicumarol. Some pastures, particularly subterranean clover in the green stage, may contain sufficient isoflavones or flavones of oestrogenic potency to affect the reproductive activity of grazing ewes (Flux, Mumford and Barclay, 1961). The oestrogenic potency of pasture can be determined by the increase in length of wethers' teats (Braden, Southcott and Moule, 1964).

Fluoracetate, found in the leaves of certain plants in Africa and Australia, can be toxic to grazing sheep and cattle, since it blocks the metabolic pathway for oxidation (Peters, 1957). Of particular interest is the finding that some amino acids may be toxic for stock (Ressler, 1962). These are found in plants but are not derived from proteins. Some sufficiently resemble the normal amino acids from proteins to compete with the latter, thus disrupting metabolism.

Pastures, of course, may also be deficient in trace organic substances. Thus muscular dystrophy occurs in sheep, cattle and pigs (especially young ones) when there is insufficient alpha tocopherol, particularly if the diet contains unsaturated fat (Blaxter and McGill, 1955). Many other examples could be given. Apart from naturally occurring excesses or deficiencies of minerals and organic matter in soils and feed, an artificial hazard has arisen, during the last 30 years, from the extensive use of pesticides. It is now appreciated more fully that the benefits these have conferred in conservation of fodder and in the diminution of worry and wastage of stock caused by parasites and insects, must be balanced against the effects of ingestion of pesticide residues by the human consumer of the meat and the undesirable changes in the ecological pattern which have been observed. Probably the most extensively used pesticide has been the organochloride compound, D.D.T.; but other organochlorine substances such as deildrin, organophosphorus compounds such as malathion, and organomercurials, have also been used extensively. The main danger arises from the persistence of such substances. They resist degradation to non-toxic derivatives; and can gradually build up on soils. Pesticide residues can accumulate in the flesh of animals feeding in such areas; but in the United Kingdom lard is so far the only meat product in which more than acceptable levels of pesticide residues have been regularly detected (Anon., 1967).

The dangers of ingesting methylmercury through environmental pollution have been recognized in recent years. Although fish appears to be the major foodstuff from which man derives this toxin, meat and more particularly pork can be implicated (Curley *et al.*, 1971).

2.3.5. *Unconventional Feed Sources*

The gravity of the world protein shortage has stimulated the search for more effective ways of producing protein of high biological value. One approach to this problem is to ensure the fullest utilization of the food which ruminants are given. The rumen microflora can degrade essential amino acids ingested by cattle and sheep and thus prevent their absorption. Treatment of the feed with formalin protects amino acids during their passage through the rumen and makes them available to the animal when they reach the small intestine (McDonald, 1968).

Another possibility is to recycle manure. Fresh feedlot manure can be mixed with concentrates and fed successfully to cattle with a considerable saving in feed per unit of beef produced (Anthony, 1969). The manure is removed daily, mixed with fresh hay, and fermented by rumen micro-organisms. Yeast can also be produced on fluidized manure, 70 per cent of the dry matter of the latter being incorporated in the yeast; which can then be eaten by stock.

It has been demonstrated that yeast can ferment mineral hydrocarbon fractions to produce protein of high biological value which is as effective for the growth of stock as soya meal or fish protein concentrates (Champagnat, 1966; Shacklady, 1970). Bacteria can also subsist on crude petroleum; and, like yeast, they can convert it into protein of high biological value for animal feeding and, simultaneously, upgrade the hydrocarbon to produce high-grade domestic fuel.

Although the process is currently prohibitively expensive, algae of various types can subsist on waste and, by direct use of light, produce high-quality protein feed.

2.4. SOME MODERN DEVELOPMENTS

As we have seen, the present forms of meat animals have arisen from the long-term direct and indirect effects of natural factors on their genetic potential; and, over a relatively short period, from the artificial selection by man of desired variants. Deliberate, scientific manipulation of domestic livestock to alter their growth and development along largely predetermined lines is now possible.

2.4.1. *Fertility*

A serious problem in commercial pig production, is infertility in the sow (Pomeroy, 1960). It may be caused by infection of the reproductive tract, or by abnormalities in the latter causing mechanical obstruction. It may arise from failure of mating in sows with normal reproductive tracts, or through death of the embryos of newly-born piglets. Sows which fail to mate may have atrophied or encysted ovaries. On the other hand, the ovaries may appear quite normal and, in such cases, the cause of infertility may be excessive fatness (the fat possibly absorbs oestrogens: Hammond, 1949). Failure of fertilization may be due to the sows being served at the wrong phase of heat (or where ovulation is unusually late) or through the boar being sterile. Embryonic or neonatal mortality may reflect a deficiency in the placental blood supply during the last stages of pregnancy and this, in turn, may reflect malnutrition of the sow during the *early* part of pregnancy (Pomeroy, 1960).

Two main approaches have been made to augment the fertility of female animals, namely by increasing the number of conceptions occurring in the normal breeding season through raising the plane of nutrition or through the injection of gonadotrophic hormones (i.e. those influencing the sex glands) and by extending the normal breeding season hormonally or by decreasing the period of exposure to daylight (Laing, 1959).

The gonadotrophins which have been used to increase the number of ova shed at normal oestrus include anterior pituitary extract (Hammond, Jr., Hammond and Parkes, 1942), and pregnant mare serum gonadotrophin (Hammond, Jr. and Battachanyha, 1944). Extension of the breeding season of the ewe, by artificial reduction of the hours of daylight exposure, has been successful (Yeates, 1949) although it would be difficult to apply under natural conditions of sheep husbandry.

Although many factors are known to affect fertility in the male, it is difficult to enhance the fertility of normal individuals. No increase in sperm production has yet been demonstrated following the injection of hormones into male animals (Emmens, 1959); on the other hand, the injection of androgens or of pregnant mare serum gonadotrophin will stimulate sexual drive. The quantity and quality of semen appear to be enhanced by psychological conditioning of the animal (Crombach, de Rover and de Groote, 1956).

2.4.2. *Artificial Insemination*

Artificial insemination was first developed on a large scale in U.S.S.R.: 16 million ewes are said to have been treated as early as 1932 (Emmens, 1959). There is little doubt that it is the most effective method to improve and multiply superior meat-producing animals. For example, under natural breeding conditions a proven bull can sire only 25-30 calves per year: artificial introduction of the semen may permit the siring of 5000 calves annually (Hill and Hughes, 1959). The efficiency of the semen depends on the mobility, morphology and numbers of the spermatoza: it is protected by glycerol; and indeed semen may then be frozen and maintained at $-80°C$ for as long as 5 years (Emmens, 1959).

It is thus possible to successfully inseminate females in distant areas and to produce offspring long after the death of the fath̩er. Work in Scandinavia has shown that the female- and male-determining spermatoza can be separated by centrifugation, thus permitting preselection of the sex of the offspring. Recent work on boar taint (Patterson, 1968a, b) has suggested a novel approach which may make insemination more effective. A substance, 3α-OH-5α-androst-16-ene, which is closely related to that responsible for boar odour, is produced in the submaxillary salivary gland of entire male pigs. It is released in considerable quantities when boars salivate excessively just prior to mating. Its musk-like odour stimulates the female. As an aerosol spray it seems likely to offer a valuable adjunct to present means of encouraging fertilization.

2.4.3. *Ova Transplantation*

Just as the number of offspring carrying the desirable characteristics of a good male animal can be vastly increased by artificial insemination, so those of a good female can be multiplied by transferring her ova, after fertilization, to be developed in cows which have themselves no characteristics justifying their use for breeding (Hafez, 1961). A cow could only produce one calf per year normally if it were raised by herself. The oestrus cycle of the donor and recipient cows have to synchronize; and follicle-stimulating hormone is given to cause the ovary to mature several times the normal number of ova.

Experiments involving the transfer of fertilized ova between ewes of the large Lincoln breed to the small Welsh mountain breed have shown that the latter can respond adequately to the demands made by embryos of greater size (Dickinson *et al.*, 1962).

2.4.4. *Sterile Hysterectomy*

Much retardation of growth and development in animals is indirectly caused by disease: in young pigs, for example, virus pneumonia and atrophic rhinitis are particularly troublesome. One way to overcome these losses is to remove unborn pigs from the uterus just before term under aseptic conditions and to rear them away from possible infection (Betts, 1961). Such animals are free from the natural pathogens of the species. They are referred to as minimal disease pigs in the United Kingdom and as specific pathogen free pigs in U.S.A. Swine repopulation with such pigs appears to be effective in the U.S.A. in eradicating respiratory diseases.

2.4.5. *Antibiotics*

For some years, in the U.S.A. particularly, there were reports that the feeding of antibiotics produced better growth rates in pigs (Cuff *et al.*, 1951) and calves (Voelkner and Cason, 1951). In the United Kingdom a scientific committee, appointed jointly by the Agriculture and Medical Research Councils (Anon., 1962b), accepted the view that the practice of feeding antibiotics has been associated with improved growth rates and feed conversion efficiency in young pigs and poultry, and believed it could be extended to calves, but not to adult livestock. Penicillin, chlortetracycline and oxytetracycline are permitted in animal feeding-stuffs without veterinary prescription. It would appear that the beneficial effects of feeding antibiotics may be due to their control of subclinical infections. In young ruminants, however, it is also possible that they may be effective by increasing food utilization more directly since they enhance the digestion of starch through depressing the microbial activity responsible for gas production (Preston, 1962). In this context, it is known that bloat in cattle can be prevented by antibiotics in the feed (Johns, Mangan and Reid, 1957). The danger of depressing the activity of the rumen micro-organisms, normally responsible for the digestion of cellulose, seems small (Hardie *et al.*, 1953–4).

There is no evidence to suggest that the animals suffer any ill effects or that other than traces of antibiotic remain in the carcase after slaughter. On the other hand, there are indications that antibiotic-resistant strains of certain pathogenic micro-organisms (e.g. *Salmonella* spp.) may become established in farm animals given antibiotics either therapeutically or as feed additives (Anon., 1962b). "R factors" — entities which confer resistance to various antibiotics—can be transferred between bacterial cells. It now appears that transfer can occur in the rumen of sheep even in the complete absence of antibiotics. This was shown when sheep were starved for 2–3 days after being inoculated with large numbers ($10°$) of donor and recipient micro-organisms (Shaw, 1973).

2.4.6. Hormones and Tranquillizers

Scientific discoveries over the last three decades have made it possible to stimulate the growth and development of meat animals by the administration of hormones from the pituitary, testes and ovary. Interest in possible use of pituitary hormones in this context is recent, since sufficiently large quantities of relatively pure preparations were not available earlier. As mentioned above, Baird *et al.* (1952) showed that the growth hormone content of the pituitary from rapidly growing pigs was markedly higher than that of the pituitary of slowly growing pigs. The daily injection of growth hormone into pigs significantly increases the total protein over non-injected controls (Turman and Andrew, 1955). Growth hormone apparently enhances the mobilization of free fatty acids from adipose tissue and acts inside the cell; whereas lipoprotein lipase is regulated by insulin and is located near the endothelium of capillaries. It is involved in the deposition of preformed lipid on the adipose tissue cell, into which it liberates fatty acids (Allen, 1968).

As is well known, castration in the male reduces the efficiency of weight gain in comparison with the entire animal, and it is thus not surprising that male hormones (androgens) stimulate protein synthesis in cattle (Burris *et al.*, 1954). There is an optimum dose level for androgens, however: excess may produce decreased growth (Rubenstein and Solomon, 1941). Females show a greater response to androgens than do males in growth rate and feed conversion (Burris *et al.*, 1954; Andrews, Beeson and Johnson, 1954).

The possibility of dangerous side effects, their cost and relatively minor action, has largely displaced androgens by oestrogens for growth stimulation. Following work on the treatment of poultry with synthetic oestrogens, experiments were extended in the U.S.A. to cattle and sheep. By 1955 about 5 million cattle were said to be receiving rations containing oestrogen (Hammond, 1957). Numerous investigations indicated that the rate of gain and the efficiency of feed conversion were improved by the feeding or implantation of stilboestrol or hexoestrol. It has been found that hexoestrol has less side effects, especially if used in excess. There appear to be no detectable residues of the hormones in the flesh of treated cattle (Perry *et al.*, 1955) or pigs (Braude, 1950). Reports at one time current in the United Kingdom, that hormone implantation caused dark-cutting beef (§10.1.2) could not be substantiated (Lawrie, 1960). One effect of hormone implantation is to increase the amount of lean meat and decrease the amount of fat in carcases (Lamming, 1956): the consequent relative absence of subcutaneous fat facilitates the observation of the underlying deoxygenated muscle and this may help explain the earlier report. The best time to implant oestrogen pellets in the flesh is 100 days before it is expected that cattle will be marketed: the procedure should not be used with young or store cattle (Hammond, 1957). It would appear that administered oestrogens act by increasing the output of growth hormone—thus making the animal temporarily younger—and emphasizing bone and muscle growth instead of that of fat.

Oestrogen administration may well also enhance growth and development indirectly by the stimulation it gives to the animal's antibacterial defences. It has been shown to increase phagocytosis (i.e. ingestion of bacteria by white blood corpuscles) and the level of serum globulin (Nicol and Ware, 1960). Stilboestrol eliminates boar odour and thus overcomes the major disadvantage of the entire male pig as an efficient growing animal (Deatherage, 1965).

The psychological as well as the physiological status of animals is now known to be mediated by means of hormones (Selye, 1950; Himwich, 1955), the hypothalamus exerting hormonal control of the pituitary and thereby of other endocrine glands. One feature of its control is the elaboration by the hypothalamus of several "releasing" hormones which appear to be peptides of relatively low molecular weight. The production of luteinizing and follicle-stimulating hormones by the pituitary is elicited by a specific decapeptide (Crighton, 1972); and another is responsible for releasing thyrotrophin from this gland. An imbalance at various points in this system could cause stress and, if chronic, the so-called diseases of adaptation. The hypothalamus also exerts its influence through the production of the hormone serotonin; and the action of the latter can be inhibited by the drugs reserpine and chlorpromazine which tranquillize the organism (Udenfriend *et al.*, 1957). Stress susceptibility would be expected to interfere with growth and development; and, in fact, it has been shown that its control by low doses of tranquillizers increases the rate of weight gain and the feed conversion efficiency of fattening cattle and sheep (Sherman *et al.*, 1957, 1959; Ralston and Dyer, 1959); whereas artificially induced stress depresses weight gains (Judge and Stob, 1963).

Removal of the thymus gland from male hamsters, but not from females, causes a regression in growth which appears to be mediated in some way through wasting of the spleen (Sherman and Dameshek, 1963); but the precise mechanism has not been elucidated so far.

CHAPTER 3

THE STRUCTURE AND
GROWTH OF MUSCLE

3.1. THE PROPORTION OF MUSCULAR TISSUE IN SHEEP, CATTLE AND PIGS

As normally prepared for the meat trade, the carcases of sheep, cattle and pigs represent those portions of the body remaining after the removal of the blood, the head, feet, hides, digestive tract, intestines, bladder, heart, trachea, lungs, kidney, spleen, liver and adhering fatty tissue. The joints into which beef carcases are commonly split are shown in Fig. 3.1. On the average, about 50, 55 and 75 per cent of the live weight of sheep, cattle and pigs, respectively, remains on the carcase (Gerrard, 1951). The carcase itself consists substantially of muscular and fatty tissues, of bone and of a residue which includes tendon and other connective tissue, large blood vessels, etc. According to Callow (1948), who dissected a series of cattle and analysed the data of Pállson (1940) and of McMeekan (1940, 1941) on sheep and pigs respectively, the weight of muscular tissue ranged from 46 to 65 per cent of the carcase weight in sheep, from 49 to 68 per cent in cattle, and from 36 to 64 per cent in pigs. Its proportion varied in a roughly inverse manner with that of fatty tissue, the latter being determined, in turn, by such factors as age, breed and plane of nutrition: there are no clear-cut differences between species. The effect of age may be seen from Table 3.1. (Cuthbertson and Pomeroy, 1962), which indicates that the proportion of muscular tissue is high, and that of fatty tissue low, in pigs aged 5 months, in comparison with those aged 6 or $7\frac{1}{2}$ months.

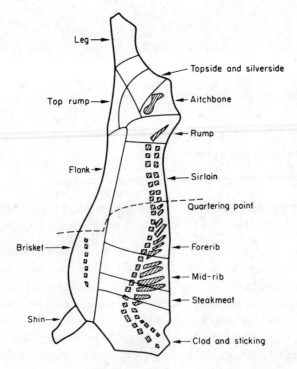

FIG. 3.1. Location of wholesale joints into which English sides of beef are commonly cut.

TABLE 3.1. *The Proportion of Muscular and Fatty Tissue and of Bone in Pig Carcases*
(After Cuthbertson and Pomeroy, 1962)

Age (months)	Per cent muscular tissue	Per cent fatty tissue	Per cent bone
5	50·3	31·0	10·4
6	47·8	35·0	9·5
7·5	43·5	41·4	8·3

The proportion of bone also decreases as the animal grows older. Sheep and cattle show a similar trend (Callow, 1948). The effects of breed and level of nutrition are shown in Table 3.2.

TABLE 3.2. *The Proportion of Muscular and Fatty Tissue and of Bone in Cattle Carcases* (after Callow, 1961)

Breed	Plane of nutrition	Per cent muscular tissue	Per cent fatty tissue	Per cent bone
Shorthorns	High–high	52·3	33·9	11·1
	Medium–medium	55·8	29·3	12·5
Herefords	High–high	54·5	31·5	11·7
	Medium–medium	58·0	27·7	12·2
Friesians	High–high	59·0	26·1	12·5
	Medium–medium	62·3	21·6	15·2

It is clear that the percentage of muscular tissue is lower, and that of fat higher, in animals on a high plane of nutrition than in those on a low plane. Moreover, the proportion of muscular tissue is relatively low in Shorthorns and relatively high in Friesians.

It would thus appear that 30–40 per cent of the live weight of the three domestic species consists of muscular tissue. Under the microscope such muscle is seen to be crossed by parallel striations: because it is associated directly or indirectly with the movement of the skeleton and is under control by the higher centres, it is also referred to as skeletal or voluntary muscle. There is also a minor amount of unstriated, involuntary muscle associated with the intestines, glands, blood vessels and other members, but it is neither appropriate nor necessary to give detailed consideration to these muscles in the present volume.

The musculature of sheep, cattle and pigs consists of about 300 anatomically distinct units (Sisson and Grossman, 1953). The approximate location of those mentioned in the text is indicated in Fig. 3.2. Muscles vary both superficially and intrinsically. They differ in overall size, in shape (which may be triangular, fan-like, fusiform, long or short, broad or narrow), in attachments (to bone, cartilage or ligaments), in blood and nerve supply, in their association with other tissues and in their action (which may be fast or slow, prolonged or intermittent, simple or in complex association with other muscles). In short, muscles are highly differentiated from one another for the performance of numerous types of movement. Some idea of the size which individual mammalian muscles can attain is given in Fig. 3.4(a) in which the two l. dorsi muscles of a Fin whale have been exposed by removal of the overlying layer of blubber. The combined weight of the two l. dorsi and two psoas muscles of an 84-ft-long Blue whale may be more than 22 tons (Sharp and Marsh, 1953). Notwithstanding their differentiation, a basic structural pattern is common to all muscles.

3.2. STRUCTURE

3.2.1. *Associated Connective Tissue*

Surrounding the muscle as a whole is a sheath of connective tissue known as the epimysium: from the inner surface of the latter, septa of connective tissue penetrate into the muscle, separating the muscle fibres—its essential structural elements, see below—into bundles: these separating septa constitute the perimysium, which contains the larger blood vessels and nerves. From the perimysium a fine connective tissue framework passes further inwards to surround each individual muscle fibre. The connective tissue round each fibre is called the endomysium. The size of these muscle fibre bundles determines the texture of the muscle (Hammond, 1932a; Walls, 1960). In muscles capable of finely adjusted movement, as in those which operate the eye, the texture is fine; whereas in those performing grosser movements it is coarse. Nevertheless, it is of interest to note that the *proportion* of connective tissue is higher in muscles of the former type (Fernand, 1949). The relative proportions of connective tissue and muscle fibres vary between muscles and, in part, account for the relative toughness of meat.

Muscle fibres do not themselves directly attach to the bones which they move or in relation to which their force is exerted; the endomysium,

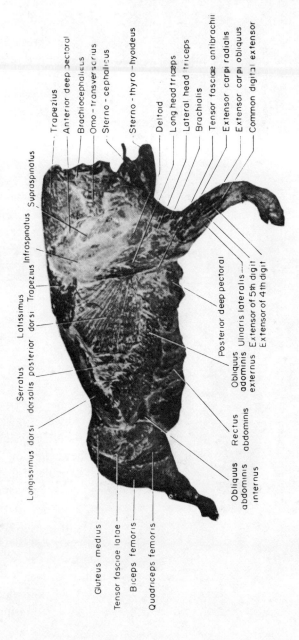

Longissimus dorsi — Serratus dorsalis posterior — Latissimus dorsi — Trapezius — Infraspinatus — Supraspinatus

Trapezius — Anterior deep pectoral — Brachiocephalicus — Omo-transversarius — Sterno-cephalicus — Sterno-thyro-hyoideus — Deltoid — Long head triceps — Lateral head triceps — Brachialis — Tensor fasciae antibrachii — Extensor carpi radialis — Extensor carpi obliquus — Common digital extensor

Gluteus medius — Tensor fasciae latae — Biceps femoris — Quadriceps femoris

Obliquus abdominis internus — Rectus abdominis — Obliquus abdominis externus — Ulnaris lateralis — Posterior deep pectoral — Extensor of 5th digit — Extensor of 4th digit

FIG. 3.2. Approximate location of various muscles in carcase. (After Cuthbertson and Pomeroy, 1963.) (Courtesy Dr. R. W. Pomeroy.)

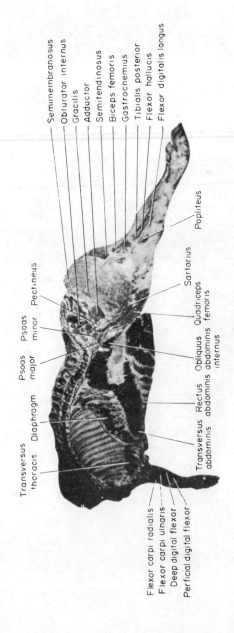

Fig. 3.2 (*cont.*)

perimysium and epimysium blend with massive aggregates of connective tissue (or *tendons*) and these attach to the skeleton.

Connective tissue includes formed elements and an amorphous ground substance in which the formed elements are frequently embedded. The latter consist of the fibres of collagen, which are straight, inextensible and non-branching; of elastin, which are elastic, branching and yellow in colour; and of reticulin, which resembles collagen but is associated with substantial quantities of a lipid containing myristic acid (Windrum, Kent and Eastoe, 1955). Reticulin is stained black by ammoniacal silver solution in contrast to collagen, which stains brown; but, on the basis of staining and other characteristics, various forms of reticulin have been reported. The structure of collagen, at various levels of organization, is shown in Fig. 3.3. (Gross, 1961). Collagen is one of the few proteins to contain large quantities of hydroxyproline. The polypeptide chains of its primary structure each have the repeating sequence — glycine-proline-hydroxyproline-glycine—one of the other amino acids. It was shown (Piez, 1965, 1968) that one chain in three had a somewhat different amino acid composition from the other two; and the two chain types were referred to as α_1 and α_2. Subsequently it has been found that there are four subtly different forms of α_1. These are now designated α_1 I-IV. The five chain types are determined by different genes (Martin, Byers and Piez, 1975). In its secondary structure, the greater part of each chain is arranged as a left-handed helix (Fig. 3.3c); and three of these intertwine to form a right-handed super helix (Fig. 3.3, e and f), which is the tropocollagen molecule or collagen protofibril.

The types of collagen found in different tissues are characterized by the nature of their three constituent polypeptide chains (cf. Table 3.3: Dutson, 1976). Types I, II and III are aggregated in fibres; but type IV is amorphous, being found in the basement membrane in which the fibres of the other collagen types are disposed (Bailey and Robbins, 1976).

At the —NH_2 end of each tropocollagen molecule (telopeptide region) the chains are non-helical. Here both intramolecular (between α chains) and intermolecular cross-links can be formed from lysine and hydroxylysine residues via δ–semialdehydes (Bailey, 1968; Bailey, Peach and Fowler, 1970). There is also evidence that non-helical areas at the C-terminal end of tropocollagen may participate in forming inter-molecular cross-links (Zimmermann, Timpl and Kuhn, 1973). It is the intermolecular cross-links which are responsible, in the main, for the mechanical strength of collagen.

It appears that every tissue has its own special modification of cross-linked collagen. Thus intramuscular collagen includes a number of disulphide cross-links (Bailey, 1974). In general, the type of cross-link reflects the ability of the tissue to hydroxylate specific lysine and hydroxylysine residues in the non-helical regions; and its ability to glycosylate lysine. Hydroxylation by specific enzymes takes place on the nascent chains prior to their release from the membrane-bound ribosomes (Miller and Udenfriend, 1970). The enzymes require ascorbic acid and oxygen for their activity. Hydroxylysine is necessary for the addition to collagen of small amounts of carbohydrate (Bailey and Robbins, 1973a). The cross-links range in stability from the very labile dehydrolysinonorleucine to the very stable heterocyclic rings of desmosine. With the exception of dehydrodihydroxylysinonorleucine, the Schiff base linkages are both heat- and acid-labile and cannot contribute to the decreased solubility of collagen with age (Robbins, Shimokomaki and Bailey 1973). During maturation of the animal, the cross-links are stabilized in as yet unidentified, non-reducible forms.

In both elastin and collagen, cross-linking reactions start with the oxidation of some of the lysine and hydroxylysine in the side chains of the monomers to allysine, under the influence of an amine oxidase which requires copper as prosthetic group. Both copper deficiency and the administration of β-aminopropionitrile inhibit the oxidizing reactions. Various diseases of connective tissue can be related to failure of one or other of the biochemical stages involved in cross-link formation (Bailey and Robbins, 1973b).

Tropocollagen molecules align in a staggered fashion (Fig. 3.3g), with an overlap of a quarter of a molecular length (2800Å) to form collagen fibrils; and these aggregate to form fibres. The fibres are laid down in a well-defined criss-cross lattice which is orientated at an angle to the long axis of the muscle (Rowe, 1974).

The structure and arrangement of elastin fibres differs according to

TABLE 3.3. *Types of Collagen and their Location (after Dutson, 1976).*

Type	Location	Molar composition	Characteristic features
I	Skin, tendon, bone, muscle	$[\alpha_1(I)]_2\alpha_2$	α_2 chains: 6–8 hydroxylysine residues/chain: low CHO
II	Cartilage, intervertebral discs	$[\alpha_1(II)]_3$	α_1 chains only: 20–25 hydroxylysine residues/chain: 10% CHO
III	Foetal skin, cardiovascular system, cardiac and skeletal muscle	$[\alpha_1(III)]_3$	α_1 chains only: 6–8 hydroxylysine residues/chain: high hydroxyproline cystine: low CHO
IV	Basement membrane	$[\alpha_1(IV)]_3$	α_1 chains only: 60–70 hydroxylysine residues/chain: high 3– and 4– hydroxyproline: 15% CHO

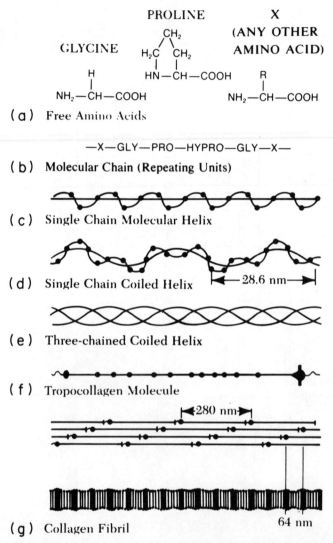

(a) Free Amino Acids

(b) Molecular Chain (Repeating Units)

(c) Single Chain Molecular Helix

(d) Single Chain Coiled Helix

(e) Three-chained Coiled Helix

(f) Tropocollagen Molecule

(g) Collagen Fibril

FIG. 3.3. Schematic illustration of the amino acid sequence and molecular structure for collagen and tropocollagen; and collagen fibril formation. Notional magnifications: (c), (d), (e): × 17,500,000 (f): × 330,000: (g): × 120,000. [From 'Collagen', *J. Gross.* Copyright ©, May, 1961, by Scientific American Inc. All rights reserved.]

their origin (Partridge, 1962). In the ligamentum nuchae of the ox, thick elastic fibres make up the greater part of the tissue, these being separated by mucopolysaccharide (i.e. a chemical aggregate of protein and complex carbohydrate) ground substance: the elastin fibres of arteries and veins are additionally associated with fibres of collagen, reticulin and smooth muscle; and the elastin fibres of elastic cartilage form a lace-like network of fibrils with large numbers of chondrocyte cells (i.e. those found in connective tissue). The quantity of elastic fibres present in the connective tissue of muscle and which is not associated with blood vessels, seems extremely small (J. R. Bendall, private communication; but cf, §4.3.5). The chondroitin sulphates are among the principal mucopolysaccharides of the ground substance. As animals age the proportion of chrondroitin 4-sulphate is altered in favour of chondroitin 6-sulphate (Schiller, 1966). The other major component of the ground substance, hyaluronic acid, has a not dissimilar disaccharide structure.

3.2.2. The Muscle Fibre

The essential structural unit of all muscles is the *fibre*. Fibres are long, narrow, multinucleated cells which may stretch from one end of the muscle to the other and may attain a length of 34 cm, although they are only 10–100 μ in diameter (Walls, 1960). In healthy animals the diameters of muscle fibres differ from one muscle to another and between species, breeds and sexes (Hammond, 1932a; Joubert, 1956). They are increased by age, plane of nutrition and training (Joubert, 1956; Goldspink, 1962a), by the degree of postnatal development in body weight rather than by the body weight itself (Joubert, 1956), and by oestradiol administration (McDonald and Slen, 1959). Some of these effects are shown in Tables 3.4 and 3.5.

Garven (1925) had noticed that a given muscle contained fibres of varying diameter, the smaller ones being more peripheral and the large ones more central in their distribution; and Hammond (1932a) observed that muscles which were more pigmented had relatively more small diameter fibres containing pigment than large non-pigmented ones. The significance of the associated chemical differences will be considered

TABLE 3.4. *Mean Fibre Diameter of Three Muscles from Lambs of Different Age and on Two Planes of Nutrition* (Joubert, 1956)

Age (days)	Muscle (diameter μ)		
	L. dorsi	Rectus femoris	Gastrocnemius
HIGH PLANE			
0	9·0	10·4	10·9
60	31·7	33·8	35·8
290	48·2	49·5	45·5
LOW PLANE			
0	7·3	8·3	8·7
60	17·3	19·8	21·3
290	35·0	36·3	39·5

TABLE 3.5. *Effect of Species on Muscle Fibre Diameter at Birth and Maturity, Showing the Importance of Rate of Postnatal Development in Body Weight.* (after Joubert, 1956)
(Relative Increases: Birth = 100)

Species	Birth		Maturity			
	Body weight (kg)	Fibre diameter (μ)	Body weight (kg)	(rel. incr.)	Fibre diameter (μ)	(rel. incr.)
Sheep	4·2	11·3	113·5	2687	50·4	446
Cattle	30·2	14·3	817·2	2707	73·3	511
Pigs	1·3	5·3	236·1	17,660	90·9	1705

later. Recently, Goldspink (1962a, b), in studying the biceps femoris of the mouse, has shown that the distribution of fibre diameters observed is not normal and that such fibres can exist in two phases—one having a small diameter (20 μ) and the other a large one (40 μ): there are few fibres of intermediate cross-section.

Surrounding each fibre, and underneath the connective tissue of the endomysium, is a sheath, the sarcolemma, which was once thought to be structureless but has now been shown by the electron microscope to represent a double membrane of which the components are about 50–60

Å apart (Robertson, 1957). Reed, Houston and Todd (1966) suggest that the sarcolemma may play an active part in contraction by transmitting the force of the myofibrils to the connective tissue structures. There may also be a spiral collagenous structure between the endomysium and the sarcolemma (Lörincz and Biro, 1963). Within the sarcolemma are the myofibrils which are surrounded by a fluid phase, the sarcoplasm; in the latter are found certain formed structures, the mitochondria or sarcosomes, the sarcoplasmic lipid bodies and the sarcotubular system (Bennett, 1960), as well as dissolved or suspended substances. The muscle cell nuclei are generally found just beneath the sarcolemma. Scopes (1970) has pointed out that there can be no sarcoplasmic proteins *within* the myofibrils since their molecular size would interfere with the contraction mechanism. Their concentration in the interfibrillar fluid, therefore, must be 25–30 per cent. In a muscle such as the psoas of the rabbit, the actual size of which is shown in Fig. 3.4b, there would be about 20,000 fibres: the grouping of such fibres is represented in Fig. 3.4c, which shows pig 1. dorsi muscle taken at 20 × magnification in longitudinal (L.S.) and transverse (T.S.) section. When the magnification is increased to 200 ×, it is possible to see (L.S.) that the fibres are crossed by parallel striations: in T.S., at this magnification, the varying size and shape of the individual fibres is evident (Fig. 3.4d). At 2000 × magnification (Fig. 3.4e) it can be seen in T.S. that each individual fibre is composed of a number of smaller units, the myofibrils; in L.S. the individual myofibrils are not so apparent, but details of the cross-striations are visible. Thus, the dark or *A*-band has a central clear area (the *H*-zone) and the light or *I*-band has a central dark division (the *Z*-line). The distance between two adjacent *Z*-lines is the functional unit of the myofibril: it is known as the sarcomere. The sarcomeres of the myofibrils are shown in Fig. 3.4f at 20,000 × magnification, in L.S. and T.S. It can now be observed that the myofibril is itself composed of numerous parallel filaments. Some of these extend from the *Z*-lines to the edge of the *H*-zone: others traverse the entire width of the *A*-band. When, finally, the magnification is increased to 200,000 × (Fig. 3.4g), these filaments which traverse the *A*-band are seen to be relatively thick; those which stop at the edge of the *H*-zone are relatively thin. The thick

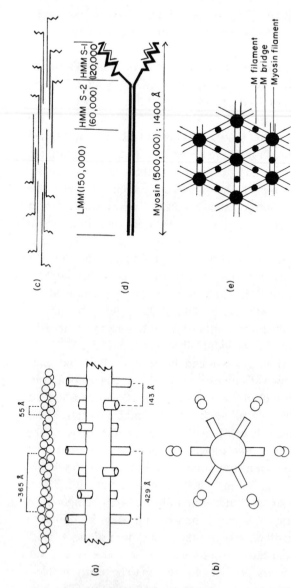

Fig. 3.5. Ultrastructure of muscle. (a) Diagram, based on X-ray analysis, showing part of a myosin filament, with one double helix of G-actin monomers above. Note that pitch of the helix, and monomer repeat distance, differ from repeat distances of the H-meromyosin heads on the myosin filament (after Huxley, 1969; courtesy Dr. H. E. Huxley, F.R.S, and American Association for the Advancement of Science). (b) Diagrammatic cross-section of myosin filament showing position of six surrounding actin filaments. (c) Sketch showing mode of aggregation of myosin molecules in forming myosin filament. Note opposite polarity of molecules on each side of *M*-zone (after Huxley, 1969; courtesy Dr. H. E. Huxley, F.R.S, and American Association for the Advancement of Science). (d) Sketch showing one myosin molecule: note double-stranded form and relative proportions of light meromyosin (LMM) and heavy meromyosins (HMMS-1, HMMS-2) (after Lowey *et al.*, 1969; courtesy Dr. Susan Lowey). (e) Diagrammatic cross-section of myofibril in region of *M*-zone, showing myosin filaments within a network of *M*-filaments and *M*-bridges (after Knappeis and Carlsen, 1968; courtesy Prof. G. G. Knappeis).

and thin filaments are now known to consist of molecules of the contractile proteins myosin and actin respectively (Hanson and Huxley, 1953, 1955; Huxley and Hanson, 1957; Huxley, 1960). It may be noted in T.S. that each myosin filament is surrounded by six actin filaments in hexagonal array. The L.S. of Fig. 3.4g also indicates that there are small projections between the myosin and actin filaments. The projections are so arranged that each sixth one is on the same radial plane of the cylinder of the myosin filament and aligned opposite to one of the six surrounding actin filaments. The actin filaments consist of two helically wound strands composed of sub-units which appear to be alike and are approximately spherical (Hanson and Lowy, 1963). This general arrangement is shown diagrammatically in Figs. 3.5a and b. A strand of the minor myofibrillar protein, tropomyosin, runs along on each side of the actin polymers; and, at 38.5 nm. intervals along the thin filaments, there is located another protein troponin, which itself consists of three units, T, C and I (Shaub and Perry, 1969). Troponin T binds to tropomyosin. In the ultimate analysis, the myosin filaments represent the lateral aggregation of the individual tadpole-like molecules of myosin. The latter aggregate—with the "tails" towards one another and the "heads" directed towards the Z-lines (Fig. 3.5c)—until a cylinder with tapering ends, and about $1 \cdot 5 \, \mu$ in length, is formed. This is the myosin filament (Huxley, 1963) and comprises about 200 myosin molecules. The myosin molecule itself is about 1500 Å in length. Each molecule consists of two apparently identical units. Each unit has a long "tail" (light meromyosin), a "collar" (heavy meromyosin S-2) and a "head" region (heavy meromyosin, S-1) (Fig. 3.5d). It seems possible that there may be additional protein associated with the latter (Lowey *et al.*, 1969; Gergely, 1970). Three light sub-units have been found in the "head" region (Gershmann, Stracher and Dreizen, 1969). Digestion of myosin with trypsin yields the heavy and light meromyosin fragments. Acetylation yields three small fragments of MW 20,000 (Locker and Hagyard, 1968); and a further multiplicity of subunits is formed on treatment with 8 m-urea. One of these sub-units contains N^E-methyl lysine; and, indeed, 3-methylhistidine has also been found as part of the myosin molecule (Hardy *et al.*, 1970). Methylation of these two amino acids in myosin occurs after peptide bond synthesis. The points of attachment of the light meromyosin shaft and of the head of the myosin molecule (S_1) to the intermediate region (S_2) are susceptible to attack by proteolytic enzymes. This suggests that these junction points could act as hinges, permitting S_1 and S_2 to swing out from the shaft towards the actin filaments (Lowey, 1968); and could mean that the S_2 portion can always attach to actin in exactly the same orientation (Huxley, 1971). Davey and Graafhuis (1976a) have shown by electron micrography that the light meromyosin backbone of the myosin filaments is arranged as a right hand tertiary coil, comprising three secondary coils–each of which is composed of three primary strands in a left hand helix. This evidence supports X-ray data indicating that the heavy meromyosin heads of the myosin molecules are regularly disposed along the myosin filament to give nine in the helical repeat distance. There appears to be no need to postulate the existence of a protein to act as a central core for the myosin filaments.

Electron micrographs have revealed the fine structure of the *M* zone in the centre of the myosin filaments. There are three to five parallel striations running perpendicular to the long axis. These *M*-bridges appear to link the myosin filaments to their six nearest neighbours. The *M*-bridges themselves are linked by thin filaments running between those of the myosin and parallel to the latter (Fig. 3.5e: Knappeis and Carlsen 1968). It would thus appear that the bridge-filament lattice of *M* substance keeps the myosin filaments centrally aligned in the sarcomere.

Another feature which appears to reflect the basic structural skeleton of the sarcomere, which has recently been discerned by the electron microscope, are so-called "gap filaments". These may be seen in the spaces which develop in muscles when these have been stretched beyond the point of overlap of A and I filaments (Carlsen, Fuchs and Knappeis, 1965). It has been suggested (Locker and Leet, 1975) that each gap filament starts as the core of an A filament in one sarcomere, extends through (and may be attached to) the Z-line and terminates as the core of the aligned filament in the adjacent sarcomere. However elusive, gap filaments have some significance for meat quality (Davey and Graafhuis, 1976b; Locker, 1976). They appear to correspond to the series elastic elements long postulated as components of muscle by physiologists. The elastic protein, referred to as "connectin", has been characterized by Muruyama *et al.* (1977). It contains 5 per cent lipid and 1 per cent carbohydrate.

The mitochondria of skeletal muscle are particles having a fine internal membranous structure: they are located between the myofibrils in longitudinal rows or situated at the Z-line and are especially prevalent in active muscles (Paul and Sperling, 1951).

A delicate network—the sarcotubular system—appears to surround each myofibril and the level of the myofibril at which it occurs is characteristic for different muscles (Porter, 1961). It was first extensively studied by Veratti (1902), forgotten for 50 years and rediscovered by electron microscopists, when it was shown to consist of two series of tubules along which it has been presumed chemical control may be swiftly and intimately exerted over muscle function (Bennett, 1960). Longitudinal tubules—to which the term "sarcoplasmic reticulum" is now taken to refer—run parallel to the myofibrils, being linked at intervals along the sarcomeres, and unite to form a terminal sac usually† before each Z-line. Between the pairs of terminal sacs (from adjoining sarcomeres) of the longitudinal elements a second series of tubules runs transversely across the fibrils, apparently as invaginations of the sarcolemma (the "T"-system). The two series of tubules do not seem to actually join, but their walls are in contact, The "T"-system tubules transmit the excitatory impulse in contraction from the depolarized sarcolemma; the sarcoplasmic reticulum is believed to control relaxation (Porter, 1961; Weber, Hertz and Reiss, 1963). In Fig. 3.6 the sarcoplasmic reticulum in pig 1. dorsi muscle is shown at a magnification of 2000×. The structure stains with osmic acid—silver nitrate. Although in L.S. the appearance presented is similar to that in the L.S. of Fig. 3.4e—which shows muscle at the same magnification when stained by Heidenhain's reagent—the two T.S. are quite different. It is clear that the myofibrillar protein stains with Heidenhain, the myofibrils

†In typical mammalian muscles. In slow-acting muscles the longitudinal tubules of the sarcoplasmic reticulum continue without interruption between successive sarcomeres (Smith, 1966; Page, 1968).

being separated by unstained areas: in Fig. 3.6 the myofibrils do *not* stain, but the sarcoplasmic reticulum surrounding each myofibril does so.

3.3. THE GROWTH OF NORMAL MUSCLE

The initiation and growth of muscle automatically implies (1) the synthesis of those complex protein molecules which are specific for the tissue and the secretion of their necessary components (amino acids), (2)

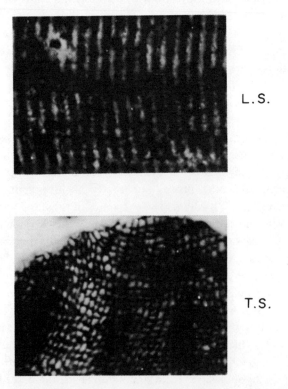

L.S.

T.S.

FIG. 3.6. The sarcotubular system in pig 1. dorsi muscle. L.S. showing regular arrangement of transverse strands of reticulum at *A–I* band junction. T.S. showing reticulum surrounding each myofibril within a fibre (× 2000). (Courtesy C. A. Voyle.)

the precise alignment of the specific proteins into the structural element peculiar to muscle (fibres) and (3) the subsequent differentiation and development of the fibres according to muscle type and function, all these processes being subject to the overall requirement of perpetuating the pattern of the parent body. Various hormones are known to expedite the growth of biological tissues and to exert control over their function either directly or indirectly: their general mechanism of action is upon the enzyme proteins which control the rate of chemical reactions whether these be synthetic or otherwise (Villee, 1960). In some cases hormones are known to act by making substrate molecules more accessible, e.g. insulin (Levine and Goldstein, 1955). One might thus explain the accretion of the amino acids required for protein building. An explanation of how these amino acids are built into the exact and reproducible position which they occupy in the polypeptide chains of which proteins are constructed has only been possible within the last 15 years (Perutz, 1962).

3.3.1. *Fundamental Basis of Protein Organization and Replication in Biological Tissues*

While hormones may expedite the building of proteins through their action on the synthesizing enzymes, the question of how the enzymes themselves are synthesized naturally arises. It is now known that the genes on the chromosomes of the cell nucleus are responsible. One gene controls the synthesis of the structure specific for one or part of one enzyme protein: it also effects the synthesis required for self-replication, thus ensuring the perpetuity of its own structure. The genes are not themselves proteins: they consist of nucleic acid, generally, de-oxyribonucleic acid (DNA). DNA consists of two chains of nucleotides coiled around each other to form a double helix (Watson and Crick, 1953). Although there are only four different nucleotides in the chains (adenosine, guanosine, cytidine and thymidine), they occur many times and are arranged in a complicated sequence. This sequence in the two chains is identical but complementary, being followed in opposite order in each.

In replication one chain of the parent double helix is transferred in forming each of the daughter double helices. The biosynthesis of the second daughter chain is catalysed by an enzyme which uses as substrate the four component deoxyribonucleoside triphosphates: it uses the daughter DNA chain as a basis for building the second complementary chain (Perutz, 1962).

It has long been clear that enzyme molecules are not synthesized by the DNA of the gene directly, the DNA being in the nucleus and protein synthesis occurring in the cytoplasm, where another type of nucleic acid involving ribose instead of deoxyribose, occurs (ribonucleic acid— RNA). It is known that a small short-lived fraction of ribonucleic acid (messenger RNA) carries the genetic message from the DNA on the gene in the nucleus to particles in the cytoplasm known as ribosomes. Activated amino acids are brought to the ribosome by other forms of RNA (transfer RNA), there being at least one molecule of transfer RNA for each amino acid. It seems likely that growth hormone regulates the rate of protein biosynthesis by controlling the synthesis of messenger RNA (Korner, 1963). One function of insulin appears to be to accelerate the translation of the messenger RNA for ribosomal and sarcoplasmic proteins in particular (Kurihara and Wool, 1968).

Each molecule of transfer RNA contains a code in the form of a short sequence of the nucleotides already referred to, which permits it to pair with a sequence of complementary nucleotides on the messenger RNA, held in the ribosomes, and thus to add the correct amino acid to the growing polypeptide chain. It has been established that a specific sequence of three nucleotides determines the selection of a given amino acid (Crick *et al.*, 1961). The four different nucleotides on the DNA chains, and hence on the protein building RNA chains, if taken three at a time, permit sixty-four different sequences. Since only about twenty amino acids are found in proteins, it would appear that each one can be determined by three different sequences. The sequence of nucleotides in nucleic acid is colinear with the sequence of amino acids on the polypeptide chain which it determines (Whitmann, 1961). Soon it was chemically confirmed that the sequence of nucleotides in messenger RNA was related, by the genetic code, to the sequence of amino acids in the protein that it specifies (Adams *et al.*, 1969). In respect of muscular tissue, polysomes which synthesize myofibrillar proteins specifically have been identified (Heywood and Rich, 1968). These comprise fifty to sixty ribosomal particles. Such are large enough to code for a protein of MW 170,000 to 200,000, i.e the mass of the main myosin subunit. These polysomes appear to correspond to that species of RNA with 26 S sedimentation characteristics. Actin and tropomyosin are synthesized by smaller polysomes: and there seems to be a correspondence between the size of m-RNA and the muscle protein for which it codes (Heywood, 1970). In embryogenesis the synthesis of actin precedes that of myosin and the latter proceeds before tropomyosin is synthesized. Sarcoplasmic proteins turnover at a faster rate than those of the myofibrils (Burleigh, 1974).

3.3.2. General Origins of Tissues

Although the way in which cells perpetuate their proteins is becoming clearer, and how histones suppress those genes which are not permitted to code for proteins, it is not as yet known how such proteins are organized spatially to produce the cell's formed elements and how the latter are further differentiated. The sciences of cytology and embryology, however, provide some clues.

It is no longer possible to regard the initial cell from which embryonic growth occcurs as having a completely undifferentiated protoplasm: the spherical symmetry of the egg is transitory and disguises the heterogeneous nature of its contents. Either from its position in the ovary or because it possesses within itself incipient polar organization, the egg is already highly polarized (Picken, 1960). The embryo becomes differentiated into "head" and "tail" regions through morphogenetic stimuli from a primary inductor (Needham, 1942). Holtfreter (1934) showed that the adult tissues from members of all phyla, if implanted into the embryonic body cavity formed at an early stage in the mass of dividing cells, induced the formation of a secondary embryo. It has since been shown that the primary inductor is extractable from such tissues.

Several substances act as hormones controlling the form of growing tissue but it seems likely that the natural primary organizer of the embryo is steroid in nature: it is thus of interest that the unorganized differentiation of most carcinoma should be caused by compounds belonging to the same chemical family as the steroids (Cook, 1933, 1934). There is now known to be a hierarchy of tissue organizers: after the primary induction of "head" and "tail" regions, secondary or tertiary inductors evoke the production of different types of tissue in the embryo and of different organs and structures within these types. The members of this series of morphogenetic hormones differ in their susceptibility to heat inactivation: the inductor for the parent cell tissue from which muscular tissue develops is relatively labile (Needham, 1942). Development and differentiation depend, however, not only on the inductor but also on the responsiveness or competence of the tissue-forming region itself. The morphogenetic hormones may not be as mobile as are the hormones which integrate the metabolic activities of the body as a whole: it is conceivable that an inductor may exert a polarizing influence upon the environment over some distance from a fixed location (Hardy, 1927). The competence of local hormonal control in directing tissue organization may be exemplified by the elaboration of contractile muscular tissue *in vitro* (Marka and Reinecke, 1964) in a cultural explant.

3.3.3. *Development of Muscular Tissue*

Skeletal muscles arise in the embryo from the mesodermic somites, i.e. from the third (and central) germinal layer of the embryo. The somite cells begin to form along each side of the embryonic axis 2–3 weeks after conception. From the somites muscle cells arise in about forty groups (mytomes). Initially these consist of a mass of closely spaced and undifferentiated cells of fusiform shape. As development proceeds, two types of cell can be distinguished, one acquiring the morphology of primitive branching, connective tissue cells, and the other that of primitive muscle cells (myoblasts). The latter at first multiply by mitotic division whereby the nuclear material is divided equally between mother and daughter cells. Later they elongate, become multinucleated and divide amitotically. Within a muscle fibre, the number of myofibrils increases, during embryonic development, from a single original fibril (Maurer, 1894) by longitudinal fission (Heidenhain, 1913). The fibrils produce the fibre by forming first a hollow tube and then filling its interior (Maurer, 1894). The first fibrils formed are unstriated even when several are in parallel and dots delineating each sarcomere (the subsequent Z-lines) appear before the fibrils form a tube (Duesberg, 1909). In mammals, the myofibrils just beneath the sarcolemma, i.e. those forming the periphery of the muscle fibre tube, are the first to become striated. Muscle nuclei are originally located in a central position but eventually migrate to the periphery of the fibre, later becoming flattened against the sarcolemma as the number of myofibrils increases.

Generally, after the second half of intrauterine life, muscles increase in size not by augmenting the number of their constituent fibres but by increasing the size of the latter (Adams, Denny-Brown and Pearson, 1962). Nevertheless, Goldspink (1962b) found that the fibres of the biceps brachii of the mouse increased in number for some time after birth: subsequent muscle development with age or with exercise is due not to a further increase in fibre numbers, but occurs because there is a greater number of fibres having a large diameter (Goldspink, 1962a); and those fibres which acquire a large diameter do so by an increment in the number of their constituent myofibrils (Goldspink, 1962c). Inanition is associated with a redistribution in the population of muscle fibre diameters, those of small diameter increasing in number at the expense of those of large diameter (Goldspink, 1962b).

During early development, fibrils grow in length from each end in complete sarcomere units (Holtzer, Marshall and Finck, 1957), i.e. the number of sarcomeres per fibril increases: after birth, the number of sarcomeres per fibril tends to remain constant and increase in fibre length is achieved by increasing the width of existing sarcomeres (Goldspink, 1962c). There is a concomitant increase in the degree of overlap of actin and myosin filaments with increasing age. This explains why the muscles of the young animal cannot develop much power (Goldspink, 1970).

For the musculature generally, the greatest rate of increase of weight occurs in the immediate postnatal period: the rate tends to diminish as growth continues.

In sheep (Hammond, 1932a; Pállson, 1940) and pigs (McMeekan, 1940) it has been shown that there is a greater rate and amount of postnatal growth in the musculature of the head and trunk, as one proceeds from the fore to the hind end of the body, and in the musculature of the limbs, as one proceeds from the feet towards the body: the latest maturing region is that where these waves of growth meet at the junction of the loin and the last rib, as has been mentioned in connection with body growth generally. Hammond (1932a) studied how the main groups of muscles in the hind limb of the sheep developed with increasing age and showed that those in the "leg" portion were relatively better developed at birth than those in the "thigh" portion: muscles of the latter group matured later. Sex also influenced the relative development of the groups, the "thigh" muscles (i.e. those of the upper portion of hind leg) being relatively more developed than those of the "leg" (i.e. those of lower portion of hind leg) in males than in females. Again, the level of fatness influences the issue. The "thigh" muscles are capable of depositing more fatty tissue between their fibres than the "leg" muscles.

The postnatal growth of individual muscles is determined by the relative maturity at birth of the area in which they are found. Thus, those in the "thigh" show a greater development than those in the "leg" (Hammond, 1932a). Joubert (1956), on the basis of fibre diameter measurements, compared the l. dorsi from the loin—a late developing area—with the rectus femoris from the "thigh" and the gastrocnemius from the "leg", of the hind limb. At birth the gastrocnemius possessed the largest fibres and the l. dorsi the smallest. Those of l. dorsi, on the other hand, showed greatest relative increase during postnatal life while the fibres of gastrocnemius increased least at this time. In mature animals the early developing gastrocnemius increased most under a high plane of nutrition: on a submaintenance diet the fibres of l. dorsi decreased in size fastest.

In the pig at birth the weights of lumbar and thoracic l. dorsi and of the neck muscles represent, respectively, 2·6, 3·6 and 4·6 per cent of the total muscle weight: 100 days later the respective values are 3·9, 5·4 and 4·8 per cent (Cuthbertson and Pomeroy, personal communication). These data again demonstrate that muscles located nearer to the rear of the animal—here the two portions of l. dorsi—have a greater postnatal development than those in the fore end.

Within a given area, however, individual muscles vary considerably in their rates of growth (Hammond, 1932a). So many factors interact in producing growth in individual muscles that generalizations are difficult, but the largest muscles have the greatest rate of postnatal development, this being possibly related to muscle function. In classifying the relative growth patterns of muscles in cattle, Butterfield and Berg (1966) have pointed out that most muscles show more than one growth phase.

The muscles of male animals tend to be larger than corresponding muscles in females. This is not entirely a reflection of differences in overall body size. It would seem that the growth of some muscles is preferentially stimulated by sex hormones (Kochakian and Tillotson, 1957). Various C_{19} steroids, with more or less androgenic activity, produced a growth stimulation in the muscles of the head, neck, chest, shoulder, back and abdominal wall which was much greater than the concomitant increase in body weight. It was concluded that the specific nature of growth varies between individual muscles. Other hormones have a differential effect on the growth of muscles. Thus, growth hormone from pituitary preferentially increases the growth of masseter, quadriceps, supraspinatus and diaphragm (Greenbaum and Young, 1953). These same muscles (with the exception of masseter) lost weight much more rapidly during starvation. Before puberty growth hormone is probably the major endocrine regulator of growth (Kay and Houseman, 1975). Clearly the protein lability of some muscles of the body is greater than that of the body as a whole. Reference has already been made to a condition, apparently controlled by a single recessive gene and presumably mediated by hormones of some kind, in which there is a marked increase in the proportion of muscular tissue in the animal (Doppelender hypertrophy—McKellar, 1960). The overall hypertrophy of the musculature is about 2–3-fold; but it is selective for individual muscles, being most pronounced in those which are the latest to develop (Pomeroy and Williams, 1962). The musculature which develops is quite normal (Lawrie, Pomeroy and Cuthbertson, 1963) and if the nature of the growth stimulus could be elucidated and regulated, it might be possible to produce cattle, sheep and pigs of enhanced meat content.

As in the case of the animal as a whole, it is normal for muscles to lay down both intracellular and extracellular fat. This occurs as a result of age or because of a high plane of nutrition (Helander, 1959).

3.4. ABNORMAL GROWTH AND DEVELOPMENT IN MUSCLE

A variety of factors can cause abnormal growth and development in muscle. Such may be superficially manifested by an unusual increase or decrease of normal muscular tissue or by the production of atypical tissue, which may be accompanied by an overall increase or decrease in size. At the present moment, most of these abnormalities would automatically preclude the affected musculature from consumption as meat on aesthetic grounds or on those of public health; but they should be considered, since they help to indicate the nature of muscle, and it is conceivable that one day some may be utilized deliberately to produce desired qualities in meat.

3.4.1. *Genetic Aspects*

The muscular hypertrophy of "doppelender" cattle and the stunted growth of "snorter" dwarf cattle have already been mentioned as being due to recessive genes. In neither case is the musculature other than entirely wholesome as meat.

Imperfections in embryogenesis account for a number of conditions where there is anomalous development in muscle or where muscles fail to develop at all. Club-foot exemplifies one of the conditions where development is faulty: histological examination shows that the muscle fibres are of uniformly small diameter. When congenital *absence* of muscles occurs, those which most frequently fail to develop are the pectorals (Bing, 1902). In recent times, the ingestion by pregnant women of tranquillizers such as thalidomide has emphasized the susceptibility to mutation of the genes controlling muscular development.

Many other abnormalities of development have been shown to be heritable. These include various diseases in muscle where inflammation by infecting organisms is not involved (muscular dystrophy). The heritable types are characterized by the relative absence of regenerative activity: they are largely degenerative; and the chain of causes is unknown (Adams, Denny-Brown and Pearson, 1962). The muscle fibres have a greatly lessened capacity to retain creatine (Ronzoni *et al.*, 1958) and potassium (Williams *et al.*, 1957), more collagen (Vignos and Lefkowitz, 1959) and a decreased ability to produce lactic acid by glycolysis due to lowered contents of aldolase, phosphorylase and creatine kinase (Dreyfus, Schapira and Schapira, 1954; Ronzoni *et al.*, 1958). In Duchenne muscular dystrophy the electrophoretic pattern of the lactic dehydrogenase enzymes (cf. Fig. 4.1) reverts to that of the embryonic muscle (Emery, 1964). The contractile proteins are relatively unaffected.

The most important histological feature of the dystrophies is the disappearance of muscle fibres, which proceeds, in phases of hypertrophy, atrophy, splitting and fragmentation, to degenerating myoblasts.

A series of heritable glycogen storage diseases are known (Cori, 1957). Certain of these are characterized by the deposition of large quantities of glycogen in muscle. They are distinguished from one another by various genetically-determined deficiencies of glycolytic enzymes, on account of which the accumulation occurs. In one condition "debranching enzyme" is deficient and the structure of the glycogen deposited is abnormal: in another phosphorylase is deficient, but the glycogen is normal. It should be mentioned, however, that the glycogen concentration in the muscles of the new-born pig is normally very high (about 7 per cent compared with 1–2 per cent in the muscles of older animals: McCance and Widdowson, 1959).

Familial periodic paralysis, in which potassium accumulates (McArdle, 1956), and a spontaneous discharge of muscle pigment with myoglobinuria (Biörck, 1949), exemplify two other types of heritable abnormalities of muscle growth.

3.4.2. *Nutritional Aspects*

Reference has already been made to the differential effects which animal age and the general plane of nutrition have on the development of various groups of muscles. Provided the diet is qualitatively adequate such growth is normal; but the absence or excess of specific substances can cause atypical development.

Dystrophic muscle which is superficially white, and may be exudative, can arise in cattle, sheep and pigs through a deficiency of vitamin E: the latter appears to be essential for the integrity of muscle (Blaxter and McGill, 1955). Histologically, there are distinct pathological features such as hyaline degeneration (cell transparency), and phagocytosis. Characteristically, long segments of fibres show "coagulation necrosis": areas of regeneration are found concomitantly (West and Mason, 1958). Biochemically, there is an increase of γ-myosin (Kay and Pabst, 1962). Vitamin E-dystrophic muscle has a greater capacity for proteolytic breakdown, which may be attributed, in part, to increased dipeptidase activity (Weinstock, Goldrich and Milhorat, 1956); a lowered capacity for respiration (Schwartz, 1962); a greater content of connective tissue protein, fat and water; and a lower content of total nitrogen (Blaxter and Wood, 1952). Structural changes in myosin are also induced by vitamin E dystrophy (Lobley, Perry and Stone, 1971). The content of 3-methyl histidine is lowered, one of the soluble subunits of myosin (Perrie and Perry, 1970) apparently fails to be synthesized and its Ca^{++}-activated ATP-ase is markedly depressed. A diet containing appreciable quantities of unsaturated fatty acids, especially linoleic acid, predisposes to vitamin E deficiency (Lindberg and Orstadius, 1961), emphasizing the antioxidant aspects of the role of vitamin E. A dietary absence of selenium also produces muscular dystrophy, which vitamin E counteracts; here its role is unknown (Blaxter, 1962).

As in the case of vitamin E deficiency, it seems possible that an excess of dietary vitamin A increases the proteolytic activity of muscle, perhaps by increasing the permeability of the membrane within which catheptic enzymes are contained (Fell and Dingle, 1963).

The ingestion of specific toxins, such as the diterpenes pimaric and abietic acids, is also thought to be responsible for the occurrence of white, exudative muscle and myoglobinuria ("Haff disease"; Assmann *et al.*, 1933).

3.4.3. *Physiological Aspects*

A white, exudative appearance is a superficial symptom of many abnormalities in muscle growth which are directly attributable to genetic or nutritional factors; as we have seen, in these microscopic examination reveals pathological features. Much interest has been shown in a condition in the muscles of pigs which resembles the nutritional or genetic dystrophies superficially, but in which virtually no pathological changes can be observed. According to Bendall and Lawrie (1964) its most immediate cause is physiological. It has been suggested that overintensive selection for high feed conversion efficiency and for leanness in pigs (e.g. Danish Landrace, Piétrain) has inadvertently also selected for pigs having an excess of growth hormone (GSH) and a deficiency of adrenocorticotrophic hormone (ACTH) in the pituitary and hyperthyroidism (Ludvigsen, 1954). Wood and Lister (1975) believe, however, that such pigs possess instead an impaired capacity to deposit fat. The leanness of stress-sensitive, PSE-susceptible pigs may be due to an enhanced capacity to mobilize fat associated with impaired insulin metabolism and a greater sensitivity to the action of catecholamines (especially norepinephrine) of the body stores of fat (Wood, Gregory and Lister, 1977).

Despite the absence of pathological features the condition has been referred to as "Muskeldegeneration" (Ludvigsen, 1954) and "la myopathie exudative dépigmentaire du porc" (Henry, Romani and Joubert, 1958); the original name "wässeriges Fleisch" (Herter and Wildsdorf, 1914) or the description "pale, soft, exudative" (PSE) musculature (Briskey, 1964) are more appropriate. Nevertheless, the histological features are uncommon and resemble those which can be artificially produced by a fast rate of post-mortem glycolysis. In longitudinal section there is frequently an alternate array of strongly contracted and adjacent passively kinked fibres; or irregularly spaced bands of dark-staining protein deposits running across the fibres (Lawrie, Gatherum and Hale, 1958, Bendall amd Wismer-Pedersen, 1962). These bands penetrate into the depth of the fibre (Fig. 3.7) and

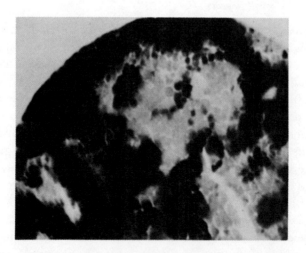

FIG. 3.7. Cross-section of muscle fibre from pig affected by so-called White Muscle disease,† showing irregular disposition of dark-staining myofibrils, presumably coated with a precipitate of denatured sarcoplasmic proteins (× 2000).

† PSE muscle

appear to consist of denatured sarcoplasmic protein, which has precipitated on the myofibrils, lowering the extractability of the latter (Bendall and Wismer-Pedersen, 1962). The sarcoplasmic precipitate includes the enzyme creatine kinase (Scopes and Lawrie, 1963). There may be a fast rate of pH fall during post-mortem glycolysis, with a normal ultimate pH (5·5), or an unusually low ultimate pH (5·0). Either would tend to denature muscle proteins and lower their capacity to hold water—in the former case because a relatively low pH would be attained whilst the temperature of the carcase was still high (Bendall and Wismer-Pedersen, 1962). Arakawa, Goll and Temple (1970) have shown that the regulatory functions of α-actinin and tropomyosin–troponin are markedly lowered in such conditions. Penny (1969) demonstrated (in porcine l. dorsi) that the lower the pH at 90 min post-mortem, the lower the water-holding capacity, the ATP-ase activity and the extractability of the myofibrillar proteins. It is evident that a fast rate of pH fall post-mortem is also effective in denaturing the *contractile* proteins. A high environmental temperature, struggling immediately before slaughter and delayed cooling of the carcase cause the condition to be manifest (Bendall and Lawrie, 1964). Briskey (1969) and Kastenschmidt (1970) presented biochemical evidence, however, which suggested that the degree of struggling at death is *not* the main reason for a high rate of post-mortem glycolysis in stress-susceptible pigs. They believed that the inherent constitution of the muscles in the latter is such that they are more readily made anoxic post-mortem and hence encourage a fast rate of lactic acid production. The efficacy of relaxant doses of magnesium sulphate administered preslaughter in slowing post-mortem ATP breakdown (Howard and Lawrie, 1956) and in preventing PSE (Briskey, 1969; Sair *et al.*, 1970) may be due to a vasodilatory action. Although the preslaughter injection of magnesium sulphate slows the rate of ATP breakdown in pigs of Pietrain, Landrace and Large White breeds, and there is a marked reduction in exudation post-mortem in the former two breeds, this is less so with the meat from Large White animals, suggesting that there may be influences other than the rate of post-mortem glycolysis affecting water-holding capacity (Lister and Ratcliff, 1971). The Ca^{++}-accreting ability of the sarcoplasmic reticulum from muscles showing exudative character is said to be less than that of normal porcine muscle (Greaser *et al.*, 1969b). This feature would exacerbate any tendency for a fast rate of pH fall post-mortem and this, in turn, increases the damage to the sarcoplasmic reticulum (Greaser, 1969a, 1974). Mitochondria from *l. dorsi* muscles of stress-susceptible Pietrain and Poland China pigs release Ca^{++} ions anaerobically at twice the rate of those in stress-resistant pigs. Halothane anaesthesia enhances the rate of release in stress-susceptible pigs. The excess anaerobic release of Ca^{++} ions by the mitochondra of the muscles of stress-susceptible pigs has thus been postulated as a "trigger" for the PSE condition; and also for malignant hyperthermia (Cheah and Cheah, 1976). "Giant" fibres are particularly prevalent in the musculature of exudative pork (Cassens, Cooper and Briskey, 1969). They have low amylophosphorylase and high ATP-ase activities and are thus biochemically intermediate between "red" and "white" fibres. Prophylaxis is said to be made possible by giving cortisone to stress-susceptible pigs (Ludvigsen, 1957). At rest the level of 17-hydroxycorticosterone in the blood serum is 50 per cent greater in stress-susceptible than in normal pigs (Topel, 1969); and, on exposure to stress, the level falls in the former, whereas it rises in normal pigs. The intravenous injection of aldosterone induces a pale, soft exudative condition in pig musculature. This effect is prevented if an oral drench of aldactazide (a competitive inhibitor of aldosterone) is administered 30 min beforehand (Passbach *et al.*, 1969). Another index of the potentially stress-susceptible pig is the presence of lactic dehydrogenase isozyme V in the blood serum: usually isozyme I is found. A high isozyme V/I ratio in blood samples would indicate a tendency to develop PSE post-mortem (Addis, 1969). There are said to be enhanced levels of creatine phosphokinase in the blood serum of stress-susceptible pigs (Allen and Patterson, 1971), and of glucose-6-phosphate in muscles sampled by biopsy (Schmidt, Zuidan, and Sybesma, 1971). These observations are compatible with a physiological explanation of the condition. Nevertheless, Bendall and Lawrie (1964) consider that increased liability to produce watery pork may represent a genetically controlled difference in the nature and quantity of glycolytic enzymes: such may have inadvertently arisen in breeding for high-feed

FIG. 3.8. Emulsions of salt soluble proteins from 6·25 g samples of pork, after heat treatment. Emulsions 1, 2, 3 and 4 contain 50, 100, 150 and 200 ml soya-bean oil respectively. (a) Meat of high water-holding capacity. (b) Meat of low water-holding capacity. (Courtesy Dr. J. Wismer–Pedersen.)

conversion rates and for large muscles. Wismer-Pedersen (1969b) has shown that the proteins from watery pork have a much lower capacity to form stable emulsions than those from normal porcine muscles (Fig. 3.8). He suggests that the greater insolubility of sarcoplasmic proteins in such meat (see above) prevents myofibrillar proteins forming the strong membrane round fat globules to which, he believes, emulsion stability is due when sausage meat is heated. It seems likely, however, that the connective tissue proteins also affect the stability of sausage meat emulsions. It is of interest, in this regard, that the epimyseal connective tissue appears to have significantly more salt-soluble collagen and a greater amount of heat-labile collagen, when derived from watery pork than from the flesh of normal pigs (McLain *et al.*, 1969).

Henry *et al.*, (1958), Lawrie (1960) and Scopes and Lawrie (1963) attributed the paleness largely to the absence of myoglobin: whereas Wismer-Pedersen (1959a) and Goldspink and McLoughlin (1964) attributed it to denaturation of myoglobin. Scopes and Lawrie (1963) found little evidence for the latter.

Complete disuse of muscles causes a physiological atrophy. Histologically, there is a reduction in the mean diameter of muscle fibres (Tower, 1937, 1939). Conversely, continuous training increases the size of muscles (Morpurgo, 1897). This reflects an increase in the number of fibres which have a large diameter rather than an increase in the width of all the component fibres (Goldspink, 1962a, b). The muscle fibres increase in diameter both by the elaboration of new myofibrils and by an increase in sarcoplasm (Morpurgo, 1897). Such coarsening of texture would tend to make the muscles tougher as meat (Hiner *et al.*, 1953).

Physiological hypertrophy is also a reflection of hormonal activity. Much of this is "normal", such as the effect of androgens (male hormones) in increasing the muscle size of males. On the other hand, disorders of the pituitary, thymus, thyroid and adrenal cortex glands are frequently associated with excessive or stunted muscular development. Little analytical work has been done on such material. Over-hydration of muscle has been noted in impaired adrenal function (Gaunt, Birnie and Eversole, 1949) and fatty infiltration in hyperthyroidism (Adams *et al.*, 1962).

3.4.4. Various Extrinsic Aspects

Atrophy is a common reaction of living muscle to injury. This response may follow directly from crushing or cutting of the muscle substance, ionizing radiation, excessive heat or cold, or high voltage electricity; or indirectly, by section of or damage to the muscle's blood supply, nerves or tendons. These circumstances are fully discussed by Adams *et al.* (1962). There is generally some degree of reversion to the primitive foetal muscle structure (Denny-Brown, 1961). Histologically, the reaction ranges from a cloudy swelling of the sarcoplasm to total dissolution of the muscle fibre. Regardless of the precipitating cause, an orderly series of changes can be observed. There is firstly an enlargement of the nuclei and a tendency for these to migrate centrally to form rows. Next there is an accumulation of granular sarcoplasm around the nuclei and then, depending on the extent of the injury, regeneration or degeneration occurs, i.e. budding of new muscle tissue or fragmentation and splitting of the tissue into spindle cells, respectively (Denny-Brown, 1961).

Intermediate doses of ionizing radiation (*ca.* 1000 rad†) before slaughter increase the water-holding capacity of the subsequent meat and decrease its catheptic activity (Silaev, 1962). Large doses (*ca.* 5000 rad) may cause disappearance of cross-striations and vacuolation of the sarcoplasm (Warren, 1943), oedema (Wilde and Sheppard, 1955), a rise in sodium and a fall in potassium and aldolase (Dowben and Zuckerman, 1963). The effects of massive, megarad, doses on muscle *in vitro* will be considered in a later chapter.

Crushing (Bywaters, 1944) and high voltage electricity (Biörck, 1949) cause substantial changes in muscles. They may lose most of their myoglobin, potassium and other soluble sarcoplasmic material.

A series of inflammatory conditions in muscle (myositis) is known and in each there is destruction of the muscle fibres and proliferation of connective tissue (Adams *et al.*, 1962). The inflammatory agent may be parasitic (e.g. trichinosis in pork), bacterial (e.g. spontaneous acute

---

†A rad is a measure of the dose of irradiation sustained and may be defined as an energy absorption of 100 ergs/g of material.

streptococcal myositis), viral (e.g. Bornholm disease, caused by Coxsackie Group B virus) or metabolic (e.g. various rheumatic conditions).

Muscle tissue itself rarely elaborates into carcinomata: these are found generally as invasions of muscle by direct extension of a primary growth in another tissue. In such cases compression atrophy may result.

CHAPTER 4

CHEMICAL AND BIOCHEMICAL CONSTITUTION OF MUSCLE

4.1. GENERAL CHEMICAL ASPECTS

In a broad sense the composition of meat can be approximated to 75 per cent of water, 19 per cent of protein, 3·5 per cent of soluble, non-protein, substances and 2·5 per cent of fat, but an understanding of the nature and behaviour of meat, and of its variability, cannot be based on such a simplification. On the contrary, it must be recognized that meat is the post-mortem aspect of a complicated biological tissue, viz., muscle, and that the latter reflects the special features which the function of contraction requires, both in the general sense and in relation to the type of action which each muscle has been elaborated to perform in the body.

As outlined in Chapter 3, the essential unit of muscular tissue is the fibre which consists of formed protein elements, the myofibrils, between which is a solution, the sarcoplasm, and a fine network of tubules, the sarcoplasmic reticulum; the fibre being bounded by a very thin membrane (the sarcolemma) to which connective tissue is attached on the outside. The spatial distribution, between these structural elements, of the 19 per cent of protein in the muscle is shown in Table 4.1 (compiled from various sources), together with other data on the chemical composition of a typical adult mammalian muscle, after rigor mortis but before marked degradative changes. The principal amino acids in fresh muscle are α-alanine, glycine, glutamic acid and histidine (Tallan, Moore and Stein, 1954).

75

TABLE 4.1. *Chemical Composition of Typical Adult Mammalian Muscle after Rigor Mortis but before Degradative Changes Post-mortem (after Lawrie, 1975)*

Components	Wet % weight
1. WATER	75·0
2. PROTEIN	19·0

(a) Myofibrillar		11·5
myosin[1] (H and L meromyosins, and several light chain		
proteins associated with them)	6·5	⎫
actin[1]	2·5	⎪
tropomyosins	1·5	⎬
troponins C, I and T	0·4	⎪
α and β actinins	0·4	⎪
M protein etc.	0·2	⎭
(b) Sarcoplasmic		5·5
glyceraldehyde phosphate dehydrogenase	1·2	⎫
aldolase	0·6	⎪
creatine kinase	0·5	⎪
other glycolytic enzymes	2·2	⎬
myoglobin	0·2	⎪
haemoglobin and other unspecified extracellular		⎪
proteins	0·6	⎭
(c) Connective tissue and organelle		2·0
collagen	1·0	⎫
elastin	0·05	⎬
mitochondrial etc. (including		⎪
cytochrome c and insoluble enzymes)	0·95	⎭
3. LIPID		2.5
neutral lipid, phospholipids, fatty	2·5	
acids, fat-soluble substances		
4. CARBOHYDRATE		1·2
lactic acid	0·90	⎫
glucose-6-phosphate	0·15	⎬
glycogen	0·10	⎪
glucose, traces of other glycolytic intermediates	0·05	⎭
5. MISCELLANEOUS SOLUBLE NON-PROTEIN SUBSTANCES		2.3
(a) Nitrogenous		1·65
creatine	0·55	⎫
inosine monophosphate	0·30	⎬
di- and tri- phosphopyridine	0·30	⎪
nucleotides	0·10	⎭

amino acids	0·35 ⎱	
carnosine, anserine,	0·35 ⎰	
(b) Inorganic		0·65
total soluble phosphorus	0·20 ⎫	
potassium	0·35 ⎪	
sodium	0·05 ⎬	
magnesium	0·02 ⎪	
calcium, zinc, trace metals	0·23 ⎭	

6. VITAMINS
  Various fat- and water- soluble vitamins, quantitatively
    minute.
  ¹Actin and myosin are combined as actomyosin in
  post rigor muscle

4.1.1. *Muscle Proteins*

The proteins in muscle (Table 4.1) can be broadly divided into those
which are soluble in water or dilute salt solutions (the sarcoplasmic
proteins), those which are soluble in concentrated salt solutions (the
myofibrillar proteins) and those which are insoluble in the latter, at least
at low temperature (the proteins of connective tissue and other formed
structures).

The sarcoplasmic proteins (myogen and globulins) are now known to
represent a complex mixture of about 50 components, many of which
are enzymes of the glycolytic cycle (cf. Fig. 4.1; courtesy R. K. Scopes).
Band F3 has been isolated as a basic protein by Scopes (1966). Although
it constitutes 2 per cent of the total sarcoplasmic proteins (in pig 1. dorsi)
it does not appear to correspond to any of the known enzymes of the
glycolytic pathway. It will be observed that several enzymes consist of
more than one molecular species ("isozymes"). Almost all the
sarcoplasmic proteins have been crystallized (Scopes, 1970). Apart from
the differences in charge implicit in Fig. 4.1, the sarcoplasmic proteins
differ in various other parameters including their relative susceptibility

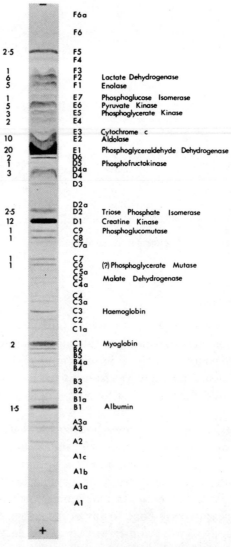

FIG. 4.1. Diagrammatic representation of electrophoretogram of soluble proteins extracted from 1. dorsi muscle of the pig and separated on starch gel. Several of the unnamed bands represent minor components of the known enzymes (e.g. C4a and C5a are lactic dehydrogenases). Phosphorylase remains insoluble at the origin (i.e. between D6 and E1). (Courtesy Dr. R. K. Scopes.)

to denaturation (Bate-Smith, 1973b; Scopes, 1964), but their individual characteristics as proteins will not be considered here.

Myosin is the most abundant of the myofibrillar proteins. Its identity was a somewhat confused issue for nearly 100 years from 1859, when the name was first given to a substance in muscle press juice which formed a gel on standing (Bailey, 1954). The molecule of myosin, which has a molecular weight of about 500,000, is highly asymmetric, the ratio of length to diameter being about 100:1. Because of its high content of glutamic and aspartic acids, and of dibasic amino acids, it is highly charged and has a strong affinity for calcium and magnesium ions. Myosin molecules are built from two types of sub-unit—light (*L*) and heavy (*H*) meromyosins (Szent-Györgyi, 1953). *H*-meromyosin, which contains all the ATP-ase and actin-combining properties of myosin, is sited on the periphery of the myosin filaments. The properties depend upon free-*SH* groups in the molecule (Bailey, 1954). Tropomyosin was discovered in 1946 by Bailey. Once extracted from muscle it is soluble at low ionic strength but *in situ* is extracted only at high ionic strength. Its amino acid composition is similar to that of myosin (Bailey, 1954) and like the latter, there are few free amino groups: it appears to be a cyclopeptide (a chain of amino acids forming a closed figure). It has been suggested that actin filaments are attached to the Z-line by a meshwork of tropomyosin (Huxley, 1963); and the tropomyosin extends along the helical groove in the actin filament (cf. § 3.2.2).

The other major protein of the myofibril is actin (Straub, 1942). It can exist in two forms, *G*-actin, which consists of relatively small globular units having a molecular weight of about 70,000, and *F*-actin, in which these globular units are aggregated end to end to form a double chain (cf. Fig. 3.5). *G*-actin polymerizes into *F*-actin in the presence of salts and small amounts of ATP. It is *F*-actin which combines with myosin to form the contractile actomyosin of active or pre-rigor muscle and the inextensible actomyosin of muscle in rigor mortis (cf. § 4.2.1). The interrelation of actin, myosin and ATP is complex (Bailey, 1954) and will not be discussed in detail. Relatively small quantities of other proteins, which are associated with the myofibrils, have been isolated; and functions have been assigned to some of them (Ebashi and Endo,

1968; Schaub and Perry, 1969; Maruyama, 1970). Thus the troponin complex promotes the aggregation of tropomyosin, binds calcium and prevents actomyosin formation; α-actinin promotes the lateral association of F-actin; β-actinin inhibits polymerization of F-actin; and the M-line substance promotes the lateral polymerization of light meromyosin, but not that of H-meromyosin. Tropomyosin B is the term now given to the protein remaining after troponin has been removed from tropomyosin as it occurs naturally. Because of its high content of α-helix, tropomyosin B is capable of contributing mechanical stability to the muscle filaments. The proteins of the M-line substance represent at least two molecular species (Porzio, Pearson and Cornforth, 1978).

There are at least three kinds of light chain component, of MW 15,000—30,000 daltons, associated with myosin (Perry, Cole, Morgan, Moir and Pires, 1975). The 18,000 dalton component (there are two present for each double-stranded molecule of myosin) is distinguished by being the specific substrate for the enzyme, myosin light chain kinase; and it has been designated the "P" light chain (Frearson and Perry, 1975). Another enzyme, myosin light chain phosphatase (Morgan, Perry and Ottaway, 1976), specifically removes phosphate from the "P" light chain. Changes in the phosphorylation status of the "P" light chain of myosin have been correlated with the physiological state of muscle (Frearson, Solaro and Perry, 1976) i.e. the interaction of myosin with actin.

Troponin is composed of three major members, refered to as C, I and T, which are concerned with the contractile process (Schaub, Perry and Hacker, 1972); and have distinct amino acid compositions. Troponin C(MW 18,000) binds calcium ions and forms an equimolar complex with troponin I. It is phosphorylated neither by 3 , 5 -cyclic AMP-dependent protein kinase nor by phosphorylase b kinase (Perry *et al.*, 1975). I (MW 37,000) inhibits actomyosin ATP-ase. It can be phosphorylated by both enzymes (at serine and threonine residues, respectively) (Cole and Perry, 1975). Troponin T (MW 37,000) binds to tropomyosin and troponin C: it is phosphorylated by phosphorylase b only.

The primary structure and molecular weights of troponins I and T differ when derived from "white", "red" or cardiac muscles. On the other hand, whereas the amino acid compositions of the troponin C derived from cardiac and skeletal muscle generally differ, the primary structures of troponin C from "white" and "red" muscles are similar (Head, Weeks and Perry, 1977).

Smooth muscle, which is found in varying amounts at different locations in the gastrointestinal tract, in the lungs and in the uterus, does not form part of the edible portion of the carcase. Although its operating mechanism is basically similar to that of striated muscle, and involves parallel filaments of myosin and actin, there are a number of differences in the proteins of the contractile machinery. Thus, the MW of smooth muscle myosin (600,000) is rather greater than that of striated muscle (Kotera *et al.*, 1969), the ratio of actin to myosin is almost twice that of skeletal muscle (Somlyo *et al.*, 1971) and there are some differences in the amino acid composition of both major and minor proteins (Carsten, 1968). As a reflection of these differences, the contractile proteins of smooth muscle are extracted at markedly lower ionic strength (Hamoir and Laszt, 1962).

The distribution of amino acids in the various myofibrillar proteins of the rabbit is shown in Table 4.1a. It will be noted that there is a higher content of aromatic residues in actin, the actinins, troponin C and *H*-meromyosin than in the other proteins. Actin and the actinins also have relatively high contents of proline. The latter is particularly low in *L*-meromyosin and tropomyosin B.

In that portion of muscle which is insoluble in concentrated salt are the mitochondria, containing the insoluble enzymes responsible for respiration and oxidative phosphorylation, the formed elements of the muscle membrane (sarcolemma) and the collagen, reticulin and elastin fibres of connective tissue. The collagen of connective tissue has the highest content of hydroxyproline of any common protein (12·8 per cent: Bowes, Elliott and Moss, 1957). The hydroxyproline content of muscle, is, therefore, frequently used as a measure of its connective tissue. There is a high proportion of hydroxy amino acids in collagen and elastin; trytophan is virtually absent; and hydroxylysine is found.

82   *Meat Science*

TABLE 4.1a. *Distribution of Amino Acids in Myofibrillar Proteins*
(as percentages of total residues)
(After Bodwell and McClain, 1971; Wilkinson *et al.*, 1972; Cummins and Perry, 1973; Head and Perry, 1974).

Protein	Aromatic amino acids	Proline	Basic amino acids	Acidic residues
Actin	7·8	5·6	13	14
α-actinin	7·7	5·9	12	14
β-actinin	7·5	5·7	13	12
Tropomyosins B, α & β	3·0	0·1	18	36
Troponin C	7·8	0·6	10	33
Troponin I	3·7	2·8	20	28
Troponin T	5·3	3·5	22	32
Myosin	5·3	2·6	17	18
H-meromyosin	7·2	3·4	15	15
L-meromyosin	2·8	1·0	19	18

The latter occurs in no other proteins. Ascorbic acid is required for the formation of collagen and is said to control the conversion of proline, after it has already been incorporated into the polypeptide chain, into hydroxyproline (Stone and Meister, 1962). In ascorbic-acid deficiency an elastin low in hydroxyproline is formed (Barnes, Constable and Kodicek, 1969). When heated in water at 60-70°C, collagen fibres shorten to about one-third or one-quarter of their initial length. When the temperature is raised to about 80°C, collagen begins to be converted into the water soluble molecule gelatin. Reticulin, unlike collagen, which it resembles in other respects, does not yield gelatin on boiling (Kramer and Little, 1953). It is of interest that the collagen of intramuscular connective tissue is more highly cross-linked (and insoluble) than that of the corresponding tendon (Mohr and Bendall, 1969).

Unlike collagen and reticulin, elastin is not broken down on exposure to heat. It is a unique protein containing a chromophoric residue which gives elastin its characteristic yellow colour and fluorescence (Partridge, 1962). The elastic properties of elastin fibres are due to an unusual cross-linking between adjacent polypeptide chains, which does not involve

S–S bridges. The polypeptide at the cross-link areas has recently been shown to contain two hitherto unknown amino acids—desmosine and isodesmosine (Thomas, Elsden and Partridge, 1963). These are salts of tetramethyl-substituted pyridine. Elastin differs from collagen in having only 1·6 per cent hydroxyproline and few polar amino acids; and the valine content (18 per cent) is much higher than that in collagen (Partridge and Davis, 1955). (cf. also § 3.2.1).

4.1.2. *Intramuscular Fat*

Although the fat of adipose tissue generally consists of true fat (i.e. esters of glycerol with fatty acids) to an extent of more than 99 per cent, the fat of muscle, like that of other metabolically active tissues, has a considerable content of phospholipids and of unsaponifiable constituents, such as cholesterol (Lea, 1962). Only three or four fatty acids are present in substantial amounts in the fat of meat animals—oleic, palmitic and stearic (Table 4.4, p. 102); and of the four types of glyceride GS_3, GS_2U, GSU_2 and GU_3 (S and U represent saturated and unsaturated fatty acids respectively), certain isomers greatly predominate. In the majority of fats which have been examined by partial degradation using pancreatic lipase, saturated acids are found preferentially in the alpha or exterior positions of the glycerol molecule (Savary and Desnuelle, 1959). Pig fat is exceptional, however, in that unsaturated acids are usually found in the alpha position. Although the fatty acids are not randomly orientated in animal fats, they can be so arranged artificially by heating with an esterification catalyst. This causes a marked improvement in the texture and plasticity of the fat and other characteristics which are useful in baking (Lea, 1962).

The phospholipids—phosphoglycerides, plasmalogens and sphingomyelin—are more complex than the triglycerides. In the phosphoglycerides one of the three hydroxyl groups of glycerol is combined with choline, ethanolamine, serine, inositol or glucose. In the plasmalogens the second hydroxyl group of glycerol is esterified with a long-chain fatty aldehyde instead of with fatty acid; and in sphingomyelin the amino alcohol sphingosine is bound by an amide link to a fatty acid and by an ester link to phosphorylcholine. There are also present in muscular tissue complex sugar-containing lipids— glycolipids. The effect of such factors as species, age and type of muscle in the composition of the phospholipids, is still little known (Lea, 1962). Of the total phospholipids in beef muscle, lecithin accounts for about 62 per cent, cephalins for 30 per cent and sphingomyelin for less than 10 per cent (Turkki and Campbell, 1967). Accompanying the triglycerides are small quantities of substances which ae soluble in fat solvents, e.g. vitamins A, D, E and K and cholesterol derivatives.

4.2. BIOCHEMICAL ASPECTS

4.2.1. *Muscle Function* in vivo

The thick filaments which were apparent in Fig. 3.4g consist essentially of myosin and the thin filaments of actin. The latter are continuous through the Z-line, but do not traverse the H-zone which bounds each sarcomere; the myosin filaments traverse the A-band only. The three-dimensional aspect of this arrangement was briefly outlined in Chapter 3 and shown diagrammatically in Fig. 3.5 when it was indicated that there are six straight rows of projections or "feet" running longitudinally along the side of each myosin filament, the sets of feet being symmetrically distributed around the periphery of the latter, so that one set of feet is opposite one of the six filaments of actin which surround each myosin filament (Fig. 3.4g). The two-dimensional aspect of this arrangement is shown in Fig. 4.2 (Bendall, 1969). This shows, in diagrammatic form, a longitudinal section of the sarcomeres (a) at rest length, (b) when extended and (c) during contraction. The thick myosin filaments are depicted with (above and below) two of the six actin filaments with which they are associated. The degrees of interdigitation, and of linkage between the myosin heads and the actin, in each condition will be apparent. Figure 4.2 also depicts the patterns seen in cross-sections corresponding to these sarcomere lengths. It will be apparent that, as the muscle is extended beyond rest length, it becomes narrower and the hexagonal array of myosin and actin filaments becomes tighter.

Conversely, when the muscle contracts, the cross-sectional area, and the distance apart of the myosin and actin rods, both increase. In muscle at rest in the living animal (or in the pre-rigor state in the dying muscle), the beads comprising the actin filaments are prevented from combining with the corresponding projections on the myosin by the magnesium complex of adenosine triphosphate ($MgATP^=$): the latter acts as a plasticizer.

A possible sequence of events in contraction may be outlined. In the myofibril the contractile proteins are associated with the regulatory complex of troponins (troponins C,T and I) and tropomyosin (§4.1.1.). These confer sensitivity to Ca^{++} ions upon the hydrolysis of $MgATP^=$ by the actomyosin ATP-ase (Perry, 1974).

Activation of the muscle usually is the result of a nerve stimulus arriving at the motor end plate, whereby the polarization of the sarcolemmal surfaces is reversed. The sarcolemma temporarily loses its

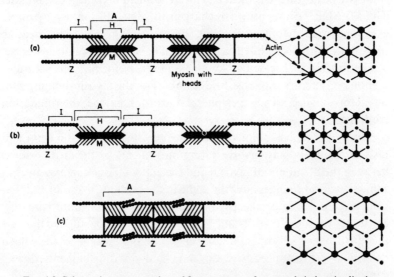

FIG. 4.2. Schematic representation of fine structure of ox muscle in longitudinal- and cross-sections. The length of the sarcomeres has been reduced tenfold in proportion to the thickness of the filaments. The beaded nature of the actin rods and the "heads" in those of myosin are indicated. (a) Sarcomeres at rest length (*ca.* 2·4 μ); (b) sarcomeres stretched to length *ca.* 3·1 μ; (c) sarcomeres contracted to length *ca.* 1·5μ. (Courtesy Dr. J. R. Bendall.)

impermeability to calcium, and Ca^{++}ions dissociate from the acidic protein by which they are normally bound in the sarcotubular system, equilibrating with those in the sarcoplasm. As a result, the Ca^{++}ion concentration rises from about $0.10\mu M$ to $10\mu M$. This saturates troponin C, the calcium-binding member of the troponin complex, causing a configurational change whereby the inhibitory protein, troponin I, no longer prevents actin from interacting with the $MgATP^=$ on the H-meromyosin heads of the myosin molecule. The contractile ATP-ase in the vicinity of the linkage is thus strongly activated, splitting $MgATP^=$ to $MgADP^-$ at a high rate and providing the energy for the actin filament to be pulled inwards towards the centre of the sarcomere i.e. the portion of the myofibril involved contracts. The link between actin and myosin is simultaneously broken, although tension will remain as there are 5.4×10^{16} cross links per millilitre of muscle; and some will be bearing tension at any given moment in contracting muscle. The $MgADP^-$ on myosin is recharged to $MgATP^=$, either by direct exchange with cytoplasmic ATP, by the action of ATP: creatine phosphotransferase or by the action of ATP: AMP phosphotransferase.

The process is repeated so long as an excess of Ca^{++}ions saturates troponin C and myosin cross bridge links with the myosin-binding sites on actin at successively peripheral locations as the interdigitation continues.

Huxley (1971) has pointed out that interdigitation of the actin and myosin filaments may involve tilting movements of the cross bridges between the S_1 submit of myosin and the actin—if one can assume that some structural changes alter the angle of the bridging material and that some system of forces keeps the filament separation approximately constant over short axial distances. Elliott (1968) has postulated that it is the disturbance of dipole-dipole and van der Waals forces which determine the distances between actin and myosin filaments during contraction.

In order to explain how the myosin cross bridges are able to link with the myosin-binding sites on actin, Davies (1963) postulated that $MgATP^=$ was bound to the H-meromyosin crossbridge by a polypeptide chain. Its helices were extended at rest by mutual repulsion generated between the negative charge on $MgATP^=$ at one end and a net negative charge at the other, where the polypeptide joined the H-meromyosin. On stimulation, Ca^{++} ions annulled the negative charge on $MgATP^=$ and this eliminated the repulsive effect on the coils of the polypeptide, causing it to assume the α-helical configuration—by the energy of formation of about forty-six hydrogen bonds—and, through the link with actin, pulling the latter inwards by an amount equivalent to the distance between successive myosin-binding sites on actin. On the $MgADP^-$ being recharged to $MgATP^=$, the polypeptide was re-extended; but now to a position opposite to the next distal myosin-binding site on actin.

When the stimulus to contract ceases, the concentration of Ca^{++} ions in the sarcoplasm is restored to rest level ($\sim 0.10\mu M$), being reabsorbed into the sarcotubular system by the sarcoplasmic reticulum pump which depends upon ATP for the necessary energy. ATP is also needed to restore the differential distribution of sodium between the two surfaces of the sarcolemma which provides the action potential on nerve stimulation. The latter process probably requires only about one-thousandth, and the calcium pump one-tenth, of the energy required in contraction *per se* (Bendall, 1969). The sarcoplasmic reticulum has itself some ATP-ase activity (Engel, 1963).

Being no longer saturated with Ca^{++} ions, troponin C and tropinin I return to their resting configurations whereby the latter prevents interaction of myosin and actin (Schaub *et al.*, 1972). It is feasible that the gap filaments (Carlsen *et al.*, 1965: Locker and Leet, 1976), which have some elasticity, assist in pulling the actin filaments outwards from their interdigitation with those of myosin so that the sarcomere's resting length is reestablished.

Apart from the major involvement of an elevated sarcoplasmic concentration of Ca^{++} ions in the interaction of actin and myosin during muscular contraction such also activates myosin light chain kinase (which phosphorylates one of the light chain components of myosin) and phosphorylase *b* kinase (which phosphorylates troponins T and I) (cf. § 4.1.1.). Moreover, Perry and Schaub (1969) have shown that purified troponin required the addition of tropomyosin for its inhibitory action on actomyosin ATP-ase. It may be presumed that these subsidiary proteins are important in the response of the contractile system (Perry *et al.*, 1975). It has been demonstrated that muscular contraction changes the angles of the lattice of the perimyseal connective tissue and the crimp length of the collagen fibres (Rowe, 1974). Collagen, therefore, may have a more positive role in contraction than has been supposed hitherto. Most other aspects of muscle contraction concern the mechanism of ensuring an adequate supply of ATP. In this both the soluble and insoluble proteins of the sarcoplasm play an essential role (Needham, 1960). The most immediate source of new ATP is resynthesis from ADP and creatine phosphate (CP), by the enzyme creatine kinase, which is one of the soluble proteins of the sarcoplasm:

$$ADP + CP \rightleftharpoons creatine + ATP.$$

Non-contractile myosin ATP-ase is responsible for the small degree of contractility necessary to maintain tone of resting muscle and body temperature: it also causes the depletion of ATP, and hence rigor mortis after death (Bendall, 1973). But *in vivo* the major source of ATP is its resynthesis from ADP by respiration, whereby muscle glycogen (or in some cases fatty acids) is oxidized to carbon dioxide and water. When energy is needed in excess of the power of the respiratory to generate ATP, the process of anaerobic glycolysis, whereby glycogen is converted to lactic acid, can do so—although much less efficiently. The mechanism of ATP resynthesis by respiration or by anaerobic glycolysis is complicated: a highly simplified outline is given in Fig. 4.3 (after Baldwin, 1967). It will be seen that much more ATP can be resynthesized by respiration than by anaerobic glycolysis. Most of the enzymes needed to convert glycogen to lactic acid, and many other substances, are in solution in the sarcoplasm. The latter include the muscle pigment, myoglobin, which is quite distinct from the haemoglobin of the blood (Theorell, 1932). It exists in two molecular species in horse (Boardman and Adair, 1956) and five species in the seal (Rumen, 1959); and it appears to act as a short-term oxygen store in muscle (Millikan, 1939). The oxygen-utilizing enzymes of respiration, in particular the

cytochrome system, and those required to convert pyruvic acid to
carbon dioxide and water and to form ATP, are located in insoluble
particles, the mitochondria. These are distributed in the sarcoplasm

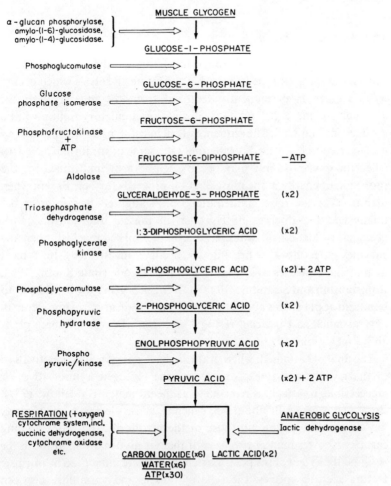

Fig. 4.3. Simplified scheme (after Baldwin, 1967), showing stages in the
conversion of muscle glycogen to carbon dioxide and water, by respiration in the
presence of oxygen, and to lactic acid under anaerobic conditions. The yields of
ATP are indicated. Substances in capitals, enzymes in lower-case.

(Cleland and Slater, 1953; Chappel and Perry, 1953). Most of the glycolytic and respiratory enzymes require co-factors which are either vitamins or trace metals; and the composition of muscle reflects this requirement.

4.2.2. *Post-mortem Glycolysis*

Since it reflects the basic function of muscle, it is appropriate to consider at this point the irreversible anaerobic glycolysis which occurs when oxygen is permanently removed from the muscle at death, although the more general consequences of circulatory failure will be outlined in Chapter 5. The sequence of chemical steps by which glycogen is converted to lactic acid is essentially the same post-mortem as *in vivo* when the oxygen supply may become temporarily inadequate for the provision of energy in the muscle; but it proceeds further. Except when inanition or exercise immediately pre-slaughter has appreciably diminished the reserves of glycogen in muscle, the conversion of glycogen to lactic acid will continue until a pH is reached when the enzymes effecting the breakdown become inactivated. In typical mammalian muscles this pH is about 5·4—5·5 (Bate-Smith, 1948; Ramsbottom and Strandine, 1948). Glycogen is generally considered to be absent at pH values above this level; but certain atypical muscles may have as much as 1 per cent residual glycogen when the ultimate pH is above 6 (Lawrie, 1955).

The final pH attained, whether through lack of glycogen, inactivation of the glycolytic enzymes or because the glycogen is insensitive (or inaccessible) to attack, is referred to as the ultimate pH (Callow, 1937). Because it is generally about 5·5, which is the iso-electric point of many muscle proteins, including those of the myofibrils, the water-holding capacity is lower than *in vivo*, even if there is no denaturation. Both the *rate* and the *extent* of the post-mortem pH fall are influenced by intrinsic factors such as species, the type of muscle and variability between animals; and by extrinsic factors such as the administration of drugs pre-slaughter and the environmental temperature. The effect of species in a given muscle and at a given temperature is illustrated in Fig. 4.4a and the type of muscle in Fig. 4.4b. Variation in time taken for the pH of the 1. dorsi of different pigs to fall from 6·5 to an ultimate of 5·5 at 37°C is considerable (Fig. 4.5); and such differences have been observed

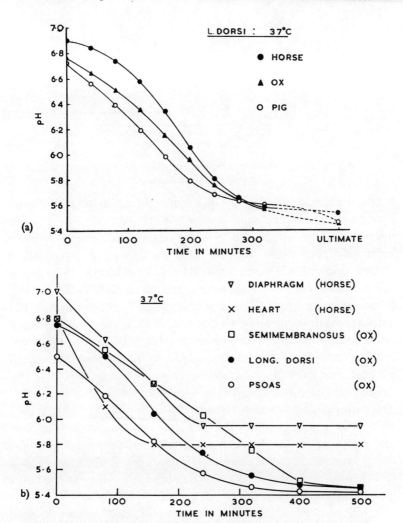

FIG. 4.4a and b. The effect of (a) species and (b) type of muscle on the rate of post-mortem pH fall at 37°C. Zero time is 1 hr post-mortem.

92   *Meat Science*

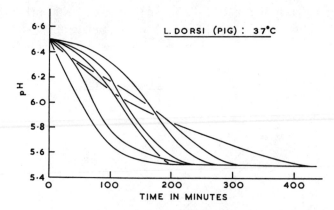

FIG. 4.5. Variability in the rate of post-mortem pH fall in l. dorsi muscles at 37°C between individual pigs.

between specific muscles of different beef animals at constant temperature (Howard and Lawrie, 1975b: Bendall, 1978). The intravenous administration of relaxing doses of magnesium sulphate before slaughter will slow the subsequent rate of post-mortem glycolysis; injection of calcium salts (Howard and Lawrie, 1956) and of adrenaline and noradrenaline (Bendall and Lawrie, 1962) will accelerate the rate. Insulin shock (Hoet and Marks, 1926) and the injection of adrenaline (sub-cutaneously: Cori and Cori, 1928, tuberculin (Howard and Lawrie, 1957a) and tremorine (Bendall and Lawrie, 1962) will produce and high ultimate pH through depleting glycogen reserves, but by a different mechanism in each case.

The rate of post-mortem glycolysis increases with increasing external temperature above ambient (Bate-Smith and Bendall, 1949; Marsh, 1954—cf. Fig. 4.6). Contrary to expectation, however, the rate of post-mortem glycolysis also increases as the temperature at which it occurs falls from about 5° to 0°C (Newsbold and Scopes, 1967). Indeed Smith (1929) found that the rate was even greater at −3°C than at 0°C i.e. as the system was freezing.

It will be obvious that, in the carcases of meat animals, various muscles will have different rates of fall of temperature post-mortem, according to their proximity to the exterior and their insulation. As a

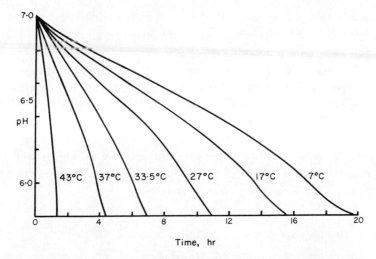

Fɪɢ. 4.6. The effect of environmental temperature on the rate of postmortem pH
fall in beef 1. dorsi (Marsh, 1954). (Courtesy Dr. B. B. Marsh.)

result, the rates of post-mortem glycolysis will tend to be higher in
muscles which are slow to cool; and vice versa. Some of the observed
differences in the rates of post-mortem glycolysis in beef muscles *in situ*
are certainly due to this factor (Bendall, 1978). It has been suggested that
the exceedingly fast rate of pH fall in the musculature of pigs affected by
the so-called white muscle condition (§3.4.3), in which the pH may have
fallen to about 5·4 in 40 min (Ludvigsen, 1954; Briskey and Wismer-
Pedersen, 1961; Bendall, Hallund and Wismer-Pedersen, 1963), may
reflect the development of an abnormally high temperature post-
mortem (Bendall and Wismer-Pedersen, 1962) or immediately pre-
slaughter (Sayre, Briskey and Hoekstra, 1963b). On the other hand,
there is no doubt that the rate of pH fall is abnormally fast even at normal
temperature in some pigs and may proceed to an exceptionally low
ultimate pH, e.g. 4·7 (Lawrie, Gatherum and Hale, 1958). It is possible
that the complement of the enzymes which effect glycolysis may vary
between individual animals. As indicated above (§3.4.1), various
genetically determined glycogen storage diseases are known (Cori, 1957)
in which certain enzymes in the muscle are deficient. Since it seems

feasible that the so-called PSE condition is heritable, a genetically controlled excess or imbalance of glycolytic enzymes could well be implicated. In the musculature of affected pigs post-mortem, certain sarcoplasmic proteins denature because of the high temperature–low pH combination (Scopes, 1964), in particular the enzyme creatine phosphokinase (Scopes and Lawrie, 1963). In its relative absence, there would be an excess of ADP and inorganic phosphate in the muscle and this could accelerate post-mortem glycolysis. It was shown that electrical stimulation of exercised pig muscle enhances ATP-ase activity causing a faster than normal rate of pH fall during post-mortem glycolysis (Hallund and Bendall, 1965).

4.2.3. *Onset of rigor mortis*

As post-mortem glycolysis proceeds the muscle becomes inextensible: this is the stiffening long referred to as rigor mortis. Its chemical significance has only recently been appreciated. Erdös (1943) showed that the onset of rigor mortis was correlated with the disappearance of ATP from the muscle: in the absence of ATP, actin and myosin combine to form rigid chains of actomyosin. The observations of Erdös were confirmed and greatly extended by Bate-Smith and Bendall (1947, 1949) and by Bendall (1951), who has written a comprehensive review of the subject (1973). The loss of extensibility which reflects actomyosin formation proceeds slowly at first (the delay period) then with great rapidity (the fast phase): extensibility then remains constant at a low level. The time to the onset of the fast phase of rigor mortis (at given temperature) depends most directly on the level of ATP which, in the immediate post-mortem period, is being slowly lowered by the surviving non-contractile ATP-ase activity of myosin (Bendall, 1973). Under local control the latter operates in an attempt to maintain body heat and the structural integrity of the muscle cell. The level of ATP can be maintained for some time by a resynthesis from ADP and creatine phosphate (CP). When the store of CP is used up, post-mortem glycolysis can resynthesize ATP; but only ineffectively (as has already been pointed out) and the overall level falls. It will be clear that this will

happen sooner if there is little glycogen; but even with abundant
glycogen the resynthesis of ATP by glycolysis cannot maintain it at a
level sufficiently high to prevent actomyosin formation. Struggling at
death will lower the initial pH and shorten the time until the fast phase,
as will depletion of glycogen by other means (starvation, insulin tetany).
On the other hand, an excess of oxygen, by stimulating respiration, will
delay the onset of rigormortis. Indeed thin portions of muscles (ca. 3 mm.
thick), if exposed to oxygen during post-mortem glycolysis, can produce
ATP with such efficiency that not only is rigor mortis delayed but CP is
resynthesized to above its *in vivo* level (Lawrie, 1950: unpublished). The
pH of the muscle also tends to rise.

With a knowledge of the temperature, the initial store of glycogen and

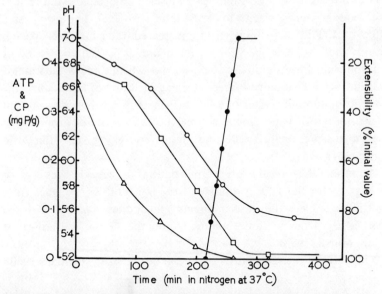

FIG. 4.7. The onset of rigor mortis in 1. dorsi muscle of the horse. Changes in
ATP, CP, and extensibility as a function of time in nitrogen at 37°C. Zero time: 1
hr post-mortem. Adenosinetriphosphate (ATP) and creatine phosphate (CP)
determined in trichloroacetic acid extracts made from muscles at various time
intervals. ATP-P and CP-P expressed as mgP/g wet weight of muscle.
Extensibility expressed as a percentage of initial value (Lawrie, 1953). □—□,
ATP; △—△, CP; O—O, pH; ●—●, extensibility.

the initial levels of ATP and CP, the time to onset of rigor mortis can be predicted accurately (Bendall, 1951). The initial pH alone gives a good general approximation (Marsh, 1954). The onset of rigor mortis is accompanied by lowering in water-holding capacity. It is important to emphasize that this is not due solely to the drop in pH (and the consequent approach of the muscle proteins to their iso-electric point) or to denaturation of the sarcoplasmic proteins (Table 5.3, p. 150). Marsh (1952a) showed that, even when rigor mortis occurred at a high pH, there was a loss of water-holding capacity, due to the disappearance of ATP and to the consequent formation of actomyosin.Whilst the Marsh–Bendall factor (sarcoplasmic reticulum pump) is still operating in post-mortem muscle, re-addition of ATP, at relatively high concentration, will cause swelling of muscle homogenates and restore the water-holding capacity towards its *in vivo* level. The plasticizing effect of ATP is thus associated with increased water-holding capacity. N.m.r. studies have shown that there are at least two phases or environments for water in muscle, in each of which some of the water is "bound" and the majority "free". During the onset of *rigor mortis* the amount of "bound" water in each environment remains constant, but there is progressive movement of "free" water from one environment to the other—presumably reflecting the cross-linking of actomyosin (Pearson *et al.*, 1974).

An idea of the typical relative time relations of these changes is given in Fig. 4.7 for the 1. dorsi muscle of the horse (at 37°C). Once rigor mortis is complete, the muscle remains rigid and inextensible, provided it is kept free from microbial contamination: there is no "resolution" of rigor (Marsh, 1954).

The patterns of rigor mortis onset can be classified (Bendall, 1960):

   (i) Acid rigor: characterized in immobilized animals by a long delay period and a short fast phase and in struggling animals by drastic curtailment of the delay period. At body temperature stiffening is accompanied by shortening.
  (ii) Alkaline rigor: characterized by a rapid onset of stiffening and by marked shortening, even at room temperature.

(iii) Intermediate type: characterized in starved animals by a curtailment of the delay period but not of the rapid phase: there is some shortening.

Shortening in rigor mortis involves only a fraction of the muscle fibres, is irreversible and is thus distinguished from physiological contraction (Bendall, 1960).

The characteristics of rigor mortis, e.g. the levels of ATP and CP initially and at onset; the pH value initially, at onset and ultimately; the initial and residual stores of glycogen; the activities of ATP-ases and of the sarcoplasmic reticulum pump, will vary according to intrinsic factors, such as species and type of muscle, and extrinsic factors, such as the degree of struggling and temperature (cf. Tables 4.6 and 4.23).

Abnormal types of rigor mortis are known. Thus, if muscle is frozen whilst the ATP level is at the pre-rigor value, an exceedingly fast rate of ATP breakdown and of rigor onset ensues on thawing ("thaw rigor"). The muscle may contract to 50 per cent of its initial length and exude much fluid or drip (Chambers and Hale, 1932). It has been suggested that the contractile actomyosin ATP-ase, which is not normally responsible for ATP depletion post-mortem, is activated on freezing and thawing (Bendall, 1973). This reflects the inability of the sarcoplasmic reticulum pump to reabsorb calcium ions effectively in these circumstances (cf. §§ 4.2.1 and 10.3.3.1).

In contrast, a much delayed onset of rigor mortis has been observed in the muscles of the whale (Marsh, 1952b). The ATP level and the pH may remain at their high *in vivo* values for as much as 24 hr at 37°C. No adequate explanation of this phenomenon has yet been given.

Besides the chemical changes which directly affect actomyosin formation, and thereby stiffening in rigor mortis, there are other concomitant reactions. Of these the most striking are in the pattern of nucleotides (Bendall and Davey, 1957). After ATP has been broken down to inorganic phosphate (Pi) and ADP, the latter is further dephosphorylated and deaminated to produce inosine monophosphate (IMP); and IMP is dephosphorylated to produce inosine. Ribose is then split from inosine, producing hypoxanthine.

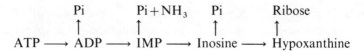

$$\text{Pi} \qquad \text{Pi} + \text{NH}_3 \qquad \text{Pi} \qquad \text{Ribose}$$
$$\uparrow \qquad\qquad \uparrow \qquad\qquad \uparrow \qquad\qquad \uparrow$$
$$\text{ATP} \longrightarrow \text{ADP} \longrightarrow \text{IMP} \longrightarrow \text{Inosine} \longrightarrow \text{Hypoxanthine}$$

Some ADP is deaminated only, forming inosine diphosphate (Webster, 1953); and enzymes exist in muscle to resynthesize nucleotides, IMP being condensed with aspartic acid to form adenylsuccinic acid in the first instance (Davey, 1961). Ammonia liberation during rigor mortis can be related, therefore, to the onset of stiffening. Electrophoresis shows that the pre-rigor pattern consists of small amounts of ADP and relatively large amounts of ATP; at post-rigor there is a large quantity of IMP, and traces of inosine, hypoxanthine, ADP, ATP, IDP and ITP (Bendall and Davey, 1957).

During and after post-mortem glycolysis some glycogen may be broken down by α-amylase to glucose and hexose—1:6—diphosphate instead of to lactic acid (Sharp, 1958; cf. Table 4.7).

4.3. FACTORS REFLECTED IN SPECIALIZED MUSCLE FUNCTION AND CONSTITUTION

It is possible to classify muscles broadly as "red" or "white" (Needham, 1926). This superficial differentiation reflects both histological and biochemical differences. So-called "red" muscles tend to have a greater proportion of narrow, myoglobin-rich fibres; so-called "white" muscles have a greater proportion of broad, myoglobin-poor fibres (Denny-Brown, 1929; Hammond 1932a; George and Scaria, 1958). Differentiation of fibres into two types can be demonstrated histochemically by about half-way through the gestation period (Dubowitz, 1966). Gauthier (1969) gives a reminder that "redness" and "whiteness" do not invariably correspond to slow and fast contraction rates, respectively. The terms are useful, however. "Red" fibres are rich in mitochondria (with abundant cristae) and have wide Z-lines. "White" fibres are poor in mitochondria (and these have few cristae) and the width of the Z-lines is about half that in "red" fibres. A (histologically) intermediate type of fibre is also found. The latter resemble "red" fibres, but have larger diameter and a narrow Z-line (cf. § 4.3.5 below). It has been suggested that the narrow diameter of "red" fibres reflects their preferential utilization of incoming protein precursors for energy- yielding purposes rather than for construction (Burleigh, 1974). Red muscles tend to operate over long periods without rest; in these it is found that the mitochrondria, respiratory enzymes and myoglobin are present in greater quantity (Paul and Sperling, 1952; Lawrie, 1952a). White fibres tend to operate in short fast bursts with frequent periods of rest and restitution: respiratory enzymes and myoglobin are present in relatively small amounts only; but lactic dehydrogenase activity is high (Dubowitz and Pearse, 1961). The concentration of the dipeptides, carnosine and anserine, which act as buffers in muscle (Bate-Smith, 1938), appears to bear an inverse proportionality to respiratory activity (Davey, 1960). Differences between muscles, however, are considerably more complex than their classification as "red" or "white" would signify. Both the dynamic (or biochemical) and static (or chemical) aspects of their constitution are elaborate. Their variability reflects the influence of a large number of *intrinsic* factors related to function. The most important of these are (i) species, (ii) breed, (iii) sex, (iv) age, (v) anatomical location of muscle, (vi) training or exercise, (vii) plane of nutrition and (viii) inter-animal variability, the nature of which is little understood. In addition, various *extrinsic* factors modify the behaviour of muscle in the immediate post-mortem period and during storage and processing; and its composition as meat. These are (i) food, (ii) fatigue, (iii) fear, (iv) pre-slaughter manipulation, and (v) environmental conditions at slaughter, in the immediate post-mortem period and during subsequent storage; but these are more appropriately considered in Chapters 5 and 7.

4.3.1. *Species*

Species is perhaps the most easily appreciated factor affecting the composition of muscle; but its effect is conditioned by the simultaneous operation of many of the intrinsic and extrinsic factors already mentioned. In comparisons between species it is thus desirable to choose definite values for these other variables. Some aspects of the chemical composition of the 1. dorsi muscles from mature meat animals are compiled in Table 4.2

TABLE 4.2. *Chemical Composition of L. Dorsi Muscle from Mature Meat Animals*

	Species				
Characteristic	Rabbit[a]	Sheep[bc]	Pig[d]	Ox[e]	Whale (Blue)[cf]
Water (% fat-free)	77·0	77·0	76·7	76·8	77·7
Intramuscular fat (%)	(2·0)	(7·9)	2·9	3·4	2·4
Intramuscular fat (iodine no.)	—	54	57	57	119
Total nitrogen (% fat-free)	3·4	3·6	3·7	3·6	3·6
Total soluble phosphorous (%)	0·20	0·18	0·20	0·18	0·20
Myoglobin (%)	0·02	0·25	0·06	0·50	0·91
Methylamines, trimethylamine oxide, etc.	—	—	—	—	0·01–0·02

[a]Bendall (1962). [b]Callow (1958). [c]Lawrie (1952a). [d]Lawrie et al. (1963). [e]Lawrie (1961). [f]Sharp and Marsh (1953) and personal communication.

Although it is obvious that the contents of water, of total nitrogen and of total soluble phosphorus are similar in all five species, there are marked differences in the other characteristics. The fat of the 1. dorsi of the blue whale has a very much higher iodine number than that of the other four. To some extent this is due to the krill on which whales subsist. Another peculiarity of whale meat is its high content of the buffers carnosine, anserine (Davey, 1960) and balenine. This fact, together with the relatively high oxygen store held by the myoglobin, helps to explain the diving capabilities of this mammal. Its musculature is constrained to operate anaerobically for prolonged periods. Indeed, in the sperm whale and seal, in which the dives may be especially lengthy, the percentage of myoglobin may reach 5–8 per cent of the wet weight of the muscle (Sharp and Marsh, 1953; Robinson, 1939). Such muscle is almost black in appearance. The low myoglobin content of rabbit and pig muscle accords with the superficial paleness of the flesh of these animals. The myoglobin of pig muscle also differs qualitatively from that of ox muscle. The results obtained using freshly cut surfaces of l. dorsi suggest that the rates of oxygenation of myoglobin are fastest in pork, intermediate in lamb and slowest in beef (Haas and Bratzler, 1965).

Wismer-Pedersen (1969) has given data on the proximate composition of the canned meat from l. dorsi of a number of African ungulates. Of those studied the meat from wart-hog had the lowest water content (68.9 per cent) and the highest content of fat (4 per cent), whereas meat from the eland had the highest water content (75·2 per cent) and the lowest content of fat 1·9 per cent). The triglycerides of red deer have relatively high contents of myristic acid compared with those in cattle: those of moose contain more than 40 per cent of stearic acid (Garton, Duncan and McEwan, 1971).

In Table 4.2 the total nitrogen content (fat free) of the l. dorsi muscle of the pig and ox are 3·7 and 3·6 respectively. However, the mean values for the entire musculature of pigs and cattle are 3·45 and 3·55 respectively (Anon., 1961, 1963). It might have been supposed from the data on l. dorsi in Table 4.2 that the intramuscular fat of pigs and cattle always had a comparable iodine number. The danger of such a generalization can be seen, however, from Table 4.3, in which data for the psoas major of boars and bulls are given.

TABLE 4.3. *Chemical Composition of Psoas Major Muscles from Boars and Bulls*

Species	Breed	Sex	Age (months	No.	Moisture (%fat-free)	Total nitrogen (%fat-free)	Intramuscular fat (%)iodine number	
Pig	Large white	Boar	5	5	77·1	3·5	1·6	71·4
Ox	Ayrshire	Bull	10	5	77·4	3·3	1·7	47·0

In this case, despite an almost identical content of intramuscular fat in both species, that in the boar has a much higher iodine number. Generally the iodine number of the fat in the pig is higher than that of the ruminant. In Table 4.4, where the fatty acid composition of the fats from cattle, sheep and pigs are compared, this difference is seen to be largely due to the higher content of linoleic acid in pig fat. This acid has two double bonds.

TABLE 4.4 *Typical Fatty Acid Composition of Fats from Cattle, Sheep and Pigs* (after Dugan, 1957)

Fatty acid	Formula	Per cent fatty acid in fat		
		Cattle	Sheep	Pigs
Palmitic	$C_{15}H_{31}COOH$	29	25	28
Stearic	$C_{17}H_{35}COOH$	20	25	13
Hexadecenoic	$C_{15}H_{29}COOH$	2	—	3
Oleic	$C_{17}H_{33}COOH$	42	39	46
Linoleic	$C_{17}H_{31}COOH$	2	4	10
Linolenic	$C_{17}H_{29}COOH$	0·5	0·5	0·7
Arachidonic	$C_{19}H_{31}COOH$	0·1	1·5	2

Dahl (1958a) has reviewed the characteristics of the fat laid down by different species. Dietary fat is probably of little influence on the depot fat of all species of ruminant, for ingested and saturated fatty acids are hydrogenated by the rumen micro-organisms. These may also effect a change in the length of the fatty acid chains. Nevertheless, there are seasonal alterations in the degree of unsaturation of the depot fats of ruminants, probably because of the ingestion of octadecatrienoic acid during pasture feeding; and there are distinct differences due to breed (Callow and Searle, 1956). Cattle regulate the degree of unsaturation of their fat by interchange between stearic and hexadecenoic acids whereas pigs do so by an exchange between stearic and oleic acids. As opposed to cattle, pigs and other non-ruminants such as the horse tend to deposit unchanged dietary fat. Indeed, pigs which have been fed large quantities of whale oil may have rancid fat *in vivo* (J. K. Walley, personal communication). A high proportion of C_{18} fatty acids is characteristic of mutton fat (Dahl, 1958a). Rabbits, eating the same grass as horses, lay down much more linoleic acid (Shortland, 1953). Species differences between the myosins of the l. dorsi muscles of ox, pig, sheep and horse have been shown immunologically (Furminger, 1964); but the degree of cross-reaction is too high to permit clear identification of unknown meats. The tropomyosins of ox, sheep, pig and rabbit have different electrophoretic characteristics ((Parsons *et al.*, 1969). This is true of the myofibrillar group generally (Champion *et al.*, 1970). Quantitative identification of species on the basis of the electrophoretic pattern of their proteins is still possible after these have been heated to 120°C for 6 min (Mattey *et al.*, 1970).

Apart from static chemical differences due to species, in a given muscle, differences of a more dynamic kind are found. Thus, for example, the activity of cytochrome oxidase varies considerably in the psoas major muscles of different species (Table 4.5). Cytochrome oxidase is the enzyme principally for linking oxygen with the chain of electron carriers by which most substances in muscle are eventually oxidized in providing energy.

TABLE 4.5. *Activity* (Q_{O2}) *of Cytochrome Oxidase in Preparations from Psoas Muscles of Various Mammals* (Lawrie, 1953b)

Species	Activity
Horse	1600
Ox	1200
Pig	1000
Sheep	950
Hare	650
Blue whale	600
Rabbit	250

It is therefore not surprising to find that the activity of this enzyme should be particularly high in the muscles of the horse, which are obviously powerful, and low in those of the rabbit; and that the staying power of the hare and the relatively easy exhaustion of the rabbit are reflected in the capacity of their psoas muscles to gain energy by oxidation (Table 4.5).

Some of the species differences in enzymic activity are reflected post-mortem. Thus at a given temperature (37 C) and in a given muscle (1. dorsi) the characteristics of the onset of rigor mortis are different in horse, ox, pig and sheep (Table 4.6, Fig. 4.4a). The mean chain lengths of glycogens from the 1. dorsi muscles of horse and ox, pig and rabbit are 17, 15 and 13 glucose residues respectively (Kjolberg, Manners and Lawrie, 1963).

TABLE 4.6. *Mean Data on Post-mortem Glycolysis and the Onset of Rigor Mortis in the L. Dorsi of Different Species*

Species	Time to on-set of fast phase of rigor mortis (min/37°/N$_2$)	Initial[a]	pH (at onset)	pH (ulti-mate)	ATP/P[b] (as % TSP) at onset	CP/P[b] (as % TSP) initial
Horse[c]	238	6·95	5·97	5·51	8·3	18·9
Ox[c]	163	6·74	6·07	5·50	13·2	13·2
Pig[c]	50	6·74	6·51	5·57	21·0	7·2
Lamb[d]	60	6·95	6·54	5·60	—	—

[a]i.e., at 1 hr post-mortem. [b]ATP/P, CP/P = phosphorus due to adenosine triphosphate and creatine phosphate respectively (TSP = total soluble phosphorous). [c]Lawrie (1953). [d]Marsh and Thompson (1958). Time to onset in sheep *ca.* 80 min.

It will be seen that while the ultimate pH is the same in all four species, the initial pH levels are high in horse and lamb and relatively low in ox and pig and that the pH at the onset of the fast phase of rigor mortis is low in horse and ox and high in lamb and pig. The level of ATP/P at the onset of rigor mortis is particularly high in the 1. dorsi of the pig. In the psoas major of the rabbit at 37°C, the fast phase of the onset of rigor mortis begins when the ATP/P has fallen to about 15 per cent soluble phosphorus (Bendall, 1951). It is also interesting to observe that the reserve of creatine phosphate—which, as mentioned in Chapter 3, is the most immediate mechanism for resynthesis of ATP—is highest in the horse 1. dorsi and lowest in that of the pig, apparently reflecting their relative capacity for energy production.

Another post-mortem difference in enzymic constitution between the corresponding muscles of different species is shown by the activity of α-amylase. This enzyme converts muscle glycogen to glucose and competes with the system whereby glycogen is converted to lactic acid. Comparative data are given in Table 4.7 from which can be seen the high rate of glucose accumulation in the muscles of pigs and rabbits in comparison with sheep and oxen (Sharp, 1958).

TABLE 4.7. *Post-mortem Activity of α-Amylase in Muscles of Different Species*

Species	Rate glucose accumulation (mg/hr/g at 20 C)
Sheep	0·08
Horse and Ox	0·04
Rabbit	0·50
Pig	0·90

4.3.2. Breed

After species, breed exerts the most general intrinsic influence on the biochemistry and constitution of muscle. A particularly striking effect of breed is found in the horse. The percentage of myoglobin in the 1. dorsi of thoroughbreds, which arch their backs strongly in running, is considerably higher than in this same muscle of the draught horse in which the 1. dorsi is moved relatively little. On the other hand, the psoas muscles show no such difference (Table 4.8).

Among cattle, there are differences between those breeds which are primarily used for milk production and those which are more suitable for meat. Thus, the percentage of intramuscular fat in the 1. dorsi muscle at the level of the 4th, 5th and 6th lumbar vertebrae tends to be markedly greater in beef cattle than in dairy-type animals after the age of 18 months (Callow, 1947; Lawrie, 1961). The percentage of intramuscular

TABLE 4.8. *Myoglobin Concentrations in Muscles of Different Breeds of Horse* (Lawrie, 1950)

Breed	(% wet weight)	
	L. dorsi	Psoas
Draught horse	0·46	0·82
Thoroughbred	0·77	0·88

fat in specially fattened beef animals (e.g. West Highland show cattle) may reach 17 per cent. Mean data for l. dorsi and psoas muscles from Herefords (a beef breed) and Friesians (predominantly a dairy breed) are given in Table 4.9.

TABLE 4.9. *Intramuscular Fat and its Iodine Number in Muscles of Cattle* (from Callow, 1962)

Breed	L. dorsi		Psoas	
	Intramuscular fat (%)	I.N.	Intramuscular fat (%)	I.N.
Hereford	7·1	54·6	5·6	50·5
Friesan	6·4	56·4	5·1	53·9

In sheep the percentage of intramuscular fat is considerably greater among improved breeds such as Hampshire and Suffolk than in semi-wild types, such as Soay and Shetland (Hammond, 1932a). In a study of the back and kidney fats of pigs, it was found that introduction of the Hampshire breed led to an increase in the number of pigs producing abnormally soft and highly unsaturated fats (Lea, Swoboda and Gatherum, 1969). They concluded that, when the cause of softness was not ingested fat, there was a strong correlation between the ratio of the monoene to stearic and palmitic acids, and the melting point.

Because of interest in pale exudative pig musculature (§ 3.4.3), the effect of breed on muscle composition in this species has recently been investigated. At all locations from the 5th thoracic to the 6th lumbar vertebrae, the l. dorsi muscle of pigs of the Large White breed has more myoglobin and a higher ultimate pH than the corresponding muscle from pigs of Landrace breed (Lawrie and Gatherum, 1962) Again, for a given percentage of intramuscular fat in the l. dorsi muscle (lumbar), its iodine number and the area of cross-section of the muscle as a whole are greater in pigs of the Welsh breed than in Landrace, and in the latter than in Large White animals (Anon., 1962; Lawrie and Gatherum, 1964). The rate of post-mortem glycolysis at 37°C in the l. dorsi muscles of Large White pigs in the United Kingdom is only one-third to one-half that in the Danish Landrace (Bendall, Hallund and Wismer-Pedersen, 1963). According to Bendall (1966), however, such breed differences disappear when pigs are curarized (or injected with myanesin) before slaughter. In these circumstances the rate of post-mortem glycolysis in the muscles of Danish Landrace pigs is as slow as that in those of Large White pigs in the United Kingdom. He suggested that electrical stunning can produce, in the pig only, a long-term stimulation of post-mortem glycolysis which would thus lead to that combination of low pH and high temperature responsible for the PSE condition (Hallund and Bendall, 1965). Were this the only reason for the superficial manifestations of the condition, however, there would remain unexplained the great variability in susceptibility shown by individual pigs. Moreover, Lister (1959) found that curare had no effect in diminishing the tendency for a swift production of lactic acid in stress-susceptible Poland China and Chester White pigs. McLoughlin (1968) found no apparent difference in the proteins of l. dorsi when sampled pre-rigor between Landrace and Large White pigs. Sayre, Briskey and Hoekstra (1963a) in the U.S.A. found that the external chain length of glycogen from the l. dorsi muscle of Chester White pigs decreases to a greater extent—but at a slower rate—during post-mortem glycolysis than that in pigs of the Hampshire and Poland China breeds; and the same workers (1963b) found that, when subjected to a temperature of 45°C for 29–60 min pre-slaughter, the l. dorsi muscles of the latter two breeds became pale and exudative during subsequent post-mortem glycolysis, whereas those of the Chester White pigs remained firm and dark. The activities of phosphorylase and phosphofructokinase were markedly higher in l. dorsi muscles of Hampshire pigs than in those of Poland China or Chester White breeds (Sayre *et al.*, 1963c).

4.3.3. *Sex*

In general, males have less intramuscular fat than females, whereas the castrated members of each sex have more intramuscular fat than the corresponding sexually entire animals (Hammond, 1932a; Wierbicki *et al.*, 1956). Table 4.10 gives comparative data on the l. dorsi from a 12-month-old steer and bull of Ayrshire-Red Poll breed. It will be seen that with the exception of the percentage of intramuscular fat (which is relatively high) and the moisture (which is correspondingly low) in the steer in comparison with the bull, there are no striking differences in composition.

TABLE 4.10. *Comparative Composition of L. Dorsi (Lumbar) of Ayrshire—Red Poll Steer and Bull*

	Steer	Bull
Intramuscular fat (%)	3·03	1·00
Intramuscular fat (I.N.)	51·39	51·06
Moisture (%)	74·09	77·30
Myoglobin (%)	0·20	0·19
Ash (%)	0·99	1·16
Total nitrogen (%)	3·61	3·50
Non-protein nitrogen (%)	0·38	0·41
Sarcoplasmic nitrogen (%)	0·94	1·08
Stroma nitrogen[a] (%)	0·36	0·28
Myofibrillar nitrogen (%)	1·93	1·81

[a]i.e. from insoluble protein, mainly originating from connective tissue.

It will be noted, however, that despite the difference in the percentage of intramuscular fat their iodine numbers are the same; and it is found that, in the lumbar region of l. dorsi, the iodine number of intramuscular fat from bulls is markedly less than that from steers at a given level of fatness (Lawrie, 1961). In comparing castrated members of each sex, it has been found that the depot fats of steers have a more saturated fat than those of heifers (Terrell, Suess and Bray, 1969). Fats from the latter have a higher percentage of oleic acid. No differences have been noted in the total cholesterol content of the depot fats between steers and heifers. Such sex differences can be further exemplified by comparing the composition of the l. dorsi muscle of control steers with those of the same age (36–40 months) and breed (Friesian) subjected to the masculizing effect of hexoestrol implants (Table 4.11), there being a somewhat lower content of intramuscular fat in the treated animals, but no other difference.

In pig, also, the major differences in muscle composition due to sex are found in the contents of intramuscular fat. The l. dorsi (lumbar) muscles of hogs (i.e. castrated males) contain about 30 per cent more intramuscular fat than those in gilts (i.e. mature females before pregnancy) of the same age (Lawrie and Gatherum, 1964).

TABLE 4.11. *Comparative Composition of L. Dorsi Muscles from Control and Hexoestrol Implanted Steers* (Lawrie, 1960)

	(Mean of 6)	
	Control	Implanted
Intramuscular fat (%)	3·37	2·42
Intramuscular fat (I.N.)	57·45	59·31
Moisture (%)	74·12	74·88
Ash (%)	1·01	1·02
Total nitrogen (%)	3·51	3·53
Non-protein nitrogen (%)	0·43	0·44
Sarcoplasmic nitrogen (%)	0·88	0·89
Myofibrillar nitrogen (%)	1·83	1·77
Stroma nitrogen (%)	0·36	0·44

4.3.4. *Age*

Irrespective of species, breed or sex the composition of muscles varies with increasing animal age, there being a general increase in most

110   *Meat Science*

parameters other than water, although the rates of increment are by no means identical in all muscles. Moreover, different components reach adult values at different times (Lawrie, 1961). Thus, in bovine 1. dorsi those nitrogen fractions representing myofibrillar and sarcoplasmic proteins have reached 70–80 per cent of their mean adult value by birth, and their subsequent rates of increase become asymptotic at about 5 months of age. Non-protein nitrogen, however, does not attain its characteristic adult value until about 12 months of age; and the concentration of myoglobin increases rapidly until about 24 months of age. Intramuscular fat appears to increase and moisture content on a whole tissue basis to decrease, up to and beyond 40 months of age. Before birth, the moisture content of muscle is very high, being over 90 per cent for a considerable portion of the gestation period (Needham, 1931). On a fat-free basis, however, the moisture content remains fairly constant after 24 months of age. Some idea of the difference in composition of a given muscle in the bovine at two different ages is given in Table 4.12. The great increase in intramuscular fat and in myoglobin content, the lesser increase in total and sarcoplasmic nitrogen and the decrease in moisture and in stroma with age are evident. These trends are also evident in pig 1. dorsi (Table 4.13) in which the composition is compared at 5, 6 and 7 months of age (Lawrie, Pomeroy and

TABLE 4.12. *Comparative Composition of L. Dorsi Muscle in Calf and Steer*

	12-day-old calf	3-year-old steer
Intramuscular fat (%)	0·55	3·69
Intramuscular fat (I.N.)	82·41	56·50
Moisture (%)	77·96	74·11
Myoglobin (%)	0·07	0·46
Total nitrogen (%)	3·30	3·52
Non-protein nitrogen (%)	0·36	0·39
Sarcoplasmic nitrogen (%)	0·62	0·87
Myofibrillar nitrogen (%)	1·52	1·61
Stroma nitrogen (%)	0·80	0·65

'TABLE 4.13. *Comparative Composition of L. Dorsi Muscles from Pigs at Three Ages*

	(Mean of 10)		
	5 months	6 months	7 months
Intramuscular fat (%)	2·85	3·28	3·96
Intramuscular fat (I. N.)	57·4	55·8	55·5
Moisture (%)	76·72	76·37	75·90
Myoglobin (%)	0·030	0·038	0·044
Total nitrogen (%)	3·74	3·74	3·87

Cuthbertson, 1963). Much of the increased saturation of intramuscular lipid in heavier pigs is due to an increase in the ratio of C_{18} to $C_{18.1}$ fatty acids in the neutral lipid fraction (Allen, Bray and Cassens, 1967). It is interesting to note that odd-numbered fatty acids (C_{11}, C_{13}, C_{15}, C_{17}) are quite prevalent in the phospholipid fraction of porcine intramuscular fat. In cattle the iodine number of the intramuscular fat falls very markedly with increasing age. In this species, one of the important factors involved is the development of the rumen microflora, which hydrogenate dietary fats. Calves, initially, tend to deposit dietary fat relatively unchanged (Hoflund, Holmberg and Sellman, 1956).

Myoglobin concentration appears to increase in a two-phase manner, an initial swift rate of increment being followed by one which is more gradual. The fast phase lasts about 1, 2 and 3 years in pigs, horses and cattle respectively. Reflecting the increases in myoglobin with age, there is a concomitant two-phase increment in the activity of the enzymes which govern respiration and, thereby, in energy production potential (Table 4.14; Lawrie, 1953a, b).

The activity of the respiratory enzymes increases in a not dissimilar fashion in various muscles. Typical values at birth and in the adult are given in Table 4.15 for horse muscles.

These activities are based on the rate of oxygen uptake (Q_{O2}) of mitochondrial membrane preparations from the muscles concerned and are thus relative. They are proportional, however, to the absolute values for the muscles themselves.

TABLE 4.14. *Comparative Rates of Increase of Oxygen-linked Factors in Psoas Muscles of Immature and Adult Horses*

The rates of increase are expressed as percentages per year of the average adult values for these factors

Age (years)	Myoglobin concentration	Cytochrome oxidase activity	Capacity for energy-rich phosphate resynthesis
0–2	42·8	37·9	43·8
2–12	2·1	0·6	1·0

TABLE 4.15. *Effect of Animal Age on Enzymic Activity in Preparations from Horse Muscles*

Muscle	Birth	Adult
(a) Cytochrome oxidase		
Heart	1000	2700
Diaphragm	200	1700
Psoas	200	1600
L. dorsi	70	900
(b) Succinic oxidase		
Heart	100	510
Diaphragm	20	260
Psoas	20	240
L. dorsi	10	130

It will be noted that the cytochrome oxidase activity of the heart has attained 33 per cent of its final value by birth, whereas that in l. dorsi is then only 8 per cent of the adult value: values for diaphragm and psoas are intermediate. This order of difference reflects the fact that the heart has been contracting powerfully for a considerable time during uterine life, whereas the other muscles have not: the latter develop preferentially in relation to the animal's need for increasing power to move about. A similar impression is given by the data on succinic oxidase activity.

The connective tissue content of muscle is greater in young animals than in older ones (Bate-Smith, 1948; Wilson, Bray and Phillips, 1954). The concentrations of both collagen and elastin diminish with increasing animal age (Table 4.16).

TABLE 4.16. *Collagen and Elastin Content of*
L. Dorsi Muscles in Cattle (Wilson et al.,
1954)

Cattle	Collagen (%)	Elastin (%)
Calves	0·67	0·23
Steers	0·42	0·12
Old cows	0·41	0·10

As the tenderness of veal and the toughness of older animals testifies, however, the *nature* of the connective tissue must be different at different ages. The connective tissue in the young animals may well contain more reticulin (Boucek, Noble and Marks, 1961). There is a higher concentration of "salt-soluble" collagen (a precursor of insoluble collagen) in young—or actively growing—muscle (Gross, 1958). The degree of intra- and inter-molecular cross-linking (cf. § 3.2.1) between the polypeptide chains in collagen increases with increasing animal age (Carmichael and Lawrie, 1967a, b; Bailey, 1968). The investigations of Bailey and his colleagues have provided detailed information on the age-related changes in the collagen of tendon, muscle and the other tissues. Whilst, in young animals, most of the cross-links are reducible, heat and acid labile and increase up to two years of age, thereafter they are gradually replaced by linkages which are thermally stable (Shimokomaki, Elsden and Bailey, 1972; and cf. § 3.2.1).

4.3.5. Anatomical Location

The most complex of the intrinsic differentiating factors is anatomical. As we have already mentioned, muscles may be broadly classified as "red" or "white" according to whether they carry out sustained action or operate in short bursts. But the variation in shape, size, composition and function of the 300 muscles in the mammalian body obviously reflects a diversity of activity and development the details of which are still largely unknown.

Chemical differences may be considered first of all. Ramsbottom and Strandine (1948) analysed fifty muscles of adult beef animals. Moisture and fat contents ranged from 62.5 and 18.1 per cent respectively in the intercostal muscles to 76 and 1·5 per cent respectively in extensor carpi radials. The ultimate pH ranged from 5·4 in semi-membranosus to 6·0 in sternocephalicus. Comparative data on chemical parameters of various beef and pork muscles are given in Table 4.17 (Lawrie, Pomeroy and Cuthbertson, 1963; Lawrie, Pomeroy and Williams, 1964). Particularly striking is the high iodine number and the low total nitrogen content in

TABLE 4.17. *Some Chemical Parameters of Various Muscles*

Muscle	Moist- ure (%)	Intramuscular fat (%)	(I.N.)	Total nitro- gen (% fat free)	Hydroxy- proline (µg/g)
(a) Beef					
L. dorsi (lumbar)	76·51	0·56	54·21	3·54	520
L. dorsi (thoracic)	77·10	0·90	56·62	3·47	610
Psoas major	77·34	1·46	52·92	3·30	350
Rectus femoris	78·07	1·49	67·82	3·40	550
Triceps (lateral heat)	77·23	0·73	62·20	3·45	1000
Superficial digital flexor	78·67	0·40	81·47	3·27	1430
Sartorius	77·95	0·58	64·04	3·33	870
Extensor carpi radialis	74·83	0·60	68·16	3·29	1160
(b) Pork					
L. dorsi (lumbar)	76·33	3·36	56·3	3·77	670
L. dorsi (thoracic)	76·94	3·26	55·5	3·69	527
Psoas major	77·98	1·66	62·8	3·58	426
Rectus femoris	78·46	0·99	71·5	3·41	795
Triceps (lateral head)	78·68	1·84	67·0	3·46	1680
Superficial digital flexor	78·87	1·90	65·3	3·35	1890
Sartortius	78·71	0·87	—	3·41	850
Extensor carpi radialis	79·04	1·39	69·7	3·36	2470

superficial digital flexor and its relatively high concentration of hydroxyproline (as an indicator of connective tissue). Using hydroxyproline as criterion, the lowest content of connective tissue may be seen to be in psoas major ($350\mu g/g$); in extensor carpi radialis, however, it can be about 2500 $\mu g/g$. Bendall (1967) measured the elastin content of various beef muscles using a technique whereby the last traces of collagen and myofibrillar proteins were removed. In most of the muscles from the choice cuts of the hind quarter and loin the elastin content was generally less than 5 per cent of the total connective tissue. In *semitendinosus,* however, it constituted 40 per cent of the total. Of the muscle of the forequarter only 1. dorsi had a comparable elastin content. Bendall concluded the elastin contributed to the toughness of cooked meat to about the same extent as denatured collagen. Although, within a given muscle, there is a hyperbolic relationship between the content of intramuscular fat and its iodine number (Callow and Searle, 1956) this clearly does not hold between different muscles. Certain differences between muscles in the iodine number or their fat have been attributed to corresponding differences in local temperature, a higher temperature being associated with a lower iodine number; and vice versa (Callow, 1958, 1962). There is obviously a wide range of values for these chemical parameters and this can be equally exemplified in corresponding muscles of beef and pork. In comparing those muscles which are common to both species it is seen that the muscles listed do not have the same relative composition in the two species. Thus while extensor carpi radialis has the lowest moisture content in beef, it has the highest value in the pig. Clearly both lumbar and thoracic 1. dorsi muscles have the highest content of intramuscular fat in the pig; in beef, however, the percentage of intramuscular fat is relatively low in these muscles. Again, the hydroxyproline content of superficial digital flexor is markedly greater in beef than in other muscles of this species. In the pig, however, the highest hydroxyproline content of this same group of muscles is found in extensor carpi radialis. Data on the ultimate pH of these muscles (not represented) show that as the percentage of moisture on a fat-free basis increases so also does the ultimate pH: there is, in fact, a significant positive correlation between these two variables in the pig.

This obtains not only between different muscles but within a given muscle also.

It is particularly interesting to note that, as judged by the hydroxyproline content, the connective tissue concentration is greater in most pig muscles than in corresponding beef muscles. Since pork is generally tender, this again emphasizes that the quality of connective tissue must be considered as a factor additional to its quantity. Studies of the fatty acid compositions of neutral lipids and phospholipids of different muscles have revealed a number of distinctions between them. For example, the phospholipid content and the ratio of C_{18} to C_{16} fatty acids in the total lipid are particularly high in the diaphragm (both in beef and pork) in comparison with such muscles as *l. dorsi* and *psoas* (Catchpole and Lawrie, 1967; Allen, Cassens, Bray, 1967; Hornstein, Crowe and Hiner, 1968).

In Table 4.18 comparative data are given on the fatty acid composition of intramuscular fats from nine muscles of an adult Large White × Landrace pig (Catchpole, Horsfield and Lawrie, 1970). In respect of the major fatty acid components (oleic, palmitic, linoleic, stearic and palmitoleic) the pattern for the nine locations is not dissimilar. Nevertheless, the ratio of linoleic to oleic differs substantially between locations; and there are noteworthy distinctions in respect of arachidonic and pentadecenoic acids. Differences in the fatty acid pattern between anatomical locations are *more* marked when muscles are fractionated into such functional components as mitochondria.

Differences between muscles in other parameters are, of course, found; those in sodium, potassium and myoglobin are shown for five pig muscles in Table 4.19. In beef animals, in contrast to pigs, *extensor carpi radialis* does not have an abnormally low content of potassium. This may reflect differences in slaughtering procedures with the two species, as potassium is found at higher concentration in well-drained muscle (Pomeroy, 1971). The apparent variability in potassium content makes it difficult to accept that the radioactive emanations from K^{40} could accurately indicate the lean meat content of carcases. Nitrogen distribution may also differ between muscles (Table 4.20), and this, together with differences in total nitrogen (Table 4.17a and 4.17b),

TABLE 4.18. *Relative Fatty Acid Composition of Total Lipids from Muscles of the Adult Pig*

Muscle	Fatty acid (as per cent total fatty acids)									
	$C_{18:1}$	$C_{16:0}$	$C_{18:2}$	$C_{18:2}$	$C_{16:1}$	$C_{20:4}$	$C_{14:0}$	$C_{15:1}$	$C_{17:1}$	$C_{13:0}$
L. dorsi (lumbar 4—6)	40	24	11	10	5	2·5	1·5	1·5	0·8	—
L. dorsi (thoracic 13—15)	37	21	12·5	11	5	4·8	1·0	3·2	1·2	—
L. dorsi (thoracic 8—12)	34	30	11	10	3·5	4·3	1·0	2·5	0·5	0·2
L. dorsi (thoracic 5—7)	38	21	13·5	10	4	4·2	1·5	2·5	1·0	0·3
Semimembranosus	35	24	14	10	4·5	4·2	1·5	2·5	1·3	0·2
Rectus femoris	29	21	16	11	5	5·8	1·0	3·7	0·5	—
Psoas	33	22	17	12	5	3·8	1·2	2·3	1·5	—
Diaphragm	35	22	15	15	5	2·0	1·5	1·0	0·8	—
Supraspinatus	34	26	14	19	6	—	—	4·8	—	—

TABLE 4.19. *Sodium, Potassium and Myoglobin in Pig Muscles*
(Lawrie and Pomeroy, 1963)

Muscle	Sodium (as % wet weight)	Potassium (as % wet weight)	Myoglobin (as % wet weight)
L. dorsi (lumbar)	0·05	0·35	0·044
Psoas major	0·05	0·37	0·082
Rectus femoris	0·05	0·38	0·086
Triceps (lateral head)	0·07	0·31	0·089
Extensor carpi radialis	0·08	0·29	0·099

TABLE 4.20. *Distribution of Nitrogen in Bovine Psoas
and L. Dorsi Muscles (as per cent Total Nitrogen)*

	Psoas	L. dorsi
Non-protein nitrogen	11·2	11·6
Sarcoplasmic nitrogen	21·3	26·0
Myofibrillar nitrogen	44·0	52·5
Stroma nitrogen	23·5	9·9

reflects both quantitive and qualitative differences in the proteins of different muscles. Indeed, starch gel electrophoresis reveals that the pattern of soluble, sarcoplasmic proteins may be unusual in certain muscles. Thus, the heart and, in the rabbit, the small red muscle deep in the proximal portion of the hind limb, differ from skeletal muscles generally in that the bands corresponding to the protein enzymes of the glycolytic pathway are virtually absent. Moreover, such lactic dehydrogenase activity as is present is associated with a completely different protein to that in other muscles (R. K. Scopes, personal communication).

Quantitative differences in myoglobin and connective tissue (as indicated by hydroxyproline) have already been considered (Tables 4.17 and 4.19); many such examples could be given. It is apparent, however, that there are also qualitative differences in proteins between muscles within a given species and at a given age. Thus the proteins of beef 1.

dorsi and psoas muscles differ in their susceptibility to freezing damage. Even when the rate of post-mortem glycolysis and the ultimate pH are the same in each, the former exudes, on thawing, nearly twice as much fluid or "drip". Moreover, the solids content of the drip from l. dorsi is about 25 per cent higher than that from psoas (Howard, Lawrie and Lee, 1960), and the relationship of total solids to ash is quite different in the exudate from the two muscles. Differences in the susceptibility to freeze-drying of the myosins prepared from porcine psoas and l. dorsi have been shown (Parsons *et al.,* 1969). While the pattern of electrophoreti-cally seperable components in both myosins is similar when prepared from fresh muscle, they differ considerably after freeze-drying, i. dorsi showing a greater degree of change. Tropomyosins from the two muscles, on the other hand, give similar patterns both before and after freeze-drying. Herring (1968) has found differences in the actomyosins extracted from naturally tough and tender muscles and Dube *et al.,* (1972) found that the myofibrillar proteins of bovine l. dorsi were less susceptible to oxidation of the sulphydril groups (on heating to about 60°C) than those of psoas muscle. Other aspects of differences in the types of protein found in various muscles are indicated by the moisture-protein ration (Lockett, Swift and Sulzbacher, 1962) and by the relative susceptibility of pig muscles to become pale and exudative post-mortem, l. dorsi and semi-membranosus being especially labile (Lawrie, Gatherum and Hale, 1958; Wismer-Pedersen, 1959a). The susceptibility of myoglobin to oxidize during chill or frozen storage differs between different muscles (Ledward, 1917a; Owen and Lawrie, 1972). When the level of ultimate pH is high, the myofibrillar proteins of l. dorsi and semimembranosus are altered less by freeze-drying than are those of psoas and biceps femoris. When the ultimate pH is normal, however, the myofibrillar proteins of l. dorsi are relatively the most susceptible to damage in freeze-drying (Table 4.21). The patterns obtained by starch gel electrophoresis of myofibrillar proteins from rabbit, ox and sheep, indicate that, within each species, these differ between different muscles (Champoin, Parsons and Lawrie, 1970).

Detailed studies of the myofibrillar proteins of "red", "white" and cardiac muscles have revealed various differences betwween specific

120   *Meat Science*

TABLE 4.21. *The Percentage of Myofibrillar Protein from Various Pork Muscles which is Soluble in* 0·92M *KCl at* pH 6·0

Muscle	Ultimate pH 6·5–7·2		Ulitmate pH 5·3–5·6	
	(Frozen)	(Freeze dried)	(Frozen)	(Freeze dried)
L. dorsi	91	85	53	41
Psoas	80	68	49	40
Biceps femoris	88	75	55	46
Semimembranosus	85	77	54	46

components. Thus the electrophoretic patterns of the so called myosin light chains (Perrie and Perry, 1970) and those of troponin I (Cole and Perry, 1975) are different when these proteins are derived from the three types of muscle. This reflects differing degrees and mechanisms of phosphorylation of the proteins concerned (Perry et al., 1975). Two subunits of tropomyosin, α and β, have been isolated (Cummins and Perry, 1973) and two of α-actinin (Robson, Goll, Arakawa and Stromer, 1970), the ration of these subunits being different in "red" and "white" muscle. The myosin of "red" muscle has a higher content of 3-methylhistidine than that of "white" (Johnson and Perry, 1970).

In addition to purely chemical differences, muscles also vary in their enzymic constitution. Differences in the activity of the enzymes of the cytochrome system have already been exemplified (Table 4.15); comparative data for other specific enzyme activities are given in Table 4.22.

As between species (Table 4.6), so also between muscles there are broad differences in the pattern of post-mortem glycolysis and of the onset of rigor mortis. Although the nature of these differences is not yet understood in detail, they are most important in relation to the texture and appearance of meat post-mortem. Under controlled conditions muscles may differ in the times to the onset of rigor mortis, in their initial and ultimate pH, in their content of initial and residual glycogen, in the rates of pH fall aerobically and anaerobically, in their initial store of energy-rich phosphate (i.e. the labile phosphorus of ATP and CP), in

TABLE 4.22. *Activity of Certain Enzymes in Various Beef Muscles*
(after Herman, 1961)

Muscle	Lactic dehydro- genase[a]	Glutamic dehydro- genase[b]	Carbonic anhydrase[c]
L. dorsi	3·53	661	0·59
Semimembranosus	3·73	730	0·63
Serratus ventralis	1·08	960	0·63
Rectus abdominis	2·58	675	0·66
Semitendinosus	3·74	813	0·47
Trapezius	2·14	836	0·47

[a] Moles lactate oxidized per kg wet weight per 3 min.
[b] Micromoles glutamate oxidized per kg wet weight per hr.
[c] Log pressure change per g wet weight per min.

their capacity for energy-rich phosphate resynthesis, and in their power to split ATP and to suppress such splitting (i.e. Marsh-Bendall factor activity). Such differences are apparent in Table 4.23, in which data from four horse muscles are represented (Lawrie, 1952a, 1953a, b, c, 1955). Similar differences are obtained between muscles of beef animals. Postmortem glycolysis will be considered again in Chapter 5.

The time to the onset of the fast phase of rigor mortis under anaerobic conditions at 37°C tends to be proportionate to the initial store of energy-rich phosphorus and of glycogen. On the one hand l. dorsi has the characteristics of a "white" muscle, capable of short bursts of activity, this being aided by the relatively large store of energy-rich phosphorus and a low capacity for the aerobic resynthesis of $\sim P$. On the other hand, the heart has a capacity for sustained activity, represented by its marked ability to resynthesize $\sim P$ aerobically, and a low $\sim P$ store. It is interesting to note that the power to suppress ATP-ase is least where—in the heart—there would be no lasting relaxation phase.

There are differences in glycogen metabolism between "red"and "white" muscles, the pathway from glycogen to glucose being more active in the former, as shown by the specific activity of residual, and trichloacetic acid-soluble, glycogens after the administration of C^{14}-glucose (Bocek *et al.*, 1966).

The activity of glucose-6-phosphate dehydrogenase, 6-phosphogluconic dehydrogenase and glycogen synthetase are also more marked in "red" muscles. On the other hand the enzymes in the pathway from glycogen to lactic acid are more active in white muscle (e.g. phosphorylase, phosphohexose-isomerase, phosphofructokinase, fructose-1:6-diphosphatase, aldolase, α-glycerophosphate dehydrogenase, pyruvate kinase, lactic dehydrogenase: Beatty and Bocek, 1970). Enzymes involved in the complete oxidation of fat and carbohydrate are more prevalent in red muscles (e.g. β-hydroxy acyl CoA dehydrogenase, citrate synthetase, isocitric dehydrogenase, malic dehydrogenase, succinic dehydrogenase and cytochrome oxidase). Red muscles have a smaller content of the calcium-activated, sarcoplasmic factor which is believed to disintegrate essential structural elements of the myofibril during conditioning (Goll, 1974), and this may explain the observation that they tenderize less markedly than white muscles.

In accordance with the lower power to suppress ATP-ase activity in "red" muscle (i.e. a lower activity of the Marsh–Bendall factor) it is of interest that the grana of the sarcoplasmic reticulum isolated from "red" muscle have negligible power to make up Ca^{++} compared with those from "white" muscle (Gergely *et al.*, 1965). This may explain the greater susceptibility of red muscles to "cold-shortening" (cf.§§ 10.3.3.1. 7.1.1.1.).

The elements of the sarcoplasmic reticulum are also morphologically different in the two types of muscle. It is further of interest that it is in the grana of the sarcoplasmic reticulum that the adenyl cyclase systems is found (Sutherland and Robson, 1966) suggesting that the relative metabolism of "red" and "white" muscles may be be mediated through cyclic 3′-5′-AMP. Some hormones, such as catecholamines, appear to direct their control of tissues through the enzyme adenyl cyclase. This is said to be located on cell membranes and to govern the synthesis of cyclic 3′-5′-AMP from ATP. Again, fructose 1,6-diphosphatase (which is believed to expedite glycogen formation from 2-glycerophosphate) is high in "white" muscles but low, or even absent, in such "red" muscles as rabbit *semitendinosus* and heart (Opie and Newsholme, 1967).

In Table 4.23 l. dorsi may be regarded as a fairly typical muscle, having residual glycogen at an ultimate pH of about 5·5 (cf. § 4.2.2). It will be seen, however, that horse psoas and diaphragm have

TABLE 4.23. *Characteristics of Post-mortem Glycolysis in Horse Muscles*

Characteristic	L. dorsi	Psoas	Dia-phragm	Heart
Time to onset fast phase rigor mortis $(min/37°C/N^2)^b$	214	173	148	50[a]
pH initial[b]	6·95	7·02	6·97	6·90[a]
at onset	5·97	6·24	6·28	6·30
ultimate	5·51	5·98	5·91	5·81
Glycogen:				
initial[b] (mg/100 g)	2249	1229	1715	584
residual (mg/100 g)	1411	606	1109	276
ATP/P at onset (as % TSP)	6·	6	7	15
CP/P initial[b] (as % TSP)	19	10	3	1
Initial $\sim P(\gamma/g)$	700	450	520·	100
Rate aerobic pH fall (pH/hr)	0·13	0·06	0·07	0·0
Rate anaerobic pH fall (pH/hr)	0·19	0·11	0·11	1·20[a]
Rel. capacity $\sim P$ resynthesis aerobically (arbitrary units)	0·24	0·51	0·51	2·40
ATP-ase activity				
(i) unwashed $(\sim P/hr/g)$	2400	1800	1800	1800
(ii) washed $(\sim P/hr/g)$	9000	4800	5400	1800
Marsh–Bendall factor activity (ii)–(i)	6600	3000	3600	0

[a] Because of the fast rate of pH fall in heart, special precautions are necessary to demonstrate the onset of rigor mortis; some data for heart are thus not strictly comparable with those from other muscles.

[b] Initial = 1 hr post-mortem, except in heart.

ATP/P, CP/P = labile phosphorus of adenosine triphosphate and creatine phosphate, respectively.

TSP = total soluble phosphorus.

$\sim P$ = sum of ATP/P and CP/P.

considerable residual glycogen at an ultimate pH of about 6. This phenomenon is also observed in beef sternocephalicus muscle. In the latter the residual glycogen has a shorter external chain length (9) than the initial glycogen (12) (Lawrie, Manners and Wright, 1959); but this does not, in itself, appear to explain the cessation of glycolysis. It is conceivable that such qualitative differences in glycogen may represent some kind of specialization of muscle function, e.g. precision of movement, as a factor additional to the ability to contract quickly or in a sustained manner. On the other hand, variations in AMP-deaminase activity between different muscles could explain some of the characteristic differences found in ultimate pH (Scopes, 1970). Using reconstituted systems he (Scopes, 1974) found that the *extent* of post-mortem glycolysis depended significantly on the proportion of phosphorylase in the *a* form.

Even within a single muscle there may be systematic differences in composition and constitution. Figure 4.8 indicates how the ultimate pH and pigmentation vary along the l. dorsi muscle in Large White and Landrace pigs (Lawrie and Gatherum, 1962). In the semimembranosus muscles of pigs, areas only 1 cm apart may be pale and exudative and

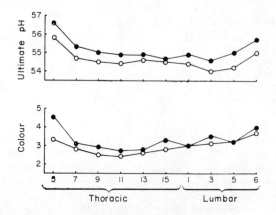

FIG. 4.8. The mean (20) ultimate pH and colour (arbitrary units) of l. dorsi muscles from Large White (●) and Landrace (○) pigs of similar weight, at the levels of the 5th, 7th, 9th, 13th and 15th thoracic and 1st, 3rd, 5th and 6th lumbar verterbrae. (Lawrie and Gatherum, 1962.)

have an ultimate pH of 4·9, on the one hand, or be pink and dry and have an ultimate pH of 5·6, on the other. In two-toned *semitendinosus* muscle in the pig, it has been shown that the concentrations of myoglobin, and of the cytochrome enzyme system, are higher in the darker (red) than in the lighter (white) portions; and the latter have a greater content of sarcoplasmic proteins (Beecher, *et al.*, 1968). In other words, the light and dark regions of a given muscle apparently reflect predominant capacities for glycolytic and oxidative metabolism, respectively, as do muscles which are uniformly "red" or "white". It is a peculiarity of the pig that such "red" fibres as this species has are clustered in the central region of the fibre bundles: in other mammalian muscles the "red" fibres have no preferred location (Cassens, 1970). Variability within a given muscle may also be exemplified by bovine l. dorsi. The percentage of intramuscular fat is consistently higher in the region of the 4th, 5th and 6th lumbar vertebrae than in the region of the 8th, 9th and 10th thoracic vertebrae at all ages from birth to 36 months. But, while the iodine number of the intramuscular fat is initially lower at the former location, it eventually becomes significantly higher due to the elaboration of a greater proportion of C_{16} and C_{18} fatty acids in the lumbar region with increasing age. The physiological implications of such a difference and of the reversal in relative iodine number are unknown.

There are marked differences in the enzymic constitution of individual muscle fibres, some being wider in diameter and predominantly glycolytic in their metabolism, others being narrower, having a greater proportion of respiratory activity (George and Naik, 1958; Blanchaer and Van Wijhe, 1962) and being supplied by more blood capillaries (Romanul, 1964). The "red" fibres are able to oxidize fat—indeed, in prolonged muscle activity, it is the principal fuel—and the inflow of lipids into muscle has been observed to supply such fibres (Vallyathan, Grinyer and George, 1970). The glycogen of "red" fibres resembles amylopectin, that of "white" fibres resembles amylose in respect of the colour produced with iodine. The high glycogen content of horse muscles (cf. Table 4.23) and of the "red" fibres of the guinea-pig (Gillespie, Simpson and Edgerton, 1970) emphasize that this criterion does not invariably signify a dependence on glycolytic, as opposed to respiratory, metabolism. Non-differentiation of fibres into such types is symptomatic of certain diseases in muscle, e.g. Dubowitz, 1963. Since differences of this order are integrated over the volume of muscle or meat normally encountered, however, they will not be further elaborated on here.

4.3.6. Training and Exercise

Implicit in the differences in constitution in a given muscle between active and inactive species and breeds, between young and old animals, and between "red" and "white" muscles in a given animal, is the concept that constant usage can cause a development of certain features and that, conversely, disuse can cause a reversion of such factors. Systematic usage over a period ("training") as opposed to fatiguing exercise immediately preslaughter, or cessation of activity in a previously active muscle, cause opposing changes in constitution. As to what training signifies, Müller (1957) has shown that hypertrophy—and presumably associated changes in muscle constitution—is not stimulated unless the exercise involves about two-thirds of the maximum resistance which the muscle can overcome. The most obvious alteration in constitution is the elaboration of myoglobin during systematic exercise and its failure to develop in inactive muscles (Lehmann, 1904; Hammond, 1932a). This is logical if myoglobin functions as a short-term oxygen store in muscle (Millikan, 1939) which facilitates its ability to develop power. There would appear to be a concomitant increase in the activity of the respiratory enzymes (Denny-Brown, 1961). Bach (1948) has shown that if the tendon of the red soleus muscle of the rabbit is transplanted to the tendon of the pale posterior tibial muscle, the soleus loses myoglobin and becomes a "white" fast-contracting muscle. Such transplants have indicated that it is the nerve fibres supplying a muscle which determine whether it will develop a large proportion of glycolytic fibres, and become fast-acting, or a large proportion of oxidative fibres, and become slow-acting (Romanul and Van der Meulen, 1967).

Another feature of training is the elaboration of increased stores of muscle glycogen, which, of course, leads to a lower ultimate pH post-mortem (Bate-Smith, 1948). This should not be confused, however, with the *depletion* of glycogen, and the high ultimate pH which exhausting exercise immediately prior to slaughter would cause (Chapter 5).

There is some suggestion that training may increase the equilibrium level of phosphorylase *a* (Cori, 1956) which is responsible for the first step in making glycogen available for energy production both in respiration and under the anaerobic conditions of glycolysis. On the other hand, Gould and Rawlinson (1959) could detect no difference in the level of phosphorylase—or in that of lactic and malic dehydrogenases—on training. As mentioned above, muscles, when working aerobically, i.e. when well trained, depend on fat rather than carbohydrate for their long-term energy requirements (Zebe, 1961).

The atrophy which arises when disuse is complete is invariably accompanied by a decrease in total nitrogen and in the percentages of sarcoplasmic and myofibrillar proteins; and by an increase in the amount of connective tissue proteins (Helander, 1957). Moderate inactivity causes a diminution in the sarcoplasmic and myofibrillar proteins only (Helander, 1958).

4.3.7. *Plane of Nutrition*

The general effects of the level of nutrition on the growth of meat animals (Hammond, 1932a; McMeekan, 1940) are reflected in the composition of the individual muscles. As the percentage of fatty tissue in an animal increases, the percentage of intramuscular fat also tends to increase (Callow, 1948). This relationship is seen to hold, in general, with the data for cattle and sheep given in Table 4.24 (Callow and Searle, 1956; Callow, 1958).

The content of intramuscular fat also reflects the plane of nutrition when this is deliberately controlled. Data for the 1. dorsi and psoas muscles of cattle are given in Table 4.25 (Callow, 1962).

Moreover, on a high plane of nutrition, a greater proportion of fat is synthesized from carbohydrate; and such fat has, consequently, a lower iodine number. With an increasing degree of emaciation, on the other hand, the relative percentage of linoleic acid increases and that of

TABLE 4.24. *Relationship between Percentage of Fatty Tissue in Carcase (FT/C) and Percentage of Intramuscular Fat (F/MT) in L. Dorsi and Psoas Muscles of Cattle and Sheep*

FT/C	F/MT			
	L. dorsi		Psoas	
	Cattle	Sheep	Cattle	Sheep
20	4·5	5·8	4·7	2·4
26	6·1	8·9	5·3	4·6
34	7·0	8·8	5·6	5·6
39	11·1	8·7	8·2	5·1

TABLE 4.25. *Percentage of Intramuscular Fat in L. Dorsi and Psoas Muscles of Cattle on Four Planes of Nutrition*

Plane of nutrition	L. dorsi	Psoas
High—high	8·3	7·1
Moderate—high	8·1	6·8
High—moderate	5·5	5·0
Moderate—moderate	7·7	6·6

palmitic decreases in the phospholipids (Vickery, 1977). Ingestion of much unsaturated fatty acid in the diet will lead to deposition of unsaturated, intramuscular fat in pigs but not in ruminants. In these, dietary fatty acids are reduced in the digestive tract. The effects of plane of nutrition on the composition of muscles from ewes of two age groups are shown in Table 4.26 (Pállson and Verges, 1952).

It is obvious that a high plane of nutrition increases the percentage of intramuscular fat and decreases the percentage of moisture in sheep, both soon after birth and in older animals, the effect being superimposed upon trends due to the age. Similar data were obtained by McMeekan (1940) in pigs at 16 and 26 weeks (Table 4.27) and these show the same trends.

TABLE 4.26. *Effect of Age and Plane of Nutrition on Composition of L. Dorsi Muscles from Ewes*

| | Plane of nutrition | | | |
| | High | | Low | |
	9 weeks	41 weeks	9 weeks	41 weeks
Intramuscular fat (^o_o)	2·13	5·00	0·51	3·24
Intramuscular fat (I.N.)	65·67	55·85	99·65	51·34
Moisture (%)	77·59	73·59	81·03	74·13

TABLE 4.27. *Effect of Age and Plane of Nutrition on Composition of L. Dorsi Muscle of Pigs*

| | Plane of nutrition | | | |
| | High | | Low | |
	16 weeks	26 weeks	16 weeks	26 weeks
Intramuscular fat (%)	2·27	4·51	0·68	2·02
Intramuscular fat (I.N.)	62·90	59·20	95·40	66·80
Moisture (%)	74·39	71·78	78·09	73·74

Janicki, Kolaczyk and Kortz (1963) have shown that, in addition to the above changes in the percentages of intramuscular fat and moisture, there is a progressive diminution in the percentage of myoglobin from 0·08 to 0·05 per cent in the l. dorsi as the plane of nutrition is increased in pigs. The moisture content of muscle may also be influenced by the *nature* of the diet (Lushbough and Urbin, 1963).

Undernutrition causes a marked increase in the water content of muscle. Thus, the muscles of pigs which had been kept severely undernourished from the age of 10 days to 1 year had a moisture content of 83 per cent in comparison with 74 per cent in the muscles of a corresponding 1-year-old, well-nourished pig (Widdowson, Dickerson and McCance, 1960).

4.3.8. *Inter-animal Variability*

The least understood of the intrinsic factors which affect the constitution of muscle is the variability between individual animals. Even between litter mates of the same sex considerable differences are found in the percentages of intramuscular fat, of moisture and of total nitrogen and in the distribution of nitrogen between sarcoplasmic, myofibrillar and stroma proteins (Lawrie and Gatherum, 1964). As has been indicated already (Chapter 2) such differences may be adventitiously determined by the position of the embryo in the uterus (McLaren and Michie, 1960) and, after birth, by the suckling order (Barber, Braude and Mitchell, 1955; McBride, 1963); but the precise reasons have not been found so far.

Recessive genes no doubt account for apparently sporadic differences in the composition of muscles of animals within a given breed. Reference has already been made to the phenomenon of doppelender cattle, in which most of the musculature is hypertrophied and the ratio of muscle to bone and fat greatly increased (McKellar, 1960; Pomeroy and Williams, 1962). Although the musculature concerned has been reported as less developed than normal and to contain more moisture and less fat (Neuvy and Vissak, 1962), recent investigations in the United Kingdom suggest, on the contrary, that the quality of the musculature generally is improved (in terms of eating quality), the content of total nitrogen being greater, the contents of moisture and of hydroxyproline being less than in normal muscle (Lawrie, Pomeroy and Williams, 1963) and the tenderness greater (Bouton, Harris, Shorthose and Ellis, 1978).The intramuscular fat is also lower in the muscles of doppelender cattle. Selected data are given in Table 4.28. Such hypertrophied muscles have a lower succinic dehydrogenase activity than normal, the metabolism on the fibres being more of the glycolytic than oxidative type (Ashmore and Robinson, 1969). Since the former are thicker it has been suggested that this feature accounts for the muscular hypertrophy as superficially observed.

Among more dynamic differences, inter-animal variability in the rate of post-mortem glycolysis in pigs may be considerable (Fig. 4.5). There is some evidence that a slow rate may be associated with the presence of the enzyme phosphoglucomutase in a dephosphorylated form (R. K. Scopes, personal communication). Clearly, substantial differences in the composition of muscle are caused by factors which are, as yet, unexplained: their elucidation will no doubt form the subject for a wide area of future research.

TABLE 4.28. *Composition of Various Muscles from Normal (C) and Doppelender (D) Heifers*

Muscle	Moisture (%)		Intra-muscular fat(%)		(%)		Hydroxy-proline (μg%g)	
	C	D	C	D	C	D	C	D
L. dorsi (lumbar)	76·51	75·63	0·56	0·27	3·54	3·70	520	350
Psoas major	77·34	77·41	1·46	0·43	3·30	3·35	350	265
Rectus femoris	78·07	76·81	1·49	0·30	3·40	3·51	550	330
Triceps (lat. head)	77·23	76·59	0·73	0·37	3·45	3·53	1000	770
Superficial digital flexor	78·67	77·79	0·40	0·42	3·27	3·40	1430	415
Sartorius	77·95	77·38	0·58	0·25	3·33	3·41	870	460

CHAPTER 5

THE CONVERSION OF MUSCLE TO MEAT

IN CONSIDERING how meat animals grow and how their muscles develop and are differentiated, the distinction between the terms "muscle" and "meat" has not been emphasized. Meat, although largely reflecting the chemical and structural nature of the muscles of which it is the post-mortem aspect, differs from them because a series of biochemical and biophysical changes are initiated in muscle at the death of the animal. Some details of the conversion of muscle to meat will now be given.

5.1. PRE-SLAUGHTER HANDLING

Although, at the most, only a few days elapse between the time when meat animals have attained the weight desired by the producer and the actual moment of slaughter, their condition may change appreciably in this period. This will happen to some extent irrespective of whether the animals are driven on the hoof or transported to the abattoir. There may be loss of weight, bruising and, if the animals are in road or rail trucks, suffocation due to inadequate ventilation. In 1971 bruising, oedema and emaciation accounted for 4 per cent, 65 per cent and 77 per cent of the total condemnations of pigs, sheep and cattle respectively, In Northern Ireland (Melrose and Gracey, 1975). In most cases of extensive bruising damage to muscles causes the release of enzymes into the blood stream; and the relative concentrations of creative phosphokinase and aspartate transaminase permits an assessment of how long before slaughter bruising occurred (Shaw, 1973).

Death of pigs in transport appears to have increased greatly in the decade 1960–70 (Thornton, 1973). There is a marked seasonal effect, deaths both in transit and lairage being correlated with the environmental temperature (Allen, Herbert and Smith, 1974). It was reported that the transport of pigs in double-decker road vehicles was particularly liable to affect the musculature adversely as meat (Williams, 1968). It is increasingly recognized that thoughtless or rough handling of animals in the immediate pre-slaughter period will adversely affect the meat, quite apart from being inhumane. Recommendations on ante-mortem care (Thornton, 1973; Houthuis, 1957) will not be discussed at length in the present volume: but some aspects of the question should be considered.

It would appear that only recently have attempts been made to study the behaviour pattern of meat animals with a view to improving pre-slaughter handling. With pigs, for example, acknowledgement that these animals tend to fight when awaiting slaughter, especially if they come from different farms, led Danish workers to employ a halter which prevents biting and damage to the flesh (Jørgensen, 1963) and droving is so arranged that the more cautious animals follow the bolder ones. With particular reference to pigs, it is clear that responses to transport and handling depend not only on the stress susceptibility of the animal as a whole, but also on which muscles are being considered. Both the metabolic capability of individual muscles and the duration and severity of transport determine whether the PSE condition will develop or whether glycogen reserves will be depleted sufficiently to produce dark meat (Anon., 1971). Much of the stress sustained in transport and handling arise during loading and unloading. Tranquillizing drugs (when permitted) may be effective in preventing fighting and struggling; and may reduce the incidence of exudative meat, injury and death.

5.1.1. *Moisture Loss*

The moisture content of pork muscle is especially liable to change because of even moderate fatigue or hunger in the immediate pre-slaughter period (Callow, 1938a, b). When fasted during transit, cattle lose weight less readily than sheep, and sheep less readily than pigs. With the latter species, the wasting can be about 3 lb/24 hr in an animal weighing about 200 lb (Callow and Boaz, 1937). In one study it was found that pigs which had travelled for 8 hr before slaughter yielded carcases averaging 0·9 per cent less than corresponding animals which had travelled for only $\frac{1}{2}$ hr pre-slaughter. This was regardless of whether they had been fed or not (Cuthbertson and Pomeroy, 1970). Moreover, the pigs may lose an extra 4 lb if they are given water on journeys over 36 hr in duration (Callow, 1954). A loss of weight of this order cannot be accounted for entirely by the breakdown of fatty and muscular tissues to produce energy and heat for the fasting pig and may be due, in part, to a loss of water-holding capacity in the muscular tissues (Callow, 1938b). An animal killed immediately on arrival at a slaughterhouse, after a short journey, may provide both a heavier carcase and heavier offal than an animal which has been sent on a prolonged journey, then rested and fed for some days in lairage (Callow, 1955). It is difficult to cause such carcase wastage in cattle.

5.1.2. *Glycogen Loss*

The influence of fasting in depleting the glycogen reserve of muscle has been known since the work of Bernard in 1877. Recognition of the importance of this fact in relation to the meat from domestic species is more recent. Callow (1936, 1938b) indicates that inadequate feeding in the period before slaughter could lower reserves of glycogen in the muscles of pigs. Bate-Smith and Bendall (1949) showed that fasting for only 48–72 hr lowered the glycogen content of rabbit psoas muscle sufficiently to raise the ultimate pH from the normal (for the rabbit) value of 5·9 to 6·5. In contrast, when steers are fasted at normal ambient temperatures for periods up to 28 days, the ultimate pH can be unaffected (Howard and Lawrie, 1956).

The importance of exhausting exercise as a factor in depleting glycogen reserves in muscle has also been recognized for a considerable period. Mitchell and Hamilton (1933) showed that exhausting exercise immediately pre-slaughter could cause a high ultimate pH in the muscles of cattle; but Howard and Lawrie (1956) found it most difficult to deplete the glycogen reserves in this species, even when pre-slaughter exercise and fasting for 14 days were combined (Table 5.1). Yet such depletion occurred, without fasting, if enforced exercise took place immediately after train travel.

TABLE 5.1. *Glycogen Concentrations and Ultimate* pH *in Psoas and L. Dorsi Muscles of Steers after Enforced Exercise and Fasting*

Treatment	L. dorsi		Psoas	
	Glycogen (mg %)	Ultimate pH	Glycogen (mg %)	Ultimate pH
Controls (fed and rested 14 days after train travel)	957	5·49	1017	5·48
Exercised 1½ hr (after train travel and 14 days fasting)	1028	5·55	508	5·55
Exercised 1½ hr (immediately after train travel)	628	5·72	352	6·15

The glycogen reserve of pig muscle, however, is especially susceptible to depletion by even mild activity immediately pre-slaughter (Callow, 1938b, 1939); a walk of only a quarter of a mile may cause a small but significant elevation of ultimate pH. Bate-Smith (1937a) suggested that if an easily assimilable sugar were fed before death the reserves of muscle glycogen might be restored to a level high enough to permit the attainment of a normal, low ultimate pH—the latter being desirable to avoid microbial spoilage (Callow, 1935; Ingram, 1948). This principle was confirmed in commercial practice by Madsen (1942) and Wismer-Pedersen (1959b) in Denmark and by Gibbons and Rose (1950) in Canada (Table 5.2).

If pigs are rested for *prolonged* periods before slaughter, in an attempt to restore glycogen reserves naturally, there is danger that animals carrying undesirable bacteria may infect initially unaffected animals, e.g. with *Salmonella*, which can endanger subsequent human con-

136   *Meat Science*

TABLE 5.2. *Effect of Feeding Sugar Pre-slaughter on the Ultimate pH of Pig Muscles*

Group treatment[a]	Muscle	Ultimate pH
(a) Held overnight without food	psoas	6·00
(b) Fed 3 lb sucrose at 22 hr and 6 hr pre-slaughter	psoas	5·54
(c) No food pre-slaughter	psoas	5·75
	biceps femoris	5·74
(d) 2 lb sugar fed 3–4 hr pre-slaughter	psoas	5·56
	biceps femoris	5·57

[a]Groups (a) and (b), Gibbons and Rose (1950); groups (c) and (d), Wismer-Pedersen (1959b).

sumers. This fact is reflected in current legislation in the United Kingdom which does not permit holding for more than 72 hr.

The existence of some influence controlling the level of muscle glycogen other than fatigue or inanition was suggested by the finding that certain steers which had been well fed and rested, and would therefore have been expected to have ample glycogen in their muscles, yielded meat of high ultimate pH (Howard and Lawrie, 1956). It appeared that these steers were of an excitable temperament. In such animals, short range muscular tension, not manifested by external movement, reduced glycogen reserves to a chronically low equilibrium level. Drugs given pre-slaughter to induce tremor considerably depleted glycogen reserves, causing a high ultimate pH, and confirmed the view that fear was an important factor in this context (Howard and Lawrie, 1957a). (The muscles of the cattle killed after excitement of train travel (Table 5.1) had a high ultimate pH, whereas those of cattle rested for 14 days after travel had normal values.)

Apart from its effect in enhancing the growth of bacteria (Ingram, 1948), a high ultimate pH, in the muscles of the cattle, causes the aesthetically unpleasant phenomenon of dark-cutting beef—known since 1774 (Kidwell, 1952)—and in those of pigs that of "glazy" bacon (Callow, 1935). These points will be considered in more detail in a later chapter.

Recognition that stress susceptibility is a factor in determining the condition of animals generally, and thereby the glycogen status of their muscles, has grown as the result of Selye's (1936) concept of the general adaptation syndrome. He noted that animals exposed to a variety of stress-producing factors such as emotional excitement, cold, fatigue, anoxia, etc., reacted by discharge of the same hormones from the adrenal gland irrespective of the nature of the stress—adrenaline from the adrenal medulla, 17-hydroxy- and 11-deoxy-corticosterones from the adrenal cortex. These substances elicit a variety of typical responses in the animal. Adrenaline depletes muscle glycogen and potassium: 17-hydroxy-corticosterone and 11-deoxy-corticosterone, respectively, restore the equilibrium level of these substances in normal animals. The release of the latter two hormones is controlled by the secretion of ACTH by the pituitary; and ACTH production is said to be controlled by a releasing-factor produced in the hypothalamus (Harris, Reed and Fawcett, 1966), the part of the brain which is reactive to external stimuli. As mentioned in § 2.4.6, an imbalance at various points in this complicated system can cause so-called diseases of adaptation (Selye, 1944, 1946). Such would be expected in individual animals which were stress-susceptible; and the imbalance could be manifested by low equilibrium levels of glycogen, disturbances in the rates of glycogen breakdown and so on (§ 3.4.3). In the plasma of pigs which yield pale, exudative flesh, for example, there is a deficiency of 17-hydroxy-corticosteroids (Topel, Markel and Wismer-Pedersen, 1967). Tranquillizers known to offset stress susceptibility have been given to calm stock in transit; but they are not without danger as they may induce a state of relaxation so profound that the animals cannot stand and may be suffocated. The metabolic stresses which affect muscle have been reviewed (Lawrie, 1966).

5.2. DEATH OF THE ANIMAL

A major requirement for desirable eating and keeping qualities in meat is the removal of as much blood as possible from the carcase, since it can cause an unpleasant appearance and is an excellent medium for the growth of micro-organisms. Except in ritual slaughter, animals are anaesthetized before bleeding. The procedure, at both stunning and bleeding is important. When special precautions are taken to ensure sterility, there is some evidence that unbled muscles undergo the tenderizing changes of conditioning to a greater extent than do those which are bled (Shestakov, 1962), but this could scarcely be regarded as a generally valid reason against bleeding.

5.2.1. *Stunning*

Whatever the method of stunning employed it is desirable that the medulla oblongata in the brain should not be destroyed. This centre, which controls the heart and lungs, should continue to function for some time, since the action of these organs helps to pump blood out of the carcase when the blood vessels in the neck are cut. Generally, cattle are stunned by a captive bolt pistol or by a blow from a pole-axe. In recent years the dressing of beef carcases has been carried out more frequently as they hang vertically rather than when supine on the abattoir floor. These changing circumstances make it rather less important to ensure that the heart is still functioning as blood can drain quite effectively from the carcase oven when heart action has ceased. In certain countries they are stunned electrically. Sheep and pigs are stunned electrically or anaesthetized by carbon dioxide. It has been observed that in sheep killed by a captive bolt pistol the epithelial lining of the intestines is shed, whereas it remains intact in anaesthetized animals (Badawy *et al.*, 1957); this could have microbial implications which will be referred to later.

In electrical stunning, the characteristics of the current must be carefully controlled, otherwise complete anaesthesia may not be attained and there may be convulsive muscular contractions. The siting of the electrodes is also important, since the current must pass through the brain. Variation in electrical resistance because of differing thicknesses in the skull can cause ineffective stunning. There are three phases in the animal's reaction: (i) as soon as the current is switched on there is violent contraction of all voluntary muscles and the animal falls over; respiration is arrested; (ii) after 10 sec (the current being discontinued) the muscles relax and the animal lies flaccid; (iii) after a further 45–60 sec the animal starts to make walking movements with its legs and respiration starts again. Usually, alternating current at 70–90 V and 0·3 A is used for 2–10 sec (Croft, 1957). Better relaxation and less internal bleeding is said to result if a high frequency current (2400–3000 c/s; Koledin, 1963) and a square wave form, instead of a sine wave (Blomquist, 1958), are employed.

There is some suggestion that electrical stunning may lower the glycogen reserves of the muscle slightly. The mean ultimate pH of quadriceps femoris from 518 electrically stunned pigs was 5·78; that in non-stunned controls was 5·67 (Blomquist, 1959). If the period between electrical stunning and bleeding is prolonged, the rather high pH may foster microbial spoilage (Warrington, 1974). In comparison with captive bolt stunning, electrical stunning has been shown to cause an elevation of amino acids in the plasma (especially of valine; the concentration of isoleucine falls somewhat) (Lynch *et al.*, 1966). It has been found that the level of corticosteroids in the blood of electrically stunned pigs is higher than that of those anaesthetized by carbon dioxide (Luyerink and Van Baal, 1969).

Carbon dioxide anaesthesia is an effective alternative to electrical stunning provided the concentration of the gas is between 65–70 per cent. If the latter concentration is not exceeded the musculature of the pigs is relaxed and the ultimate pH is slightly lower, and less variable, than with electrical stunning (Blomquist, 1957). One disadvantage of using a carbon dioxide chamber is that pigs differ somewhat in their susceptibility to anaesthesia by the gas, and that individual control of the animals is not feasible. Moreover, there is evidence that, prior to anaesthesia, animals suffer considerable stress; and, indeed, it has been suggested that carbon dioxide anaesthesia does not comply with the generally accepted definition of pre-slaughter stunning.

Von Mickwitz and Leach (1977) surveyed the various methods of stunning employed in the European Economic Community. They rated concussion stunning of cattle as the most effective, followed by captive bolt stunning of sheep and electrical stunning of pigs. Electrical stunning of sheep and captive bolt stunning of calves were deemed ineffective procedures. They concluded that any attempt to standardize stunning methods must specify proper pre-slaughter treatment of animals as an integral part of the overall procedure.

Irrespective of the mode of stunning employed at death three reactions occur: stimulation of the nervous system, anoxia and release of catecholamines (Anon., 1971). In principle, and whether or not they are practicable, stunning procedures should be designed to minimize muscle ATP-ase activity.

5.2.2. Bleeding

In cattle and sheep, bleeding is effected by severing the carotid artery and the jugular vein; and in pigs by severing the anterior vena cava. If the knife penetrates too far, blood may collect beneath the scapula and cause taint by early decomposition (Thornton, 1949). To avoid entry of micro-organisms, the cut made is minimal, especially with bacon pigs which are subsequently placed in a scalding tank. It has been said that bleeding after electrical stunning is more effective than after the use of the captive bolt pistol, but that it is less so than with carbon dioxide anaesthesia (Blomquist, 1957). Even with effective bleeding only about 50 per cent of the total blood is removed (Thornton, 1949), different muscles retaining more or less blood according to their nature. In the horse, for example, 50 per cent of the total pigment left in the heart after bleeding is haemoglobin from the blood, whereas in psoas and l. dorsi the corresponding values are about 25 and 10 per cent respectively (Lawrie, 1950). It has been shown that electrical stimulation (§7.1.1.1) of the carcase after severance of the neck vessels increases the weight of blood which drains from the main veins and arteries and the organs; but does not affect its removal from the musculature (Graham and Husband, 1976).

Since the introduction of electrical stunning there has been an increased frequency of "blood splash", i.e. the appearance of numbers of small dark red areas in the muscles. These had previously been noted when pigs or lambs were shot. Blood splash is more frequently observed in l. dorsi and in various muscles of the hind limb. Microscopic examination has shown that blood splash arises where capillaries have ruptured through over-filling with blood (Anon., 1957a). The occurrence of blood splash does not signify that bleeding has been incomplete. When the current is applied there is a considerable rise in blood pressure, muscles are contracted and their capillaries are almost empty of blood. Subsequently the muscles relax and if the blood pressure is not released by external cutting, blood is forced into the capillaries again with sufficient force to rupture many of them and enter the muscle itself (Leet, Devine and Gavey, 1977). Emotional stress causes vasodilatation of the blood vessels in skeletal muscle, and may enhance fibrinolytic activity in entrained blood. These effects, especially if combined with electrical stunning, could perhaps explain the higher incidence of "blood splash" reported in excitable animals (Jansen, 1966). The remedy appears to be to bleed the pigs within 5 sec of administering the anaesthetizing current (Blomquist, 1959). Bleeding should be performed as soon as possible after stunning whatever the method of stunning employed.

5.2.3. *Dressing and Cutting*

Following bleeding, carcases are "dressed" i.e. the head, feet, hides (in the case of sheep and cattle) excess fat, viscera and offal (edible and inedible) are separated from the bones and edible muscular tissue. Cattle and pig carcases, but not those of sheep, are split along the mid ventral axis into two sides. It is not appropriate here to detail dressing procedures; these are fully considered in other texts (Gerrard, 1951). The present monograph is primarily concerned with the muscular tissue—the predominant edible portion of the carcase.

Until recently it was commercial practice to chill dressed carcases prior to preservation or processing (cf. Chapters 7, 8 and 9); and, after chilling (which signified after *rigor mortis*), to prepare primal, wholesale cuts (cf. Fig. 3.1; and Gerrard, 1951) from them. Traditionally, skeletal reference points and straight cutting lines have been used. These have contributed to variability in retail joints since the boneless primal cuts are aggregates of several muscles rather than muscles isolated individually by "seaming out" along the muscle fascia—as in certain continental practice (Strother, 1975).

Prior to the introduction of vacuum packaging, wholesale cuts were sold with bone intact to avoid evaporative losses and minimize contamination. Now, however, about 15 per cent of home killed beef in Britain is deboned centrally and delivered to retailers as boneless primal cuts. Not only is it likely that deboning of beef carcases will become a standard abattoir operation in the future; such will be effected on hot carcases immediately after slaughter. It has been demonstrated that losses due to evaporation and exudation in vacuum-packed, hot-deboned beef are markedly reduced. Moreover, control of eating quality is greater since muscles can be "seamed out" as anatomical entities. In the absence of bone, and because the meat cuts are less bulky, chilling and freezing can be more rapidly and economically effected. "Cold-shortening" can be avoided by deboning in rooms at 5–15°C and holding the vacuum packed cuts for at least 10 hours at these temperatures (Schmidt and Gilbert, 1970; Follet, Norman and Ratcliff, 1974). The principles have been extended to the hot cutting of lamb and mutton carcases (McLeod *et al.*, 1973), cuts being shrink-wrapped and held at 10°C for 24 hours before freezing. Tenderness, far from being diminished, was enhanced in some cuts over that of cuts from carcases which had been chilled intact before cutting. Shrink wrapping, by moulding the warm fat and musculature, produces pleasing cuts from the initially untidy portions (Locker, Davey, Nottingham, Haughey and Law, 1975). It also eliminated weight losses.

Weight losses, and in particular, exudation in deeper muscles where the combination of body temperature and low pH denature proteins have been much reduced also by partial excision of beef muscles on the warm sides immediately after slaughter and exposing the "seamed out" muscles to air at 0°C (Follet, 1974). The bulk of the musculature, in these circumstances, prevents temperatures falling fast enough to cause "cold-shortening".

5.3. GENERAL CONSEQUENCES OF CIRCULATORY FAILURE

Stoppage of the circulation of the blood at death initiates a complex series of changes in muscular tissue. The more important of these are outlined in Fig. 5.1. It will be appreciated, from what has been indicated in Chapter 4, that the speed and extent of these changes may be expected to differ in different muscles.

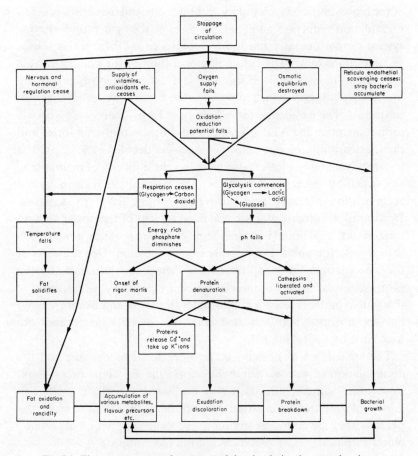

FIG 5.1. The consequences of stoppage of the circulation in muscular tissue.

At the moment of death of the animal as a whole, its various tissues are continuing their particular types of metabolism under local control. Although muscle is not actively contracting at such a time, energy is being used to maintain its temperature and the organizational integrity of its cells against their spontaneous tendency to break down. The non-contractile ATP-ase of myosin, and not the contractile ATP-ase of actomyosin, is one of the enzymes involved in this context (Bendall, 1951). The most immediate change caused by bleeding is the elimination of the blood-borne oxygen supply to the muscles and the consequent fall in oxidation reduction potential. As a result the cytochrome enzyme system cannot operate, and the resynthesis of ATP from this source becomes impossible. The continuing operation of the non-contractile ATP-ase of myosin depletes the ATP level, simultaneously producing inorganic phosphate which stimulates the breakdown of glycogen to lactic acid. The ineffectual resynthesis of ATP by anaerobic glycolysis cannot maintain the ATP level and, as it drops, actomyosin forms and the inextensibility of rigor mortis ensues (as detailed in § 4.2.3). The lowered availability of ATP also increases the difficulty of maintaining the structural integrity of proteins. The lowered pH, caused by the accumulation of lactic acid, also makes them liable to denature. Denaturation is frequently accompanied by loss of the power to bind water and the falling pH causes the myofibrillar proteins to approach their iso-electric point. Both events cause exudation. Denaturation of the sarcoplasmic proteins also makes them liable to attack by the proteases or cathepsins of muscle, which are probably held inactive *in vivo* within particles known as lysosomes (De Duve and Beaufay, 1959) but are liberated and activated when the particle membranes are weakened by the falling pH.

The breakdown of proteins to peptides and amino acids, and the accumulation of various metabolites from the glycolytic process and from other sources, affords a rich medium for bacteria. Although growth of the latter is somewhat discouraged by the extent to which the pH falls, they are no longer subject to the scavenging action of "white" blood corpuscles (since blood circulation has stopped).

A further aspect of the stoppage of the circulation is the cessation of long-term hormonal control of tissue metabolism. As it fails, the temperature falls and fat solidifies. The tendency for the fat to oxidize and become rancid is facilitated by failure of the blood to renew the supply of anti-oxidants, and by the accumulation of pro-oxidant molecules in the tissues.

5.4. CONDITIONING (AGEING)

Although muscle is increasingly liable to suffer microbial spoilage in direct proportion to the time and temperature of holding post-mortem, hygienic abattoir operations will generally ensure satisfactory storage for a few days at room temperature and for about 6 weeks if the meat is held just above its freezing point ($-1.5°C$). Various processes applied to the commodity, such as curing, freezing, de-hydration and irradiation, will vastly extend storage life; but, in so far as they are artificial, they are not relevant in this chapter. In the absence of microbial spoilage, the holding of unprocessed meat above the freezing point is known as "conditioning" or "ageing"; and it has long been associated with an increase in tenderness and flavour (cf. Bouley, 1874). During the first 24–36 hr post-mortem, the dominant circumstance is post-mortem glycolysis. This has already been considered in some detail in §§ 4.2.2 and 4.2.3. Even before the ultimate pH has been reached, however, other degradative changes have commenced. These continue until bacterial spoilage or gross denaturation and desiccation of the proteins have made the meat inedible. The extent of these changes, which affect the nature and amount of both proteins and small molecules, is generally limited, however, by the cooking and consumption of the meat.

5.4.1. *Protein Denaturation*

Muscle, like all living tissues, represents a complexity of organization among molecules which is too improbable to have arisen, or to be maintained, by their random orientation. The structure of the proteins which characterize contractile tissue can only be preserved against the tendency of the component atoms and molecules to become disorientated by the provision of energy (as ATP). Such energy is not available after death and the proteins will tend to denature. Denaturation may be defined as a physical or intramolecular rearrangement which does not involve hydrolysis of the chemical bonds linking the constituent amino acids of the proteins' polypeptide chains (Putnam, 1953). It is generally accompanied by an increase in the reactivity of various chemical groups, a loss of biological activity (in those proteins which are enzymes or hormones), a change in molecular shape or size and a decrease in solubility. Proteins are liable to denature if subjected, during post-mortem conditioning, to pH levels below those *in vivo*, to temperatures above 25°C or below 0°C, to desiccation and to non-physiological salt concentrations.

Of the proteins in muscle, it has been generally accepted that the collagen and elastin of connective tissue do not denature during conditioning (Ramsbottom and Strandine, 1949; Wierbicki *et al.*, 1954). This view was supported by the concomitant absence of soluble, hydroxyproline-containing molecules, indicating that neither collagen nor elastin were proteolysed (Sharp, 1959); proteolysis would not normally precede denaturation. When, however, collagen is denatured, for example, by heating beef muscles to 60–70°C for 20–25 min, there is a continuous nonenzymic, breakdown to hydroxyproline-containing derivatives (Sharp, 1963).

During post-mortem conditioning, the proteins of the myofibril and of the sarcoplasm denature in varying degree. Immediately after death and before the onset of rigor mortis, muscles are pliable and tender when cooked. The principal proteins of the myofibril, actin and myosin, are dissociated and myosin is extractable at high ionic strength (Weber and Meyer, 1933; Bailey, 1954). With the onset of rigor mortis as we have considered above, the muscle becomes inextensible and is tough when cooked (Marsh, 1964). As conditioning proceeds, the muscle becomes pliable once more (and increasingly tender on cooking); but this is *not* due to the dissociation of actomyosin (Marsh, 1954); inextensibility remains.†

The extractability at high ionic strength of total myofibrillar proteins decreases by about 75 per cent with the onset of rigor mortis, from the value immediately post-mortem; but on subsequent storage at 2°C the extractability again rises—up to and even beyond the initial level (Locker, 1960a). It is significant that, in addition to a predominance of actomyosin, the myofibrillar proteins extractable at high ionic strength

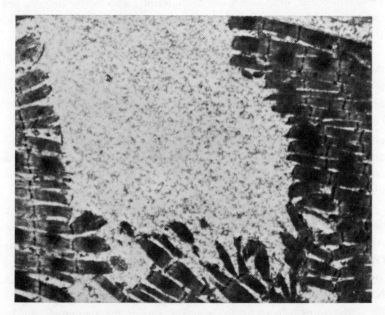

FIG. 5.2. Electron micrograph of a break across an aged, stretched muscle fibre. Each broken fibre has parted at the Z-line (× 5000). (Courtesy Dr. M. R. Dickson.)

†Busch, Goll and Parrish (1972) followed the onset of rigor mortis by observing changes in isometric tension. This increases as extensibility decreases; but, whereas extensibility remains low, isometric tension diminishes again during the so-called resolution of rigor. Increase in isometric tension post-mortem is more marked in "red" than in "white" muscles. This difference appears to be related to dissimilarities in the sarcolemma of these two types of muscle.

now include α-actinin, tropomyosin and the troponin with which the latter is associated *in vivo* (Ebashi, 1964; Valin, 1968). This suggests that the process of conditioning detaches the actin filaments from the Z-line with which their union, probably via tropomyosin (Huxley, 1963), is weaker than with myosin. Figure 5.2 demonstrates that aged myofibrils break at the Z-lines on mild homogenizing (Dickson, 1969: Davey and Dickson, 1970). The actin filaments collapse on to those of myosin, leading to lengthening of the *A*-bands (Davey and Gilbert, 1967), and there is increased weakness at the *A-I* junction, as shown by an increased gap between the *A* and *I* bands of the sarcomere (Davey and Graafhuis, 1976b).

The process is apparently initiated by the release of Ca^{++} ions from the sarcoplasmic reticulum (the capacity of which to accumulate Ca^{++} ions decreases during conditioning: Newbold and Tume, 1976) and operates through a calcium-activated sarcoplasmic factor (CASF). (Busch, Stromer, Goll and Suzuki, 1972). It is significant that the Ca^{++}-chelating agent, ethylene diamine tetraacetate, should prevent these ageing changes; and Penny *et al.* (1974) shewed that, when CASF was added to freeze-dried beef, it caused Z-line disintegration (and tenderness).

Penny (1970) had earlier found evidence for weakening of the link between actin and α-actinin after 15 days' ageing of beef *l. dorsi*. Although CASF does not appear to act on actin or myosin *per se* (Penny, 1974; Robson *et al.*, 1974), Penny (1968) shewed that, if rabbit myofibrils were aged after isolation from muscle, the myosin-actin bonds were weakened; and Strandberg *et al.*, (1972) found that some of the -SH groups of actomyosin were lost during the ageing of beef. In 1974 Penny concluded that CASF acted upon α-actinin and later (1976) he demonstrated that progressive time- and temperature-dependent changes occur in the troponin complex during the ageing of pork whereby the proteins bound to actine diminish.†

During conditioning or ageing, the Z-lines in "white" muscles appear to be more labile than those in the "red" variety (Goll, 1970). Thus, they alter more rapidly in rabbit and porcine muscles than in those of the bovine (Henderson, Goll and Stromer, 1970): and more in bovine *semitendinosus* than in *psoas* (Goll, 1974). Tenderness changes little in bovine *psoas* over 4 days' ageing at 2°C, whereas in *semitendinosus*—it increases markedly during this period. It is significant that the latter has about three times the activity of CASF as bovine *psoas*. It may be noted that "white" muscles are less susceptible to "cold shortening" than "red"; and that this has been attributed to their greater ability to control intramuscular concentrations of calcium ions because of a more effective sarcotubular system (§ 10.3.3).

Notwithstanding these observed alterations in Z-line integrity on ageing, there is evidence that the CASF acts on so called "gap filaments" and not on the Z-line material itself (Locker, 1976). Thus, when *stretched* muscle is aged, subsequent cooking causes the "gap filaments" to disappear whilst the Z-lines remain intact (Davey and Graafhuis, 1976b).

The extractability of myofibrillar proteins is affected by the ultimate pH of the muscle, a high ultimate pH tending towards greater extractability (cf. Table 4.21). The temperature post-mortem is also important, a high temperature being associated with lower extractability (Wierbicki *et al.*, 1956). This is partly due to the precipitation of sarcoplasmic proteins on to those of the myofibril (Bendall and Wismer-Pedersen, 1962). Some denaturation of the latter also occurs, however. This is implied by the greater difficulty of splitting muscle fibres into myofibrils after aseptic storage for 30 days at 37°C than at 5°C (Sharp, 1963); but in this case changes in the sarcoplasmic reticulum between each myofibril may be responsible (Lawrie and Voyle, 1962). Even at 35°C denaturation of *isolated* myosin is relatively speedy (Penny, 1967); and it can be presumed that some denaturation of actomyosin *in situ* occurs during post-mortem glycolysis.

†Subsequently, Penny & Ferguson-Price (1979) shewed that, during conditioning of beef muscles, troponin T (MW 37,000) is proteolysed with the concomitant production of four peptides, of which the principal member has a MW of 30,000. It was concluded that at least two endogenous enzymes were involved—CASF above pH6 and cathepsin B below it. The proteolysis of troponin T increase of tenderness correlated well when conditioning took place between 3° and 15°C (Penny & Dransfield, 1979). At higher temperatures (25–35°C), when protein denaturation is a contributory factor, and at 0°C, when cold shortening may be anticipated, toughness was greater than the degree of proteolysis of troponin T would have predicted.

An important aspect of changes in the myofibrillar proteins post-mortem, which is reflected in their extractability and tenderness, is the degree of shortening which occurs during the onset of rigor mortis (Locker, 1960a; Locker and Hagyard, 1963; Marsh, 1964). In muscles which go into rigor mortis in an extended condition, the filaments of actin and myosin overlap and cross-bond at fewer points, and the amount of actomyosin formed is small. Such meat is tender on cooking. On the other hand, when muscles go into rigor mortis in a contracted condition, there is considerable shortening since the actin and the myosin filaments interpenetrate extensively. There is much cross-bonding and the meat is relatively tough on cooking. Normally, muscle goes into rigor mortis in an intermediate condition wherein the overlapping of actin and myosin, the degree of cross-bonding and the toughness are somewhere between the two extremes (cf. Fig. 4.2). It has been shown that the rate of tenderizing during conditioning is minimal in muscles which have shortened substantially at onset of rigor mortis (Davey, Kuttel and Gilbert, 1967). The degree of shortening during rigor mortis is temperature dependent (cf. §§ 7.1.1 and 10.3.3).

By far the most labile proteins of muscle post-mortem are those of the

TABLE 5.3. *Percentage of Sarcoplasmic Protein precipitating from Extracts of Post-rigor Beef L. Dorsi*
(after Scopes, 1964)

Temp.:	0°	10°	15°	20°	25°	30°	37°	45°
pH								
4·5	4·4	3·8	4·2	4·0	4·4	4·7	5·1	8·1
4·8	6·6	5·7	4·8	6·4	6·6	7·4	5·3	15·0
5·2	5·0	4·9	5·5	6·2	7·8	10·5	18·5	35·0
5·7	3·1	2·9	3·2	3·1	4·2	6·2	12·2	34·0
6·0	2·1	1·9	2·2	2·5	3·2	6·3	8·5	29·0
6·5	0·6	0·8	0·7	2·1	2·8	3·4	6·6	24·5
7·1	0·4	0·4	0·6	0·5	1·2	2·1	5·2	22·0

Extracts exposed to temperature/pH conditions for 4 hr.

sarcoplasm, the diversity of which is represented in Fig. 4.1 (p. 78). It has been realized for many years that proteins precipitate when muscle extracts of low ionic strength are allowed to stand at room temperature, the process being accelerated by raising the temperature and by the addition of salt and acid (Finn, 1932; Bate-Smith, 1937b). The behaviour of sarcoplasmic proteins in extracts from beef l. dorsi muscle under various temperature–pH combinations is shown in Table 5.3.

It will be seen that an increase of temperature causes increasing precipitation of sarcoplasmic proteins at all pH values studied; that at all temperatures maximum precipitation occurs at a pH of 4·8–5·2; but that at some temperature between 37° and 45°C, a high ultimate pH no longer protects sarcoplasmic proteins against precipitation (Scopes, 1964). Even after heating at 60°C for 10 hr a proportion of the sarcoplasmic proteins are still soluble and will separate electrophoretically; but after 2 hr at 80°C almost all sarcoplasmic proteins except myoglobin have become insoluble (Laakkonen, Sherbon and Wellington, 1970). Obviously, even the attainment of a normal ultimate pH (about 5·5) during post-mortem glycolysis must be associated with the precipitation of some of the sarcoplasmic proteins (on the presumption that *in vivo* behaviour reflects that *in situ*). A high temperature during post-mortem glycolysis causes additional precipitation. This is exemplified in Fig. 5.3, from which it will be clear that one of the most labile of the sarcoplasmic proteins in the muscles of beef, rabbit and pig is the enzyme creatine kinase (Scopes, 1964). Particularly severe precipitation of sarcoplasmic proteins occurs during post-mortem glycolysis in the muscles of pigs which appear pale and are exudative post-mortem (cf. § 3.4.3; Scopes and Lawrie, 1963). In these there is a combination of low pH and high temperature (Bendall and Wismer-Pedersen, 1962), and sarcoplasmic proteins precipitate on to those of the myofibril lowering their extractability and water-holding capacity. As observed histologically, the precipitated sarcoplasmic proteins form bands across the muscle fibre (Fig. 3.7) and lower the extractability of the myofibrillar proteins, even although the latter may not be denatured themselves (Bendall and Wismer-Pedersen, 1962). The greater prevalence of such bands in affected musculature of ultimate pH

5·4 than in those of ultimate pH 4·7 and their presence in muscle of high ultimate pH (Lawrie *et al.*, 1963) follows from the behaviour indicated in Table 5.3. There is clearly a critical temperature, between 37–45°C, above which a high ultimate pH fails to keep sarcoplasmic proteins in

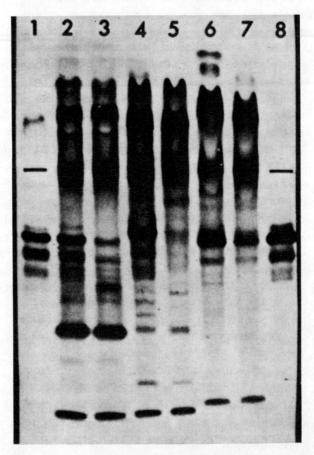

FIG. 5.3. Starch gel electrophoretograms showing relative stability of sarcoplasmic proteins in extracts from l. dorsi muscles of various species undergoing rigor mortis at 0° or 37°C. (1) Purified beef creatine kinase. (2) Beef, 0°C. (3) Beef, 37°C. (4) Rabbit, 0°C. (5) Rabbit, 37°C. (6) Pig, 0°C. (7) Pig, 37°C. (8) Purified pig creatine kinase. (Courtesy Dr. R. K. Scopes.)

solution. That pigs affected by the so-called PSE condition seem to have a higher temperature than normal immediately post-mortem (Bendall and Wismer-Pedersen, 1962) and that the condition is said to be induced artificially by holding pigs at 45°C for a period before slaughter (Sayre *et al.*, 1963b) substantiates this view. It is interesting that, as already indicated, some adverse change should also occur in the myofibrillar proteins at about this temperature (Marsh, 1962).

After the ultimate pH has been reached, further changes occur in the sarcoplasmic proteins, there being a general alteration in the nature of the components (Deatherage and Fujimaki, 1964).

Denaturation of the principal muscle pigment, myoglobin, which is another of the sarcoplasmic proteins, accelerates the oxidation of its iron to the ferric form, the pigment turning brown (metmyoglobin). Although, considering the muscle as a whole, this is not an extensive process, it is, nevertheless, a very important one for it occurs preferentially near exposed surfaces or where the oxygen tension is about 4 mm (Brooks, 1935, 1938). Such factors as desiccation can initiate the denaturation and discoloration, especially where the ultimate pH is relatively low. It is also linked with still surviving activity in the oxygen utilizing enzymes (succinic dehydrogenase and cytochrome oxidase) which persists for some time at 0°C. This matter will be referred to again below.

As far as meat quality is concerned, perhaps the most important manifestation of the post-mortem denaturation of the muscle proteins is their loss of water-holding capacity, because in practice it is a more universal phenomenon than discoloration. The point of minimum water-holding capacity of the principal proteins in muscle (i.e. the isoelectric point) is 5·4–5·5 (Weber and Meyer, 1933). Since, as we have seen in Chapter 4, the production of lactic acid from glycogen, at any given temperature and rate, will, *generally*, cause the pH to reach 5·5, normal meat will lose some fluid ("weep"). This will, obviously, be less if the ultimate pH is high, however (Empey, 1933).

The contribution by the sarcoplasmic proteins to overall water-holding capacity, once lost by precipitation during the attainment of even a normal ultimate pH, cannot be regained by applying a buffer of high ultimate pH to the muscle. Thus, the relatively low water-holding capacity of fibres prepared from muscle of low ultimate pH remains lower than that of fibres prepared from muscle of an intrinsically high ultimate pH, even when placed in a medium having the latter pH value (Penny, Voyle and Lawrie, 1963).

For a given muscle, water-holding capacity is at a minimum at the ultimate pH; thereafter, on subsequent conditioning of the meat, it tends to increase (Cook *et al.*, 1926). This may be due to an increased osmotic pressure, caused by the breakdown of protein molecules to smaller units (proteolysis will be discussed below); but much intramolecular rearrangement, not involving splitting but causing changes in the electrical charges on the protein, may be responsible (Bendall, 1946). There is concomitantly an increase in the pH of the meat when it is held above the freezing point (Sair and Cook, 1938); Wierbicki *et al.*, 1954; Bouton, Howard and Lawrie, 1958). The pH rise is more marked when the temperature of holding is high and is greater in pork than in beef (Lawrie *et al.*, 1961).

These changes in pH are accompanied by changes in ion–protein relationships. Arnold *et al.* (1956), found that sodium and calcium ions are continuously released into the sarcoplasm by the muscle proteins, and potassium ions are absorbed after the first 24 hr. Because of the large excess of potassium ions absorbed on to the muscle proteins, the net charge on to the latter increases, and, thereby, the water-holding capacity.

5.4.2. *Proteolysis*

Denatured proteins are particularly liable to attack by proteolytic enzymes (Anson and Mirsky, 1932, 1933; Lineweaver and Hoover, 1941). The increase in tenderness, observed on conditioning, was found many years ago to be associated with an increase in water-soluble nitrogen (Hoagland, McBride and Powick, 1917; Fearson and Foster, 1922), due to the production of peptides and amino acids from protein. There has been much controversy as to which proteins undergo proteolysis during the holding of meat at temperatures above the freezing point.

Although extensive proteolysis of the collagen and elastin of connective tissue might appear to be the most likely change causing increased tenderness the proteins of connective tissue are not normally changed in this way during conditioning in skeletal muscle. This was conclusively shown by Sharp (1959). There is no increase in water-soluble hydroxyproline-containing derivatives, even after storage of sterile, fresh meat for one year at 37 C. Soviet workers, however, claim to have detected a three fold increase in the N-terminal residues of elastin during meat ageing at an ultimate pH of 5·6 (Solovev and Karpova, 1967). Despite the absence of massive proteolysis of native collagen during conditioning, such as would require the action of a true collagenase capable of cleaving all three chains in the helical region of tropocollagen (Gross, 1970), there is evidence for the operation of a lysosomal enzyme (Valin, 1970) which can attack the cross-links in the non-helical telopeptide region of collagen. Etherington (1972) also studied an enzyme which is found in low concentration in rat muscle and has the ability to attack collagen. As the pH optimum is 3·5, however, it presumably must operate in isolated microenvironments in the muscle. In 1974 he isolated two collagenolytic cathepsins from bovine spleen which cleaved the non-helical, telopeptide region of native tropocollagen between the lysine-derived cross-links and the triple helix of the main body of the molecule. This resulted in longitudinal splitting and dissociation of the protofibrils. The enzymes operated at pH 4–5 (28°C). Subtle enzyme actions of this nature, if operating during conditioning, would not be reflected by a release of soluble, hydroxyproline-containing substances.

Collagen fibres appear to swell during conditioning, a feature which may signify that cross-links are, in fact, being broken. As tenderness increases, there is a concomitant increase in the titre of free β-glucuronidase (Dutson and Lawrie, 1974). This enzyme can attack the mucopolysaccharide of the ground substance or carbohydrate moieties in collagen itself. One of the points of attachment of carbohydrate to collagen is the ε-amino group of lysine; and the ε-aminoglycosylamines are probably involved in binding collagen to the ground substance (Robins and Bailey, 1972). It may be, therefore, that splitting of both carbohydrate and peptide links contributes to increased tenderness in conditioning.

Preceding the repair of damaged muscles, collagen and elastin are evidently removed *in vivo* (Partridge, 1962). There is a general increase in phagocytic (Rickenbacher, 1959) and in proteolytic activities—the latter due to the liberation of catheptic enzymes from lysosomes (Hamdy, May and Powers, 1962). Anti-inflammatory (anti-rheumatic) drugs, such as cortisone, inhibit the formation of the acid mucopolysaccharides of the ground substance of connective tissue by suppressing sulphation (Whitehouse and Lash, 1961) and decrease the amount of free hydroxyproline (Kivirikko, 1963). Vitamin C deficiency interferes with collagen formation by inhibiting the hydroxylation of soluble proline (Stone and Meister, 1962). Again, during post-partum involution of the uterus, enzymes are elaborated which are capable of breaking down connective tissue proteins to their constituent amino acids (Woessner and Brewer, 1971). It has been postulated that the collagen fibril is first attacked extracellularly by a secreted neutral collagenase and that its subsequent digestion is intracellular (Etherington, 1973), by macrophages (Parakkal, 1969; Eisen, Bauer and Jeffrey, 1971). These reactions imply that *in vivo* muscle is capable of elaborating enzymes which proteolyse connective tissue proteins, in abnormal circumstances, even if they are not present, or are inactive, during conditioning.

Notwithstanding the absence of massive proteolysis in the collagen and elastin of fresh sterile meat, even after 1 year at 37°C, such breakdown does occur in sterile meat which has been heated. For example, in beef held at 37°C, after heating for 15 min at 70°C, soluble hydroxyproline rose from about 2 per cent to about 23 per cent of the total hydroxyproline during 97 days (Sharp, 1964). In corresponding beef which had been heated for 45 min at 100°C (being thus cooked), the value rose from 12 per cent initially to 55 per cent over the same period of subsequent holding at 37°C. Histological examination revealed that the connective tissues of the perimysium had been weakened, since fibre bundles were easily separated from one another. In view of the preceding treatment, however, the breakdown of collagen (or elastin) in these circumstances can scarcely have been due to enzymic action: progressive physical changes in the connective tissue proteins are probably involved (Gustavsen, 1956).

As mentioned in § 5.4.1, the absence of changes in the extensibility of muscle in conditioning—and subsequent to actomyosin formation during the onset of rigor mortis—despite the concomitant increase in tenderness, indicated that the latter phenomenon did not involve dissociation of actin from myosin (Marsh, 1954). A similar conclusion was reached by Locker (1960b). He applied Sanger's method of N-terminal analysis (1945) to the salt soluble proteins of beef muscle during conditioning at low and high temperature and failed to detect any significant increase in the number of protein N groups. It must be appreciated, however, that significant changes in muscle proteins, which might alter the tenderness of meat, could occur without extensive proteolysis, if a few key bonds were broken, as indicated above.

Since neither the proteins of connective tissue nor of the myofibrils are subjected to extensive proteolysis during conditioning, the considerable

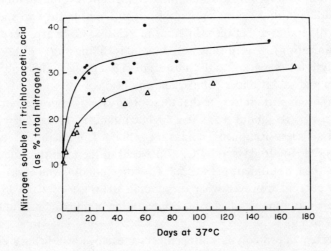

FIG. 5.4. Production of nitrogen soluble in trichloroacetic acid during aseptic storage of muscle at 37°C. ●—●, rabbit muscle; △—△, beef muscle. (Courtesy Dr. J. G. Sharp.)

increments in the soluble products of protein breakdown must arise from the sarcoplasmic proteins. As we have seen, these denature in varying degree during post-mortem glycolysis (§ 5.4.1); and chromatography of extracts prepared from muscle after increasing periods of storage show a gradual diminution of various components (Deatherage and Fujimaki, 1964).

During storage at 37 C of sterile l. dorsi muscles of beef, the total soluble protein nitrogen was found to fall from 28 to 29 per cent of the total nitrogen to 13, 11 and 6 per cent after 20, 46 and 172 days respectively (Sharp, 1963). The lowered concentration of sarcoplasmic proteins was due rather to their proteolysis to amino acids and not to precipitation, which could only account for a small amount of the diminution: the nitrogen soluble in trichloroacetic acid rose from 11 per cent of the total protein to 17, 23 and 31·5 per cent respectively in these same periods. Moreover, in terms of a specific amino acid, the percentage of total tyrosine soluble in trichloroacetic rose from 11 per cent initially to 13, 17 and 35 per cent over 20, 46 and 172 days respectively (Sharp, 1963). Comparable changes were found in rabbit l. dorsi although the rates of proteolysis are different in the two species (Fig. 5.4); and even between different muscles (J. G. Sharp, personal communication). According to Radouco-Thomas *et al.* (1959), proteolysis is less marked in the muscles of pigs and sheep than in those of lamb and rabbit under comparable conditions.

It is most important to note that these observations refer to a normal ultimate pH (i.e. about 5·5). At a higher ultimate pH the degree of proteolysis is less (Radouco-Thomas *et al.*, 1959). Thus, in rabbit l. dorsi after storage for 16 days at 37°C, 17 per cent of the total tyrosine was soluble when the ultimate pH was 5·8. The corresponding value was only about 9 per cent, however, when the ultimate pH was 6·8 (Sharp, 1963); and there was a smaller degree of disintegration of muscle fibres during homogenizing.

The extent of proteolysis is also temperature dependent, being greater at 37°C than at 5°C, although the degree of histological breakdown, as shown by the cohesiveness of fibres after homogenizing, is much greater at 5° than at 37°C. This is, presumably, because there is a greater degree

TABLE 5.4. *Dimensions of Fibres present in Greatest Number in Low Speed Homogenates of Sterile, Stored Beef L. Dorsi Muscle of Normal Ultimate* pH

Storage characteristics	Length (μ)	Diameter (μ)
Control (2 days at -20 C)	650–1300	200–600
30 days at 37 C	250–430	43–170
30 days at 5 C	50–170	14–86

of denaturation of the myofibrillar proteins at the higher temperature (Table 5.4; Sharp, 1963) which would oppose breaking up of the tissue.

It is, thus, evident that there are naturally occurring enzymes in muscle which operate, during post-mortem conditioning to hydrolyse sarcoplasmic proteins to peptides and amino acids. An early attempt to study those enzymes—often referred to as cathepsins—was made by Balls (1938) who showed that one from beef had an optimum pH of about 4. A similar finding was reported for rabbit muscle (Snoke and Neurath, 1950). Three enzyme fractions were separated from beef muscle, with optima at pH 5, 8–9 and 10 when using soluble protein from the muscles of this species as substrate (Sliwinski *et al.*, 1961). The enzyme with optimum pH at 5, is activated by ferrous iron and that with optimum pH at 8–9 by a removal of calcium ions (Landmann, 1963). It is important to note that the pH optimum of the former cathepsin as isolated is in the range which would be encountered in muscle of normal ultimate pH. This may explain the relative absence of proteolysis at high ultimate pH which has already been mentioned (Randall and Macrae, 1967). However, low ultimate pH may enhance proteolytic activity way. The lysosomes, which contain enzymes having proleolytic activity and acid pH optima (De Duve, 1959a), have lipoprotein membranes which, whilst intact at *in vivo* pH levels under normal conditions, rupture when the Ph falls post-mortem, or when there has been extensive tissue damage (Hamdy *et al.,* 1961), and liberate the proteolytic enzymes. The permeability of these membranes appears to be controlled by the vitamin A status of the tissue, hypervitaminosis A being associated with undue fragility (Fell and Dingle, 1963). It is also lowered following tissue breakdown (De Duve, 1959b) as in the dystrophies due to recessive genes or to vitamin E deficiency (Tappel *et al.*, 1962); and in such dystrophies the activity of the lysosomal proteolytic enzymes is increased.

It is evident that some proteolytic activity may be due to residual blood in the muscle (Shestakov, 1962); and in 1974 Bailey and Kim showed that the proteinases from the porcine leucocyte lysosomes can degrade myofibrillar proteins. The question of whether the proteolytic activity observed in muscle post-mortem is a property of lysosomes intrinsic to the tissue or of those belonging to entrained phagocytes was resolved by Canonico and Bird (1970) who demonstrated that the former had relatively greater contents of acid phosphatases than of cathepsins. More recently, Venugopal and Bailey (1978) compared the lysosomes proteinases of the muscular tissue and leucocytes of beef and pork. They found that cathepsins D and E,† which had pH optima of 4·0 and 2·5, respectively, were the most active proteolytic enzymes found in both tissues; and that all the enzymes from the lysosomal leucocytes were more active than their counterparts in the lysosomes of the muscular tissue (cf. Table 5.5).

5.4.3. *Other Chemical Changes*

By the time the ultimate pH has been reached, ATP has been largely broken down to inosinic acid, inorganic phosphate and ammonia (§ 4.2.3). Although some degradation of inosinic acid to phosphate, ribose and hypoxanthine will have occurred at this stage, the latter process is substantially a function of time, temperature and pH after the attainment of the ultimate pH (Solov'ev, 1952; Lee and Webster, 1963). According to Howard, Lee and Webster (1960) conditioning is organoleptically at an optimum when the hypoxanthine level has reached 1·5–2·0 μmoles/g. This is attained after 10–13 days at 0°C, 4–5 days at 10°C, 30–40 hr at 20°C and 10–11 hr at 30°C (Lee and Webster, 1963). The rate of hypoxanthine formation is increased by a high ultimate pH, however, and this circumstance must be considered when assessing the time-temperature history of meat.

†Terminology of Barret (1977).

TABLE 5.5. *Specific Activity of Bovine Lysosomal Proteinases*
(after Venugopal and Bailey, 1978)
(pH of measurement in brackets)

Source	Enzymes						
	Carboxypeptidases		Cathepsins		Collagenase	Dipeptidyl-aminopepti-dase I
	A (5·0)	B (6·0)	B (7·8)	D (4·0)	E (2·5)	(7·0)	(6·8)
Leucocytes	30	23	110	2751	1482	0·75	140
Muscle (diaphragm: 10,000 g fraction)	12	9	24	1878	1132	0·15	28

In view of the development of flavour which accompanies conditioning it is of interest that many years ago hypoxanthine, or its precursor
nosinic acid, was reported to enhance flavour when added to meats
(Kodama, 1913). It has been shown that inosinic acid (or inosine and
inorganic phosphate) when heated with a glycoprotein containing
alanine and glucose and (also isolated from the water-soluble extracts of
beef), produces a basic meat flavour and odour (Batzer, Santoro and
Landmann, 1962). The breakdown of protein and fat during
conditioning also contributes to flavour by producing hydrogen
sulphide, ammonia, acetaldehyde, acetone and diacetyl (Yueh and
Strong, 1960); but prolonged conditioning, e.g. 40–80 days at 0°C, is
associated with loss of flavour (Hoagland, McBryde and Powick, 1917).
And, of course, where oxidative rancidity occurs in fat, the products
affect flavour in a highly adverse manner (Lee, 1939). Oxidative
rancidity in fat is retarded by a high ultimate pH as also is the oxidation
of myoglobin (Watts, 1954) with which it is frequently linked. These
phenomena will be considered in more detail in a later chapter.

Apart from the increase in free amino acids arising from proteolysis,
their concentration is also augmented by the breakdown of various
peptides. During conditioning, for example, the dipeptides carnosine
and anserine are progressively hydrolysed to β-alanine and histidine
(Bouton et al., 1958). The accumulation of free amino acids, and of
soluble carbohydrates, such as glucose (by the action of α-amylase on
glycogen; Sharp, 1958), glucose-6-phosphate (one of the intermediaries
in the glycolytic pathway), ribose (from nucleotide breakdown) and
other sugars in traces, is potentially undesirable. During the preparation
of dehydrated meat, for example, the carbonyl groups of the
carbohydrates will combine with the amino nitrogen of amino acids
non-enzymically to form unsightly brown compounds which are also
troublesome in having a bitter taste. The Maillard reaction, as it is
known, may also take place between the sugars and intact protein (Lee
and Hannan, 1950).

Although conditioning enhances the water-holding capacity of
proteins to some extent, the loss due to denaturation changes and to
post-mortem pH fall predominates, and meat exudes fluid post-mortem.

CHAPTER 6

THE SPOILAGE OF MEAT
BY INFECTING ORGANISMS

CHANGES which take place during the conversion of muscle to meat, both immediately post-mortem and later, on keeping the commodity above the freezing point, were described in Chapter 5. It was emphasized that these occurred in meat irrespective of the presence or absence of extraneous organisms. But meat, like all man's foodstuffs, is acceptable to other organisms and is susceptible to invasion by them. Their invasion of the meat (infection), the consequent production of unattractive changes (spoilage), the factors controlling their growth and the question of prophylaxis will now be separately considered.

6.1. INFECTION

The organisms which spoil meat may gain access through infection of the living animal (endogenous disease) or by contamination of the meat post-mortem (exogenous disease). The consumer is more likely to encounter the latter. Nevertheless, both aspects are important. It should be noted that serious human infections can be acquired from apparently healthy animals (Dolman, 1957).

6.1.1. *Endogenous Infections*

Before considering diseases caused in man by consumption of meat from infected animals, brief reference should be made to those which are transmitted by contact, namely anthrax, bovine tuberculosis and brucellosis. These are caused by the microbes *B. anthracis*, *M. tuberculosis* and *Brucella* spp. respectively. Anthrax is mainly contracted by contact with the hides and hair. Although the main vehicle for infection with bovine tuberculosis is raw milk, contact with affected carcases is also a serious source (Dolman, 1957). The skin (and the mucus membranes) is also the route of infection from carcases carrying *Brucella* spp. These diseases tend to be localized in certain areas of the world.

Most other diseases arising from *in vivo* infection in meat animals are acquired by consumption of infected carcases. The infections may be caused by bacteria or by parasitic worms. Perhaps the most important bacterial diseases in this category are those caused by members of the genus *Salmonella*. The consumption of inadequately cooked meat is the usual method of infection. *S. typhimurium* is found in lambs, calves and adult bovines, the principal source of their infection being on the farm (Nottingham and Urselmann, 1961). *S. cholerae suis* is mainly confined to pigs. Even healthy carriers may transfer *Salmonella* to normal animals whilst these are being held awaiting slaughter (Galton *et al.*, 1954). In an investigation in Australia nearly half of the animals passed as healthy had *Salmonella* spp. in the rumen liquor (Green and Bronlee, 1965). A very marked increase between 1961–65 in the outbreaks of salmonellosis in calves, involving *S. typhimurium*, was attributed to the use of heavily infected premises for holding and sale (Melrose and Gracey, 1975).

More prevalent are the infections acquired by ingestion of meat infested with parasitic worms. Stoll (1947) calculated that there may be a world total of 27 million cases of trichinosis and 42 million of taeniasis (caused by the tapeworms of beef and pork). There are also about 100,000 cases of echinococcosis (disease caused by certain other tapeworms).

Trichinella spiralis is a small nematode worm with many potential hosts including man. Infection may prove fatal (Zenker, 1860). Human trichinosis is a serious public health problem in the U.S.A. due to the practice there of feeding uncooked garbage to hogs in certain areas. The disease is found only where raw, inadequately cooked or improperly cured meat (especially pork) is eaten. Even in remote areas of the world the disease may be endemic, as in the Arctic where the flesh of whale, polar bear and walrus may be implicated. Fresh pork may be rendered harmless by exposure to sufficient heat, cold, salt, smoke or ionizing radiations. For example, exposure to $-38°C$ for 2 min will kill the larvae (Gould, Gomberg and Bethell, 1953). The effect of salt has been elucidated (Gammon *et al.*, 1968). It appears that *Trichinella spiralis* can survive the phase of salt equilibration during curing processes; but it begins to die off after 1 week; and none survives 1 month.

For the development of the adult beef tapeworm. *Taenia saginata*, which may grow to many feet in length, it is essential that a bovine should eat grass contaminated with the ova of the organism derived from the human intestine and that parts of the bovine containing the subsequent larvae of the organism (*Cysticercus bovis*) should be eaten raw by man. The predilection of the meat consumer for underdone beef may explain the greater prevalence of this kind of parasitic infection. Maintenance of the life cycle of the pork tapeworm (*T. solium*) requires an analogous relationship between pig and man. The corresponding larval stage in porcine muscle is known as *C. cellulosae*. Infestation with pork tapeworm is the more serious because the organism may develop into larvae in the human brain. Control of both diseases can be achieved by avoiding insanitary disposal of human faeces near cattle or swine feeding areas and by proper cooking. Exposure for 6 days to a temperature of $-9.5°C$ will destroy the cysts (Dolman, 1957). "Measly" beef or pork, as the infested meat is called, is generally detected by thorough meat inspection.

Although human diseases caused by other tapeworms are not acquired directly by consuming infested meat, the domestic association of man with dogs, the usual host of *Echinococcus granulosis* (the parasite responsible), leads to human infection, as in sheep-rearing areas where sheep, man and dog are in close contact.

Trematodes (especially *Fasciola hepatica*, the liver fluke) are communicable to man, but not through infected meat.

6.1.2. *Exogenous Infections*

Whereas the infections mentioned in § 6.1.1 arise from established disease in the live animal and may involve both parasitic worms and bacteria, meat spoilage and associated food poisoning reflect infection of the meat by bacteria (or fungi) after death. Where there is proper meat inspection to eliminate infected carcases from distribution, the predominant mode of meat deterioration by invading organisms will be by exogenous infection.

6.1.2.1. *Bacteraemia*

Notwithstanding the predominantly post-mortem aspect of exogenous infection, the condition of the animal's blood immediately before and at slaughter is also appropriately considered in this context. In the large intestine there may be 33×10^{12} viable bacteria (Haines, 1937). Invasion of the tissues and organs of the body from the gut via the blood stream (bacteraemia) is opposed, however, by the mucous lining of the intestinal tract (Kohlbrugge, 1901), through agglutination of bacteria by circulating antibodies (formed from the gamma globulins of the blood in response to some previous minor exposure to the organisms concerned) and through phagocytosis of bacteria by the cells of the reticulo–endothelial system (in lymph nodes, in the blood and, possibly, in the tissues themselves). There is an equilibrium between invasion of the tissues and removal of the invading organisms such that the tissues of healthy animals are normally free from bacteria (Haines, 1937). Using bacteria labelled with C^{14} it has been confirmed that bacteria entering the lymphatic system from the intestines up to 24 hours post-mortem are destroyed by surviving action of the reticulo-endothelial system (Gill, Penney and Nottingham, 1976). This explains the possibility of rearing disease-free pigs after sterile hysterectomy (Betts, 1961) referred to in § 2.4.4. In some species it would appear that the reticulo–endothelial system is more effective than in others, since venison, for example, can be hung for a considerable period at room temperature without undue precautions. Phagocytic activity, together with the gamma globulin content of the blood, can be enhanced by the administration of oestrogens (Charles and Nicol, 1961) and of certain other substances (Nicol, McKelvie and Druce, 1961).

Invasion of the blood stream by organisms from the gut may be increased by fatigue in the animal (Haines, 1937; Burn and Burket, 1938; Robinson *et al.*, 1953), *prolonged* starvation (Ficker, 1905) or even feeding (Desoubry and Porcher, 1895; Gulbrandsen, 1935). The mode of slaughter can also be implicated since breakdown of the intestinal mucosa was observed in sheep which had been shot (Badawy *et al.*, 1957). The bolt of a captive bolt pistol may carry a bacterial load of the order of 4×10^5 organisms cm^2 of metal (Ingram, 1971). These observations explain the traditional reluctance to give animals food later than 24 hr pre-slaughter and why the flesh of fatigued animals does not keep so well—although, in the latter, a high ultimate pH is a contributory factor. The organisms from the gut which can be distributed to the muscles by the blood include various Streptococci (*Strep. bovis* in cattle and sheep; *Strep. faecalis*, *Strep. faecium* and *Strep. durans* mainly in sheep: Medrek and Barnes, 1962), *Clostridium welchii* and *Salmonella* spp.

If an infected knife is used, or organisms are inadvertently introduced from the skin whilst the main blood vessels are being severed, bleeding can itself lead to bacteraemia and to the infection of the animal's tissues (Empey and Scott, 1939; Jensen and Hess, 1941).

6.1.2.2. *Sources and nature of external contamination*

External contamination of the meat is a constant possibility from the moment of bleeding until consumption. In the abattoir itself there are a large number of potential sources of infection by micro-organisms. These include the hide, soil adhering thereto, the contents of the gastro-intestinal tract (if inadvertently released during dressing operations), airborne contamination, aqueous sources (the water used for washing the carcase, immersing wiping-cloths or for cleaning the floors), the instruments used in dressing (knives, saws, cleavers and hooks), various vessels and receptacles, and, finally, the personnel (Empey and Scott, 1939). Some idea of the microbial loads which may be expected in an Australian slaughterhouse killing beef pre-war is given in Table 6.1. It is particularly important to avoid dirt from hides or fleece settling on exposed meat surfaces (Bryce-Jones, 1969). The fleece of sheep is a

TABLE 6.1 *Typical Microbial Counts in Sources of Microbial Contamination in an Abattoir*
(after Empey and Scott, 1939)

Sources and method of calculation	Temp. of incubation (°C)	Bacteria	Yeasts	Moulds
Hides (no. cm²-surface)	20	3.3×10^6	580	850
	—1	1.5×10^4	89	89
Surface soils (no. g dry wt)	20	1.1×10^8	5×10^4	1.2×10^5
	—1	2.8×10^6	1.4×10^4	1.0×10^4
Gastro-intestinal contents:	20	9.0×10^7	2.0×10^5	6.0×10^4
Faeces (no. g dry wt)	—1	2.0×10^5	70	1700
Gastro-intestinal contents:	20	5.3×10^7	1.8×10^5	1600
Rumen (no. g dry wt)	—1	5.2×10^4	50	60
Airborne contamination				
(no. deposited from air/	20	140	—	2
cm²/hr)	—1	8	—	0.1
Water used on slaughter	20	1.6×10^5	30	480
floors (max. no./ml)	—1	1000	10	50
Water present in recep-				
tacles from immersion	20		1.4×10^5	
cloths (no./ml.)	—1		40	

significant source of salmonella contamination of the carcase: it can become a reservoir of these organisms after a day's holding at the abattoir lairage (Grau and Smith, 1974). There seems little difference, microbiologically, between flaying on the rail or in a "cradle" (Nottingham, Denney and Harrison, 1973). By dosing sheep with cyclopropamide up to 10 days before slaughter, manual removal of the fleece can be readily carried out off the slaughter floor (Leach, 1971). Since recent legislation has prohibited the use of wiping cloths, alternative ways of removing excess blood, etc., from the surface of the carcase have had to be considered (Akers, 1969; Bryce-Jones, 1969). Pressure hosing is said to lead to loss of desirable surface appearance ("bloom") through uptake of water by the connective tissue. This latter can be avoided by applying warm water (about 43°C) as a spray followed by *rapid* drying. The "bloom" reappears after the carcases have been at chill temperature for a few hours subsequently. The application of markedly higher temperatures to sheep carcases—immersion in water at 80°C for 10 seconds has been shown to destroy about 99 per cent of contaminating coliforms initially present on surface tissues (Smith and Graham, 1978). Bacteria are liable to multiply rapidly in lukewarm water; and care must be taken to ensure that no pockets of moisture remain (if necessary by wiping with approved disposable, absorbent paper). Wetting carcases does not spoil them provided the moisture is removed rapidly; and that the dirt is removed and not merely redistributed. In general it is preferable, of course, to avoid surface contamination by strict hygiene than to remove it.

It will be seen (Table 6.1) that the initial contamination acquired by beef surfaces during dressing operations under earlier conditions included more than 99 per cent of bacteria amongst those organisms viable at ordinary temperature (20°C). These populations contained less than 1 per cent of organisms viable at − 1°C, although the percentage of yeast and moulds was greater in the populations viable at − 1°C than at 20°C. The chief source of the superficial microflora was the hide of the slaughtered animals; the types of organisms in both localities was the same. Of the organisms viable at − 1°C, four principal bacterial genera were represented, namely *Achromobacter* (90 per cent), *Micrococcus* (about 7 per cent), *Flavobacterium* (about 3 per cent) and *Pseudomonas* (less than 1 per cent). Of the mould genera the most common were *Penicillium, Mucor, Cladosporium, Alternaria, Sporotrichium* and *Thamnidium.* In Fig. 6.1 the effect of incubating a piece of meat touched by the hand of a workman carrying mould spores is shown.

Inadequate cooling of the carcase at the abattoir will permit the proliferation of putrefactive organisms, the most common type causing bone taint (Savage, 1918; Acevado and Romat, 1929). These are external in origin and gain access to the animal by cuts and abrasions on the skin (Cosnett *et al.*, 1956). Bone taint was defined by Haines (1937), as "the development of putrid or sour odours in the deep-seated parts of meat, usually near the bone". The bacterial flora of lymph nodes and of tainted meat are similar (Nottingham, 1960), consisting of gram-positive rods. It seems likely that when the pH is relatively high and the temperature falls insufficiently quickly, bacteria proliferate within the lymph nodes (ischiatic and popliteal) and spread into the surrounding meat (Cosnett *et al.*, 1956).

Although some sources of contamination are obviously removed when the carcases leave the slaughter floor, contamination by contact with unhygienic surfaces, by personnel and by airborne organisms will remain as a possibility in all operations during the subsequent history of the meat—chilling, freezing, processing, cutting, packaging, transport,

FIG. 6.1. Effect of incubating meat surface after contamination through contact with a hand bearing mould spores. (Courtesy J. Barlow.)

sale and domestic handling. The organisms derived from infected personnel or healthy carriers include *Salmonella* spp., *Shigella* spp., *E. coli*, *B. proteus*, *Staph. albus* and *Staph. aureus*, *Cl. welchii*, *B. cereus* and faecal streptococci: those from soil include *Cl. botulinum*. Together with those distributed to the tissue by the blood (§ 6.1.2.1), they constitute the source not only of much meat spoilage but also of food poisoning since they are conditioned to grow preferentially at body temperature. Inadequate cooking of contaminated meat or meat products which have been kept warm beforehand or reheating of partly cooked meat can be responsible. Since some of the organisms form spores or toxins, however, even cooking may fail to prevent infection, poisoning and even death (e.g. with *Cl. botulinum*, the toxin of which is one of the most potent poisons known). Some features of food poisoning organisms are summarized in Table 6.2 (Anon., 1957b). There are six serologically distinguishable types of *Cl. botulinum*—A, B, C, D, E and F. Spores of A and B survive boiling for several hours but the organisms will only grow slowly below 10°C. Spores of type E are killed

TABLE 6.2. *Some Characteristics of Bacterial Meat Poisoning*

Causal organism	Time from ingest to onset symptoms	Reservoir of infecting organisms	Characteristic symptoms
Salmonella	8–72 hr, often 8–12	Gut of animals	Abdominal pain; diarrhoea; nausea; pyrexia; prostration
Staphylococcus	1–6 hr, often 2–4 hr	Skin, nose, cuts in man animals	As above; plus salivation and vomitting but sub-normal temperature
Enterococcus *Cl. welchii* *Strep. Faecalis*	2–18 hr	Gut of animals	Abdominal cramp; diarrhoea; no pyrexia or prostration
Cl. Botulinum	2 hr–8 days, often 12–48 hr	Soil	Difficulty in swallowing; double vision; no pyrexia; respiratory paralysis

by heating to 80°C for 30 min, but they will grow at 3·3°C in a beef-stew medium (Schmidt, Lechowich and Folinazzo, 1961). Fortunately, *Cl. botulinum* E if present, would be outgrown by psychrophils in chilled meat. The only other non-mesophilic pathogen which might be encountered, *Listeria monocytogenes* grows only slowly (Mossel, Dijkmann and Snijders, 1975). Types C and D are rarely implicated in human botulism: type F is so far known to have been involved in only one outbreak, caused by home-prepared liver paste. The geographical distribution of the various types is probably related to temperature; soil type and other unknown ecological factors. The toxins produced by *Cl. botulinum* are quite resistant to heat and to the enzymes in the digestive tract; in fact type E toxin is activated by trypsin (Duff, Wright and Yarinsky, 1956).

Of 164 food poisoning outbreaks in England and Wales in 1953 (Anon., 1957b) forty-four were due to *salmonellae*, forty-seven to *staphylococci*, nineteen to *Cl. welchii* and fifty-four to other organisms, mostly unidentified.

6.2. SYMPTOMS OF SPOILAGE

In satisfying their requirements for nourishment and survival, invading organisms alter meat in a variety of ways. Some of these are not deleterious: a few are beneficial, but the vast majority are not and, indeed, may even be lethal, as we have seen.

The superficially recognizable effects of invasion by parasites are sometimes striking (Thornton, 1973) but, as they are generally detected by public health inspectors and are rarely recognizable or encountered by the consuming public, they will not be considered here. The types of spoilage caused by micro-organisms broadly depends on the availability of oxygen, although, as will be considered below, many other factors are involved (Table 6.3; Haines, 1937).

The nature, range and sequence of the changes in meat caused by the biochemical activities of a single species of invading organism, can be exemplified by the behaviour of *Cl. welchii*, an anaerobe (Gale, 1947; Wilson and Miles, 1955). First, the meat liquifies because the organism

TABLE 6.3. *Superficially Recognizable Symptoms of Microbial Spoilage of Meat*

Oxygen status	Type of micro-organism	Symptoms of spoilage
Present	Bacteria	Slime on meat surface: discoloration by destruction of meat pigments or growth of colonies of coloured organisms; production off-odours and taints; fat decomposition
Present	Yeasts	Yeast slime; discoloration; off-odours and tastes; fat decomposition
Present	Moulds	Surface "stickiness" and "whiskers"; discoloration; odours and taints; fat decomposition
Absent	Bacteria	Putrefaction accompanied by foul odours; gas production; souring

excretes a collagenase which hydrolyses the connective tissue between the fibre bundles, causing them to disintegrate. This is followed by gas production. The free amino acids present are attacked by deaminases with the production of hydrogen, carbon dioxide and ammonia; and glycogen, if present, is fermented to give acetic and butyric acids. These activities cause foul smells and unpleasant tastes. Another enzyme produced by *Cl. welchii* decarboxylates histidine to histamine, which affects membrane permeability. Certain highly invasive strains of *Cl. welchii* produce hyaluronidase, which attacks mucopolysaccharides in the ground substance between cells and permits further penetration by the micro-organisms. In addition to all these actions, which are relatively harmless to the consumer, *Cl. welchii* produces toxins in the meat. On being ingested, these have various biological actions including haemolysis of the blood and destruction of tissue cells and, in severe infections, death. But the changes caused by individual organisms—and the corresponding symptoms of spoilage—are usually somewhat more limited in scope.

Surface slime is the superficially observable effect of the coalescence of a sufficiently large number of individual colonies of micro-organisms: the further apart these colonies are in the first place, i.e. the lower the initial infection, the longer the time will be until slime forms (Fig. 6.2;

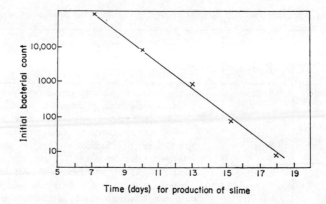

FIG. 6.2. The relationship between initial microbial load and the time for slime to develop on the surface of meat (Haines, 1937).

Haines, 1937). Slime formation signifies a general suitability of the temperature and moisture of meat surfaces and the adjacent air for growth; but the chemical nature of these two phases will select the type of organism found. Thus, there will be substantial representation of the genus *Achromobacter* on chilled beef (Empey and Scott, 1939), of *Micrococcus* on sides of pork and on matured bacon (Brooks *et al.*, 1940); and of *Lactobacillus* on vacuum packed, sliced bacon, if stored between 5° and 30°C (Kitchell and Ingram, 1963). Slime formation on sausages, however, can be due to a white yeast (Haines, 1937).

Discoloration may be due to alteration or destruction of meat pigments. Myoglobin may be oxidized to brown metmyoglobin; it may combine with H_2S, produced by bacteria, to form sulphmyoglobin (Jensen, 1945); or be broken down to form yellow or green bile pigments by microbially produced hydrogen peroxide (Niven, 1951; Watts, 1954). Yeasts, growing on the fat surfaces of vacuum-packed, chilled beef, have been found to cause the development of brown spots after six weeks' storage at 0°C (Shay and Egan, 1976), due to their action on haem. Discoloration may also be due to the elaboration of foreign pigments of *Pseudomonas*, pink pigments of various types of micrococci, sarcinae and yeasts, and the red colour of *B. prodigiosus* (Haines, 1937). Moulds of the genera *Cladosporium*, *Sporotrichium* and *Penicillium* produce black, white and blue-green colours respectively. Black or red discoloration can be produced in salt meat and meat products by certain halophilic pseudomonads (Gibbons, 1958). Green cores can be formed in sausages by *L. viridescens* (Niven and Evans, 1957). Green, blue and silver surface luminescence can be caused by the activity of harmless bacteria belonging to many genera—a phenomenon known since ancient times (Jensen, 1949).

Putrid odours are produced mainly by anaerobes through the decomposition of proteins and amino acids (yielding indole, methyl-amine and H_2S) and sour odours through the decomposition of sugars and other small molecules (Haines, 1937). Such may be encountered in the interior of improperly cured hams, the organism responsible in this case being *B. putrifaciens* (McBryde, 1911): it may be caused by various gram-positive rods in inadequately cooled beef carcases (bone taint; § 6.1.2.2). The growth of anaerobes is associated with a more offensive decomposition than that of aerobes. There are several reasons for this (Haines, 1937). For example, the low energy yield of anaerobic processes compared with aerobic ones makes it necessary for anaerobes to break down a proportionately greater quantity of material than aerobes for a given degree of multiplication. Again, evil-smelling substances tend to be liberated particularly under reducing conditions.

If *Pseudomonas fragi* is present during the storage of pork at 2°–10°C, some proteolysis of myofibrillar proteins occurs; and this will raise the emulsifying capacity of the meat (Borton *et al.*, 1970). Neither in their experiments nor in those of Dainty *et al.*, (1975), who studied beef surfaces at 5°C, was there detectable proteolysis before spoilage odours and slime had developed.

Many types of micro-organisms cause spoilage by producing free fatty acids and yellow or green pigments (Jensen, 1949) from the superficial fat in meat; and, indeed, such changes are frequently the limiting factors in storage.

Although, quite apart from microbial techniques, there are a large number of objective chemical tests which can be used to assess the degree of microbial spoilage in meat (Thornton, 1949; Rubashkina, 1953;

Herschdoerfer and Dyett, 1959) human sensory evaluation of superficial symptoms has not lost its value.

6.3. FACTORS AFFECTING THE GROWTH OF MEAT SPOILAGE MICRO-ORGANISMS

Implicitly, the micro-organisms spoiling meat can gain therefrom their basic requirements for growth—sources of carbon, nitrogen, bacterial vitamins, etc.—although the degree of accessibility of these nutrients will vary. A suitable temperature, moisture availability, osmotic pressure, pH, oxidation–reduction potential and atmosphere are also essential; but these factors are interrelated and their individual importance varies with the particular circumstances being considered. Other less fundamental factors affect microbial growth. These include ionizing radiations, although their effect is more logically considered under prophylaxis; and some so far unidentified agencies. It was observed, for instance, that the growth of psychrophiles at 0°C in extracts of beef l. dorsi muscles was inversely related to the time elapsing between death of the animal and the onset of rigor mortis: no explanation of this effect has been established so far (Brown, Coote and Meaney, 1957). It is important to emphasize that the observed status of these factors, in or on meat at a given time, does not necessarily define whether or not the meat is (or is likely to be) spoiled. The products of past microbial activity will remain after the death of the organisms responsible and, in the case of toxins, may prove dangerous as well as distasteful. Moreover, against immediately unfavourable conditions, certain organisms form resistant spores which survive cooking and canning. In these, metabolic activities are largely suspended; but viability may remain and the rapid growth of the organism recommences when favourable circumstances again arise. Infection can thus be latent. Spores of *B. anthracis* have been known to survive as potential centres of infection for 60 years (Umeno and Nobata, 1938). Authentic evidence that spores of *Thermoactinomyces spp.* can survive for 1900 years has been presented (Seaward, Cross and Unsworth, 1976).

6.3.1. Temperature

The most important single factor governing microbial growth is temperature (Haines, 1937). Broadly, the higher the temperature the greater is the rate of growth (Fig. 6.3; Haines, 1934). Many meat micro-organisms will grow to some extent at all temperatures from below 0°C to above 65°C, but, for a given organism, vigorous growth occurs in a more limited temperature range. It is customary to classify meat spoilage organisms in three categories. Psychrophiles have temperature optima between −2°C and 7°C, mesophiles between 10°C and 40°C and thermophiles from 43° to 66°C (Jensen, 1945). The distinction is by no means absolute, however, as certain gram-negative rods, which are generally regarded as mesophiles, will grow at −1·5°C (Eddy and Kitchell, 1959).

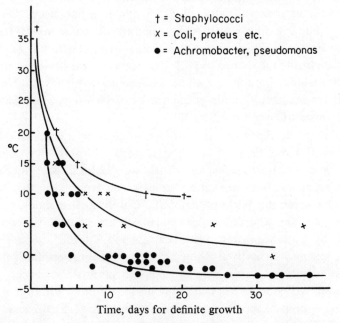

FIG. 6.3. The effect of temperature on the rate of growth of various bacteria (Haines, 1934).

An interesting aspect of temperature optima is the finding that the beef prepared from cattle in tropical areas will carry a relatively small percentage of organisms capable of growing when the meat is kept at chill temperatures (− 1·5 C) and will thus keep better than beef prepared from temperate zone cattle. The predominant microflora on beef surfaces is derived from the soil and is adjusted to grow at soil temperatures, which are high in the tropics (Empey and Scott, 1939).

Another reflection of temperature optima is the difference in behaviour of ham and gammon, despite that they are both produced from the leg of pork (Ingram, 1952). Hams are only lightly injected with curing salts. When taint occurs it does so at relatively high storage temperatures and is caused by mesophiles (faecal clostridia and streptococci) which are probably intrinsic to the animal body. Gammons, however, are injected with brine, the microbial flora of which consists of psychrophilic, salt-tolerant organisms (mainly micrococci). They will thus grow and cause taint even at chill temperatures. On the other hand, if curing is ineffective, spoilage of gammons by faecal streptococci can occur (Ingram, 1952). Similarly, bone taint in beef, as we have already mentioned in § 6.1.2.2, represents the development of mesophiles under conditions where the temperature is favourable for growth (through faulty cooling), and there exists a reservoir of infection in the animal (Cosnett *et al.*, 1956).

Although the types of micro-organisms growing on prepackaged fresh beef, lamb or pork are the same at 3° and 7°C (mainly *Achromobacter* and *Pseudomonas fluorescens;* Halleck, Ball and Stier, 1958), an apparent species difference has been reported in that both anaerobic or aerobic packs of lambs at 5°C were spoiled mainly by *M. thermosphactum*, whereas, under similar conditions, beef was spoiled mainly by gram-negative bacteria (Barlow and Kitchell, 1966). These differences may be partly attributed to the fact that the residual rate of oxygen utilization is considerably higher in lamb than in beef. The temperature of storage has marked influence on the micro-organisms growing in prepackaged cured meats. If prepackaged sliced bacon, for example, is kept at 37°C its normal psychrophilic flora is replaced by mesophilic organisms, which include pathogenic staphylococci (Ingram,

1960). At temperatures of storage from 5 to 30 C the halophilic micrococci and lactic acid bacteria, which constitute the greater part of the flora of packaged sliced bacon, both increase in numbers, but the lactic bacteria do so rapidly and they come to constitute a greater proportion of the population. On continued storage, the lactic acid bacteria reach maximum numbers and stop growing, but the micrococci continue to increase. Above 20 C, however, the type of *Micrococcus* changes and organisms related to *Staph. aureus* predominate (Ingram, 1960). There is a marked, concomitant effect on bacon flavour—at 20 C the spoilage odour is sour and at 30 C putrid (Cavett, 1962)—and on the relative quantities of nitrate and nitrate present (Eddy and Gatherum, unpublished data). It is conceivable that micrococci reduce nitrate and that gram-negative rods destroy nitrite, as in bacon curing brines (Eddy, 1958). Since temperatures alter the rate of bacterial respiration and the system is closed, the atmosphere within a pack, being of restricted volume, should contain more oxygen and less carbon dioxide if kept at low temperatures (Ingram, 1962). The reaction of within-pack atmospheres with temperature has to be considered as an additional determinant of bacterial flora and growth in such products; and it is of course, related to the nature of the wrapping medium and its relative permeability to various gases.

Micro-organisms may remain viable well outside the ranges quoted. They have been reported to survive for 10 hr at -252 C (MacFadyen and Rowland, 1900) and, as spores, for $5\frac{1}{2}$ at $100°C$ in the presence of moisture, and for $2\frac{1}{2}$ hr ar $200°C$ in the dry state (Tanner, 1944). The effect of freezing must be distinguished from that of low temperature itself, however, since although $-12°C$ will stop all microbial growth in frozen carcases, some organisms will grow in a super-cooled liquid at $-20°C$ (Richardson and Scherubel, 1909).

In general, a reduction in the number of micro-organisms occurs when meat is frozen; but yeasts and moulds will grow at $-5°C$ although not at $-10°C$ (Haines, 1931). Carefully controlled experiments have failed to substantiate the prevalent view that thawed meat is *intrinsically* more perishable than meat which has not been frozen (Sulzbacher, 1952; Kitchell and Ingram, 1956). Even so, under commercial handling conditions, the moister surface of thawed meat would tend to pick up greater numbers of bacteria and hence be potentially more liable to spoil (Kitchell, 1959). Even with storage at 0 C spoilage could occur through the activities of psychrophiles, e.g. *Ps. fluorescens* (Petersen and Gunderson, 1960).

The effect of temperature on microbial growth may differ according to the nature of the nutrients available. Thus, *Lactobacillus arabinosus* needs phenylalanine, tyrosine and aspartic acid for growth at 39°C, phenylalanine and tyrosine at 37 C and none of these amino acids at 26 C (Borek and Waelsch, 1951). It is important to appreciate that, if there has been heavy microbial growth before freezing, a high concentration of microbial enzymes (e.g. lipases) may have been produced. Thus, even if microbial growth is arrested by the process of freezing, the enzymes may continue to produce deleterious quality changes even down to about −30°C (Sulzbacher and Gaddis, 1968).

6.3.2. *Moisture and Osmotic Pressure*

After temperature, the availability of moisture is perhaps the most important requirement for microbial growth on meat, although some types of bacteria may remain dormant for lengthy periods at low moisture levels; and spores resist destruction by dry heat more than by moist heat (Tanner, 1944). Typical data from an experiment with cuts of lamb, showing the growth-promoting effects of moisture and temperature, are given in Table 6.4. The organisms present belong to several genera—*Pseudomonas, Achromobacter, Proteus* and *Micrococcus* (Jensen, 1942).

The availability of moisture is complementary to that of osmotic pressure, which is a function of the concentration of soluble, dializable substances (salts, carbohydrates, etc.) in the aqueous medium. High solute concentrations tend to inhibit growth; desiccation of the substrate and not low temperature as such generally restricts microbial growth on frozen-meat products. Nevertheless, there is great variation between species and, although most of the organisms which will grow on meat are

TABLE 6.4. *The Effect of Surface Moisture and Temperature on Microbial Growth on Lamb Cuts* (after Jensen, 1942)

Time (hr)	Aerobic bacteria/g			
	2–3 C		7–10 C	
	Wet surface	Dry surface	Wet surface	Dry surface
24	400,000	40,000	1,000,000	200,000
72	760,000	42,000	Putrid	4,000,000

inhibited by salt, there are many salt-tolerant organisms which grow successfully on bacon brines.

The water relations of meat-spoilage organisms have been studied in detail by Scott, who has used the term "water activity" (a_w) in this context. The a_w of a solution is the ratio of its vapour pressure to that of pure water at the same temperature: it is inversely proportional to the number of solute molecules present (Scott, 1957). In general, moulds and yeasts tolerate higher osmotic pressures than bacteria (Haines, 1937), bacteria growing from an a_w of just under 1·0 down to an a_w of 0·75, and yeasts and moulds growing slowly at an a_w of 0·62 (Scott, 1957).

Scott (1936) showed that decreasing the a_w decreased the rates of growth of moulds, yeasts and bacteria on meat surfaces. The optimum a_w for several food poisoning strains of *Staph. aureus* was shown to be about 0·995 (Scott, 1953). Below this value, the rate of growth markedly diminished (Fig. 6.4). At 38°C the level of a_w at which this organism would grow on dried meat was 0·88, corresponding to 23 per cent of available water. A similar study of the water requirements of *Salmonella* was made by Christian and Scott (1953); and of *Vibrio metschnikovi* by Marshall and Scott (1955) the latter having a very well-defined optimum a_w which was critical for growth (cf. Fig. 6.4). Temperature and pH are among various factors which affect the a_w (Scott, 1957).

Fresh meats have an a_w which is frequently about 0·99, and they are thus liable to spoil through the growth of a wide range of organisms

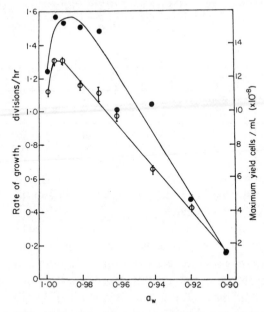

FIG. 6.4. Relationship between the mean rate of growth (○), maximum yield of cells (●), and a_w for fourteen strains of *S. aureus* under controlled conditions (Scott, 1953). (Courtesy Dr. W. J. Scott.)

(Scott, 1957). The importance of surface drying in restricting microbial growth on beef was demonstrated by Scott and Vickery (1939).

Because of the interaction of oxygen availability and a_w, it is feasible that in prepackaged meats, where the oxygen tension is low, growth of micro-organisms might be inhibited at a higher a_w (Ingram, 1962). Scott (1953) found, for example, that the growth of *Staph. aureus* would proceed at an a_w of 0·86 aerobically, but only above 0·90 anaerobically. On the other hand, when meat is prepackaged and sliced, surface growth will be possible between the pieces, and the surface drying which would normally inhibit growth on stored meat would not operate (Ingram, 1962). Whenever the mode of packaging limits evaporation and weight loss there will be an increased humidity within the pack and the danger of bacterial growth will be greater. Nevertheless, the microbiological undesirability of a wrap which is impermeable to water vapour may be offset if it is relatively permeable to oxygen and carbon dioxide (Shrimpton and Barnes, 1960).

With bacon, a high salt/moisture ratio extends its storage life (Hankins *et al.*, 1950).

The effect of salt concentration in altering the types of micro-organisms capable of growing on meat products can be exemplified by comparing the behaviour of those isolated from bacon brines and pork sides (Table 6.5; after Kitchell, 1958).

TABLE 6.5. *Plate Counts, at Two Salt Concentrations, of Micro-organisms from Bacon Brines and Pork Sides*

Source	Counts	
	1%NaCl	10%NaCl
Bacon brines	$1 \cdot 43 \times 10^6$ per ml	$11 \cdot 14 \times 10^6$ per ml
Pork sides	$15 \cdot 8 \times 10^3$ per cm^2	$8 \cdot 4 \times 10^3$ per cm^2

It is obvious that the micro-organisms of bacon brine are predominantly of types capable of growing in the presence of 10 per cent salt, and relatively incapable of growing in the presence of 1 per cent salt: whereas, the converse is true for the micro-organisms of pork sides. High salt concentration shifts the balance of the microbial population towards halophilic organisms. Nevertheless, a certain affinity exists between the micro-organisms of raw pork and those of matured bacon (Shaw, Stitt and Cowan, 1951); but both differ from those of brine. The ability to reduce nitrate and/or nitrite is one of the metabolic activities found preferentially among the bacteria capable of growing at high salt concentration (Table 6.6).

Bacilli are known which will tolerate 15 per cent NaCl and in canned hams will vigorously reduce nitrate and nitrite with the production of sufficient nitrous oxide to "blow" the cans (Eddy and Ingram, 1956).

In the maturation of bacon, colour fixation is due to the reaction of the pigment of fresh meat (myoglobin) with nitric oxide. The curing brine contains nitrate which is reduced to nitrite, and the latter to nitric

TABLE 6.6. *Proportions of the Strains of Micrococci,
isolated from various sources, which reduce either Nitrate
or Nitrite*
(after Kitchell, 1958)

Source	No. of strains examined	Per cent of reducing strains
Bacon brines	59	90
Immature bacon	22	83
Pork sides	31	68

oxide, by microbial action. An increase in salt concentration in the brine, however, suppresses these processes by lowering the metabolic rate of the halophilic micro-organisms responsible and vice versa: the effect is more marked at 5° than at 10°C (Eddy and Kitchell, 1961). The microbial reduction of nitrate and nitrite also occurs in the bacon itself during maturation (Eddy, Gatherum and Kitchell, 1960). The reduction of nitrite, in contrast to that of nitrate, may well occur in bacon through the activity of tissue enzymes and in the absence of micro-organisms (Walters and Taylor, 1963).

Salt itself, depending on its origin, may harbour various bacteria, including halophiles which produce red colonies and thus spoil the product being preserved. These may be troublesome in the fish industry (Bain, Hodgkiss and Shewan, 1958) and with imported gut casings. Although, they have not appeared in the spoilage of bacon as such, they may well be responsible for a discoloration of bacon brines which has been sporadically reported (D. P. Gatherum, personal communication). According to Yesair (1930) certain salts may harbour proteolytic anaerobes and should thus be avoided for meat curing.

Certain species of *Lactobacillus* will tolerate the high sugar concentrations used in ham curing brines in the U.S.A., and will grow on cured unprocessed hams producing polysaccharides with concomitant deterioration in flavour and appearance (Deibel and Niven, 1959).

6.3.3. *pH*

As we have already considered, the post-mortem pH of meat will be determined by the amount of lactic acid produced from glycogen during anaerobic glycolysis (§ 5.1.2); and this will be curtailed if glycogen is depleted by fatigue, inanition or fear in the animal before slaughter. Since pH is an important determinant of microbial growth, it will be obvious that the ultimate pH of meat is significant for its resistance to spoilage. Most bacteria grow optimally at about pH 7 and not well below pH 4 or above pH 9 (Fig. 6.5; Cohen and Clark, 1919); but the pH of maximal growth is determined by the simultaneous operation of variables other than the degree of acidity or alkalinity itself. Some of the bacteriological enzymes which cause spoilage may have different optima from that of the organism itself. Thus, whereas bacterial proteolytic enzymes operate best near neutrality, the enzymes which attack carbohydrates tend to have optima below 6; and organisms such as lactic acid bacteria, of which the predominant activity is carbohydrate breakdown, have optima between pH 5·5 and 6.

In fresh meat, the encouragement given to bacteria by a high ultimate pH, especially in the deeper areas of the carcase which are slow to cool, causes "bone taint" (§§ 6.1.2.2 and 6.3.1).

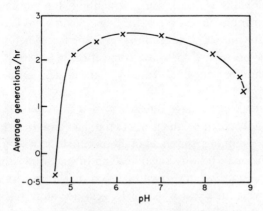

FIG. 6.5. The effect of pH of the medium on the rate of growth of *E. coli*.
(Cohen and Clark, 1919.)

A particularly striking example of the adverse effects of high ultimate pH in spoiling cured meats was described by Callow (1937). In Northern Ireland, during re-organization of the pig industry in the early 1930s, it was required that pigs should be slaughtered at factories rather than on the farms of origin. An outbreak of soured hams resulted which was attributable to the greater glycogen depletion in the muscles of the factory-killed pigs during transit or in the excitement of slaughter (Table 6.7).

TABLE 6.7. *Relation between Ultimate* pH *of Psoas Muscle and Subsequent Spoilage in Cured Hams* (Callow, 1937)

Degree of spoilage	No. of hams	Mean ultimate pH of psoas
None	148	5·65
Slight	47	5·71
Severe	18	5·84

It will be apparent that an elevation in mean ultimate pH of only 0·2 units was critical. Of forty-six micro-organisms which were isolated from tainted hams, eighteen were substantially inhibited below pH 5·7 and a further fourteen below pH 5·4. Sugar feeding has been advocated to increase the muscle glycogen reserves immediately before death; and although the procedure does have some effect in lowering the ultimate pH to an inhibitory range (cf. Table 5.2), the benefits on storage life are not great.

The outbreak of spoilage referred to by Callow in 1937 concerned hams—a mildly cured product; where the salt content in the product is higher, as in gammons, the effect of ultimate pH is not so critical (Table 6.8); and this may be why sugar feeding of bacon pigs has not been universally adopted so far. It will be seen that, in general, the micro-organisms which are less resistant to acid are more resistant to salt (mostly micrococci) and that the species which are not salt tolerant will not be inhibited by acid (mainly gram-negative rods).

TABLE 6.8. *Optimal* pH *Values and Salt Concentration for Ham Spoilage Organisms*
(after Ingram, 1948)

A. pH *range*	3·1–4·0	4·1–5·0	5·1–6·0	6·1–7·0
No. species having optimum pH within zone	1	7	31	7
Mean optimum salt concentration of these species (%)	5·0	6·9	8·2	11
B. *Range salt concentration* (%)	0–5	5–9	10–15	15
No. species having optimum salt concentration within zone	11	14	14	7
Mean optimum pH of these species	5·1	5·4	5·6	6·0

It might be thought that fresh meat, where the latter organisms would be preferentially found, would tend to spoil rather readily since salt is absent; but the muscles of beef and lamb, which are generally not cured, usually attain an ultimate pH of 5·5 or below. In cured products pH has another effect on microbial growth. It determines the proportion of the nitrite which is present as undissociated nitrous acid and thus inhibitory to bacterial growth (Table 6.9; Castellani and Niven, 1955).

TABLE 6.9. *Effect of* pH *on the Aerobic Nitrite Tolerance of* Staph. aureus

pH	Nitrite concentration (ppm)		Undissociated nitrous acid (ppm)	
	Growth	No growth	Growth	No growth
6·90	3500	4000	1·12	1·28
6·52	1800	2000	1·37	1·52
6·03	600	700	1·38	1·61
5·80	300	400	1·20	1·60
5·68	250	400	1·32	2·12
5·45	140	180	1·25	1·50
5·20	80	150	1·12	2·10
5·05	40	80	0·92	1·84

It will be clear that an increase of 1 pH unit requires a tenfold increase in nitrite concentration to prevent growth; but that the undissociated nitrous acid is fairly constant. Nitrite happens to have a specific action in inhibiting *Cl. botulinum* (Roberts, 1971). The anti-microbial action of nitrite has been reviewed by Spencer (1971). It is likely to play an important part in the stability of uncooked, cured meats; and in the stability and safety of cooked, cured meats (Greenburg, 1972). In regard to the latter, however, it is present at too low a concentration to inhibit clostridia at the pH values found in such products, suggesting that some additional factor is involved. Perigo, Whiting and Bashford (1967) believe that when nitrite is sufficiently heated, it is involved in a reaction with the medium which causes the production of some inhibitory substance, which differs from nitrite *per se* in that, for example, its inhibitory action is only slightly pH-dependent. An inorganic compound derived from nitrite is possible (Spencer, 1971). Nitrite (at 20 ppm) lowers the concentration of salt required to stabilize mild-cured, vacuum-packed, green bacon for three weeks at 5°C from 4 to 2·5 ent cent (Wood and Evans, 1973). *Nitrate,* in the concentrations found in cured meats, is without direct effect on bacteria.

pH is also likely to be important with canned meat products since the resistance of faecal streptococci to heat at 60°C for 1 hr is apparently enhanced by a high value (Bagger, 1926).

6.3.4. *Oxidation-reduction Potential*

Immediately after death, whilst temperature and Ph are still high, it would be expected that the dangers of proliferation of, and spoilage by, anaerobes would be great. That such does not generally occur appears to be due to the level of the oxidation–reduction potential (E_h; Knight and Fildes, 1930) which usually does not fall for some time (Fig. 6.6; Barnes and Ingram, 1956). Growth of clostridia on horse muscle does not take place until the E_h has fallen from about + 150 mV to about − 50 mV. The greatest rate of change in E_h occurs immediately after death and is probably due to the removal of the last traces of oxygen by the still surviving activities of the tissues' oxygen utilizing enzyme systems. In whale meat, however, there is usually a greater reserve of oxygen because of the higher myoglobin content and of the low enzymic activity in the muscles of this species (Lawrie, 1953a, b) and the E_h may remain high for some time post-mortem (Robinson *et al.*, 1953; Ingram, 1959, unpublished data).

The effect of E_h on microbial growth is to prolong the initial lag phase: the eventual growth rate is not affected (Barnes and Ingram, 1956), since once the organisms become adjusted to a high E_h the rate is the same as at a low E_h. The E_h in meat is not, of course, a function of oxygen tension only; the concentration of molecules having a marked electropositive character is also important. Thus, the presence of nitrate in cured meats probably exerts an indirect antibacterial effect through raising the E_h of the system. Under anaerobic conditions at low pH (5·5) nitrate protects bacteria against nitrate (Eddy and Ingram, 1956).

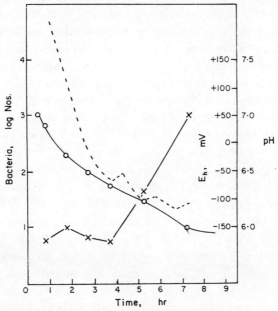

Fig. 6.6. Changes in pH ($\bigcirc$), E_h (— — —) and numbers of viable *Clostridia* (×) in horse muscle after death (Barnes and Ingram, 1956). (Courtesy Dr. E. M. Barnes.)

6.3.5. Atmosphere

Implicit in the concept of the oxidation–reduction potential and in the contribution of oxygen tension to maintaining it at a high level, is the importance of the latter in determining the growth of surface spoilage organisms on meat and meat products. A major grouping of micro-organisms can be made on the basis of the oxygen tension which they need or can be made to tolerate—aerobes, anaerobes and facultative anaerobes—although it is not possible to unequivocally correlate the growth of anaerobes with the amount of oxygen present.

The exposed surfaces of fresh meat at chill temperatures would normally support the growth of aerobes such as members of the genera *Achromobacter* and *Pseudomonas*. If the meat is wrapped, however, in a material which is impermeable, or only partially permeable, to the atmosphere a different situation obtains. Both the pressure and composition of the initial atmosphere within the pack can change. In an impermeable wrap, where the oxygen supply is restricted, the growth of pseudomonads is hindered, and they are temporarily overgrown by organisms which tolerate low oxygen tension; whereas in permeable wraps spoilage tends to follow the same course as that on exposed surfaces (Ingram, 1962). Nevertheless, the partial pressure necessary to maintain aerobic bacteria is frequently much lower than that attained in an oxygen-impermeable film; and much of the inhibition to aerobic micro-organisms (including yeasts and moulds as well as bacteria) which arises may be due to the accumulation of carbon dioxide (Ingram, 1962). Haines (1933) showed that this gas specifically inhibited the growth of aerobes. With poultry, the delay in spoilage was found to increase regularly with increase in carbon dioxide concentration up to 25 per cent (Ogilvy and Ayres, 1951). But the inhibitory action of carbon dioxide is a selective one, moulds being sensitive and yeasts comparatively resistant (Ingram, 1958). Among bacteria lactobacilli are relatively resistant and they are reported to occur in vacuum-packed fresh meat (Halleck, Ball and Stier, 1958) and bacon (Hansen 1960); whereas *Pseudomonas* and *Achromobacter* spp. are susceptible (Haines, 1933). It has been shown that surviving respiration of muscle in vacuum packs can produce 3–5 per cent of carbon dioxide within 3 hr of packaging fresh *pork* (Gardner, Carson and Patton, 1967). In these circumstances the pork-spoilage bacteria *Kurthia zopfi*, pseudomonads and enterobacteria are inhibited, but lactobacilli and *thermosphactum* are not suppressed. Sulzbacher and McLean (1951) originally found that the latter represented 15 per cent of the flora of fresh pork. *Thermosphactum* is rarely found in cured meats, although such factors as carbohydrate encourage its presence in sausage. Comminution and packaging create conditions favourable for its multiplication. Gardner and Patton (1969) believe that routine examination for *thermosphactum* gives a good guide as to the presence of potential spoilage organisms. Since it is the psychrophilic organisms which are inhibited by carbon dioxide, an impermeable wrap is only likely to delay spoilage of meat products at chill temperatures. In general, the storage life of *bacon* could not be increased much by vacuum packaging since carbon dioxide has little effect on the micrococci and lactobacilli which are mainly responsible for its spoilage (Ingram, 1962).

The metabolism of micro-organisms in wraps or cans will gradually decrease the remaining oxygen, and replace it with carbon dioxide (Ingram, 1962). These gas exchanges depend on the magnitude and nature of the microflora and react upon the latter. Thus, in wrapped bacon the disappearance of oxygen will cause disappearance of micrococci and their replacement by faecal streptococci and lactobacilli; and the rising concentration of carbon dioxide will cause domination of the streptococci by the lactobacilli (resistant to this gas) (Ingram, 1962; Hansen, 1960).

The interaction of atmosphere and micro-organisms within packs tends to upset the usual correlation between spoilage and bacterial count: spoilage often becomes evident only after the number of the micro-organisms has been maximal for some time (Hansen, 1960). Wrapped meat in display cabinets can reach temperatures several degrees higher than the corresponding packaged meat, possibly because of a greater retention of radiant energy. This helps to account for cases of microbial spoilage of packaged meat even when good hygiene, and strict temperature control in the cabinet, were observed (Malton, 1971).

The current interest in maintaining the bright red colour of oxymyo-globin on the surface of fresh, prepackaged meats has led to the successful use of in-pack atmospheres containing up to 80% of oxygen. The incorporation of 20% of carbon dioxide in such circumstances controls the microbial spoilage which would otherwise arise at high oxygen tensions. Its efficacy is markedly better at 0° than at 5°C (Kitchell, 1971). Because meat surfaces are aerobic, post-mortem glycolysis would be expected to be delayed , and the pH higher, than in the anaerobic interior (cf. § 4.2.3.). Rises in pH of the intact surfaces of beef and lamb carcases were observed by Carse and Locker (1974); but differences in the surface pH did not appear to effect any corresponding differences in microbial growth.

6.4. PROPHYLAXIS

6.4.1. *Hygiene*

Veterinary and public health inspection must be relied upon to ensure that most of the meat which is endogenously infected with spoilage organisms, because of disease in the live animal, will never reach the consumer. Control of exogenous contamination requires the exercise of hygiene in slaughter-houses, meat stores, during transport, in wholesale and retail distribution and in the home. Such control is obviously difficult and, indeed, it is largely because of exogenous contamination that consumers encounter meat spoilage and meat poisoning. In recognition of this fact, most countries have statutory public health regulations designed to discourage unhygienic practice in handling meat and foods generally. Such regulations promulgate recommended procedures in the cleaning and maintenance of equipment, and in regard to personnel, at all points from pre-slaughter care of the animal to consumption of the meat (Anon., 1957). These will not be given here.

An important aspect of meat hygiene is the design of abattoirs (Anderson, 1955). In general whatever contributes to a smooth flow of animals will implicitly eliminate potential sources of contamination. In particular, inadequate lairages should be avoided, since overcrowding of animals increases the risk of infection by contact. It is especially important to make provision for the efficient removal from the carcase meat of blood, hides, guts and other portions of the animal which are likely to be heavily contaminated by micro-organisms (Anon., 1938, 1957; Nottingham, 1963). In many large abattoirs in Australia and New Zealand this is achieved by killing above ground level and having chutes leading from the slaughter hall through which non-edible portions of the carcase proceed by gravity to the processing plant below. All equipment in the slaughter hall should be thoroughly and frequently cleansed by scrubbing, steaming and flushing with a solution of an approved antimicrobial agent. Until recently it was believed that methodical wiping of the surface of the carcase after dressing operations with a clean cloth was valuable in lowering contamination (Anon., 1938). Legislation has now prohibited the use of such cloths, and the application of a spray of warm water, followed by rapid drying, or pressure hosing, is employed for this purpose (Akers, 1969).

Provision for speedy and adequate chilling of the carcases is essential. In this context, although it is microbiologically desirable to place these into mechanically-operated chill rooms as soon as possible, the size of the chillers available and the rate of loading may dictate the accumulation of a group of carcases in an external area before they are loaded. The space concerned must be designed to permit a through current of air to pass over the warm carcases (Anderson, 1955). Walls and floors should be frequently washed with warm water, scrubbed with hot cleaning solution, rinsed, steamed and fumigated. It has been customary to use formaldehyde vapour for fumigation (e.g. in Australia; Anon., 1938); but it is sometimes necessary to leave the chill rooms vacant for 24–36 hr thereafter. Recently, lactic acid has been successfully used. It achieves the same reduction in micro-organisms in 3 hr when sprayed as preheated lactic acid at a concentration of 300 mg/cm^3 of air (Shaw, 1963). Moreover, it is non-toxic. Ultraviolet light, ozone and carbon dioxide have been employed in discouraging the growth of micro-organisms on chilled meat products (Haines, 1937). The two former tend to cause oxidative rancidity in the fat and to accelerate the formation of brown metmyoglobin in the lean. The fact that ozone is toxic and that ultraviolet light fails to reach crevices limits their usefulness. Moreover, whilst ultraviolet light is effective against various psychrophilic bacteria and moulds, yeasts are relatively unaffected (Kaess and Weidemann, 1973).

The desirability of developing microbiological standards for meat has been considered from time to time. Clearly, whilst they would be feasible with packaged and comminuted products, it would be difficult to apply them to carcase meat. Such specifications might be workable if they served to verify good manufacturing and distribution practices: they could not, *per se*, achieve high quality (Mossell, *et al.*, 1975). Standards should be derived from the results of surveys of products taken from production lines which have been examined for good manufacturing practice. Mandatory for the establishment of microbial standards would be precisely defined sampling procedures for assessing the numerical values specified (Mossell *et al.*, 1975).

6.4.2. *Biological Control*

Given the operation of efficient public health inspection and the exercise of hygiene, microbial spoilage can be controlled biologically, for the factors influencing growth, which we have considered above, can be manipulated to inhibit it. This fact is reflected in the processes used for preservation. The need by micro-organisms of a favourable temperature range for growth explains the possibility of preserving meat products by the imposition of sub-optimal temperatures (chilling, freezing) or of super-optimal temperatures (pasteurizing, sterilizing, cooking). Their requirement for moisture permits preservation by dehydration, freeze drying and by pickling in salt or sugar. The preferential development of anaerobes at a high ultimate pH can be prevented to some extent by ensuring that there is adequate glycogen in the muscles at the moment of death (§ 5.1.2). This involves avoiding fatigue, hunger and fear, which not only lower muscle glycogen but may cause bacteraemia (§ 6.1.2.1). The spoilage of meat surfaces by aerobic psychrophiles can be minimized by keeping the relative humidity of the atmosphere low and by incorporating in it about 10 per cent of carbon dioxide, to which such organisms are susceptible (as in the carriage of chilled beef from Australia: Empey and Vickery, 1933). Similarly, the storage life of prepackaged meat can be enhanced by incorporating carbon dioxide into the pack (Knight and Ayres, 1952). Since the rationale for biological control is implicit in § 6.3, it will not be considered further at this point.

6.4.3. *Antibiotics*

It might be thought that the growth of micro-organisms on meat could be prevented easily by chemical treatment. Until 30 years ago, however, almost all chemicals which might have been used to kill or to prevent the growth of micro-organisms were also toxic to the human consumer. A new approach to food preservation has become possible through the discovery of antibiotics. Appreciation of the fact that certain micro-organisms produced substances inimical to the growth of others—antibiotics—is attributable to Fleming (1929), who observed the production of what is now known to be penicillin by the fungus *Penicillium notatum*. Many other antibiotics, produced by bacteria, fungi or actinomycetes, have become known since then. Antibiotics are 100 to 1000 times more effective than permitted chemical preservatives. The low toxicity of many antibiotics to human beings, despite their power against micro-organisms, was firmly established in 1941 (Abraham *et al.*); but it was not until 10 years later that the possibility of preserving foodstuffs by antibiotics was clearly demonstrated (Tarr, Southcott and Bissett, 1952). The efficacy of the process has been reviewed by Wrenshall (1959).

Although many antibiotics are selective in their action, those which have been applied most frequently in the food industry are the so-called broad spectrum antibiotics, such as the tetracyclines, which are inhibitory to a wide range of both gram-negative and gram-positive bacteria:† few are active against yeasts and moulds. It is important to emphasize that, at practical concentrations, these antibiotics slow bacterial growth and hence delay spoilage: they do not sterilize.

Widespread adoption of antibiotics in a non-medical context has been delayed—in particular to avoid the establishment by their indiscriminate use of human infection caused by organisms which have developed a resistance against them. Numerous antibiotic-resistant strains of micro-organisms are now known (Goldberg, 1962). Against this hazard the use, for food preservation, of antibiotics which are not prescribed in medicine would seem appropriate. Such a substance is nisin, which is prepared by controlled fermentation of sterilized skim milk by the cheese starter organism *Strep. lactis* and in the United Kingdom is permitted in canned meats, provided these have been heated sufficiently to destroy *Cl. botulinum* (Taylor, 1963). The possibility of 'R-factor' transfer must also be carefully considered (cf. § 2.4.5).

Another aspect of the use of antibiotics as preservatives requiring caution is the question of toxicity—due to residues of still active material in the treated products. Although one of the antibiotics most frequently used with meats, aureomycin, has been shown to be non-toxic when taken orally over long periods, its use in foods, at any rate in U.S.A., has been sanctioned only on the assumption that it is completely destroyed in cooking. Nevertheless, it has been detected in chops after frying (Barnes, 1956). The need for discretion is therefore obvious. It is also conceivable that antibiotics might eliminate the organisms normally responsible for creating the symptoms commonly associated with spoilage; and the meat could be contaminated with dangerous pathogens which did not indicate their presence by producing, for example, off-odours. When considering the use of tetracyclines for preserving meat in tropical or sub-tropical areas where refrigeration is not available, it is essential to establish whether the pathogenic hazard is increased or diminished by the treatment. This will depend on the numbers of resistant pathogens likely to be present. These will be

† Bacteria can be broadly classified according to whether they stain permanently with methyl violet (gram positive) or not (gram negative).

increased if the animals have been fed the same antibiotic for growth stimulation (Barnes and Kampelmacher, 1966).

Antibiotics should not be used to replace good hygiene; but when employed with an appreciation of the dangers indicated above, and in conjunction with mild refrigeration (or some other process such as treatment with pasteurizing doses of ionizing radiations), they afford a means of preservation which does not materially alter the product.

6.4.4. *Ionizing Radiations*

In relatively recent times, another approach to the problem of preventing the growth of contaminating organisms on meat has developed. This involves treatment of the commodity with ionizing radiations from electron or X-ray generators; or from a source of radioactivity (Brasch and Huber, 1947). Of the many types of ionizing radiations, only high-energy cathode rays, soft X-rays and γ-rays find application with foodstuffs (Hannan, 1955). The standard unit of dosage is the radiation which corresponds to the absorption of 100 ergs of radiation energy per gram of the absorbing substance (rad). It is more usual to measure dosage in terms of million rad (Mrad). The characteristic chemical property of these radiations is their ability to ionize receptor molecules, forming free radicals which cause other chemical changes in the area affected. Biologically, these effects can kill micro-organisms and parasitic life without raising the temperature of the product by more than a few degrees. The first significant publications on this effect were by Wycoff (1930a, b). In general, the larger and more complex the organism, the more sensitive it is to radiation damage (Table 6.10; D. N. Rhodes, personal communication).

Among bacteria, there is a fiftyfold difference in the dose required for 90 per cent inactivation. It is feasible that radiation resistance in micro-organisms is associated with cystine-rich compounds, which may act by affording protection against the initial molecular changes induced by the radiation (Thornley, 1963).

Lea, Haines and Coulson (1936, 1937) found that the fraction of a population of micro-organisms inactivated by a given dose was

TABLE 6.10. *Lethal Dose of Ionizing Radiation required for Various Species*

Dose (rad)	$LD_{99.97}$ for species (i.e. 10^4 reduction in activity)
$10–10^3$	Higher animals
10^4	Dividing tissue of plants, sprout prevention
$10^4–10^5$	Insects, parasites
10^5	Vegetative bacteria
$10^6–10^7$	Bacterial spores, viruses
10^8	Enzymes

independent of the number of organisms originally present and that the degree of inactivation was determined by the total dose received and not by the rate at which it was delivered. They suggested that each micro-organism has a small "target" area in which several ionizations had to occur to prove lethal: presumably the nucleic acid of the nucleus is the critical area (Weiss, 1952).

To destroy all micro-organisms, including viruses, would require 10 Mrad (cf. Table 6.10). But viruses are not at present regarded as a serious food poisoning hazard. Three to five Mrad produces the degree of sterility achieved in canning practice (Ingram and Rhodes, 1962): the spores of *Cl. botulinum* need 4·5 Mrad (Schmidt, 1961). Nevertheless, there is at least one type of non-sporing organism—a red micrococcus isolated from ground beef—which requires a dose of 6 Mrad (Anderson *et al.* 1956). Pasteurizing doses (about 0·5 Mrad) will destroy food-poisoning organisms such as salmonellae and Staphylococci, and spoilage organisms, and thus prolong storage life, as with chilled beef (Drake, Gernon and Kraus, 1961) and sausages (Coleby *et al.* 1962). Parasites in meat, such as *Cysticercus bovis* and *Trichinella spiralis* are killed by 0·01–0·1 Mrad (Tayler and Parfitt, 1959). Among psychrophilic food-spoilage organisms there are further minor differences in susceptibility to radiation, such that, even after only 0·25 Mrad, the spoilage microflora which, in poultry at 0 C, is initially dominated by *Pseudomonas* and *Achromobacter* spp., is replaced by yeasts. When spoilage eventually occurs, however, and the bacteria have resumed dominance of the flora, non-pigmented pseudomonads are most numerous in both control and irradiated surfaces (Thornley, Ingram and Barnes, 1960).

Although there are exceptions, one of the most important factors affecting the radiation resistance of micro-organisms is the presence of oxygen during irradiation. For example, the complete removal of oxygen, or the presence of reducing substances, may increase the radiation resistance of *E. coli* threefold (Niven, 1958). The removal of water by freezing or drying also protects micro-organisms against radiation damage, probably by decreasing the possibility of free radical formation.

It would seem more practicable to combine an irradiation dosage which is lower than normally necessary to achieve sterility with another process (e.g. refrigeration, vacuum packaging, antibiotics, curing, heating). The bactericidal effects of combined processes are more than additive, for one treatment generally increases sensitivity to another (Ingram, 1959). Thus, for example, the heat resistance of spores of *Cl. botulinum* is only about one-third as great after treatment with 0·9 Mrad of γ-radiation; and as the radiation itself kills a proportion of the spores, the heat treatment needed to sterilize is reduced to about a quarter of that needed without irradiation (Kempe, 1955; Ingram and Rhodes, 1952). It must be remembered that radiation pasteurization *per se* does not inactivate any preformed botulinum toxin whereas heat pasteurization does so (Gordon and Murrell, 1967). Again, chilling seems necessary to supplement a pasteurizing dose of irradiation, which might allow food-poisoning organisms to survive. Refrigeration is also a necessary adjunct with antibiotics and vacuum packaging to inhibit pathogens (Ingram, 1959).

The physiological nature of the micro-organisms which infect meat is reflected by the methods which can be used to discourage their growth; and these, in turn, are reflected by the processes which are used in practice to effect meat preservation. These will now be considered.

CHAPTER 7

THE STORAGE AND PRESERVATION OF MEAT

1. TEMPERATURE CONTROL

THE processes used in meat preservation are principally concerned with inhibiting microbial spoilage, although modes of preservation are sought which minimize concomitant depreciation of the quality of the commodity. The extent to which this secondary aim can be achieved is largely determined by the time of storage envisaged. The intrinsic changes which muscles undergo in becoming meat (Chapter 5) have not generally been considered in devising preservative processes, although it is increasingly recognized that their nature and extent may well determine the behaviour of the meat. Methods of meat preservation, however different superficially, are alike in that they employ environmental conditions which discourage the growth of micro-organisms (cf. § 6.3). They may be grouped in three broad categories based on control by temperature, by moisture, and, more directly, by lethal agencies (bactericidal, bacteriostatic, fungicidal and fungistatic), although a particular method of preservation may involve several antimicrobial principles. Such control is becoming rather more deliberate and specific with increased scientific knowledge; but it was remarkably effective even when based on empirical observation.

It will have been obvious from the considerations in Chapter 6 that temperatures below or above the optimum range for microbial growth will have a preventative action on the latter. Meat and meat products may thus be preserved by refrigeration on the one hand or by heat treatment on the other.

7.1. REFRIGERATION

7.1.1. Storage above the Freezing Point

7.1.1.1. Fresh and chilled meat

That meat altered adversely sooner when kept during warm weather than under cooler conditions must have impressed early man. Appreciation of this fact led to the storage of meat in natural caves where the temperature was relatively low even in the warm season of the year. Later, as dwellings were built, cellars were constructed for food storage. Much more recently ice, gathered from frozen ponds and lakes in winter, was used to keep cellar temperatures low (Leighton and Douglas, 1910). The principles of artificial ice formation and of mechanical refrigeration date from about 1750 (Raymond, 1929). Commercial scale operations based on mechanical refrigeration were in use 100 years later. Even after it became the practice to chill meat carcases before either wholesale distribution or subsequent freezing, the idea persisted in the meat industry that carcases should be placed in an area at ambient temperature to permit the escape of "animal heat" before chilling in a mechanically refrigerated chamber. In seeking the reason for this view it is feasible that low surface temperatures on the meat in the chillers had been erroneously regarded as representing those throughout the carcases and that refrigeration had been discontinued whilst deep temperatures were still high—thus giving rise to bone taint (Haines, 1937; Cosnett et al., 1956) and other symptoms of microbial spoilage. From the viewpoint of discouraging microbial growth, the weight of evidence suggests that carcases should be cooled as quickly as possible (Tamm, 1930; Scott and Vickery, 1939) provided that the temperature of the deepest portion of the carcase is used as an indicator of the efficacy of the process (Kuprianoff, 1956). Since, however, the surfaces of the meat carcases are initially considerably higher than those of the chill room, evaporation of substantial quantities of water may occur. Even where this does not cause surface desiccation, it is obviously economically undesirable. The problem of cooling carcases with the minimum of desiccation has been extensively studied (Scott and

Vickery, 1939), and various combinations of air speeds and humidities have been considered. The achievement of rapid cooling requires a high air speed in the chill rooms or large air circulation volumes (60–100 changes of air/hr; Kuprianoff, 1956). Although a higher air velocity will tend to cause a greater weight loss, it permits the use of a high relative humidity. At the beginning of chilling, the air temperature can be as low as $-10°C$ for pigs and sheep and air speeds as high as 600 ft/min. For beef carcases air speeds of 400 ft/min and an air temperature of $-1°C$ have been recommended (Kuprianoff, 1956). Once the difference in temperature between the meat surface and the air becomes small, the air speed must be reduced to avoid desiccation. Air, super-saturated with water vapour and moving at high speed, has been used to minimize evaporation from hot sides whilst providing a high capacity for heat removal (Hagan, 1954).

Obviously, the greater the bulk of the carcase and the greater its fat cover the longer it will take to cool with a given air speed and temperature (cf. Fig. 7.1; Bouton, Howard and Lawrie, 1957). Workers

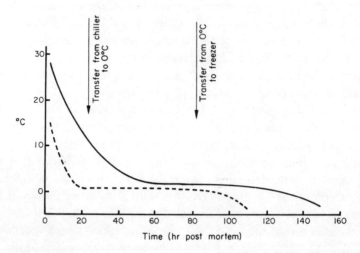

FIG. 7.1. Typical time-temperature curves for two grades of beef during chilling (at 0°C) and freezing (at $-10°C$) (Bouton *et al.*, 1957). ——— = grade 1, about 360 lb side weight. - - - - - = canner grade, about 200 lb side weight.

at the Meat Research Institute, Bristol, have obtained valuable comparative data on the rates of fall of temperature in the deep leg locations of beef sides under carefully controlled conditions (Bailey, 1976). The sides averaged 100, 180 and 260 kg. Air temperatures of 0 , 4 and 8°C were employed at air speeds of 0·5 to 3 metres per second. Whereas it took 80 hours for the deep leg temperature of 260 kg sides to attain 10°C, in air at 8°C travelling at 0·5 metres per second, this temperature was reached in only 16 hours with 100 kg sides in air at 0°C travelling at 3 metres per second. For any given conditions in chilling, the weight losses from small, poorly covered sides will be greater than those from large sides having a good fat cover (Table 7.1; Bouton *et al.*, 1957).

TABLE 7.1. *Mean Weight Losses from Good and Poor Quality Beef Sides under various Chiller Conditions*

Conditions	% Weight loss	
	Good-quality sides	Poor-quality sides
1 day at 0°C + 2 days at 20°C 3 days at 0°C 14 days at 0°C	1·7 0·7 1·6	3·8 0·9 3·2

It is important to point out that over-effective chilling of hot carcases can lead to toughness. If the relationship between the refrigeration system and the bulk of meat exposed to it are such that the temperature of the muscles can be reduced below about 15–19°C, whilst they are still in the early pre-rigor condition (pH about 6·8), there is a tendency for shortening and, thereby, toughness on subsequent cooking (Locker and Hagyard, 1963; Cook and Langsworth, 1966). This is the phenomenon referred to as "cold-shortening". The tendency is greater the closer the temperature attained by the pre-rigor muscle approaches the freezing point. At 2°C the shortening is as great as that which occurs when muscles go into *rigor mortis* at 37°C.

Cold-shortening can be avoided by cooling the meat swiftly to about 15°C and holding it at this temperature to allow the onset of *rigor mortis*. The temperature can then be lowered as quickly as is compatible with minimal surface desiccation. Moreover, not all the muscles of carcases, even if their temperature falls below about 15°C whilst they are in the early pre-rigor condition, are free to shorten. Their attachments on the skeleton may restrain them sufficiently to prevent it. In the conventional mode of carcase suspension by the Achilles tendon, certain muscles are more liable than others to shorten; and, by altering the posture of the suspended carcase in various ways, the pattern of muscles which shorten may be changed. Thus pelvic hanging of lamb and beef carcases, by preventing shortening in muscles which are normally able to respond to cold stimulus, can bring about a degree of tenderness which would otherwise require more than a week's conditioning (Herring, Cassens and Briskey, 1965; Davey, Gilbert and Curson, 1971; Bouton, Harris, Shorthose and Smith, 1974). Such altered carcase postures, however, while permitting control of cold-shortening during the fast chilling of muscles early pre-rigor, could be inconvenient in abattoir operations; and an alternative method of minimizing cold-shortening has been devised by workers in New Zealand. It has been found that electrical stimulation of the carcase immediately after death (e.g. 3000 volts AC; or 21 volts DC at 10 pulses per second for 4 minutes), so accelerates the rate of post-mortem that the pH quickly falls below 6·4; when muscles are no longer responsive to cold shock (Carse, 1973; Chrystall and Hagyard, 1976; Shaw, Harris, Bouton, Weste and Turner, 1976). Electrical stimulation shortens the time to rigor mortis through two phases of acceleration of glycolysis, the first during stimulation and the second, less precipitate phase, following stimulation. Fast chilling can thus be applied to the warm carcases without causing cold-shortening; and, incidentally, carcases can be frozen swiftly without the danger of pre-rigor freezing and the subsequent disadvantages of "thaw rigor" (see below). Nevertheless, there is a phase in post-mortem glycolysis when the muscles, although no longer reactive to cold-shortening, are still pre-rigor and when "thaw rigor" is still a possibility. Pelvic hanging appears necessary for maximum tenderness in electrically-stimulated carcases which are placed into blast freezers within 30 minutes of stunning (Shaw *et al.*, 1976). The greatest rate of pH fall over a two minute period of stimulation in lamb was achieved with 9–15 pulses per second and 200 volts DC. (Chrystall and Devine, 1976–77, 1978).

As an alternative to electrical stimulation immediately after death, which may not always be practicable in certain abattoirs, the procedure can be applied after carcase dressing; and in this case the current is applied at 14 pulses per second, with a peak voltage of 580. (Hagyard and Hand, 1976–77). Provided the stimulation is not delayed beyond 30 minutes post-mortem, a sufficient acceleration of post-mortem glycolysis is achieved to avoid susceptibility to cold-shortening. It is envisaged that electric stimulators will be standard equipment in all lamb slaughtering chains in New Zealand before long (Locker, 1976).

Since stimulation of ATP breakdown is the cause of cold-shortening (§ 10.3.3); and since the accelerated post-mortem glycolysis signifies the attainment of low pH values whilst the carcase is still near the *in vivo* temperature, it is not clear how the exudation which arises in PSE pork and in slowly cooling, deep muscles of beef, are avoided. An explanation for the absence of toughness in electrically stimulated muscle can be suggested however (Dr. J. R. Bendall: personal communication). Although Ca^{++} ions are released from the sarcotubular system, and stimulate the contractile ATP-ase of actomyosin, both by cold-shortening and electrical currents, the system can reabsorb them in the latter case because the temperature is still high. Provided the electrical stimulus is discontinued whilst there is still sufficient ATP to relax the myofibrils, shortening and toughening will be avoided. In cold shock, however, the contractile actomyosin ATP-ase continues to be stimulated because the low temperature prevents effective removal of calcium from the enzyme locality. The situation may be similar to that in pre-rigor frozen muscles fibres when they are thawed very rapidly (cf. § 7.1.2.2). Thaw rigor is avoided in those (unusual) circumstances because calcium ions are reabsorbed by the sarcotubular system before much

ATP can be broken down; and the muscle relaxes after brief shortening.†
The growth of trade in vacuum-packages, deboned primal cuts of meat has emphasized the variability in the degree of exudation and discoloration which develops. In the deeper locations of beef carcases, even with fast chilling, the problem is not cold-shortening but delay in temperature fall. As a result, *in vivo* temperatures persist, there is a consequent fast rate of post-mortem glycolysis (cf. § 4.2.2) and the pH attains acid values swiftly. These conditions, being similar to those in PSE pork, lead to loss of water-holding capacity by the proteins; and to much exudation. By exposing the deeper locations of beef carcases to the chilling environment, must faster rates of chilling are attainable. These slow the rate of post-mortem glycolysis; and they are reflected by substantial reductions in exudate from vacuum-packed primal cuts, by diminished discoloration and by some increase in tenderness (Follet, 1974; Follet, Norman and Ratcliff, 1974). Such exposure is achieved by "seaming out" the fascia of the major muscles, leaving them attached to the carcase at one end. The bulk of the muscles prevents their temperature being lowered below 10°C until the pH has fallen beyond the point of susceptibility to cold-shortening. Microbial contamination is only marginally increased by the procedure.

With the advent of hot deboning of beef carcases and of hot cutting of lamb, and their preparation as shrink-wrapped cuts (cf. 4.2.3), much faster refrigeration, economies of space and substantial reduction of evaporative and exudative losses, in comparison with those which apply when carcases are chilled before butchering, have been achieved (Locker *et al.*, 1975); and abattoir operations are likely to alter accordingly. Such

†Other investigators (Dutson, 1977: Savell, Dutson, Carpenter & Hostetler, 1977) postulated that the release of Ca^{++} from the sarcotubular on electrical stimulation may enhance proteolysis by the calcium-activated sarcoplasmic factor; and, as the pH falls further, whereby lysosomal membranes are damaged, cathepsins may be liberated. The accleration of such proteolytic activity by the high temperature-low pH combination could explain the observed tenderness in muscles which have been stimulated electrically in the immediate post mortem period as a factor additional to the avoidance of 'cold shortening'. Indeed, under certain conditions of electrical stimulation no differences in sarcomere length can be detected between electrically stimulated and control muscles, although the former are more tender as meat (Dutson 1977: Savell *et al.*, 1977). Other histological changes, however, have been detected in electrically stimulated muscles.

procedures would clearly involve a risk of cold-shortening (or thaw rigor). If, however, beef sides are electrically stimulated (3000 volts, 2 minutes) immediately after carcase dressing, rigor mortis occurs within 5 hours and thus permits concomitant fast chilling without the danger of toughening and without any increase in the microbial load, despite the degree of hot butchering which is applied (Gilbert and Davey, 1976).

Given adequate cooling of the hot carcases and cuts, the deterioration of fresh chilled meat is due to surface changes. The natural surface consists of fat and connective tissue; and during cooling the consistency of the latter changes, so that further loss of water by evaporation is restricted. On the other hand, muscle surfaces continue to lose water at a fairly fast rate; and this desiccation leads to an increased concentration

TABLE 7.2. *Time for Bacterial Slime to develop on Meat Surfaces exposed under Moist Conditions*
(after Haines and Smith, 1933)

Temperature (°C)	Time (days)
0	10
1	7
3	4
5	3
10	2
16	1

of salts at the surface which causes oxidation of the muscle pigment to brown or greyish metmyoglobin (Brooks, 1931) and a darkening of colour due to optical changes in the tissue (Brooks, 1938). Different muscles show differing susceptibility to such browning due to differing tendencies to desiccation (Ledward, 1971a). If surfaces are more moist, moulds of various colours will tend to grow (cf. Chapter 6), and these may affect the fat, causing rancidity and off-odours due to other changes. If the surfaces are moister still, bacteria can grow and, in sufficient numbers, produce off-odours and aggregate in visible colonies (slime). Apart from moisture, these features are a function of time and temperature (cf. Table 7.2).

When meat is removed from chill storage, moisture tends to condense on the cool surfaces, especially when the relative humidity of the atmosphere is high. This phenomenon is known as "sweating". Apart from its potential effect in encouraging microbial growth, it causes the collagen fibres of connective tissue to swell and become white and opaque. This change is reversible, however, and there is no evidence that "sweating" causes a permanent loss of "bloom" (Moran and Smith, 1929), the term given by the trade to a pleasing superficial appearance in the meat. The most exacting requirements for meat storage above the freezing point were those encountered in the shipment of chilled beef from Australia and New Zealand to the United Kingdom, when temperatures must be maintained at $-1.4°C$ (Scott and Vickery, 1939; Law and Vere-Jones, 1955). The essential difference between so-called chilled meat and the fresh commodity is the length of time during which it is expected to resist substantial change. By far the most important consideration is the minimizing of microbial contamination during preparation of the commodity (§ 6.1.2.2) and the strictest hygiene is essential (§ 6.4.1). On the one hand, a high relative humidity in the storage chambers will prevent desiccation and loss of bloom; on the other hand, it will encourage microbial growth. A balance has to be established between these two extremes over storage times which may extend up to 60 days. During this time beef quarters will lose about $1\frac{1}{2}$–2 per cent of their weight by evaporation (Hicks, Scott and Vickery, 1956). Although some degree of desiccation is desirable, excessive drying, of course, must be avoided, especially because of its effect on the layer of connective tissue separating the muscles from the exterior. Although this layer is very thin, it imparts a pleasing, translucent appearance to the surface of the carcase, even when there is little subcutaneous fat. When the layer becomes desiccated the superficial appearance deteriorates remarkably (Fig. 7.2).

The rate of evaporation from different parts of a carcase may vary by a factor of 10 (Hicks *et al.*, 1956). With lambs held 10 days at $3°C$, the connective tissue over the fat on the loin reached equilibrium with the atmosphere in the cold store at an a_w of 0·862, but the a_w in the panniculus muscle was still 0·906.

With chilled beef carcases, the control of microbial growth on the surface of the neck muscles is the most difficult to achieve (Scott and Vickery, 1939). Successful storage is related to conditions prevailing whilst the hot carcase is cooling, when there should be fast rates of temperature fall combined with a high speed of air movement over the beef, provided the possibilities of "cold-shortening" and of desiccation are carefully considered. This will have little effect on areas of exposed muscle where a high rate of moisture diffusion from within can be

FIG. 7.2. The effect of desiccation on chilled beef during a 45-day period at 0°C. The meat was initially covered with a moisture-impermeable wrap, which later slipped, exposing the top of the leg. (Courtesy K. C. Hales.)

maintained during storage. In regions such as the panniculus, however, where rates of moisture diffusion to the surface are low (Scott and Vickery, 1939), a high rate of moisture removal, whilst the carcase is cooling, will deplete surface moisture to an extent incompatible with the retention of bloom during storage.

Callow (1955a) reviewed the various means which were employed to discourage microbial growth on the surface of chilled meat during prolonged storage at relative humidities high enough to prevent unaue desiccation. The use of formaldehyde in this context, whilst successful, was prohibited on the grounds of toxicity in 1925. In due course it was shown that replacement of air by 100 per cent carbon dioxide in the chillers would prevent microbial growth but cause brown discoloration because of metmyoglobin. Nevertheless, concentrations up to 20 per cent had a negligible effect on colour (Brooks, 1933), and 10 per cent severely inhibited the growth of the two most common types of bacteria found on chilled meat (Haines, 1933), and, thus, indirectly, doubled the effective storage life by slowing down the rate of fat oxidation (Lea, 1931). In 1933 the first shipment of chilled beef in 10 per cent carbon dioxide was carried from New Zealand to the United Kingdom without trace of microbial spoilage. Much of the success of chilled beef carriage under carbon dioxide—by 1938, 26 per cent of the beef from Australia and 60 per cent of that from New Zealand was so carried to the United Kingdom—was attributable to the efforts of shipping companies to construct gas-tight holds. Leakage rates were reduced from about 30 to 0.25 ft^3 gas/ton of beef (Empey and Vickery, 1933).

Although oxidation of fat and the formation of brown metmyoglobin proceed slowly on the exposed surfaces of carcases from the moment such exposure commences, the changes are generally negligible by the time the meat is sold. These changes began to become apparent, however, when carcases could be kept above the freezing point and free from microbial spoilage for upwards of 40–50 days—as with chilled beef under carbon dioxide. The diminution in the chilled meat trade since the last war, for economic reasons which will not be considered here, lessened interest in the question. But the recent development of prepackaged methods of sale, in which large areas of surface are exposed and the superficial appearance of the meat is especially important, has created conditions favouring and revealing undesirable changes in the commodity even over relatively short periods of time.

TABLE 7.3. *Some Properties of Packaging Materials*
(after Mills and Urbin, 1960)

Material	Clarity	Permeability		Limiting temperature	
		Water vapour	Gases	Heat (C)	Cold
Kraft paper	Opaque	High	Poor	150	Very low
Greaseproof	Translucent-opaque	High	Fair	—	Depends on use of plasticizer
Vegetable parchment	Translucent-opaque	High	Good	90 (if dry)	Depends on use of plasticizer
Aluminium foil	Opaque	Negligible	Negligible	370	−85 C
Waxed paper	Transparent-opaque	Low	Poor	38–50	—
Cellophane	Transparent	Very high	Low (dry), higher (if moist)	190	Depends on type
Cellulose acetate	Transparent-opaque	Poor	Medium	150	Brittle below −18°C
Polyethylene	Transparent-translucent	Low	High	82	−50°C
Polyvinyl-idene chloride	Transparent-translucent	Negligible	Very low	145	Good at −18°C

7.1.1.2. Prepackaging and storage changes

The sale of prepackaged meat reflects technical advances in the production of plastic films and the development, with changing economic circumstances, of self-service stores (Bryce-Jones, 1962). Some properties of the packaging materials, which are commonly used, are given in Table 7.3. They may be combined in laminates, or coated, to alter their individual characteristics for specific purposes. For many processed and fresh meats, bags made from copolymers of vinylidine chloride and vinyl chloride are heat-shrunk, so as to conform closely to the contours of the product, after evacuation of air. Such packs have an attractive appearance and good storage life, primarily because oxygen has been eliminated. A useful summary of the properties of films used to package meat and meat products was given by Ramsbottom (1971).

Prepackaging is applied to frozen and cured meats as well as to fresh. At this point, however, only the latter will be considered.

The impression is current that, as a means of preservation, prepackaging represents an advance over older methods of sale by diminishing microbial hazards. But this cannot be taken for granted (Ingram, 1962), since meat prepared in small pieces is subjected to much more initial handling than, for example, that cut from joints; and unless the operations during prepackaging are hygienically controlled, they may provide additional opportunities for contamination. With fresh meats, a bright red surface colour is particularly desirable. As a result, oxygen-permeable wraps tend to be used for this commodity to permit the formation and retention of a layer of oxy-myoglobin on the surface. Obviously, oxygen is not so freely able to saturate the surface in such a pack as when the meat is completely exposed. Oxygen tension tends to become limiting not only because of difficulty of entry, but also because surviving activities in the oxygen-utilizing enzymes of the meat deplete the atmosphere within the pack of this gas and produce carbon dioxide (cf. § 4.3). The partial pressure of the gases constituting the internal atmosphere of the pack will influence the type of micro-organism which can grow on the meat, and, in turn, their metabolism will further change the internal atmosphere (Ingram, 1962). Moreover, the characteristics of the prepackaging films which are used are generally such as to prevent loss of water vapour. Whilst this would oppose weight loss, the absence of surface desiccation tends to encourage microbial growth, especially that of bacteria. Again, although prepackaging (once it is complete) may prevent further contamination of the meat from the exterior it may encourage consumers to expose the meat to high temperatures and other conditions which they would not consider suitable for unwrapped meat, with consequent dangers from spoilage or food poisoning. It is important to emphasize that prepackaging of meat is an adjunct to preservation by control of temperature or of other factors involved in deterioration.

It will be clear that there are several general factors likely to cause differences between the microbial status of stored, prepackaged meat and that cut from carcases or large joints. More specifically, inherent differences between the muscles of meat animals (Chapters 4 and 5) may become apparent. Although such differences exist in the intact carcases, they are exaggerated in prepackaging for the reasons already indicated—namely, exposure of individual muscles under conditions when their different susceptibilities to microbial growth, fat oxidation, discoloration and exudation are emphasized. Much variability in the keeping quality of prepackaged fresh meat can be explained in this way. Thus, as indicated above, functional differentiation of muscles will be reflected in such features as moisture content, salt concentration, pH, degree of exudation, the surviving activity of oxidizing enzymes, the degree of protein denaturation, the content of amino acids and other micronutrients and, thereby, microbial growth.

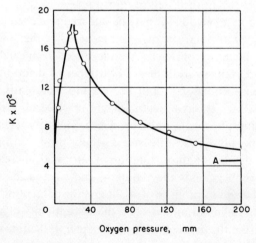

FIG. 7.3. The relationship between oxygen pressure (mm) and rate of oxidation of muscle pigment (Brooks, 1935). A = value at atmospheric oxygen tension.

As mentioned in § 7.1.1.1, the formation of brown metmyoglobin and the oxidation of fat are among other aspects of changes during storage which prepackaging emphasizes. It is particularly important that the reaction by which metmyoglobin is formed is maximal not at a high oxygen tension but when the partial pressure of the gas is 4 mm (Fig. 7.3; Brooks, 1935). Such a situation could well arise in fresh prepackaged meat, depending on the permeability of the wrap used. When fresh meat is packaged under vacuum the purplish-red colour of reduced myoglobin predominates; and, indeed, metmyoglobin, if initially formed, tends to be reduced (Ball, 1959).

Normally, fresh meat exudes fluid (weep) from cut surfaces post-mortem after attaining its ultimate pH (§ 5.3, 5.4.1 and 10.1.2); but with the large areas of exposed surface in prepackaged cuts, the phenomenon is much more noticeable. It may be exaggerated if the contents of the pack are under tension from the wrapping material. Among procedures employed to make weep less apparent is the incorporation of an absorbent tray in the pack. This soaks up fluid as it exudes from the meat. The weight of meat offered for prepackaged sale, as we have mentioned above, will tend to emphasize the differences between individual muscles in their degree of exudation.

Deterioration in meat lipids may be due to direct chemical action or through the intermediary activity of enzymes (either indigenous or derived from micro-organisms). As a rule, direct chemical deterioration is not so important in fresh meat. Two types of deterioration occur: hydrolysis and oxidation. Lipolytic enzymes split fatty acids from triglycerides (§ 4.1.2) leaving, ultimately, free glycerol. With phospholipids, inorganic phosphate is also produced. The fatty acids liberated in meat are generally not so offensive as those produced in milk (Lea, 1962). Since the rate of auto-oxidation of fatty acids increases with the number of double bonds they contain, and since acids with several double bonds tend to produce off-flavours, the content of unsaturated fatty acids has an important effect on the susceptibility of a given fat to oxidation. From the considerations in Chapter 4, the rate of oxidation of intramuscular fat would thus tend to be higher in (a) non-ruminants than in ruminants (e.g. in whale meat and pork in comparison with beef and mutton), (b) in the less improved breeds, (c) in young animals rather than in older ones, (d) in muscles with relatively low contents of intramuscular fat, (e) in the lumbar region of l. dorsi in the pig rather than the thoracic region, the reverse being true in beef animals, (f) in animals on a low plane of nutrition and (g) in animals receiving large proportions of unsaturated fat in their diet, particularly in non-ruminants. A considerable number of such differences may operate simultaneously. The relative tendency of pork muscles to become rancid and discoloured exemplifies this complexity. Porcine *psoas* muscle has a higher proportion of unsaturated fatty acids, especially in the phospholipid fraction (Owen, Lawrie and Hardy, 1975), than the *l. dorsi* of this species; and more myoglobin, which, when present in the met-form, can act as a pro-oxidant. Yet, during prolonged storage at − 10°C, minced porcine *l. dorsi* undergoes oxidative rancidity, and concomitant metmyoglobin formation, to a markedly greater extent than *psoas*. This anomalous behaviour appears to be related to the higher ultimate pH of the latter (Owen *et al.*, 1975). At high pH the activity of the cytochrome system of enzymes is much enhanced (Lawrie, 1952b) and this increases their metmyoglobin-reducing activity (Cheah, 1971). Moreover, such enzymes are found at higher concentration in *psoas* (Lawrie, 1953a). In *psoas* muscle, therefore, the relatively high ultimate pH, by minimizing pro-oxidant conditions, more than offsets the inherently greater tendency of its lipids to oxidize. Clearly, a considerable number of factors must be known before accurate prediction of the behaviour of a given muscle can be made.

The pro-oxidant effect of haematin compounds in fat oxidation is reciprocal since unsaturated fatty acids accelerate the oxidation of myoglobin (Niell and Hastings, 1925). Since myoglobin and fats are brought into intimate contact with one another in meats, their coupled reaction will contribute to rancidity and discoloration (Lea, 1937; Watts, 1954). Nevertheless, it should be pointed out that the behaviour of haem pigments and unsaturated fats, when in juxtaposition, is not fully understood (D. A. Ledward, personal communication). Thus, Kedrick and Watts (1969) postulated that at low lipid:haem ratios, haem compounds can stabilize peroxides or free radicals, and exert an anti-oxidant effect. Ultraviolet light (and other ionizing radiations) and ozone, which have been used to discourage microbial growth on meat held above the freezing point, accelerate fat oxidation. Various anti-oxidants such as polyhydroxy phenols (e.g. propylgallate, hydroxyanisole) have been incorporated successfully in meat products to retard fat oxidation (Barron and Lyman, 1938; Lineweaver, Anderson and Hanson, 1952). Of anti-oxidants which have been fed to animals in the hope of enhancing the post-mortem anti-oxidant potential of their tissues only tocopherols, such as vitamin E, are stored to any extent (Barnes *et al.*, 1943; Major and Watts, 1948). Monosodium glutamate is said to be quite an effective anti-oxidant, particularly in frozen meat (Sulzbacher and Gaddis, 1968), although its use in foods has been criticized recently.

7.1.2. *Storage below the Freezing Point*

The efficacy of freezing in preserving meat has obviously been long understood by the Eskimoes and other peoples inhabiting regions with Arctic climates. An extreme example is the reported edibility of meat from mammoths adventitiously frozen for 20,000 years in northern Siberia under conditions preventing desiccation (Stenbock-Fermor, 1915; Tolmachov, 1929). Bone marrow from a horse which had been frozen in Alaska for 50,000 years was served at a dinner in New York (R. C. S. Williams, personal communication, 1969). Modern views on the freezing of meat are based on an understanding of the changes caused by the process as well as on its preservative aspects.

7.1.2.1. *Effects of freezing on muscular tissue*

The advantages of temperatures below the freezing point in prolonging the useful storage life of meat, and in discouraging microbial and chemical changes, tend to be offset by the exudation of fluid ("drip") on thawing. Proteins, peptides, amino acids, lactic acid, purines, vitamins of the B complex and various salts are among the many constituents of drip fluid (Empey, 1933; Howard, Lawrie and Lee, 1960; Pearson, West and Leucke, 1959). The extent of drip is determined by factors of two kinds. In one category are the factors which determine the extent to which the fluid, once formed, will in fact drain from the meat. Among these are the size and shape of the pieces of meat (in particular the ratio of cut surface to volume), the orientation of cut surface with respect to muscle fibre axis, the prevalence of large blood vessels and the relative tendency for evaporation or condensation to occur in the thawing chamber. Factors of this kind are of greater importance with beef than with pork or mutton, for with the former more cutting is required to produce an easily handled quantity.

Factors in the second category are much more fundamental. They are concerned with the nature of the freezing process in muscular tissue and with the water-holding capacity of the muscle proteins, thus determining the volume of the fluid which forms on thawing. In general, the proportion of the total water in muscle which freezes increases rapidly at first as the temperature is lowered further below the freezing point; then more slowly, approaching an asymptote of about 98·2 per cent at $-20°C$ (Moran, 1930). Because not all the water in muscle freezes, the latent heat is lower than would be anticipated. The non-frozen portion appears to increase as the fat content of the muscles increases (Fleming, 1969).†

However, as well as the extent, the *rate* at which the temperature of the meat falls is a most important consideration: the time taken to pass from $0°C$ to $-5°C$ is usually regarded as an indicator of the speed of freezing. The fastest times so far obtained are of the order of 1 sec. These have been achieved by placing a single muscle fibre in isopentane at $-150°C$. At such rapid rates water freezes between the actual filaments ($\simeq$ molecules) of myosin and actin in aggregates so small that they do not distort the structure, even at the level of observation possible with the electron microscope (Menz and Luyet, 1961). These minute aggregates still appear to be crystalline and not amorphous and vitreous (Luyet,

†Love and Eherian (1963) showed that damage to proteins in fish muscle increases progressively as temperature is lowered to $-183°C$, because more and more structural water is irreversibly frozen out of them.

1961). As the time to freeze increases, structural damage to the muscle also increases. To assess it, Love (1955) has used the concentration of deoxyribose nucleic acid phosphorus (DNAP) in the expressible fluid of the muscle during a series of studies on fish. Since in undamaged muscle DNAP is found exclusively in the nucleus of the muscle cells, and thus inside the cell membrane (sarcolemma), its appearance in the extracellular fluid indicates a degree of damage sufficient to rupture the sarcolemma.

Some comparative data, compiled from the publications of Love (1958) and Love and Haraldsson (1961), are given in Table 7.4. It will be seen that the sarcolemma is still undamaged when the freezing time has been extended from 1 sec to 5 min (although with the latter time there would be considerable distortion of the myofibrils inside the muscle fibre: Menz and Luyet, 1961). It will also be seen that as the time to freeze increases beyond about 5 min, damage to the sarcolemma proceeds through a series of maxima and minima corresponding to different kinds of ice formation, firstly within and eventually outside the fibre. With those freezing times less than about 75 min and where there is little damage to the sarcolemma (e.g. 5 and 50 min), the muscle can be thawed with little formation of drip—irrespective of ultimate pH—the water which separated as ice being completely reincorporated by the proteins. The rates of freezing feasible commercially are much too slow to cause intracellular ice formation. With such rates of freezing, ice crystals tend to form first outside the fibre, since the extracellular osmotic pressure is less than that within the muscle cell (Chambers and Hale, 1932). As extracellular ice formation proceeds, the remaining unfrozen extracellular fluid increases in ionic strength and draws water osmotically from the super-cooled interior of the muscle cell. This freezes on to the existing ice crystals, causing them to grow, thus distorting and damaging the fibres. Moreover, the high ionic strength denatures some of the muscle proteins (Finn, 1932; Love, 1956; and § 4.4.1), and this factor quite apart from the translocation of water, largely accounts for the loss of waterholding capacity of the muscle proteins and for the failure of the fibres to reabsorb, on thawing, all the water removed by freezing—this being manifested as drip (Moran, 1927). On electrophoresis and ultra-

TABLE 7.4. *Relation between Freezing Rate and DNAP (as an Indicator of Cell Damage) in Press Juice from Thawed Fish Muscle (after Love, 1958; Love and Haraldsson, 1961)*

Approximate time to freeze (0 to −5°C) (min)	DNAP concentration	Type of ice formation	Presumed explanation
5	Low	Many very small *intra*cellular crystals	Sarcolemma not damaged
25[a]	High	Four *intra*cellular ice columns	Unfrozen intracellular contents too thinly spread over surface between ice crystals and sarcolemma to avoid damaging latter
50	Low	Relatively small single *intra*cellular column	Layer of unfrozen intracellular contents sufficiently thick to separate ice from sarcolemma and protect it
75[b]	High	Very large single *intra*cellular column	Unfrozen intracellular contents too sparse to protect sarcolemma from ice damage
100	Low	Relatively small *extra*cellular crystals	Water osmotically drawn from cell through intact sarcolemma to form crystals outside, which are too small to distort fibres
200–500	High	*Large extra*cellular ice crystals	Extracellular crystals are sufficiently large to distort muscle fibres and damage sarcolemma
<750	Low	Very large *extra*cellular ice masses	Ice masses so large that fibres press together: the sarcolemma of interior members thus protected from damage

[a]Denotes slowest freezing rate at which more than one ice crystal forms within muscle cell. [b]Denotes slowest freezing rate at which ice forms *intra*cellularly.

centrifugation, changes in the pattern of separated proteins between fresh and frozen muscle are detectable (Howard *et al.*, 1960). The sarcoplasm of fresh muscle shows only one isozyme of glutamate–oxalacetate transaminase. After freezing the mitochondrial isozyme is liberated; and the presence of both in a sarcoplasmic extract is thus an indication that freezing has taken place (Hamm and Kormendy, 1966). Protein damage is a function of time and temperature of freezing (Meryman, 1956). At −4°C, for example, increasing damage is caused to both sarcoplasmic and myofibrillar proteins as time of storage increases (Awad, Powrie and Fennema, 1968). The number of protein components separated by gel electrophoresis of urea-treated bovine actomyosin decreased from six to three over 8 weeks' storage at −4°C. Specific sarcoplasmic protein components also became insoluble. Nevertheless, despite the prolonged freezing times which are inevitable when dealing with meat in commercial handling—carcases, cuts or steaks—the degree of drip may be greatly lessened by various procedures. These will be considered in § 7.1.2.2.

7.1.2.2. Frozen carcase meat

Large-scale preservation of meat by freezing dates from about 1880, as far as the United Kingdom is concerned, when the first frozen beef and mutton arrived from Australia. Increasing industrialization in Britain was accompanied by increasing population and decreasing livestock: there was a surplus of meat animals in the southern hemisphere, especially in New Zealand and Australia: and freezing offered a means of preserving meat during the long voyages involved between the two areas (Critchell and Raymond, 1912). By 1960 Britain was importing more than 500,000 tons per year of frozen beef, veal, mutton and lamb (Commonwealth Economic Committee, 1961).

The rate of freezing is dependent not only on the bulk of the meat (Fig. 7.1) and its thermal properties (e.g. specific heat and thermal conductivity), but on the temperature of the refrigerating environment, on the method of applying the refrigeration and, with smaller cuts of meat, on the nature of the wrapping material used. Table 7.4A gives the thermal conductivities, at various temperatures, of muscle, bone and fat of several meat species (Morley, 1966).

TABLE 7.4A. *Thermal Conductivity of Meat*

Sample	Temperature (C)	Thermal conductivity 10^{-3} J sec^{-1} cm^{-1} C^{-1}
Miscellaneous		
Gelatin Gel	+20	6·2
Ice	−19	24·7
Muscle		
L. dorsi (lumbar), beef	+16	5·2
	−19	13·0
L. dorsi (lumbar), pork	+16	5·2
	−19	18·0
L. dorsi (lumbar), lamb	−19	17·7
Fat		
Sirloin, beef	+16	2·1
	−19	2·7
pork	+16	2·0
Kidney, beef	+16	1·9
(rendered)	+16	1·3
Bone (cancellated)	+16	2·6
Femur, beef	−19	3·3
Bone (compact)		
Femur, pork	+19	5·8
Rib, beef	+19	5·4
Radius, beef	+19	5·7

The low conductivity of fat at both ambient and freezing temperatures, and the greatly increased conductivity of meat when frozen, are apparent. Such data enable accurate cooling and freezing rates to be calculated for commercial operations (Earle and Fleming, 1967).

It is not appropriate here to discuss freezing techniques in detail: these are considered in various publications (cf. Tressler and Evers, 1947); but some comparative data will be given.

It used to be normal commercial practice in Australia to chill beef quarters for 1–3 days at about 1°C and then to freeze them for 3 to 5 days at −10°C (Vickery, 1953); but there is a present tendency to increase rates of freezing either by using smaller cuts than quarters (Law and Vere-Jones, 1955) or by placing the hot meat directly after slaughtering

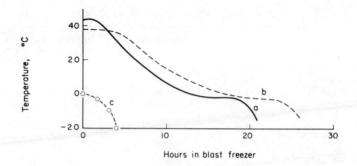

FIG.7.4.Time-temperature curves for beef placed whilst warm into a blast freezer (Howard and Lawrie, 1957b). (a) Temperature in deepest portion of side: blast at 1000 ft/min, −40°C. (b) Temperature in deepest portion of side: blast at 250 ft/min, −30°C. (c) Temperature at centre of thick section of sirloin.

into a blast tunnel freezer without prior chilling (Jasper, 1958; Howard and Lawrie, 1956). The latter procedure is now used extensively in preparing New Zealand lamb. Apart from rapidity of freezing, it involves biochemical factors which will be considered below. Some idea of the rate of freezing of beef quarters in a blast tunnel can be gained from the time–temperature curves in Fig. 7.4 (Howard and Lawrie, 1957b). Curve (a) records the temperature in the deepest part of a hind quarter of good quality beef when placed hot in a tunnel operating at 100 ft/min and −40°C. The time from entry to completion of freezing is about 18 hr compared with 24 hr for beef of similar quality in a tunnel operating at 250 ft/min and −35°C (curve (b)). A thick section of sirloin under the latter conditions froze in about 2 hr (curve (c)). The process obviously eliminates weight losses caused by evaporation during chilling and lessens those during freezing (Table 7.5); but apparently causes the frozen quarters to be more susceptible to loss during subsequent storage at −10°C. Even so, the overall loss is less. The loss in weight of carcases of New Zealand lamb over 90 days is generally about 4 per cent (Griffiths, Vickery and Holmes, 1932).

It is still customary in Britain to store frozen meat at −10°C; yet weight losses by evaporation at −30°C are only 20 per cent of those at −10°C (Cutting and Malton, 1973). Moreover, wastage at the latter

TABLE 7.5. *Weight Losses during Chilling, Freezing and Frozen Storage of Beef Quarters* (Howard and Lawrie, 1956)

Process	Quarters blast frozen without prior chilling (as % hot weight)	Quarters normally frozen after chilling (as % hot weight)
Chilling	—	1·50
Freezing	0·60	1·33
Storage at −10°C for 20 weeks	0·74	0·36
Total	1·34	3·19

temperature increases the need to trim discoloured surfaces. Packing in polythene reduced evaporation at −10°C to about the same level as that of meat at −30°C without such packaging.

When unprotected meat surfaces are blast frozen, there is considerable freezer burn. Freezer burn is the name given to the whitish or amber-coloured patches seen on the surface of frozen meats. The patches are caused by the sublimation of ice crystals into the atmosphere of the cold store, thus creating small air pockets on the meat which scatter incident light (Brooks, 1929a). This happens because the vapour pressure of water over the coils of the refrigerating machinery is much less than that above the meat surface.

Kaess and Weidemann (1961, 1962, 1963) made an exhaustive study of freezer burn. The phenomenon involves the formation of a condensed layer of muscular tissue near the surface. This prevents access of water from below, thus enhancing surface desiccation. Freezer burn is maximal during storage when the meat has been frozen rapidly under conditions where evaporation has been prevented; and conversely.

The construction of cold stores which are entirely surrounded by an insulating air jacket has made feasible a substantial reduction in evaporative loss during the storage of frozen meat. In Moscow a store capable of holding 35,000 tons of meat had been so jacketed (Gindlin,

Frid and Yakovlev, 1958) many years ago; but the extension of prepackaging methods of meat handling has largely invalidated this technical development. Currently there is growing interest in importing frozen meat from Australia and New Zealand in standardized insulated containers. Apart from speeding loading and unloading operations this would obviate any risks from exposure to ambient temperatures. Containers measuring 20 × 8 × 8 ft are in service (Middlehurst, Parker and Coffey, 1969). When used to hold 60-lb cartons of frozen boneless beef, such containers require additional refrigeration at varying times, dependent on the initial temperature of the frozen meat when loaded into the containers and the ambient temperature. "Clipon" refrigeration units can be attached for this purpose. Temperatures should not be permitted to rise above $-4°C$ with frozen beef, lamb or mutton, or above $-5°C$ with offal, as otherwise damage and distortion due to softening occur (Haughey and Marer, 1971).

TABLE 7.6. *Rates of Freezing in Relation to Temperature and Type of Freezing*
(after Dunker and Hankins, 1953)

Ambient temperature (°C)	Type of freezing	Approximate time to freeze 3° to −12°C (hr)
−17	Air blast	12
	Plate freezer	16
	Still air	19
−56	Air blast	2
	Plate freezer	3·5
	Still air	4

With pieces of meat smaller than quarters or joints considerably faster rates of freezing are naturally possible, the actual rate depending on the temperature of the refrigerating environment, on its nature (Table 7.6) and on the wrapping material which may be employed (Table 7.7).

It will be seen that such meat freezes fastest in an air blast and slowest in still air, direct contact with freezing plates giving intermediate values;

TABLE 7.7. *Effect of Wrapping on Freezing Rate of Lean Beef (6 × 6 × 23 in.) Frozen in an Air Blast at -17 C* (after Dunker and Hankins, 1953)

Type of wrapping	Approximate time to freeze 3 C to −15 C (hr)
Nil	7
Greaseproof paper	9·5
Cellophane	10
Aluminium foil	12
White parchment	12
Polyethylene	14·5

and that certain types of wrap will double the time to freeze over that for corresponding unwrapped meat (Dunker and Hankins, 1953), depending on their insulating properties (cf. Table 7.3).

Even the rates of freezing in Table 7.6, being greater than 75 min will cause extracellular ice formation (Table 7.4) and thus potential drip on thawing. Nevertheless, the extracellular crystals formed are much smaller and more finely distributed than those in normal commercial practice (Moran, 1932; Cook *et al.*, 1926). The consequently lower order of fibre distortion and of translocation of water is associated with a somewhat smaller degree of drip (Ramsbottom and Koonz, 1939). It should be pointed out that these benefits from the formation of small, *extracellular* ice crystals will be lost if the frozen meat is subsequently held at too high a temperature because of the phenomenon of recrystallization (Moran, 1932; Meryman, 1956).

If the temperature of storage is not far below the freezing point, the smallest ice crystals will sublime and recrystallize on to those which are somewhat larger, thus increasing the size of the latter still further; and damage to the tissue, manifested by drip on thawing, will increase accordingly.

Apart from its effect on the size of extracellular ice crystals, the rapid freezing of meat without prior chilling influences the water-holding capacity in another way, since post-mortem glycolysis will still be proceeding in the muscles (§ 4.2.2). If the muscle should be frozen before the ATP level has fallen appreciably (i.e. pre-rigor), there will be a greatly enhanced ATP-ase activity on thawing which will cause marked shortening and the exudation of excessive quantities of drip which may amount to 30–40 per cent of the muscle weight ("thaw rigor": Moran, 1929; Bendall and Marsh, 1951) unless the muscle is held taut (e.g. *in situ* on the carcase: Marsh and Thompson, 1958). In attempting to explain the phenomenon of thaw rigor, Bendell (1960) has pointed out that the rate of contraction depends mainly on the rate of thawing. To elucidate this problem he employed thin strips of muscle wherein the time of heat transfer was negligible. He found that during thaw rigor in such strips both creatine phosphate (C.P.) and ATP fell very swiftly from their initial level, post-mortem glycolysis being complete in a fraction of an hour. The rate of ATP breakdown was ten times greater than in normal *rigor mortis* at 37°C and this could only be explained by presuming that the contractile ATP-ase had been stimulated by pre-rigor freezing and thawing: the non-contractile ATP-ase of myosin is responsible for ATP breakdown during the onset of *rigor mortis* normally. Bendall further observed that the shortening of the muscles was complete before the ATP level had declined significantly, whereas if shortening occurs at all in normal rigor it does so at the stage when the ATP level is falling swiftly. It can be shown that there is a characteristic notch in the shortening curve—indicative of relaxation. When even faster thawing of pre-rigor frozen muscle is achieved (by the use of quantities of muscle containing only a few fibres) contraction is almost instantaneous (about 30 sec) and develops considerable power, being then followed by almost complete relaxation. On the basis of these results, and investigations on model systems, Bendall concludes that the first effect of thawing is to cause an extensive salt flux whereby Ca^{++} ions are released by the sarcotubular system and stimulate the breakdown of the considerable level of ATP present in the pre-rigor frozen muscle. Where thawing is more or less instantaneous, calcium is quickly recaptured by the sarcotubular system. Since, thereby, the stimulation of actomyosin ATP-ase is so brief, ATP is still virtually at its pre-rigor level, H-meromyosin cannot cross bond with actin and relaxation ensues. Luyet and co-workers (Luyet, Rapatz and Gehenio, 1965) have demonstrated the visual changes in this sequence of events on film.

The rate of ATP breakdown in thaw-rigor is also affected by the rate of pre-rigor freezing: fast frozen muscles metabolize ATP faster than slow frozen muscles. This is again a reflection of the degree of stimulation of the contractile ATP-ase of actomyosin by calcium ions which appear to be released by the sarcotubular system to a greater extent in the former case (Scopes and Newbold, 1968). Both in thaw rigor and cold shortening phosphorylase is markedly activated by the AMP produced (Newbold and Scopes, 1967; Scopes and Newbold, 1968).

According to Shikama (1963) the activity of isolated myosin ATP-ase is substantially lost by exposure to temperatures below $-20°C$ for even 10 min, due to disruption of the ordered array of water molecules adjacent to the protein surface. This suggests that the rate of ATP breakdown on thawing muscle which has been frozen pre-rigor might be somewhat less if the temperature attained on freezing was sufficiently low. Arrest of ATP breakdown sometimes fails to occur despite rates of freezing which are theoretically fast enough to achieve it (Howard and Lawrie, 1956); it is feasible that the rate of ATP breakdown can be *enhanced* by cold shock (and cause "cold-shortening") or under critical conditions where localized concentrations of salt arise just before the tissue, as a whole, freezes (Smith, 1929). Moreover, when pre-rigor frozen muscle is held for a few days at $-2°C$ (Marsh and Thompson, 1958) or for a few weeks at $-12°C$ (Davey and Gilbert, 1976), there is a slow breakdown of the ATP whereby the prerequisite for the shortening and exudation is removed.

Where the rate of freezing is insufficient either to arrest ATP breakdown (as in pre-rigor freezing) or to speed it up (as by salt concentration in slower freezing or by "cold-shock") it may be sufficient, nevertheless, to slow it. This would be associated with a greater water-holding capacity (§ 5.4.1) and less drip on thawing. The rate of ATP breakdown can be further slowed by pre-slaughter injection of relaxing doses of magnesium sulphate (Table 7.8; Howard and Lawrie, 1957b), and drip on thawing is diminished even more.

TABLE 7.8. *Percentage Drip from Beef Psoas Muscles under Different Conditions*

Treatment	Normal freezing after chilling	Blast freezing without prior chilling
Control	9·1	6·6
Pre-slaughter injection with magnesium sulphate	7·9	4·4

Conversely, the pre-slaughter administration of calcium salts, by increasing ATP breakdown during post-mortem glycolysis, enhances drip formation (Howard and Lawrie, 1956).

There are other ways in which drip can be minimized despite the extracellular ice formation which is inevitable with carcase meat. Conditioning of meat before freezing (§ 5.4) diminishes drip—possibly by increasing intracellular osmotic pressure and thus opposing the egress of fluid to the extracellular ice crystals (Cook *et al.*, 1926; Bouton *et al.*, 1958). Part of the conditioning effect may be due to alterations in ion–protein relationships since, during holding, sodium and calcium ions are released and potassium ions absorbed by the myofibrillar proteins (Arnold, Wierbicki and Deatherage, 1956).

The work of Empey (1933) showed that one of the most important factors determining the availability of drip fluid was pH. Even with the relatively low rates of freezing in carcase meat, which produce extracellular ice formation, the induction of a high ultimate pH can virtually eliminate drip (Fig. 7.5). The necessary glycogen depletion may be brought about in various ways (cf. §§ 4.2.2 and 5.1.2). With quarters of meat, however, the diminution in drip caused by high ultimate pH is not so marked, because much of the fluid in these circumstances is derived from blood vessels and other extracellular spaces rather than from the muscular tissue as such (Howard, Lawrie and Lee, 1960).

It is interesting to note that even with the same rate of post-mortem

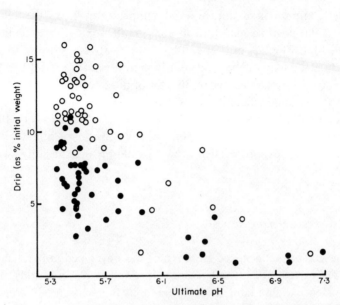

FIG. 7.5. The relationship between the percentage of drip on thawing and the ultimate pH in psoas (●) and l. dorsi (○) muscles of the ox (Lawrie, 1959).

pH fall, and at the same ultimate pH, drip from the l. dorsi muscle is generally twice as great as that from psoas; and it has a different composition (Howard *et al.*, 1960). Clearly, different muscles have different intrinsic susceptibilities to damage during freezing and thawing (Fig. 7.5). Especially with the advent of frozen cuts and individual portions of meat, there has been increasing interest in establishing optimum modes of thawing. Various investigations have been undertaken to clarify the issue. Thus, Bailey, James, Kitchell and Hudson (1974) found that, for a given temperature, frozen pork legs thaw faster in water than in air, although the appearance after the latter treatment was preferable. According to Vanichsensi *et al.* (1972) the thawing of frozen lamb shoulders in water (45°C for 2–2½ hours) is suitable for short term batch or continuous processing immediately prior to coming out. For a batch process with a cycle time of 8–10 hours, however, air thawing at 2–18°C and high humidity is better.

The long periods of storage which temperatures below the freezing point make possible may lead to considerable oxidative rancidity in exposed fat. The fats of beef and lamb are relatively resistant to such oxidation and may still be good after 18 months' storage at − 10°C (Lea, 1938). The more highly unsaturated fat of pork becomes rancid rather more quickly; and that of rabbit, which may have an iodine value of 180, turns yellow and oxidizes after only 4 months at − 10°C (Vickery, 1932). As indicated above, the formation of brown metmyoglobin tends to develop in the lean in parallel with fat oxidation and rancidity (Watts, 1954).

7.1.2.3. *Prepackaging aspects*

The sale of prepackaged frozen meat has developed in parallel with the fresh article for several reasons. In the first place, it adds to the convenience of handling, since there is a great extension of storage life making it attractive for institutional, and other bulk catering. Secondly, and in relation to the increasing availability of freezing compartments in domestic refrigerators, it gives the consumers a new facility in creating a reserve of quasi-fresh food against unexpected demands. Although temperatures below the freezing point are beneficial in permitting prolonged storage, they may make more severe demands on the packaging material than do chill or ambient temperatures (cf. Table 7.3). The meat is exposed for times long enough to cause desiccation and for oxidation of the fat and the pigments, notwithstanding the slowness of these changes because of the low temperature. The wrapping must effectively prevent—or disguise—them at temperatures for which many packing materials are unsuitable. Over prolonged storage periods, exposure to strong light, as in display cabinets, will accelerate oxidation of fats (Lea, 1938) and cause discoloration (especially at wavelengths between 5600–6300 Å: Townsend and Bratzler, 1958), and this is one reason for the use of an opaque wrap for frozen prepackaged products. Another reason is that frozen meat, by its hardness, is liable to pierce the films of polyethylene or polyvinylidene chloride which are often used.

To avoid this the film can be prevented from making close contact with the meat surfaces by the walls of the carton base. Because of the space above the meat, sublimation of ice can occur, causing extensive desiccation on the surface. An opaque wrap—stamped with a photographic representation of the contents when cooked—offsets the superficially unpleasant impression this would create. Moreover, instructions are frequently given to cook without thawing, thus disguising drip—the major disadvantage of frozen meats. Even so, the pieces of meat used in prepackaging are sufficiently small to permit really fast freezing, with a consequently diminished tendency to drip on thawing (Bouton and Howard, 1956). If the pieces of meat are free from sharp edges and are thus not liable to rupture the packaging film, the latter may be shrunk on to the meat surfaces, thus eliminating the possibility of surface desiccation.

From what has already been indicated in relation to fresh meat (§ 7.1.1.2) the lower the temperature of frozen storage, the longer is the

TABLE 7.9. *Approximate Times for Appearance of Distinct Rancidity in Fat or Discoloration of Lean in Unwrapped Meat*

Meat	Storage temperature			
	−8°C	−15°C	−22°C	−30°C
Beef (rib roasts)	3 months	6 months	12 months	—
Pork (loin without rind and back fat)	—	3 months	6 months	12 months

time before oxidative rancidity in fat and the production of brown metmyoglobin in the lean develop. These features, and the greater susceptibility to spoilage of pork than beef, have been emphasized in the work of many investigators (Emerson, Brady and Tucker, 1951; Palmer *et al.,* 1953; Dahl, 1958b): Table 7.9 is taken from the latter.

Glazing the meat with water greatly retards these changes since it protects the meat itself from desiccation and by preventing access of oxygen to the surface retards oxidation (Dahl, 1958b). In the U.S.A. the wrapping of frozen cuts in edible coating (such as acetylated monoglycerates) has been advocated. They can be applied to frozen meat ($-20°C$) by dropping the latter in a bath of the coating substance at $130°C$ for 5 sec. Even at $-30°C$ such coatings will not crack; and will retain their efficacy against desiccation.

Experiments with slices of l. dorsi (about 1 in. thick) and ground hamburger beef have shown that cryogenic freezing in liquid nitrogen gave initially lower weight losses than those with blast-freezing at $-30°C$. Subsequently, however, cooking losses from the cryogenically frozen material were greater. It has been suggested that cryogenic freezing causes cracks to develop in the product from which moisture is readily lost on cooking (Jakobsson and Bengtsson, 1969). There is a definite relation between the ability of wrapping materials to retain moisture and a desirable flavour and odour in the cooked meat. For frozen prepackaged meat, aluminium foil, polyethylene and polyvinylidene chloride are particularly good in this respect (Emerson *et al.*, 1953; Bouton and Howard, 1956). Palatability can be enhanced by packing in nitrogen (Steinberg, Winter and Hustralid, 1949) or in vacuum (Hiner, Gaddis and Hankins, 1951) although it is also more expensive. Dahl recommends $-30°C$ as the desirable temperature of storage for frozen meat, but this might be difficult to achieve commercially on a large scale. Fluctuating temperatures are particularly damaging for discoloration, rancidity and desiccation (Emerson *et al.,* Townsend and Bratzler, 1958).

Although the low temperatures involved in the storage of frozen prepackaged meat diminish the risk of microbial contamination, they do not eliminate it (§ 6.1.2.2). The same dangers of contamination during preparation, which apply to fresh prepackaged meat, apply here (§ 7.1.1.2). Spores from diseases caused by sporulating organisms or toxins may survive freezing. In the first place, bacteria would be able to multiply in the meat if it were to stay much above freezing temperatures before consumption. In the second case, sufficient toxin may form before bacterial growth is stopped by freezing to affect consumers subsequently eating the meat after frozen storage.

The salient points on the freezing of meat may be summarized.

Post-rigor meat

1. The faster the rate of freezing the less will be the drip on thawing. Not all research workers agree on this aspect. In recent studies, Dr. C. L. Cutting (personal communication) has found no significant differences in the degree of drip between duplicate samples of beef l. dorsi muscle, although these had been subjected to a wide range of freezing rates post-rigor. A high speed of freezing will also tend to enhance tenderness.

2. A high ultimate pH (however it arises) will give greatly enhanced water-holding capacity and diminish drip on thawing if the meat is subsequently frozen; but it may lead to excessive tenderness and to loss of colour and flavour.

3. Increased tenderness and enhanced water-holding capacity (with diminished drip on thawing) will develop if the meat is "conditioned" for some days after reaching the ultimate pH. (This applies particularly to beef.)

Pre-rigor Meat

The consequences of freezing are determined by the freezing rate which is feasible in particular circumstances.

1. With intact sides of pork and beef the rate of heat removal is likely to be too slow to cause much "cold-shortening"; and there will be virtually none of the meat frozen pre-rigor.

2. When freezing is applied to pre-rigor meat of smaller dimensions both "cold-shortening" and "thaw-rigor" (due to pre-rigor freezing) are increasingly likely. When very fast freezing rates are possible, pre-rigor freezing will ensue before "cold-shortening" can develop.

3. "Cold-shortening" can be avoided by ensuring that the temperature does not fall below 10–15°C before about 10 hours' post-mortem, by altering the mode of suspension of the side or by electrical stimulation of the warm carcase.

4. The extreme disadvantages of "thaw-rigor" can be avoided if the time and temperature of frozen storage are such as to allow the ATP level to fall before thawing.

7.2. THERMAL PROCESSING

Preservation of meat by thermal processing dates from the beginning of the nineteenth century when Appert (1810), whilst not aware of the nature of the processes involved, found that meat would remain edible if it were heated in a sealed container and the seal maintained until the meat was to be eaten. This method of preservation has developed into the canning industry (although glass containers as well as metal cans may be employed). The United Kingdom consumption of canned meat is now about a quarter of a million tons per year and constitutes 7·5 per cent of the total meat eaten (Commonwealth Economic Committee, 1963). Canned meat and meat products may be subjected to heat at two levels—pasteurization, which is designed to stop microbial growth with minimum damage; and sterilization, in which all or most bacteria are killed, but which alters the meat to a considerably greater degree.

An important consideration in achieving sterility is the fact that certain micro-organisms form spores which may be exceedingly heat-resistant (cf. § 6.3.1). To destroy the spores of certain thermophiles would require a degree of heating which would greatly lower the organoleptic attributes of the commodity. In canning practice "commercial sterility" is achieved by giving a degree of heat treatment sufficient to kill non-sporing bacteria and all spores that might germinate and grow during storage without refrigeration. To avoid the growth of any thermophiles potentially present it is essential to cool the cans rapidly after processing and to prevent storage at high ambient temperatures. The eating quality of canned, cured meats can only be retained by using a low degree of heat treatment (pasteurizing) which is insufficient to kill spores; but in such products the curing ingredients reinforce the bactericidal and bacteriostatic effects of the heat.

7.2.1. *Pasteurization*

Pork is more susceptible to heat damage than other meats; moreover, the ingredients used in making certain products from pork (as in hams) tend to weaken the structure still further. As a result, the heat treatment given to such commodities as canned hams cannot be sufficient to kill all micro-organisms. The definition of pasteurized or semi-preserved meats indicates that such products do not remain unchanged, and consumable, for any length of time in temperate climates unless special precautions are taken during transport and storage (Maillet, 1955). Although containers of semi-preserved meats are labelled to recommend low-temperature storage, this was frequently disregarded when United Kingdom consumption of continental canned hams and other such products increased after the Second World War, since there was a current impression that all canned meats were sterile. The widespread spoilage of the product, manifested by "blown" cans and otherwise, altered this view and has led to appropriate handling precautions (Hobbs, 1955). It is nevertheless a fact that pasteurized cured meats are usually remarkably free from microbial spoilage. Perigo, Whiting and Bashford (1967) found evidence that, on heating during the pasteurizing process, nitrite reacts with some component of the medium to produce a substance which is strongly inhibitory to the growth of clostridia. This may help to explain the fortunate—but unexpected—stability of this type of product.

Spoilage of canned hams may be attributed to various associations of bacteria, including faecal streptococci of porcine origin. The organisms responsible can be classified (Table 7.10: after Mossel, 1955).

The frequent presence of micrococci (which have only normal heat tolerance) indicates that under-processing often occurs (Ingram and Hobbs, 1954).

Although it is not possible to sample the interior of a ham during heating to determine the bacterial count, the process has been followed in ham which has been minced under sterile conditions. Typical data are given in Table 7.11 (after Grever, 1955).

No actual increase in bacterial numbers occurred; and after the centre temperature reached about 45–55°C there was a definite decrease in numbers. Apart from ensuring that the meat used in the preparation of semi-preserved products is kept cool before canning, and has the minimum bacterial load deriving from the animal or from slaughter operations, it is important to ascertain that the minor ingredients which

TABLE 7.10. *Classification of Bacteria causing Spoilage in Pasteurized Canned Meat Products*

Degree of resistance to pasteurization	Genera or species	Type of spoilage
(1) Occasional	*Salmonella*	Human disease—public health risk
	Lactobacillus	Greening
	Achromobacter–pseudomonas	Putrefaction
	Coliforms	Swelling
(2) Frequent	*Strept. faecalis*	Off-flavours
	Micrococcus	Swelling
(3) Complete	*Bacillus*	Swelling and off-flavours
	Clostridium	Swelling

may be used—such as spices, condiments, curing salts, sugar, milk powder—are sterile: they frequently harbour micro-organisms which may resist canning. Some of these may be harmful, for example spore-bearing anaerobes in spices. Black pepper, pimento and mustard seed, in their natural state, are reservoirs for moulds of *Penicillium* and *Aspergillus* spp. The latter can include *Aspergillus flavus* (Hadlok, 1969).

TABLE 7.11. *Pasteurization of Hams at 75°C: Aerobic Counts on Nutrient Agar*

Pasteurizing (hr)	Temperature of ham (°C)	Bacterial count
0	10	$1 \cdot 25 \times 10^6$
1	15	$2 \cdot 0 \times 10^6$
2	30	$2 \cdot 1 \times 10^6$
3	44	$1 \cdot 15 \times 10^6$
4	55	$2 \cdot 5 \times 10^5$
5	62	$7 \cdot 9 \times 10^3$
6	66	700
7	69	< 10

Many muscle enzymes are inactivated in the temperature range used in pasteurizing, especially the more complex ones such as hexokinase: others such as creatine kinase are not inactivated until a temperature of 60°C is reached: but an enzyme such as adenylic kinase can stand a temperature of 100°C at pH 1 and, clearly, would still be operative (Dixon and Webb, 1958). Fortunately, changes effected by the latter are of minor importance. Nevertheless, it is obvious that in semi-preserved meats, wherein the temperature is not raised much above 60°C, there may still be residual enzymic activity. This could be undesirable even though the microbial status of the product was satisfactory.

From the point of view of minimizing damage to texture, it is preferable to administer the dose of heat required for stabilizing the microbial status of the product by a short period at high temperature, rather than by longer period at lower temperature (Ball, 1938). In the future, the severity of the heat may be minimized if it is combined with the use of antibiotics, irradiation or infrared treatment.

7.2.2. Sterilization

The majority of canned meats are "commercially" sterilized, i.e. they are processed to the point at which most micro-organisms and their spores have been killed: this permits more or less indefinite storage life in the can, at any ambient temperature, provided it is kept sealed; but the product is markedly different from fresh meat, and may alter chemically and physically in the course of time. Canned meat has remained edible for 114 years (Drummond and Macara, 1938). In the early days of canning, the meat products were heated in an open water bath. Under these conditions, the temperature of the cans failed to attain 100°C and a long processing time was necessary to achieve commercial sterility. Increasing the boiling point of the water by adding salts such as calcium chloride made possible a great reduction in the processing time. By 1874 a controllable pressure steam retort had been invented; and between 1920–30 information on the heat resistance of bacterial spores, and on heat penetration into cans, permitted the preparation of time–temperature processing schedules, to control the canning process instead of relying upon empiricism (Howard, 1949). The concept of thermal death time (TDT) proved most useful in evaluating the efficacy of thermal processes (Bigelow and Esty, 1920). It is also referred to as the Fahrenheit value (F), with a subscript to represent temperature, the unit F_0 being most frequent and representing the time, in minutes, needed to achieve sterility at a temperature of 250°F (121°C). The decimal reduction value (D) is the time in minutes required to kill 90 per cent of the bacteria cells at a given temperature. By plotting the log of F or D against heating temperature a straight line is obtained. Its gradient is known as the z-value; and it may be defined as the number of Fahrenheit degrees by which the temperature must be raised to obtain a tenfold increase of death rate of bacterial cells. For spores of *Cl. botulinum* and of some other sporulating anaerobes (in phosphate buffer) z has a value of 18 (Doty, 1960).

As in the case of semi-preserved meats, underprocessed or faulty cans are liable to microbial spoilage, which may take various forms. A frequent result is the production of gas in sufficient quantities to swell or "blow" the can (cf. Table 7.10). Although its pH is generally on the acid side of neutrality, meat is regarded as a low acid food. Since the most lethal food-poisoning organism, *Cl. botulinum*, has a lower limit of growth at pH 4·5, all foods such as meat which support its growth are given heat treatment sufficient to destroy it. Its F_0 value is 2·8; and at 100°C the toxin is destroyed in 10 min. The presence of curing ingredients in products such as canned hams makes them less liable to harbour *Cl. botulinum* and this permits pasteurization (Halvorson, 1955). *Cl. sporogenes*, another spore-forming organism capable of growth on meat, is more heat resistant than *Cl. botulinum* and is used to evaluate heat processing (Desrosier, 1959). Certain thermophilic bacteria capable of withstanding very severe heat treatment may also be present. To eliminate these would require a degree of processing which would seriously affect the meat and lower its nutritive value. These organisms are controlled, as far as possible, by avoiding initial contamination (Howard, 1949). The thermoresistance of bacteria in meat products appears to bear some relation to the type of meat. Thus *S. faecalis* is more resistant to thermal inactivation in comminuted salt pork than in the corresponding beef product (Zakula, 1969). The effect has been attributed to differences in the a_w.

Since most proteins are denatured by heat (Putman, 1953), sterilized canned meats suffer considerable change in the process. There is an increase in free –SH groups (Bendall, 1946) and the proteins may coagulate and precipitate. The texture of canned meat after sterilization is thus more like the cooked than the fresh commodity. If heat treatment is excessive, marked deterioration in aesthetic appeal and eating quality occurs. Moreover, since meat (especially pork) contains appreciable quantities of thiamin (vitamin B_1) and ascorbic acid (vitamin C) and these are destroyed by heat, the nutritive value of the canned product will be lower than that of fresh meat. It must be remembered, however, that meat is not primarily eaten for its vitamin content; and that these vitamins would, in any case, be largely destroyed in cooking. The loss of such labile nutrients will be exaggerated if the cans are subsequently stored for long periods at high ambient temperatures. The colour of canned meats will also tend to resemble that of the cooked commodity, since the high temperatures will change the red pigment (myoglobin) to brown myohaemochromogen (Lemberg and Legge, 1949). If the interior of the cans is not lacquered, there may be discoloration due to the reaction of H_2S (produced from the meat proteins) with the plate metals (Howard, 1949).

Except, of course, where there is microbial spoilage, flavour changes during canning are not generally a problem since, as has been mentioned, canning represents a degree of cooking and meat is generally cooked before consumption.

There is some suggestion that the actual biological value of the proteins of meat may be lowered if processing temperatures are maintained at 113°C for periods longer than about 5 min (Beuk, Chornock and Rice, 1949).

In more recent times a degree of heat adequate to kill micro-organisms, but insufficient to seriously damage texture, has been achieved by agitation of the cans during the canning process (Fischer, Blair and Petersen, 1954) and by flash-heating the meat to temperatures *ca.* 150°C (Ball, 1938) *before* placing it in sterile cans (Martin, 1948). The latter two processes are not readily applicable to meats, however; but the former process has resulted in a 50 per cent reduction in the heating time required for corned beef and pork (in a loose mix with muscle juices: Jul, 1957).

CHAPTER 8

THE STORAGE AND PRESERVATION OF MEAT

II. MOISTURE CONTROL

FROM the considerations in § 6.3 it is apparent that deprivation of available moisture can not only prevent the growth of the micro-organisms found on meat but may also kill them. Water may be made unavailable by direct removal, as in dehydration and freeze dehydration, or by increasing the extracellular osmotic pressure, as in curing. With these processes the prevention of microbial change and the preservation of edibility involves the creation of a commodity which necessarily differs more from the fresh meat than does refrigerated meat, although on subsequent cooking these differences in nature are less apparent.

8.1. DEHYDRATION

As with refrigeration, the efficacy of drying had been empirically recognized in meat preservation since very early times. The idea that dehydration could preserve muscular tissue was obviously known in Egypt 5000 years ago and utilized in preparing mummies. A variety of dried and cured meats was available 3000 years ago: indeed, muscle fibres can still be recognized in material from Jericho (A. McM. Taylor, personal communication).

Early drying procedures, which are still continued in remoter areas of the world, involved exposure of strips of lean meat to the sun, as in the

241

manufacture of pemmican by North American Indians, or a combination of light salting followed by air drying, as in the preparation of charqui (in South America) and biltong (in South Africa) (Sharp, 1953). Such products are considerably different from fresh meat—and to most tastes lower in eating quality.

The large-scale commercial production of dehydrated meat in a form which, when cooked, was similar in nutritive value and in palatability to the fresh commodity resulted from research carried out during the Second World War (Dunker, Hankins and Bennett, 1945; Sharp, 1953). To effect the necessary degree of moisture removal by the current of hot air used in the process, it was essential to have a high surface: volume ratio in the meat: minces were, therefore, used. The use of raw, minced meat proved unsatisfactory, since it quickly became case-hardened, thus opposing further moisture removal. By first cooking the meat in slices, however, mincing it and then drying it under carefully controlled conditions (the temperature being kept below 70°C: Dunker *et al.*, 1945; Sharp, 1953) a product could be prepared which was almost indistinguishable in flavour and texture from raw minced meat, when comparisons of the fully cooked meats were made. Although minced and precooked dehydrated meat obviously cannot serve the same purposes as fresh meat, it was designed to conserve the essential nutrients and eating quality of the latter without refrigeration and in small bulk—against emergency conditions. It was never issued as such to the domestic consumer, although it was utilized for certain manufactured meat products; but it proved most useful for the Armed Forces.

The data in Table 8.1 illustrate the saving in space involved. It is important to note that although 1 ton of both canned corned beef and dehydrated beef occupies 54 ft^3, the density of essential nutrients is more than twice as high in the latter, since canned beef contains about 53 per cent water and the dehydrated meat quoted contained a mean of 7·5 per cent water (Sharp, 1953).

Before outlining some of the considerations involved in preparing a dehydrated meat of satisfactory quality, it is desirable to mention briefly some of the implicit biochemical aspects.

TABLE 8.1. *Comparative Density of Different Forms of Beef* (after Sharp, 1953)

Commodity	Ft³/ton	Ft³/ton meat solids
Frozen quarters	95	264
Frozen quarters (boneless)	78	173
Canned corned beef	54	157
Dehydrated beef (compressed to specific gravity 1)	54	75

8.1.1. Biochemical Aspects

The difference between dehydrated and fresh meat will obviously be minimized if the water removed from the former can be incorporated again on rehydration. The degree of reincorporation depends on the surviving water-holding capacity of the muscle—in terms both of microscopic structure and of the chemical state of the muscle proteins.

Loss of water from both raw and precooked meat is accompanied by diminishing space between groups of muscle fibres and between the individual fibres and by a progressive reduction in muscle fibre diameter (Wang *et al.*, 1953). The rate of moisture removal and of muscle fibre shrinkage is more rapid with precooked than with raw meat and proceeds further. Potassium was found to accumulate on the periphery of the dehydrated muscle fibres. Since this circumstance would denature the proteins in this location, thus obstructing re-entry of water on rehydration, experiments on muscle from which potassium has been removed by electrolysis were carried out (Wang *et al.*, 1954). On rehydration, electrolysed muscle absorbed about twice as much water as control material: this was attributed to its pH (2·8) which was considerably on the acid side of the isoelectric point. This procedure could not be developed in practice. Ease of rehydration is said to be enhanced by the use of irradiated meat (M. C. Brockmann, personal communication).

244   *Meat Science*

With hot-air drying procedures, lack of rehydratability is largely due to changes similar to those occurring during heat denaturation. In the range 0–20°C (as measured by the amount of so-called bound water; Grau and Hamm, 1952) the water-holding capacity of meat decreases with increasing temperature (Wierbicki and Deatherage, 1958) presumably by its effect upon the sarcoplasmic proteins (cf. Table 5.3). Between 20–30°C there was no change in the degree of hydration (Fig. 8.1). Between 30–40°C polypeptide chains in the muscle protein unfold

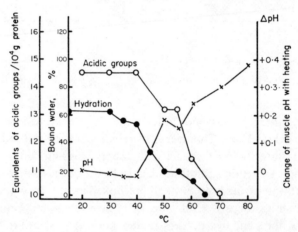

FIG. 8.1. The effect of temperature on degree of hydration, pH and acidic groups of beef muscle homogenates (Hamm, 1960). Courtesy Prof. R. Hamm.)

and new electrovalent or hydrogen bonds form (Wierbicki and Deatherage, 1958); and there is a slight fall in the degree of hydration at the iso-electric point (about 5·5). Although the heat coagulation of isolated actomyosin *in vitro* starts at about 35°C (Locker, 1956), muscle proteins are more stable *in situ* (Engelhardt, 1946), and marked changes in hydratability do not occur until the temperature rises above 40°C (Fig. 8.1). Between 40°–50°C, however, there is a loss in water-holding capacity which is associated with a corresponding diminution in the titratable acidic groups. There is a further decrease in the water-holding capacity between 50–80°C, but this is less marked (although loss of acidic groups continues). Above 80°C, free H_2S begins to form and increases with increasing temperature (Tilgner, 1958). The loss of free acidic groups explains the considerable rise in the pH of the meat (cf. Fig. 8.1) and the iso-electric point of the muscle changes to higher pH values (Fig. 8.2), thus tending to offset the increase in water-holding capacity which the higher pH would normally cause (Hamm, 1960). It is important to note that relative differences in the water-holding capacity of fresh meat are retained after heating. For example, meat of high ultimate pH which has a high water-holding capacity when fresh, has also a higher water-holding capacity after heating than that of normal ultimate pH (Bendall, 1946); Hamm and Deatherage, 1960). This circumstance is important in the production of frankfurters (Grau, 1952) and canned ham (Koeppe, 1954).

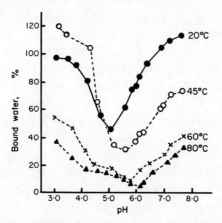

FIG. 8.2. The effect of temperature on the pH-hydration curve of beef muscle of ultimate pH 5·5 (Hamm, 1960). Courtesy Prof. R. Hamm.)

The collagen of associated connective tissue also changes as the temperature is raised. Thus, at about 60°C collagen A is transformed into collagen B. At somewhat higher temperatures the latter swells and softens as it takes up water and finally disintegrates, forming gelatin. The latter does not occur appreciably below 100°C. These changes in collagen with heating will tend to increase the water-holding capacity of the meat (Hamm, 1960), but the reactions of sarcoplasmic and myofibrillar proteins are quantitatively much more important and clearly the lower the heating temperature during drying the less will be the loss of water-holding capacity and the greater the degree of reconstitutability.

8.1.2. Physical Aspects

Various physical factors determine the efficacy of a hot-air draught in dehydrating precooked minced meat.

In the first place while the size of the meat particles is not important in itself, within the range 0·3–0·8 cm diameter, it influences the density of loading of the drying trays and thus has an effect on the time of drying. Thus the time taken for finely minced particles to reach a water content of 5 per cent was 3, 5 and 6½ hr with loading of 1, 2 and 4 lb/ft² respectively (Sharp, 1953).

As will be apparent from § 8.1.1, the temperature of drying is important. Heat damage is characterized by toughness, grittiness and burnt flavour. Whilst the water content is still about 77 per cent air temperatures of 80°C can be tolerated for 2 hr without loss of quality; but even 50°C can produce some deterioration when the water content is low. Nevertheless, quality is maintained at a satisfactory level when the drying temperature is 70°C throughout the process (Dunker et al., 1945; Sharp, 1953). A typical drying curve showing water content and meat temperature is given in Fig. 8.3 (Sharp, 1953). The operating conditions refer to an air speed of 600 ft/min, an air temperature of 60°C, a relative humidity of 40 per cent and a tray loading of 2 lb/ft². It will be observed that the temperature of the meat remains relatively low (at the web bulb temperature) until about half the moisture has been driven off. It is at this same point that a relatively high fat content begins to retard the rate of drying although it has little influence initially. This results in a serious increase in the time of dehydration if the fat content is above about 35 per cent of the dry weight; and where it is above 40 per cent of the dry weight the spongy texture of the dry meat can no longer hold the molten fat and it drips away (Sharp, 1953; Prater and Coote, 1962). On the other

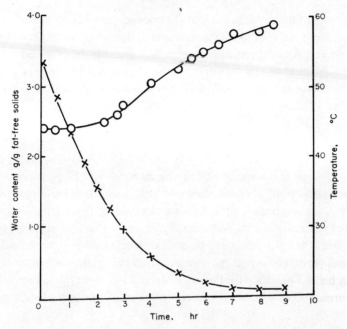

Fig. 8.3. Typical drying curve for meat. Drying temperature 60°C (dry bulb), 44°C (wet bulb), R. H. 0·40 (Sharp, 1958). × − − × = water content. ○ − − ○ = meat temperature. (Courtesy Dr. J. G. Sharp.)

hand, when the fat content is below about 35 per cent of the dry weight, dehydrated meat of satisfactory water content can be obtained in a continuous hot-air drier and at a fixed drying time, despite considerable variability in the fat content. In general, however, a low-grade meat from a leaner type of carcase is preferred for the preparation of dehydrated meat in these circumstances.

The degree of precooking is an important factor. If the meat is overcooked its connective tissue framework will be changed to gelatin, and although it will give dry granules which reconstitute quickly, it will break down under compression (§ 8.1.3). An undercooked meat, however, will have a slow drying rate and a slow rate of reconstitution, yielding a dry and brittle texture. Since the aqueous liquor exuding from the meat during the precooking period contains various soluble substances, it must be returned to the cooked meat before dehydration commences to retain the full meat flavour and nutritive value of the fresh commodity. Any fat rendered out on cooking may be returned to the meat according to the fat content desired—about 40 per cent in the standard preparation specified by the United Kingdom Ministry of Food in 1942.

8.1.3. *Organoleptic Aspects*

For long-term storage, such dehydrated meat must be compressed to exclude pockets of air or moisture and kept in an airtight and moisture-proof container, preferably a tin-plate can (Sharp, 1953), since its finely divided porous state makes it specially liable to attack by oxygen. Non-oxidative changes, whether enzymic or chemical, are of secondary importance except at high storage temperatures. Thus, while restriction of oxygen will maintain the flavour of dehydrated meat for 12 months or longer at 15°C, non-oxidative deterioration may develop under nitrogen at 37°C.

In the *absence* of oxygen the main changes during storage are caused by the Maillard reaction (Henrickson *et al.*, 1955; Sharp, 1957), wherein carbonyl groups of reducing sugars react with the amino groups of proteins and amino acids non-enzymically. A dark brown coloration and a bitter, burnt flavour develop. Glucose and glucose-6-phosphate are formed in muscle post-mortem, the rate of formation being much higher in pork and rabbit than in beef. In the former two species the breakdown of muscle glycogen by α-amylolysis is more intense (Sharp, 1958). The rate of non-enzymic browning increases with pH (Sharp, 1957) and is not inhibited above 37°C unless the moisture content of the meat is 2 per cent or less. Dehydrated raw meat deteriorates to a greater extent than the cooked product, possibly because the residual amylolytic activity is greater. To keep the reactants at the lowest possible concentration, meat must be dehydrated immediately after the death of the animal or held for some time below − 10°C before dehydration. The removal of glucose by glucose oxidase is not practicable commercially. Because of the Maillard reaction, dehydrated meat can become unpalatable in 6 months when kept at high temperature (Sharp and Rolfe, 1958). Concomitant losses in the water-holding capacity of the proteins cause brittleness of texture. The storage life can be extended considerably, however, by drying to very low moisture contents.

In the *presence* of oxygen, the storage of dehydrated meat (of high moisture content) at high temperature causes it to become pale and yellow, due to the conversion of myoglobin to bile pigments. A mealy odour develops and fat oxidation occurs giving rise to paint-like odours. In dehydrated raw meat there is still considerable lipolytic action (Table 8.2). Precooking the meat before drying greatly reduces, but does not destroy, its lipolytic activity which is greater the higher the storage temperature and the residual moisture content. Fat rancidity does not develop when the moisture content is reduced to 1·5 per cent but at such a level flavour and texture are likely to be seriously affected. The stability of the fat to oxygen is increased by the incorporation of anti-oxidants such as gum guaiac or ethylgallate in the meat during precooking (Anon., 1944). But other changes then become apparent. These are characterized by the mealy odours already mentioned (Tappel, 1956). Rancidity may also be avoided by gas-packing the dehydrated meat: only a slight odour, like that of crab meat, is then apparent and the latter disappears during reconstitution and cooking. Dehydrated cured meat is especially liable to undergo oxidative rancidity because of the production of a pro-oxidant during curing.

TABLE 8.2. *Free Acidity of Fat in Air-dried Raw Beef after 12 Months' Storage*
(Sharp, 1953)

Moisture content	(As per cent oleic acid) Temperature of storage	
	20°C	37°C
7·5	17	36
5·0	12	24
3·2	6	13

Generally the moisture content of dehydrated meat is too low to permit bacterial growth, but if it rises above 10 per cent mould growth may occur after some weeks (generally, *Penicillium* and *Aspergillus* spp.).

Ideally, foods undergoing dehydration should be heated at a temperature such that microbial growth cannot occur before the moisture content has dropped sufficiently low to prevent it. It appears, however, that even if *Cl. botulinum* were present, it could not form appreciable amounts of toxin during the period of dehydration (Dozier, 1924). Precautions must be taken, however, to prevent contamination during the period of reconstitution.

TABLE 8.3. *Loss of Thiamin in Dehydrated Pork stored at Various Temperatures*

Storage temperature (°C)	Per cent thiamin retained		
	7 days	14 days	21 days
−29	100	100	100
3	100	100	96
27	—	89	77
37	70	55	43
49	15	7	0
63	4	0	0

As with thermally processed meats the thiamin content of dehydrated meat diminishes during storage, especially at high temperatures (Table 8.3: Rice *et al.*, 1944).

In general, when compressed into blocks of specific gravity 0·8 to 1·0 in sealed cans under nitrogen, dehydrated pork, mutton or beef will keep without deterioration in flavour and odour for 3 years or more at moderate storage temperatures (Sharp, 1953) although the degree of reconstitution decreases after about 12 months (Grau and Friess-Schultheiss, 1962).

8.2. FREEZE DEHYDRATION

The necessity of using cooked mince to produce a satisfactory product with air drying procedures has been mentioned above: the possibility of vacuum drying, with advantages in quality resulting from the reduced heat treatment required, were realized in commercial operations at the end of the Second World War when vacuum contact-dehydration (VCD) plant was developed in Denmark (Hanson, 1961). Nevertheless, although the VCD method permitted technological advances, the meat so processed was difficult to reconstitute. The possibility of removing water from meat by sublimation from the frozen state rather than by evaporation of liquid, has been apparent for some years, since freeze drying was a well-known procedure in the production of highly priced pharmaceuticals and biological materials in laboratory scale operations. It has been appreciated as the mildest method known for drying meat (Wang *et al.*, 1954b; Regier and Tappel, 1956). No satisfactory way of applying the process to production line operations was initially foreseen. Between 1955 and 1960, however, a large-scale process for freeze drying was developed in the United Kingdom. It is fully described by Rolfe (1958). Since it incorporated plates to enhance heat exchange during the initial phase of sublimation and to supply heat to them to aid drying during the second phase, the process was called accelerated freeze drying (AFD). AFD permitted the freeze drying of hundreds of pounds of *raw* meat per run: in only 4 hr the moisture content could be reduced to about 2 per cent. Moreover, whole steaks (about 1·5 cm thick) could be processed; and they rehydrated quickly and easily. In short, meat could be handled in portions similar to those available to the consumer of fresh meat—or of that prepared by refrigeration, curing, canning or irradiation. The low operating temperatures and speed of the process, the avoidance of translocation of salts, etc., during drying and the honeycomb texture created by the direct sublimation of ice from the minute interstices of the tissue, caused little damage to the meat proteins. The quality of the product thus resembled fresh meat. The use of spikes, to conduct the heat into the centre of the drying tissue, permits the freeze drying of 2½ lb roasts in 5–8 hr (Brynko and Smithies, 1956).

8.2.1. Histological Aspects

If operated at a low plate temperature, the freeze drying process causes relatively little gross histological change (Wang *et al.*, 1954b; Luyet, 1962). Whereas evaporation of water from the fluid phase involves the movement of salts with the water front towards the surface of the meat, with consequent distortion of the muscle, sublimation of water vapour occurs direct from each crystal nucleus of ice during freeze drying; and any distortion is limited to the areas around these nuclei (Luyet, 1961, 1962). Such distortion obviously depends on the size and number of the ice nuclei, which in turn, is a function of the rate of freezing (§ 7.1.2.1). The smaller they are the less will be the histological damage, and the finer the honeycomb of air spaces left after sublimation. With a sufficient speed of freezing, ice crystals will form inside the myofibrils between the molecules of actin and myosin causing no alteration in structure, even at the level of observation given by the electron microscope (Menz and Luyet, 1961). It is obvious, of course, that such rates of freezing are impossible with even the smallest piece of meat encountered by the consumer. In any case, even with much slower rates, where ice crystal size and distribution is *relatively* gross, the honeycomb structure left on sublimation can be too fine to permit easy rehydration (Wang *et al.*, 1954b), because air bubbles are trapped within the structure. The pre-frozen steaks used in the AFD process have a relatively open honeycomb structure which facilitates drying (Rolfe, 1958; Hanson, 1961). They also rehydrate easily. If attempts are made to freeze-dry steaks which have been placed whilst unfrozen into the vacuum chamber, their water will tend to freeze by evaporative cooling, and, by causing local concentrations of salt on the surface, will create thereon a skin of denatured protein (cf. § 7.1.2.1) which will oppose re-entry of water (Rolfe, 1958). On the other hand, if a small quantity of water forms in the meat by thawing between pre-freezing and placing in a vacuum chamber, it quickly re-freezes and sublimes satisfactorily. Nevertheless, if the rate of such re-freezing is exceptionally fast, very small intra-cellular ice crystals will form causing a texture which will oppose rehydration (Wang *et al.*, 1954b).

Even when operated under optimum conditions, the AFD process appears to cause some change in meat: when homogenized the myofibrils tend to adhere along their length as observed at the histological level (Voyle and Lawrie, 1964). It is thus interesting to note that the sarcoplasmic reticulum, which is located between the myofibrils (§ 3.2.2), will no longer stain with the Veratti reagent after freeze drying, although electron microscopy indicates that the structure is still present (Voyle and Lawrie, 1964).

If the plate temperature is below 60°C the historical appearance of the reconstituted muscle is similar to that of fresh (Aitken *et al.*, 1962): above this temperature there is progressively greater historical change which is paralleled by difficulty in reconstitution.

8.2.2. Physical and Biochemical Aspects

Unlike the heating involved in hot air dehydration (cf. Fig. 8.2), freeze dehydration will not change the iso-electric point of muscle if operated under optimum conditions. Moreover, instead of lowering the water-holding capacity generally, it tends to do so only at the isoelectric point (Fig. 8.4). According to Hamm and Deatherage (1960b), this loss of

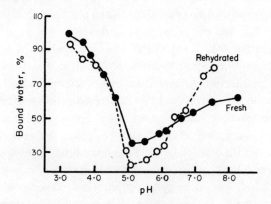

FIG. 8.4. The effect of freeze drying on the pH-hydration curve of beef muscle (Hamm, 1960). ● = fresh muscle. ○ = freeze-dried and rehydrated muscle. (Courtesy Prof. R. Hamm.)

water-holding capacity is not due to the freezing aspect of the freeze-drying process. The plate temperature during the final phase of drying is implicated. Although the latter has little effect on the total moisture content after reconstitution (Table 8.4), it affects the amount of moisture which is firmly bound (here defined as that remaining after centrifuging).

TABLE 8.4. *The Effect of Plate Temperature on Various Characteristics of Freeze-dried Meat after Rehydration*
(Aitken *et al.*, unpublished)

Characteristic	Control (frozen)	Temperature of plate (°C)				
		20°	40°	60°	80°	100°
Total moisture (per cent)	77·2	75·4	75·9	75·5	76·8	75·3
"Bound" water (per cent)	65·3	63·8	63·9	63·1	62·8	53·8
Meat solids (per cent) in reconstitution water	12·3	10·1	9·9	10·9	10·3	5·4

There is a distinct drop between 80° and 100°C in the latter. Moreover the percentage of total meat solids which is leached out by the reconstitution water is considerably less at a plate temperature of 100°C, indicating that there has been heat denaturation of sarcoplasmic proteins causing their insolubility. The contribution of sarcoplasmic proteins to water-holding capacity is also indicated by the effect of the time of reconstitution of freeze-dried meat on its bound water content. This decreases appreciably at times of reconstitution greater than 1 hr, due to the leaching out of sarcoplasmic proteins. When the plate temperatures are about 20–30°C, the accelerated freeze-drying process does not affect the extractability of the myofibrillar proteins at any pH between 5 and 7 in comparison with frozen material (Scopes, 1964). On the other hand, where the plate temperature is about 60–70°C (as is normal commercially), there is a drop in the solubility of the myofibrillar proteins, indicating some measure of denaturation (Table 8.5: Penny, Voyle and Lawrie, unpublished data), and a change in the electrophoretic pattern, indicating some alteration in the actomyosin complex (Thompson, Fox and Landmann, 1962).

TABLE 8.5. *The Percentage of Myofibrillar Protein Soluble in 0·95 M KCl-Glyceroxphosphate Buffer*, pH 6

Muscle	A. Control (low ultimate pH)		B. Adrenaline treated (high ultimate pH)	
	Frozen	Freeze dried	Frozen	Freeze dried
L. dorsi	53	41	91	85
Psoas	49	40	80	68
Biceps femoris	55	46	88	75
Semimembranosus	54	46	85	77

Clearly, in the AFD process under commercial conditions, there is some loss of water-holding capacity attributable to the effect of the plate temperature on the myofibrillar and sarcoplasmic proteins; and these changes may explain the woodiness in texture already referred to. Occasionally, even with optimum operating conditions, excessive woodiness and difficulty of reconstitution is encountered. This can be explained on the basis of exceptionally severe denaturation changes in the sarcoplasmic and myofibrillar proteins of animals, wherein post-mortem glycolysis has been very fast or where the ultimate pH has been unusually low, for example in the white muscle condition of pigs (§§ 3.4.3, 4.2.2, 5.4.1). The induction of a high ultimate pH by pre-slaughter injection of adrenaline will enhance the water-holding capacity of these proteins. This is manifested, in both cattle and pigs (Penny, Voyle and Lawrie, 1963, 1964), by the behaviour of the myofibrils from the fresh meat at various environmental pH levels; and the differences between muscles of originally high or low ultimate pH are retained after freeze drying (Fig. 8.5). It is also reflected in easy reconstitution of the dehydrated muscles (Table 8.6); and organoleptically by the virtual absence of woodiness of texture (cf. § 8.2.3).

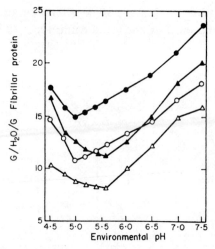

FIG. 8.5. The effect of environmental pH on water-holding capacity of myofibrils prepared from fresh or freeze-dried muscle of high or normal ultimate pH (Penny *et al.*, 1963). ● = fresh, ult. pH 6·7. ○ = rehydrated, ult. pH 6·7. ▲ = fresh, ult. pH 5·6. △ = rehydrated, ult. pH 5·6.

TABLE 8.6. *Reconstitution Ratios* (g H_2O/g *Dry Wt) of Dehydrated Muscle from Adrenaline-treated (High Ultimate* pH) *and Control (Low Ultimate* pH) *Steers*

Muscle	High ultimate pH	Low ultimate pH
Semimembranosus	3·10	1·99
Biceps femoris	3·12	1·96
Psoas	3·58	2·08
L. dorsi (lumbar)	3·22	2·02
L. dorsi (thoracic)	3·34	1·98
Deep pectoral	3·65	1·95

It is important to note that rehydration of freeze-dried meat having originally a low ultimate pH in a fluid of high ultimate pH does not enhance its water-holding capacity to the same extent as does the rehydration of freeze-dried meat having an originally high ultimate pH in water (Fig. 8.6). This may well reflect the fact that damage to sarcoplasmic proteins (and, to some extent, those of the myofibril) by the normal low ultimate pH attained during post-mortem glycolysis (Scopes and Lawrie, 1963; Bendall and Wismer-Pedersen, 1962; Scopes, 1964) cannot be completely overcome merely by raising the pH again. It may be that the protective action of high ultimate pH involves some change in the mode of chemical union between proteins and residual water. The high water-holding capacity of pre-rigor meat can also be retained by salting before the onset of rigor mortis and subsequently freeze-drying the commodity (Honikel and Hamm, 1978). The AFD process removes all the loosely held or capillary-condensed water in muscle (about 310 g/100 g dry protein), and much of the chemically bound water (about 37 g/100 g dry protein) which is attached in two layers of differing bond strength to hydrophilic groups on the proteins (Hill, 1930; Hamm, 1960), since the residual moisture content in the freeze-dried product is about 2·5 g water/100 g dry protein. In general, pork muscle is more susceptible to damage during freeze drying than in corresponding beef muscle.

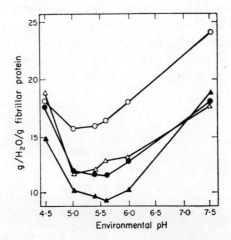

FIG. 8.6. The effect of adjusting the pH of homogenates of beef biceps femoris muscle, of high or normal ultimate pH, on water-holding capacity of myofibrils (Penny *et al.*, 1963). ○ = ult. pH 6·7. ● = ult. pH 6·7, adjusted to pH 5·6. ▲ = ult. pH 5·6. △ = ult. pH 5·6, adjusted to pH 6·7.

That proteins may survive freeze dehydration in a substantially unaltered condition is indicated by the finding that the ATP-ase activity of actomyosin in rehydrated meat may still be 80 per cent of its initial value and that the muscle fibres (as observed histologically) will still contract on the addition of ATP (Hunt and Matheson, 1958). After isolation from muscle, the ATP-ase activity of the heavy microsomal fraction and its ability to accumulate Ca^{++} ions survive freeze drying (Diehl, 1966). On subsequent storage, however, calcium-binding power is lost, due to a structural deterioration of the sarcoplasmic reticulum membranes which comprise the heavy sarcosome fraction. This may explain the myofibrillar cohesion concomitantly observed in muscle samples which have been freeze-dried intact (cf. § 8.2.1). The mildness of the AFD process is further exemplified by the survival of oxymyoglobin. Myoglobin on the exposed surfaces of the steaks used in the AFD process is particularly susceptible to oxidation or denaturation forming the brown pigments metmyoglobin or myohaemochromogen (§ 5.4.1). Yet spectroscopic study of aqueous extracts (Table 8.7) and of the meat surface (by reflectance measurements) shows that the spectrum is mainly that of oxymyoglobin, indicating that a considerable quantity of the myoglobin in the meat is not denatured by freeze drying. This is especially so at a low plate temperature (Penny, 1960a) suggesting that it is the temperature during the second phase of drying which is the important factor causing denaturation (Fig. 8.7).

TABLE 8.7. *The Effect of the AFD Process on the Proportion of Myoglobin Derivatives in Aqueous Meat Extracts*

	Met-myoglobin	Oxy-myoglobin	Myoglobin
Fresh meat	5·2	91·8	3·0
Freeze-dried meat (60°–70°C plate temp.)	30·7	69·3	0
Freeze-dried meat (30°C plate temp.)	14·7	85·3	0

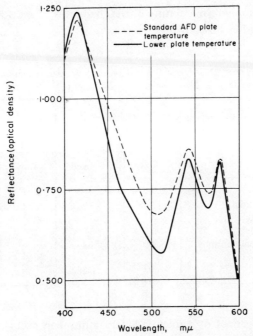

Fig. 8.7. The effect of plate temperature during freeze drying on the reflectance spectrum of dehydrated beef (Penny, 1960a). − − − − = standard plate temp. ⎯⎯⎯ = low plate temp. (Courtesy Dr. I. F. Penny.)

8.2.3. Organoleptic Aspects

It will be apparent from Table 8.7 that although the raw steaks processed by accelerated freeze drying retain much of the bright colour of fresh meat, there is a somewhat higher concentration of brown metmyoglobin on the surface. Prolongation of storage exaggerates this discoloration, which becomes worse the higher the storage temperature and the longer the time of storage (Penny *et al.*, 1963). But, as in the case of the air-dried product (§ 8.1.3) non-enzymic Maillard browning (Sharp, 1957) is also involved. The reactants glucose and glucose-6-phosphate disappear even at a residual moisture level of 2 per cent, although the reaction is faster at higher moisture levels (Matheson,

1962). The non-enzymic nature of the changes will be evident in Table 8.8: cooking has little effect.

TABLE 8.8. *The Effect of Freeze Dehydration and Storage on Glucose and Glucose-6-Phosphate in Raw and Cooked Pork*

	Glucose (mg/g dry wt)		Glucose-6-phosphate (mg/g dry wt)	
	Raw	Cooked	Raw	Cooked
Fresh	4·9	3·6	3·0	1·5
Freeze dried, initial	3·4	3·2	2·6	1·7
Freeze dried, stored for 1 month at 37°C				
(a) 2% residual moisture	1·0	1·4	1·5	1·0
(b) 10·5% residual moisture	0·4	0·4	0	0

Other aspects of organoleptic deterioration can occur at extremely low residual moisture levels. These include fat oxidation following surviving lipolytic activity (Lea, 1934).

In comparison with fresh or frozen meat, freeze-dried meat is somewhat lower in tenderness and juiciness (Penny *et al.*, 1963). The data on tenderness are shown in Table 8.9 wherein this attribute is given for various beef muscles as assessed by taste panel: objective measurements of tenderness by tenderometer (Table 8.10) confirm taste-panel results.

Some of this difference is attributable to "woodiness", although it will be seen that this characteristic is also noted in fresh (frozen) meat. The benefits of high ultimate pH (induced by pre-slaughter injection of adrenaline) in protecting muscle proteins and in enhancing their water-holding capacity, are reflected in greatly enhanced tenderness and diminished "woodiness" and these benefits are retained after freeze drying (Tables 8.9 and 8.10; Penny *et al.*, 1963). Results for pig muscles are similar (Penny *et al.*, 1964).

TABLE 8.9. *The Sum of the Tenderness[a] Rankings given by Eight Tasters for Control (Low Ultimate* pH*) and Adrenaline-treated (High Ultimate* pH*) Beef Before and After Freeze Dehydration* (after Penny *et al.,* 1963)

Muscle	A. Control (low ultimate pH)		B. Adrenaline-treated (high ultimate pH)	
	Frozen	Freeze dried	Frozen	Freeze dried
Semimembranosus	23	24	12	16
Biceps femoris	26	25	11	15
Psoas	23	25	12	14
L. dorsi (lumbar)	19	21	19	17
L. dorsi (thoracic)	26	25	11	12
Deep pectoral	25	27	10	16
Total	142	147	75	90
No. times "woodiness" detected	10	16	2	9

[a]i.e. low numbers in the table represent desirable degrees of tenderness and vice versa.

An interesting aspect of the adrenaline treatment was the differential effect it had on the various muscles in altering their resistance to shear, the semimembranosus showing the greatest increase in tenderness. The eating quality of freeze-dried meat falls both with increasing storage temperature and increasing moisture content (Thompson *et al.*, 1962). For instance, if held at 37°C it is worse than at −20°C—as manifested by tenderness, juiciness, flavour, shear force and non-enzymic browning (as measured by reflectance at 400 mμ). Again, however, a high ultimate pH in the meat is beneficial not only in enhancing eating quality but in minimizing the storage changes (Table 8.11).

Apart from the question of non-enzymic browning, the percentage of metmyoglobin is increased by a higher temperature of storage; but this also is less marked when the ultimate pH is high (Penny *et al.*, unpublished data).

TABLE 8.10. *Measurement of Work Done (Ergs × 10⁶/cm) by Tenderometer in Shearing Beef*

Muscle	A. Control (low ultimate pH)		B. Adrenaline-treated (high ultimate pH)	
	Frozen	Freeze dried	Frozen	Freeze dried
Semimembranosus	24·5	25·6	9·8	15·4
Biceps femoris	12·6	15·2	12·1	13·6
Psoas	12·9	12·4	9·2	9·5
L. dorsi (lumbar)	15·2	17·7	11·5	11·8
L. dorsi (thoracic)	12·9	17·2	6·9	9·1
Deep pectoral	18·6	19·2	14·8	18·3

TABLE 8.11. *Effect of Storage on Freeze-dried Beef L. Dorsi Muscle* (after Penny *et al.*, 1963)

Storage temperature (°C)	Ultimate pH 5·6		Ultimate pH 6·7	
	−20	37	−20	37
Tenderness	3·4	2·0	4·3	4·1
Juiciness	4·3	3·1	4·4	4·4
Flavour	4·0	4·4	4·7	4·3
Shear force (ergs × 10⁶/cm)	12·7	18·4	11·5	11·5
Reflectance (at 400 mμ)	0·15	0·50	0·13	0·35

From the nutritive point of view freeze drying does not alter the biological value of the meat proteins (Hanson, 1961) and, indeed, may enhance it (Adachi, Sheffer and Spector, 1958). Although there is a loss of about 30 per cent of the thiamin content of the meat during freeze drying, this would occur on cooking in any case. The process causes a similar loss in riboflavin from mutton but not from beef or pork (Hanson, 1961).

Rehydration of freeze-dried meat with aqueous solutions of tenderizing enzymes such as papain, helps to offset the somewhat adverse effect of freeze drying on tenderness (Wang and Maynard, 1955; Penny, 1960b). In the U.S.A. freeze-dried steaks are now available in a moisture-proof pack with a compartment containing dried proteolytic enzymes, the latter being added to the reconstitution water on rehydration.

Apart from its value under emergency conditions, freeze dehydration can provide a very palatable and nourishing meat which will resist spoilage for a considerable period without refrigeration in remote areas, and it has been successfully used during the ascent of Everest and in trans-Antarctic expeditions. Because of its lightness and high protein content, it is likely to prove valuable in future space flights. This will occur when these involve the provision of living quarters over extended periods. The weight of all other forms of meat would seem to preclude their use in such a context.

8.3. CURING

The empirical observation that salting would preserve meat without refrigeration was made several thousand years ago. By 1000 B.C. salted and smoked meats were available (Jensen, 1949). The efficacy of the process, and of the many variants which have developed (including the use of sugar), arises primarily from the discouragement to microbial growth caused by the enhanced osmotic pressure in such products. As time has passed, cured meats have come to be valued for their organoleptic quality *per se* and there has thus been a tendency to lower the concentration of the curing ingredients. This has made these mildly cured or semi-preserved products more liable to spoilage and reintroduced the need for some degree of refrigeration. Recognition of the value of sodium nitrate in producing an attractive colour may well have been due to adventitious impurities in the sodium chloride employed. At the end of the nineteenth century it has become recognized that meat-curing brines contained nitrite, that this was the colour-fixing agent and that the nitrite was produced by a reduction of nitrate.

Preservation was originally effected by sprinkling salt on to the meat surfaces. In due course the meat was placed in brine; but both dry salt curing and tank curing have been practised until the present time. More recently, vascular pumping, or multiple injection of salt solution has been employed to hasten curing. Granulated salt was formerly called "corn" and accounts for the term corned beef. It is of interest to note that the crystalline form and size of the salt used may affect its preservative properties. Smoking over a wood fire was originally employed to enhance the preservative action of curing, but it is now used mainly because people like the flavour of the smoked product.

As we have seen, the characteristics of the muscles of pork, beef and mutton are different (§ 4.3) and this is reflected in the organoleptic quality of the cured meats made from them. As a result, now that other methods of preservation are available, salted mutton and beef have fallen in popularity, whereas the various forms of salted pork, which are widely regarded as attractive, continue to be extensively prepared. Predominant consideration will, therefore, be given here to cured pork. Nevertheless, because of the limited supply and high price of pig carcases in New Zealand, there has been renewed interest in the possibility of curing of mutton and lamb (Moore, Locker and Daines, 1976–77). Lamb is far superior to mutton in this respect; and the product, although distinguishable from cured pork, is equally acceptable.

The part of the pig's carcase which was most difficult to cure was the top of the hind limb where the depth of meat was greatest. Consequently prolonged curing was frequently required, sometimes up to 80 days (Jensen, 1949). Perhaps for this reason the methods employed for curing this area are particularly diversified. Where it is cut off from the side and separately cured it is referred to as ham. The names of the available types in the United Kingdom—e.g. Yorkshire, Suffolk, Cumberland, Bradenham, Belfast—indicate more or less subtle variations in the process. Where the area concerned is cured on the side it is referred to as gammon.

Before considering the biochemical factors involved in curing, it is desirable to outline the procedure used in the production of Wiltshire sides, since this underlies most other curing methods.

8.3.1. *Wiltshire Cure*

Much of the following description is based on that given by Callow (1934). Pigs, preferably well rested, are anaesthetized (by electrical shock or carbon dioxide: § 5.2) and bled. The carcase is placed into a scalding tank at about 63°C to loosen the hair which is then generally removed mechanically. The carcase is then singed to remove coarse hair, sprayed with cold water and cleaned. The backbone is chopped out during butchering operations and the carcase (now as sides) is cooled either at ambient temperatures or in a chiller. After cooling, the sides are trimmed. This involves removal of the psoas muscle, the scapula and the aitch bone (bones of pelvis). The trimmed sides are next chilled to the temperature of the curing cellar (3–7°C) where curing takes place in four stages: (i) brine (pickle) is pumped into the sides, (ii) the sides are either sprinkled with dry salt or placed in a tank of brine, (iii) the sides are removed and stacked for some time in a maturing cellar (at 3–7°C) and (iv) the sides may be smoked. Higher temperatures speed the curing and maturation processes but increase the danger of spoilage from the growth of undesirable bacteria and moulds. It has been suggested that the processing time for cured sides would be considerably shorter and their microbial status better, if they were stitch-pumped at body temperature immediately after slaughter, then placed in brine at − 10°C (Kassai and Kárpáti, 1963). Henrickson *et al.*, (1969) compared the effects of curing pork with brine at 35°C (followed by swift chilling) with normal practice. The rate of salt penetration—and the extent of nitrosomyoglobin formation—were both somewhat greater in the former case.

For speed, the brine is introduced by pumping under a pressure of about 75–100 lb/in². The concentration of sodium chloride in the injected brine (pump pickle) is about 25–30 per cent. It also contains 2·5–4 per cent of potassium or sodium nitrate; and in some cases 0·5–1 per cent sugar. About 18–25 injections are required, most being given to the gammon region. The total amount of brine injected is about 5 per cent of the weight of the side. The "shoulder pockets" (scapula cavities) are filled with solid salt and the sides placed in curing tanks.

In a large tank the sides are stacked about 12 deep and lightly covered with sodium chloride and potassium nitrate in the ratio 10 : 1. They are battened down, brine is run in and the sides remain submerged in it for 4–5 days. The composition of this brine (tank pickle) is between 20 and 28 per cent with respect to sodium chloride and 3–4 per cent with respect to potassium nitrate when first prepared; but before it can be used in curing it must be seeded with specific, salt-tolerant micro-organisms. They are encouraged to grow by traces of protein leached from meat previously immersed in the brine and they are responsible for converting nitrate to nitrite. The latter is essential for colour fixation. The number of micro-organisms (and hence the nitrite content of the pickle) can be controlled by increasing the sodium chloride content of the brine if the nitrite is too high and by omitting the sprinkling of the sides if it is too low (Ingram, Hawthorne and Gatherum, 1947).

After removal from the brine tanks the sides are stacked in cellars for 7–14 days or longer. During this period, known as maturation, the sodium chloride, the nitrate and the nitrite become more evenly distributed throughout the musculature and the typical colour and flavour bacon develop.

The bacon thus produced may be consumed unsmoked (green) but probably the greater proportion is smoked for 2–3 days. Apart from adding flavour, the smoke contains phenols and phenanthrene derivatives. These have a preservative action and also delay rancidity in the fat on the surfaces of the bacon sides. If the temperature is allowed to rise too high during smoking, on the other hand, deep-seated bacterial growth may be encouraged.

A relatively recent development in the preparation of bacon is sliced curing (Holmes, 1960). In this process slices of pork muscle 2–8 mm thick are passed for 2–15 min through a brine containing 8–10 per cent sodium chloride and 0·02 per cent sodium nitrite. Maturation occurs over a few hours. The process gives a uniform product in less than a day instead of the 10–21 days of the traditional Wiltshire process. The brines can be filtered under pressure to remove organisms which gradually accumulate, thus regenerating the brine and permitting a substantial saving in costs (Dyett, 1969).

The addition of nitrite obviates reliance on micro-organisms to produce it from nitrate; but the level must not rise above 0·05 per cent otherwise there is a danger of toxicity through destruction of blood pigments and of vitamin A (Roberts and Sell, 1963). In this connection it may be mentioned that if all the nitrate added during traditional curing were converted to nitrite, the level of the latter would rise to 0·25 per cent (Eddy, Gatherum and Kitchell, 1960). Fortunately, most of the nitrate appears to be changed in some other way or is not broken down (Eddy *et al.*, 1960). That bacon could be made by the direct addition of nitrite and without bacterial intervention was shown about 25 years ago (Brooks *et al.*, 1940). Endeavours have been made to avoid the remote possibility of excess production of nitrite from nitrate in the traditional Wiltshire cure, by omitting the use of nitrate in the pickle and adding only about 200 ppm of nitrite. Such bacon is said to develop the flavour associated with the traditional cure provided it is permitted to mature for a reasonable period (e.g. upwards of 2 weeks). In such a cure the nitrite content clearly *cannot* exceed 200 ppm. Another recent development in curing is the "tumbling" of pork in rotating drums. In effect this procedure involves massaging the pieces of meat against one another in the presence of about 0·6% of their weight of salt. This draws out salt-soluble proteins (mainly actomyosin) to the meat surface and enhances the overall water-holding capacity. Tumbling can shorten the curing period to 24 hours (U.S. Pat. No. 3 076 713, 1960).

In general, the composition of cured meat differs markedly from fresh (McCance and Widdowson, 1946). As would be expected, its ash content is high (about 5 per cent). There is also less water (about 45–55 per cent if tank cured and about 25 per cent if dry salt cured compared with about 75 per cent raw), less protein (about 14 per cent compared with 20 per cent) and considerably more fat.

8.3.2. Biochemical Aspects

8.3.2.1. Curing

The biochemical mechanisms of curing was extensively investigated by Callow (1932, 1933, 1936). During curing, the initial outward flow of water and soluble proteins from the muscle to the brine by virtue of the higher osmotic pressure of the latter, is eventually reversed. This is because the salt, which diffuses inwards, forms a complex with the proteins of the meat which has a higher osmotic pressure than the brine. Normally, diffusion of sodium chloride into the muscles is rapid, equilibrium being established in about 48 hr in 25 per cent brine (Callow, 1930). The slower the diffusion inwards, however, the longer is the period of outflow of water from the muscle. Slow inward diffusion is favoured by immersion of the meat in relatively weak salt solutions and by a close microstructure in the tissue. The amounts of protein extracted are a function of salt concentration, the maximum being in 6–9 per cent brine. Smaller amounts are extracted by distilled water or brine of higher salt concentrations (Callow, 1931). Nevertheless, the accumulation of salt is linear with the salt concentration of the brine (Wistreich, Morse and Kenyon, 1959).

The greater water-binding capacity of the salt protein complex is indicated by the fact that about 61 g out of the 73 g of water in 100 g lean pork could be expressed mechanically, whereas only about 26 g of the 63 g water in 100 g lean bacon could be so removed (Callow, 1927a). Studies on the electrical resistance of meat and bacon suggest that this difference arises because of the more swollen structure in the latter (Banfield and Callow, 1934, 1935). It is particularly interesting that the electrical resistance of the muscles of pork sides which have been cooled quickly and in which, therefore, post-mortem glycolysis is relatively slow (§ 4.2.2) is higher than that of those which have been cooled slowly and in which, therefore, post-mortem glycolysis is relatively fast. The high resistance of the muscles of rapidly cooled sides gradually falls to the level of that of slowly cooled sides over some 14 days' storage at 0°C. It is conceivable that slow denaturation of the sarcoplasmic proteins (§ 5.4.1), changes in the binding of ions by the proteins (K^+ is taken up,

Ca^{++} is slowly released on storage: Arnold *et al.*, 1956) or the slow synaeresis of actomyosin filaments could be implicated. The degree of synaeresis or shortening of actomyosin filaments increases with the speed of onset of rigor mortis (§ 4.2.3). Its extent could be initially restricted by fast cooling; but shortening might slowly continue on storage to the point immediately attained in slowly cooled muscles. Any or all of these circumstances could lower the resistance of the fluid phase of the muscle; but the phenomenon has not so far been elucidated.

It may be mentioned that quick chilling, whilst lowering shrinkage losses at this stage in processing, appears to be associated with an increase in the loss of fluid from the muscles during curing and maturation. As a result there is no overall gain (Gatherum, 1956, unpublished data; Jul, Nielsen and Petersen, 1958).

Another circumstance causing high electrical resistance is a high ultimate pH (Callow, 1936). Partly because of the greater difficulty of salt penetration into such muscles, and of the direct effect of high ultimate pH in stimulating bacterial growth (§ 6.3.3), bacon made therefrom tended to taint frequently when curing by the dry salt method was common. Indeed, tainted bacon was associated with factory killing but not with farm killing, for the journey from farm to factory caused sufficient fatigue and depletion of muscle glycogen (§ 5.1.2) to give a high ultimate pH (Callow, 1936). Taint arises less frequently with tank curing, because a high concentration of salt builds up quickly and discourages bacterial growth—even if the pH is high. It may be undesirable, nevertheless, because of its fiery colour and sticky consistency ("glazy" bacon). On the other hand, organoleptic advantages are claimed for bacon of relatively high ultimate pH, including increased tenderness, and decreased shrink on curing and cooking (Kauffman *et al.*, 1964). A high ultimate pH has been deliberately induced in bacon by pre-slaughter injection of adrenaline (Rongey, Kahlenberg and Naumann, 1959) and by incorporating phosphate in the curing brine (Hall, 1950; Brissey, 1952).

It may be mentioned that the salt flavour of bacon is not closely related to its salt content, since apparently only some of the salt has time to affect the palate before the bacon is swallowed (Ingram, 1949a). This effect is particularly marked in the swollen structure of bacon at high ultimate pH. Attempts have been made to cure pork with acid brines (about pH 4·5) in order to enhance antimicrobial action, but increased disappearance of nitrite, precipitation of protein in the brine and somewhat lowered eating quality in the bacon more than offset the moderate increase in storage life brought about thereby (Ingram, 1949b). The slower penetration of salt into pork muscle of high ultimate pH has been attributed to the physical effect of greater muscle fibre size rather than to a direct chemical change (Körmendy and Gantner, 1958).

Proper resting before slaughter, or the feeding of sugar (Bate-Smith, 1937a; Gibbons and Rose, 1950; Wismer-Pedersen, 1959b), builds up muscle glycogen, giving a lower ultimate pH and increasing storage life (although this latter point has been disputed). According to Wismer-Pedersen (1959b) the ultimate pH of the muscle of sugar-fed pigs was about 0·2 pH units lower than that of controls. They gained more weight during curing (5·65 per cent compared with 5·49 per cent) and shrunk less during maturation (2·75 per cent compared with 3·16 per cent). Wismer-Pedersen believed that the enhanced water-holding capacity of the meat of low ultimate pH (contrary to expectation) was due to the greater ease of salt penetration possible with its more open structure and the consequently greater formation of salt–protein complex. The higher concentration of reducing sugars in the muscles of the sugar-fed pigs may also have been partly responsible.

It would be anticipated that the lower water-holding capacity of the muscles of pigs affected by the so-called PSE condition (§§ 3.4.3 and 4.2.2) would be reflected in their reaction to curing. This was studied by Wismer-Pedersen (1960). Ground meat from muscles, in which post-mortem glycolysis was fast, and in which the structure was watery, had a poor absorption of salt compared with normal meat, the weight of brine absorbed being about 7 per cent in the former and 40 per cent in the latter. The weight gain of sides from watery pork during curing was about 3 per cent whereas it was about 7 per cent in normal pork. It must be presumed that the greater penetrability of the watery pork to salt, which would have been expected to increase water binding, is more than offset by loss of water-holding capacity through damage to the proteins under the abnormally severe conditions of post-mortem glycolysis.

Freezing affects the structure of muscular tissue (§ 7.1.2.1): the penetration of salt into pork which has been frozen and thawed is about 20 per cent greater than into fresh meat (Table 8.12; Callow, 1939); and when dealing with frozen carcases curers shorten the tanking period by 1 day in every 5.

TABLE 8.12. *Salt Content of Unfrozen and Thawed Pork Muscle during Curing*

Time of immersion in 25% brine (min)	Salt (%)	
	Unfrozen	Frozen and thawed
5	1·5	2·2
10	2·1	2·7
20	3·0	3·6
60	4·5	5·6

Apart from the salt concentrations of the brine (and the time of contact with the meat) and the microscopic structure of the musculature, various other factors affect the penetration of salt during curing. An increased temperature will increase the velocity of penetration (Callow, 1934; Wistreich *et al.,* 1959; Holmes, 1960; Henrickson *et al.,* 1969); but this obviously requires the strictest hygiene since it increases the risk of microbial spoilage. Curing brines containing phosphates (especially polyphosphates) have been used to enhance the water-binding capacity of bacon and hams (Taylor, 1958). In some cases, the effect may be due to an elevated pH; but pyrophospate is said to have a specific effect because it resembles ATP and interacts with actomyosin (Bendall, 1954). On the other hand, Hamm (1955) believes that the polyphosphates increase water-binding capacity by sequestering calcium ions.

8.3.2.2. *Maturing*

Little is yet known about the reactions which cause the development of flavour when sides of pork, after immersion in curing brine, are removed and stacked in cellars to mature. But there has been much research on the development of colour, both desirable and undesirable during processing.

The attractive red colour of cured meats before cooking is essentially that of nitrosomyoglobin. *In vitro* nitric oxide can combine directly with myoglobin, and indeed a process for producing bacon by subjecting pork to a high pressure of nitric oxide gas has been devised in the U.S.A. Normally, however, the sequence of events in cured meats is more complicated. In the latter, nitrite firstly reacts with oxymyoglobin (i.e. in the presence of oxygen) to form metmyoglobin (Greenberg, Lester and Haggard, 1942). Although in the absence of oxygen, nitrite reacts with

$$NO_2^- + MygO_2 \longrightarrow NO_3^- + MygOH + O_2$$

(Nitrite)   (Oxymyoglobin)   (Nitrate)   (Metmyoglobin)

haemoglobin to form equimolar quantities of methaemoglobin and nitrosohaemoglobin, if substances capable of reducing methaemoglobin and nitrite are not present (Brooks, 1937), with myoglobin these conditions produce only metmyoglobin (C. L. Walters, personal communication). Subsequently, although brine micro-organisms *can* convert nitrite to nitric oxide (Eddy *et al.,* 1960), the reduction of both metmyoglobin to myoglobin and of nitrite to nitric oxide is probably brought about by surviving activity of enzyme systems of the muscle itself (Watts and Lehmann, 1952; Walters and Taylor, 1963, 1964). Some years ago, Fox (1962) and Fox and Thomsom (1963) showed that nitric oxide can react directly with metmyoglobin and that the complex could then be reduced to nitrosomyoglobin. The rate of formation of nitrosomyoglobin is proportional to the concentration of nitrite up to the point where the nitrite: metmyoglobin ratio is 5 : 1. Beyond this point nitrite appears to be inhibitory; and this may explain why the conversion of myoglobin to the cured meat pigment is frequently incomplete despite apparently much more than adequate nitrite concentrations. Detailed studies have elucidated the details of nitrosomyoglobin formation. The mechanism is as follows: (i) nitrite oxidizes myoglobin to metmyoglobin; (ii) nitrite also oxidizes ferrocytochrome *c* to nitrosoferricytochrome *c* (catalysed by cytochrome oxidase); (iii) the nitroso group is transferred from nitrosoferricytochrome *c* to the metmyoglobin by NADH-cytochrome *c* reductase action, forming nitrosometmyoglobin; and (iv) the nitrosometmyoglobin is reduced to nitrosomyoglobin by enzyme systems of the muscle mitochondria (even in the presence of nitrite concentrations causing rapid oxidation of oxymyoglobin). Nitrosometmyoglobin also autoreduces to nitrosomyoglobin under anaerobic conditions; but aerobically it breaks down to give metmyoglobin (Walters and Taylor, 1965; Walters, Casselden and Taylor, 1967).

In processing sausages, emulsion curing has been employed in recent years. This involves cooking the meat emulsion, immediately after adding the curing ingredients, for 90 min at 75°C. The formation of nitrosomyoglobin in these conditions is much better in the absence of air (Ando and Nagata, 1970). In comparison with entire porcine muscles, colour development was decreasingly satisfactory with fractions consisting of sarcoplasm, mitochondria, microsomes or myofibrils—a finding of interest in relation to the colour fixing mechanism.

Although reduction of nitrite to nitric oxide can be effected either by bacteria or by the muscle's own enzyme system, the reduction of nitrate can be effected only by the former. Hence the need for careful control of bacon curing brines, when nitrite is employed, to ensure that the necessary microbial reduction of nitrate will occur. Moreover, various contaminating organisms in the brine can exert a deleterious effect on the cured meat, e.g. souring, putrefaction and excessive sweetening caused, respectively, by *Lactobacillus, Vibrio* and *Bacillus* (Leistner, 1960). When nitrite is added as such (Brooks *et al.*, 1940; Holmes, 1960) colour fixation is a purely chemical process.

The stability of the red colour of bacon is enhanced if nitrosomyoglobin is converted to nitric oxide myohaemochromogen in which the globin portion of the molecule is denatured, e.g. by salts or heat, as in cooking. Thus the same agents which cause discoloration in fresh meat are advantageous in retaining the colour of cured meats (Watts and Lehmann, 1952).

Incorporation of ascorbic acid in the curing brine accelerates the reduction of metmyoglobin and probably the conversion of nitrite to nitric oxide (Riedesel and Watts, 1952). Yet nitrite alone converts oxymyoglobin to metmyoglobin; and ascorbic acid alone gives a mixture of metmyoglobin and choleglobin (Lemberg and Legg, 1950, cf. Table 10.1). Choleglobin may also form in meat when micro-organisms producing hydrogen peroxide are present. In fresh meat, hydrogen peroxide is quickly destroyed by catalase; but the latter is destroyed during curing and thus cured meats are more liable to become green. Another green pigment, which may appear during maturation, is associated with the production of hydroxylamine during the reduction of nitrate (Iskandaryan, 1958).

At an elevated pH the oxidation of nitrosomyoglobin to metmyoglobin is retarded (Urbain and Jensen, 1940). Moreover, the activity of the muscle enzyme systems which are capable of reducing metmyoglobin and nitrite is also increased (Lawrie, 1952b; Walters and Taylor, 1963). As mentioned above, a high pH may be induced in muscle by the pre-slaughter injection of adrenaline; a similar result may be achieved by the incorporation of an alkaline phosphate in the cure (Hall, 1950; Brissey, 1952). Metmyoglobin, formed by exposing cured bacon to the atmosphere can be reduced by surviving enzyme systems in the cured musculature, and reconverted to nitrosomyoglobin, by repacking the bacon *in vacuo* and storing it at 5°C for 1–2 weeks (Cheah, 1976). Lactic dehydrogenase and NADH are involved.

8.3.2.3. *Smoking*

Smoke, generally produced by the slow combustion of sawdust derived from hard woods (consisting of about 40–60 per cent cellulose, 20–30 per cent hemicellulose, and 20–30 per cent lignin), inhibits microbial growth, retards fat oxidation and imparts flavour to cured meat (Callow, 1927a, 1932). Traditionally, smoking was uncontrolled and consisted in burning the wood beneath the meat. The process can be more speedily carried out, and a product of consistent quality produced, by controlled smoking in a kiln and by electrostatic deposition of wood smoke particles (Cutting and Bannerman, 1951; Forster and Jason, 1954).

Part of the bactericidal action of smoke is due to formaldehyde (Callow, 1927b; Hess, 1928); but the composition of wood smoke is complex. According to Foster and Simpson (1961) it consists of two phases—a disperse, liquid phase containing smoke particles and a dispersing gas phase. Direct deposition of smoke particles makes a negligible contribution to the process: vapour absorption by surface and interstitial water is much more important. The vapour phase can be separated into acids, phenols, carbonyls, alcohols and polycyclic hydrocarbons (Hollenbeck and Marinelli, 1963). The major components include formic, acetic, butyric, caprylic, vanillic and syringic acids, dimethoxyphenol, methyl glyoxal, furfural, methanol, ethanol, octanal, acetaldehyde, diacetyl, acetone and 3,4-benzpyrene; but there are said to be more than 200 components (Wilson, 1963). The various alcohols and acids are derived from the celluloses and hemicelluloses which decompose at a lower temperature than lignin. The latter decomposes above 310°C, yielding phenolic substances and tars.

The detection of carcinogenic compounds such as 3,4-benzpyrene and 1,2,5,6-phenanthracene has led to studies of the effect of smoke generating conditions on their production. They are formed from lignin above 350°C and must be present, generally, since the temperature of the combustion zone is about 1000°C (Milner, 1963). Although it is felt that the danger of carcinogenesis from smoked meat is extremely small (Keller and Heidtmann, 1955) there have been many attempts to produce carcinogen-free smoke, for example, by condensation, followed by fractional distillation. The selected fraction is diluted with water in which the benzpyrenes are insoluble (Lapshin, 1962). The use of such liquid smokes is increasing on the continent; and they may be supplemented by the addition of specific phenolic substances having a fruity flavour and odour (Wilson, 1963). The composition of liquid smoke has also been elucidated by gas liquid chromatography (Fiddler, Doerr and Wasserman, 1970).

The flavour, imparted by smoking, varies according to the conditions used to produce the smoke (Tilgner *et al.*, 1962). Moreover, the same smoke will produce different aromas with different meats. To some extent, therefore, the flavour of the smoked product depends on the reaction between the components of the smoke and the functional groups of the meat proteins. Thus phenols and polyphenols react with —SH groups and carbonyls with amino groups (Krylova, Bazarova and Kuznetsnova, 1962). Organoleptic evaluation of the phenolic substances present in wood smoke suggests that guaiacol is the most effective (Wasserman, 1966).

8.3.3. *Organoleptic Aspects*

Unlike dehydration or freeze dehydration, curing is not designed to preserve meat in a condition resembling that of the fresh commodity. Indeed, cured meats are valued for the differences in organoleptic quality produced by curing. It may be mentioned that the biological value of the proteins is not lowered by curing (Dunker *et al.*, 1953) and the vitamins of the B group are almost unaffected (Schweigert, McIntire and Elvehjem, 1944). During storage, cured meats deteriorate in the first instance because of discoloration, secondly because of oxidative rancidity in the fat and thirdly on account of microbial changes—the latter having become of somewhat greater importance since the advent of prepackaged methods of sale.

Although the pigment of cured meats (nitrosomyoglobin or nitric oxide myohaemochromogen) is stable in the absence of oxygen, or even under vacuum (Urbain and Jensen, 1940), its oxidation to metmyoglobin is very rapid when oxygen is present (Watts, 1954). Unlike myoglobin itself, where the rate of oxidation is maximal at 4 mm oxygen partial pressure, the rate of nitrosomyoglobin oxidation increases directly with increasing oxygen tension (Brooks, 1935). The only practical and effective anti-oxidant so far extensively used is ascorbic acid, either incorporated in the curing brine or sprayed on to the surface of the product after maturing (cf. § 8.3.2.2.).

Nitrosomyoglobin and nitric oxide myohaemochromogen are much more susceptible to light than myoglobin. Cured meats may fade in 1 hr under display lighting conditions, whereas fresh meats will not alter over 3 days (Watts, 1954). The latter are not affected by visible light, although they oxidize under ultraviolet radiation. The pigments of cured meats are equally affected by both. Since light accelerates oxidative changes only in the presence of oxygen, however, vacuum packaging, or packaging under nitrogen, can eliminate the effect—although, of course, adding to the cost of the product. Occasionally, a particularly swift fading of the red pigment of cured meat is observed. In such cases the labile form may be nitric oxide metmyoglobin and not nitrosomyoglobin or nitrosomyohaemochromogen, since *in vitro* the former is very easily dissociated by oxygen forming brown metmyoglobin (A. McM. Taylor, personal communication). If this is so, it suggests that the enzyme systems in the muscle which reduce nitrite and metmyoglobin are not identical.

In uncooked bacon and hams the maximum formation of nitrosomyoglobin is attained with a high ultimate pH, whereas in the cooked products a low ultimate pH gives a greater proportion of cured pigment (Hornsey, 1959).

Salt has an accelerating effect on the oxidation of fat. As a result, cured meats are more liable than fresh to spoil through oxidative rancidity in the fat (Lea, 1931). For this reason it is preferable to import frozen pork and cure it than to import frozen bacon (Callow, 1931). The process of curing reduces the resistance of pork fat to oxidation to a much greater extent than would be expected if the direct influence of temperature were the sole factor involved. This is said to be because salt accelerates the action of a lipoxidase present in the muscle (Lea, 1937). Smoking decreases oxidative rancidity, partly on account of the phenolic anti-oxidants it contains (cf. § 8.2.3.3). Exclusion of oxygen by storage under carbon dioxide in the case of sides (Callow, 1932) effectively prevents fat oxidation in cold storage; but the concentration of the gas required is dangerous and also difficult to maintain. For packaging, as already indicated, gas packs employing nitrogen, or vacuum packs, are effective.

Unfortunately, ascorbic acid, notwithstanding that it preserves the colour of cured meats, can accelerate the oxidation of fat when the tocopherol content of the fat is low (Abrahamson, 1949; Scarborough and Watts, 1949) or in the absence of other specific fat anti-oxidants. Ascorbic acid has an inhibitory effect on fat oxidation, however, when a metal-chelating agent (e.g. polyphosphate) is present (Lehmann and Watts, 1951). As in the case of nitrosomyoglobin, light accelerates the oxidation of fat (Lea, 1939). In addition to the independent oxidation of unsaturated fatty acids and pigments in cured meats, each accelerates the oxidation of the other (Robinson, 1924; Niell and Hastings, 1925; Tappel, 1952). The effect is eliminated in cooked cured products, since it depends on the presence of relatively undenatured proteins.

Apart from the general preservative effect of salt, the storage life of cured meats is enhanced by the specific antimicrobial action of nitrite in the curing brines (§ 6.3.3). As indicated in § 7.1.1.2, however, the recent development of prepackaging has introduced new potential hazards of spoilage from microbial action. Thus, while the procedure obviously lowers the risk of contamination of the product after wrapping, it increases the possibility of contamination during preparation, especially as large areas of cut surface are frequently exposed (Ingram, 1962). The relatively high salt content of bacon, and its own halophilic microflora, tend to discourage the growth of the kind of micro-organisms likely to be introduced during handling: but with cooked, cured products and, especially, semi-preserved items, the nature and number of introduced contaminants might have a pronounced effect on the organoleptic behaviour of the product and, if they happened to be pathogens, on its safety.

Because vacuum packaging helps to prevent the oxidation of fat and pigments in cured meats, it is frequently employed. As a result the atmosphere within the pack may be altered by surviving microbial activity. For example, oxygen (residual) may be absorbed and carbon dioxide generated (Ingram, 1962). This circumstance would inhibit the normal microflora of cured meats, causing their replacement by other micro-organisms capable of changing flavour, odour and perhaps the safety of the products, e.g. lactic acid bacteria will grow, causing souring

(Kitchell and Ingram, 1963). Higher temperatures of storage will, of course, increase the number of micro-organisms; and the eating quality decreases faster. It is of interest, however, that bacterial numbers reach their maximum many days *before* the eating quality is noticeably affected (Cavett, 1962; Kitchell and Ingram, 1963). Unpacked bacon generally goes off organoleptically when the bacterial load has attained only 10 per cent of its final maximum (Haines, 1933). The development of unpleasant odours may be related to the preferential growth of certain types of micrococci which split fat and protein. Above 20°C organisms like *Staph. aureus* dominate the microflora (Cavett, 1962), when the spoilage odour is "scented-sour"; and at 30°C it is putrid. The tendency for prepacked cured meats (like other pre-packed products) to be subjected to temperature conditions which would not be considered suitable for meat in more traditional form, makes such spoilage a distinct possibility.

Although the potential nitrite content of bacon, represented by the nitrate employed, is not attained in normal practice because of destruction of both nitrite and nitrate by bacterial or tissue enzymes (Eddy *et al.,* 1960; Walters and Taylor, 1963) dangerously high concentrations of nitrite (0·27 per cent) can occur, if rarely, in vacuum-packaged bacon (Bardsley and Taylor, 1962). The necessary conditions are as yet unknown, but temperatures of storage about 15–20°C cause maximum nitrite accumulation (Eddy and Ingram, 1965).

The possibility that carcinogenic nitrosomines may be produced from nitrite in curing processes has been raised (Lijinsky and Epstein, 1970), but so far there has been no evidence to indicate that any public health hazard exists with cured meats. A random survey of hams showed that less than one part per billion of *N*-nitroso dimethylamine was present (Fiddler *et al.,* 1971). Heating of fat, especially at high temperature, increases the concentration of this substance (Patterson and Mottram, 1974). It should be mentioned that about 65 per cent of the nitrite ingested by man is that present in human saliva (Greenberg, 1975). At the low concentration of nitrite in cured meats, amines form nitrosoamines only with difficulty (Walters, 1973). Nevertheless, there have been vigorous efforts to lower the residual nitrite contents of such products. Although the pigment nitrosomyoglobin requires only 5 ppm of nitrite for its formation, a stable pink colour—and the variability of myoglobin concentration between muscles—necessitates 50 ppm. For the development of bacon flavour, 5–100 ppm is needed; and, most importantly, a minimum of 100 ppm is required to inhibit *Cl. botulinum* (Anon., 1974a). *Cl. botulinum* has been demonstrated in pork in the United Kingdom; and in pasteurized, cured meat heat treatment, nitrite concentration and storage temperature are important factors in determining whether growth of *Cl. botulinum* types A and B will occur (Roberts and Ingram, 1976). The frequent production of toxin at 15°C emphasizes the need for refrigerated storage of pasteurized cured meat products and the dangers which might arise if nitrite were to be markedly reduced in such products, without any compensatory safeguard.

8.3.4. *Intermediate Moisture Meat*

The need by expeditions and similar groups for palatable and nutritious food which would be stable under tropical conditions (Brockmann, 1970) and for astronauts (Klicka, 1969) has led to the development of intermediate moisture food technology. The intention is to lower water activity to the point at which bacteria will not grow, even at high ambient temperature, without lowering the water content to the point at which the product becomes unpalatable. As usually applied, the method involves the soaking of the food in an infusing solution of higher osmotic pressure so that, after equilibration, its water activity is lowered to the desired level. Equilibration can be accelerated by raising the temperature, as in the cook-soak-equilibration procedure (Hollis, Kaplow, Klose and Halik, 1968).

As applied to meat, the lean is cut into portions about 1 cm in volume and immersed in about one and a half times their weight of infusing solution. This is aqueous, containing about 10 per cent chloride, 0·5 per cent of an antimycotic and sufficient glycerol (between 33–40 per cent) to achieve a water activity of about 0·82–0·86. The mixture is heated to 70°C for 15 minutes in cans (Pavey, 1972). After a subsequent period of about 15 hours at room temperature, the meat pieces are surface-dried and stored in impermeable Cryovac bags. Such meat will remain acceptable for several months at 38°C, although it undergoes textural and colour changes. At first it becomes more tender, there being a concomitant breakdown of collagen: later there is increasing toughness which is associated with Maillard-type cross-linking reactions (Obanu, Ledward and Lawrie, 1975).

CHAPTER 9

THE STORAGE AND PRESERVATION OF MEAT

III. DIRECT MICROBIAL INHIBITION

In Chapters 7 and 8 methods of preserving meat were considered which depended essentially in discouraging microbial growth through the creation of unfavourable environments in the meat. As would be apparent from Chaper 6, other modes of preservation are possible. These involve action more directly inhibitory or lethal to moulds and bacteria. The latter may be destroyed by ionizing radiation or poisoned, either by specific microbial poisons (antibiotics) or by substances of general toxicity for biological tissues which are virtually harmless to consumers at the levels effective against micro-organisms (chemical preservatives).

9.1. IONIZING RADIATION

Of the many types of ionizing radiation which are known, only high energy cathode rays or soft X-rays from generators and γ-rays from radioactive sources (e.g. Co^{60}) are useful in practice (Hannan, 1955). Whatever the type of radiation used, it is important that the energy level of the rays should not exceed about 9 MeV since otherwise an induced radioactivity may arise in certain elements in the meat (McElhinney *et al.*, 1949), although this effect would not be large at energy levels below about 15 MeV (Hannan, 1955). In fact, energy levels above a few MeV are not practicable.

The relative characteristics of cathode rays, soft X-rays and γ-rays will not be discussed here; the former are more useful for the treatment of surfaces, the latter where treatment in depth is necessary. Within broad limits the important factor is the *total* dose received by the product, but there is evidence that if it is delivered at a high rate there may be a greater biological effect and less chemical change than at a low rate (Hannan, 1955).

The advantages of ionizing radiation for food preservation include their highly efficient inactivation of bacteria, the low *total* chemical change they cause and the appreciable thickness of material which can be treated after packing in containers—even those made of metal. Some of the disadvantages will be considered below.

9.1.1. *Chemical and Biochemical Aspects*

As the adjective signifies, ionizing radiations produce ions and other chemically excited molecules in the exposed medium; but this is only the first of a series of chemical effects many of which are not beneficial and have to be offset against their antimicrobial action. The activated molecules react further and in unusual ways, forming free radicals, polymers and, in the presence of oxygen, peroxides. In meat, and in other foods, where there is a substantial aqueous phase, destruction of organic molecules also takes place indirectly—largely through their reaction with the H atoms and OH radicals of irradiated water molecules, whereby they are reduced or oxidized respectively (Dainton, 1948; Hannan, 1955).

Proteins are the principal organic constituents of meat. The changes produced in them by ionizing radiations are determined both by the intrinsic nature of the proteins and by the dose. In general, the amount of change detected by the consumer arises from alterations in only a small proportion of the total molecules exposed. The effects in meat are less than they would be in some other foods since much of the water it contains is bound—thus limiting secondary reactions. Moreover, many substances are present which can act as free radical acceptors. There is little destruction of amino acids as combined in the proteins, but soluble amino acids are deaminated (Strenström and Lohmann, 1928) forming keto acids and aldehydes, and, in the case of S-containing amino acids, H_2S (Dale and Davis, 1951). Nevertheless, structural modifications occur in the proteins, even with low doses, which do not cause any apparent alteration (Frick, 1938). Observed chemical changes include loss of solubility at the iso-electric point (or "denaturation"), polymerization and degradation to aggregates of lower molecular weight (Svedberg and Brohult, 1939). As with proteins denatured by other means, there is a rise of pH (Batzer *et al.*, 1959).

With a dose of 5 Mrad (approximately that required for microbial sterility) meat proteins show a noticeable loss of water-holding capacity (Schweigert, 1959). The changes are paralleled by the response of isolated myofibrils to added ATP. At low ionic strength myofibrils which have been subjected to 5 Mrad synaerese less on addition of ATP than do non-irradiated controls: at high ionic strength irradiated myofibrils swell less on the addition of ATP (Lawrie *et al.*, 1961). The latter effects indicate, amongst other features, a measure of enzymic inactivation. Such effects have been intensively studied, and in some cases they are due to the oxidation of the SH-groups of the enzyme proteins (Barron and Dickman, 1949). Nevertheless, most enzymes require more than 5 Mrad for inactivation and this can be a serious problem in the storage of irradiated foods, since, although there may be sufficient freedom from bacteria to permit storage at high temperatures, the latter may accelerate adverse enzymic change. In particular, proteolytic enzymes may survive up to 70 Mrad (Schweigert, 1959), although the proteolytic activity of beef muscle is reduced 50 per cent by 1·6 Mrad.

Notwithstanding the relative resistance to irradiation of amino acids in proteins, a soluble protein has been prepared from heated meat which gives a so-called "wet dog" odour when it is irradiated; and there may be concomitant destruction of about 13 per cent of the amino acids (Hedin, Kurtz and Koch, 1961). (More recently Rhodes (1966) found little evidence for amino acid destruction with doses up to 20 Mrad). The effect is more noticeable in beef than in pork and appears to be associated with a gelatin-like protein derived from collagen (Hedin *et al.*, 1961).

Collagen shrinks when irradiated in a dry state and becomes soluble in water if irradiated wet (Perron and Wright, 1950), and, indeed, irradiation caused softness and tenderness of texture as an immediate effect (Coleby, Ingram and Shepherd, 1961). The hydrothermal shrink temperature of collagen decreases with increasing dosage. After 5 Mrad it falls from 61°C to 47°C; and after 40 Mrad to 27°C, i.e. it shrinks at room temperature (Bailey, Bendall and Rhodes, 1962). The effect is probably due to the destruction of some of the hydrogen bonds which hold together the triple helix (cf. Fig. 3.3).

Changes in the pigment proteins of meat on irradiation are sometimes beneficial. Thus, under some conditions, myoglobin may yield a bright red compound having an absorption spectrum similar to that of oxymyoglobin but rather more stable (Ginger, Lewis and Schweigert, 1955). It is formed more particularly in pork: the myoglobin of beef tends to oxidize to brown metmyoglobin on irradiation (Coleby *et al.*, 1961). On the other hand, irradiation of cooked meat reconverts the brown colour to red (cf. § 10.1). In the presence of air, some of the meat pigments may be converted into green sulphmyoglobin (Fox *et al.*, 1958), especially where the ultimate pH is about 5·3, by H_2S produced from smaller molecules such as amino acids.

It has already been mentioned that the soluble amino acids are much more liable to attack than those in proteins, yielding ammonia, H_2S, etc. The principal components of the volatile off flavour produced on irradiation are methyl mercaptan and H_2S (Batzer and Doty, 1955). Studies with S^{35} have shown that most of the methyl mercaptan is derived from methionine. Although H_2S is produced from both methionine and glutathione it is mainly derived from other amino acids (Martin *et al.*, 1962). The quantities of methyl mercaptan, ethyl mercaptan, diethylsulphide, isobutyl mercaptan produced all increase as the dose rate rises from 1 to 6 Mrad (Merritt *et al.*, 1959).

Ionizing radiation brings about changes in meat lipids which resemble those of oxidative rancidity (Coleby, 1959). In the absence of oxygen, fatty acids are decarboxylated (Whitehead, Goodman and Breger, 1951) and, if unsaturated, they are polymerized (Burton, 1949); but in the presence of oxygen, hydroperoxides and carbonyls are formed (Dugan and Landis, 1956). The quantity of carbonyls produced increases with increasing dose (Table 9.1; Batzer *et al.*, 1959). Since, however, it does not increase with increasing fat content, it is clear that most of the carbonyls produced on irradiation are not derived from the oxidation of neutral fat.

TABLE 9.1. *Effect of Irradiation Dose and Fat Content of Beef on Carbonyl Production (× 10^{-5} M Carbonyl/g Meat)*

Irradiation dose (Mrad)	% Fat in meat			
	6	8	13	23·3
0	1·27	3·22	0·98	0·92
2	4·31	4·93	2·13	2·30
4	6·60	8·74	3·40	3·57
6	8·63	11·50	4·65	5·06
8	11·20	12·88	6·46	7·25
10	11·50	10·35	7·42	4·95

There is a regular increase in acetaldehyde, acetone and methylethyl-ketone with increasing dose (Merrit *et al.*, 1959).

The carbohydrates of meat tend to be oxidized in the 6 position, yielding gluconic acids and aldehydes (Phillips, 1954).

Although irradiation affects only a relatively small proportion of the molecules, this fact becomes rather more important when the molecules concerned are present in small amounts—as in the case of vitamins, although, of course, this applies also to other methods of preservation. Vitamin C and thiamin are particularly affected, destruction of the latter representing, perhaps, the greatest nutrient loss with irradiated meat (Groninger, Tappel and Knap, 1956) although vitamin B_{12} is the most radio-sensitive vitamin (Markakis, Goldblith and Proctor, 1951).

Irradiation of cured meats converts nitrate to nitrite; but the amount of nitrite produced is insufficient to constitute a hazard, especially as it also is destroyed by irradiation (Hougham and Watts, 1958).

The potential drawback of ionizing radiation in meat processing is not so much the destruction of the proteins (which is negligible) or of vitamins (which is not negligible but of no nutritional importance) or even the production of off-flavours and off-odours (which can be serious organoleptically). It is the possibility of producing minute quantities of biologically potent and toxic chemicals, e.g. carcinogens from sterols (Weiss, 1953). As experiments involving a long-term ingestion of irradiation foods continue, however, this danger appears to be receding.

In the United Kingdom, even if the process were to remain prohibited in respect of food for human consumption it could have valuable indirect application. Thus, about 250 tons of frozen horse-meat is imported each year for the manufacture of foods for domestic pets: 60 per cent of it is contaminated with *Salmonella spp.*—which represents a potential hazard to those having dogs or cats. A plant has been designed, however, which can treat all the horse-meat imported at present with 650,000 rad from a Co^{60} source of a week's operation.

9.1.2. Organoleptic Aspects

9.1.2.1. Immediate effects

It will have been apparent from § 9.1.1 that, depending on the dose, various organoleptic changes will arise on irradiating meat. Odour and flavour can be adversely affected by the production of H_2S and mercaptans, carbonyls and aldehydes—this being worse in beef than in pork or lamb (Huber, Brasch and Waly, 1953); colour by the production of metmyoglobin and sulphmyoglobin; and texture and water-binding capacity by denaturation changes in the structural proteins. The tenderizing effect caused by changes in the collagen molecules would only be apparent at doses so high that the meat would be inedible. To achieve sterility in the meat—and the possibility of indefinite storage without refrigeration—upwards of 5 Mrad would be required (§ 6.4.4) and this would cause marked deterioration in the attributes of eating quality. Attempts have consequently been made to minimize such adverse effects. Although the presence of oxygen exacerbates irradiation-induced chemical change, in general, its removal has not given appreciable benefits (Hannan, 1955). Radio-chemical changes can be decreased considerably, however, by irradiating in the frozen state and the meat quality is much improved if the commodity is frozen and held at a very low temperature before irradiation (Table 9.2). In these circumstances removal of oxygen is advantageous (Huber *et al.*, 1953).

TABLE 9.2. *Effect of Prestorage at Various Temperatures on Odour, Flavour and Colour of Raw Beef given 1·5 Mrad* (Huber *et al.*, 1953)

Prestorage treatment		Organoleptic rating[a]		
Time (Hr)	Temp. (°C)	Odour	Flavour	Colour
24	3	2·5	2·8	1·5
24	— 15	3·0	3·5	1·5
72	3	3·0	2·8	2·8
72	— 15	4·8	4·5	4·5
72	— 35	5·0	4·0	4·5
72	—180	4·5	4·5	4·5
96	3	3·8	3·0	3·5
96	— 15	4·8	4·3	4·5

[a]Average taste panel of five members: controls rated as 5.

The beneficial effects of low temperatures may well be due to the virtual removal of the aqueous phase, thus preventing secondary chemical changes (Hannan, 1955). A somewhat larger dose may be required to achieve sterility in meat at such low temperatures, but the order of this requirement is much less than the decrease achieved in irradiation damage to the meat (Hannan, 1955). Irradiated frozen meat could subsequently be stored at a relatively high temperature but, of course, it would be subject to the disadvantages of drip in these circumstances.

The possibility of minimizing irradiation damage by the incorporation of protective compounds has been considered on the assumption that they would react with the activated molecules and free radicals produced and thus prevent them attacking the organic molecules of the meat. The potential additives and their irradiation products must be non-toxic. Ascorbic acid, nitrite, sulphite and benzoate have been used in this context (Huber *et al.*, 1953; Pratt and Eklund, 1954). It is interesting to note that irradiation odour was markedly decreased by adding ascorbate after irradiation. This suggests that it may act by directly reducing irradiation products rather than by reacting with free radicals during irradiation. The major difficulty with the use of protective compounds in practice is that of ensuring their effective distribution throughout the meat.

Another approach is the use of in-package odour scavengers; activated charcoal has been employed with some success (Tausig and Drake, 1959). Pre-irradiation storage above the freezing point does not lessen organoleptic damage (Batzer *et al.*, 1959).

9.1.2.2. *Storage changes*

Since the purpose of any method of meat preservation is to permit its storage in a form as near as possible to that of the fresh commodity, non-microbial changes during storage are as important as the immediate effects of the preservative process employed. The prolonged storage period at relatively high temperatures, which is possible with radiation sterilized meats, permits various chemical and biochemical changes which would be precluded during the more limiting conditions with other methods of preservation. Among the purely chemical changes is non-enzymic browning (§ 8.1.3). Both because of the increased storage times and temperatures, and because irradiation produces carbonyls, Maillard-type browning is greater in irradiated meat (Lea, 1959).

The immediate effects of irradiation in causing fat oxidation have been mentioned: during storage of meat irradiated at low temperature there is a possibility of further oxidation due to an after-effect, first noted by Hannan (1955).

Coleby, Ingram and Shepherd (1961) found that the initial irradiation odours and flavours of beef and pork exposed to 5 Mrad gradually changed, during storage at 37°C, to stale and bitter flavours; and the not unpleasant pink colour of irradiated pork tended to turn brown.

The most important detrimental changes during the storage of irradiation sterilized meat, however, are those due to surviving activity of proteolytic enzymes (§ 5.4.1). Some protein denaturation occurs on irradiation. This increases during storage, especially at high temperature; and the resultant loss in water-holding capacity causes considerable exudation (Cain *et al.*, 1958; Schweigert, 1959). The storage for 1 year at 37°C of beef and pork steaks, which had been irradiated in depth and had received 5 Mrad, caused a marked increase in total soluble nitrogen. Protein equivalent to about 25 per cent of the original total nitrogen was broken down to peptides and amino acids; and insoluble aggregates of crystalline tyrosine formed on the meat surface (Lawrie *et al.*, 1961). This proteolysis principally involved sarcoplasmic proteins, for there was no increase in soluble hydroxyproline (indicative of connective tissue breakdown) and, microscopically, the myofibrils *appeared* to be unchanged. Although it was evident that the actomyosin complex had not been proteolysed, its altered nature was reflected in a diminution of ATP-ase activity and accounted for some of the loss in water-holding capacity. Apart from exudation, the stored, irradiated meat had a coagulated, crumbly texture similar to that of lightly cooked meat. Zender *et al.*, (1958) and Radouco-Thomas *et al.*, (1959) found that the texture of sterile rabbit muscle was almost completely broken down during storage at 25° or 37°C over some months. To some extent the greater breakdown can be attributed to the fact that the rabbit was sterilized by irradiation only on the surface, and that within it proteolysis was unimpaired. Doty and Wachter (1955) indicated that the proteolytic enzymes of meat are diminished somewhat by irradiation. There appeared to be species differences in the degree of post-mortem proteolysis since, under comparable conditions, beef is not so extensively broken down as rabbit (Sharp, 1963).

It is evident that there are some proteolytic enzymes in meat which substantially survive even a sterilizing dose of ionizing radiation. Consequently, degradative changes and organoleptic deterioration will occur if the meat is held at the storage temperatures which sterilizing doses of irradiation make possible from the microbiological standpoint. Attempts have been made to overcome this defect in the product. One approach is to heat the meat, before irradiation, to inactivate the proteolytic enzymes. Cain *et al.,* (1958) subjected fresh and heated beef and pork (71° and 77°C, respectively) to 2–3 Mrad and stored the meat for about 8 months at 22°C. Although there was extensive fluid loss, protein breakdown and formation of tyrosine crystals in the fresh meats, the corresponding pre-heated meats were acceptable in texture and flavour. These workers also noted that bacon stored satisfactorily for 8 months at 22°C after irradiation—possibly because its proteolytic enzymes had been denatured by the curing salts. Enzyme inactivation by pre-heating is best achieved by exposure to a relatively high temperature for a short time (e.g. 163°C for 2 hr) than to a lower temperature for a longer time (e.g. 50–80°C for 20 hr): the latter causes undesirable texture changes due to partial breakdown of connective tissue (Whitehair *et al.,* 1964). After such pre-heating, of course, meat can no longer be considered fresh and thus one of the intended advantages of irradiation—the preservation of meat in a state close to that of the fresh commodity—is automatically lost. If taste panel testing of cooked meat were the only criterion of acceptability, this would be less serious than the aforementioned organoleptic changes in sterilized fresh meat stored at high temperature.

9.1.3. *Radiation Pasteurization*

There is growing realization that, whereas the prolonged storage of fresh meat at high temperatures after sterilizing doses of ionizing radiation would be offset by proteolytic and other deterioration, a substantial extension of the storage life of meat preserved by refrigeration would be possible if this were combined with a low dose. Although such "pasteurizing" doses would increase the useful life of the meat, they would be too low to cause organoleptic changes (Ingram, 1959). There would be little advantage with frozen meat, since this is not directly affected by micro-organisms (although pasteurizing doses of irradiation might increase its storage life after thawing), but spoilage of fresh or chilled meat, stored at 0–5°C, can be usefully discouraged. This is especially so since the micro-organisms which tolerate such temperatures are particularly sensitive to irradiation (Ingram, 1959). It is apparent that meat stored at 0–5°C, after irradiation with 50,000–1,000,000 rad, can be held from 5 to 10 times as long as unirradiated meat before microbial spoilage (Morgan, 1957; Shea, 1958; Niven, 1963).

Despite the general susceptibility of the cold-tolerant micro-organisms to pasteurizing doses of irradiation, certain more resistant species are bound to survive—even in small numbers, e.g. *Microbacterium thermosphactum* (McLean and Sulzbacher, 1953). Such micro-organisms spoil meat by producing a sour odour rather than the stale, musty odour from the pseudomonads which grow in stored, unirradiated chilled meat.

Although irradiation with pasteurizing doses can prolong the refrigerated storage life and meat microbiologically, other concomitant changes of non-microbial origin may become apparent. Doses as low as 50,000 rad can cause flavour changes detectable by trained individuals: doses above 200,000 rad intensify those off-flavours and make them noticeable to a higher percentage of consumers (Niven, 1963). Symptoms of accelerated oxidation may be found in beef irradiated with 25,000–100,000 rad (Lea, Macfarlane and Parr, 1960) indicated by the development of a tallowy odour and flavour; and the yellow carotenoid may be perceptibly bleached. Lea *et al.* concluded that, where the surface of the meat was exposed to the atmosphere, the margin between desirable and undesirable effects of pasteurizing doses of irradiation (as in the carriage of chilled beef between Australia and the United Kingdom) scarcely justified its adoption. On the other hand, where the surface of the meat is covered with an oxygen impermeable wrap, oxidative changes are largely eliminated and recontamination of the irradiated surfaces is avoided. In these circumstances the process may be beneficial. An extensive experiment with pasteurizing doses, in combination with chill temperatures (1°C), has been carried out on lamb and beef shipped from the United Kingdom to Australia and New Zealand (Rhodes and Sheppard, 1966). 400,000 rad was the maximum dose of surface irradiation which could be tolerated without causing detectable colour or odour changes. Such a dose delayed microbial growth on the surfaces of lamb carcases (in packs free of air), or in beef joints, for more than 8 weeks. Although, since frozen lamb is an accepted standard commodity, the procedure would not be commercially attractive with lamb, it could have real advantages with beef— a commodity which commands a markedly higher price when chilled than when frozen. A bacteria-proofed container, applied before treatment, is necessary to prevent recontamination; auto-oxidation is simultaneously eliminated by making the packaging material relatively impermeable to oxygen. Thus the need for carbon dioxide to prevent the growth of moulds would be dispensed with, eliminating the considerable expense of gas storage. However, the mechanical problem of avoiding rupture of the pack in handling arises. Similarly, pasteurizing doses of irradiation, combined with light refrigeration, may be of benefit with prepackaged cuts. At the moment, the practical usefulness of irradiation preservation of meat would seem to be within such contexts.

9.2. ANTIBIOTICS

The events leading to the use of certain so-called broad-spectrum antibiotics in food preservation have been outlined in § 6.4.3. The choice of a suitable antibiotic depends on the type of spoilage to be controlled, on the stability and solubility of the antibiotic at the pH of the food, on its stability to heat and on its lack of toxicity. Two aspects of the use of antibiotics are particularly important (Deatherage, 1955) and should be reiterated. Firstly, since they are mainly bacterio-static rather than bactericidal, they are most effective where the total bacterial population is low—discouraging their indiscriminate use with highly contaminated or partially spoiled meat. Secondly, since they do not sterilize foods, they delay rather than prevent spoilage; and they may alter the bacterial flora since the latter will differ in sensitivity. One disadvantage of antibiotics, therefore, is the possible development of resistant micro-organisms in the meat after susceptible bacteria, which normally compete with them for the available nutrients, are eliminated. As already indicated (§ 6.4.3), this difficulty can be overcome to some extent by employing, for preservative purposes, antibiotics which are not applied in human medicine; but, in commercial practice, elimination of normal spoilage organisms, and thereby of the unpleasant superficial symptoms of contamination, could conceivably permit the growth of dangerous bacteria whose toxic by-products would not be easily detectable before consumption of the meat. This danger can be circumvented by combining the use of antibiotics with refrigeration (Barnes, 1956), since pathogens will not grow rapidly at chill temperatures; and it is in this context that antibiotics are most useful. Nevertheless, under experimental conditions, antibiotics have also been used successfully against potential deep spoilage organisms where meat is to be exposed to a high temperature for a short time, rather than subjected to prolonged storage. Nothwithstanding their disadvantages, they can give the benefits of enhanced storage life without themselves causing any chemical or biochemical change in the meat. Few are effective against yeasts and moulds.

With antibiotics there is a remote possibility of toxicity from residues which are not destroyed during cooking (§ 6.4.3). This danger can be overcome to some extent by legislating for permissible limits for residues; and generally the level of antibiotics initially present in meat declines during storage and before the meat is consumed (Weiser, Kunkle and Deatherage, 1954).

Virtually no work has been done on the relative efficacy of antibiotics in different muscles; but there is some suggestion that they may be destroyed more rapidly in muscles of high ultimate pH—or where bacterial growth causes the pH to rise (E. M. Barnes, personal communication).

In general, the storage of fresh meat at chill temperatures is curtailed by the development of micro-organisms on the exposed surfaces belonging to the genera *Pseudomonas* and *Achromobacter* (§§ 6.2 and 6.3.1), although deep spoilage organisms may be involved in some cases where cooking has been delayed or there is bone taint. Since, under such conditions, the microflora is mixed, the use of a "broad-spectrum" antibiotic (e.g. oxytetracycline or chlortetracycline) can appreciably delay spoilage by both types of organisms. The meat so preserved will of course be thereby more liable to the non-microbial changes already indicated in the case of fresh and chilled meat (§ 7.1.1).

The antibiotics may be injected (intraveneously or intraperitoneally) into the animals pre-slaughter (McMahan *et al.*, 1955, 1956; Ginsberg *et al.*, 1958), perfused after death (Deatherage, 1955, 1957), sprayed on to the carcases or cut surfaces and, if packaging operations are involved, incorporated into the film (Firman *et al.*, 1959). Alternatively, the meat may be dipped in an antibiotic-containing solution (Tarr *et al.*, 1955).

Many examples of the efficacy of such treatment could be given. Thus Goldberg, Weiser and Deatherage (1953) showed that the storage life of ground beef could be extended to 9 days at 10°C by the incorporation of 0·5–2 ppm of chloramphenicol, chlortetracycline or oxytetracycline. Controls, and samples treated with penicillin, bacitracin or strep-tomyocin, spoiled in 5 days. In particular, the storage of fresh comminuted meat, such as pork sausages, can be doubled or trebled by the use of antibiotics (Wrenshall, 1959).

The relative efficacy of antibiotics as administered by pre-slaughter injection, by spraying and by the use of impregnated wraps is shown in Table 9.3.

TABLE 9.3. *Microbial Counts on Steaks treated with Chlortetracycline (CTC)*
in Various Ways and stored at 5°C
(after Firman *et al.*, 1959)

Treatment			Micro-organisms ($\times 10^6$/g meat) (days at 5°C)		
Pre-slaughter injection	Surface	Type of film	0	5	10
—	—	Plain	0·013	8·56	897
—	—	CTC	0·012	0·73	276
—	CTC	Plain	0·002	0·14	225
—	CTC	CTC	0·001	0·19	88
CTC	—	Plain	0·005	0·001	14
CTC	CTC	Plain	0·006	0·012	6
CTC	—	CTC	0·0001	0·002	1
CTC	CTC	CTC	0·005	0·005	0·25

It is evident that each procedure has antimicrobial action but that pre-slaughter injection is the most effective: distribution of the antibiotic is clearly more complete when it can be carried by the animal's blood stream into the most minute interstices of the muscle. Moreover, the inhibitory antibiotic is present *in situ* before contaminating organisms can start to multiply.

Although the tetracyclines extend the refrigerated storage life of meat, moulds and yeasts tended to grow after about 14 days at 2°C (Barnes, 1957). On the other hand, Niven and Chesbro (1956) showed that sorbic acid could be used to suppress yeasts in minced beef. Should the temperature of such meat products rise to 15°C antibiotic resistant pathogens, unhindered by the presence of normal spoilage organisms, may be able to multiply, e.g. *Salmonella typhimurium* (Hobbs, 1960). Animals are more likely to be carrying antibiotic-resistant organisms if they have been fed with antibiotic supplements (Barnes, 1958; and cf. § 2.4.5).

The tetracycline antibiotics and irradiation appear to be complementary in extending the refrigerated life of fresh meat (Niven and Chesbro, 1956). Low-level irradiation of meat tends to change the spoilage flora from a gram-negative one to a gram-positive one (Maclean and Sulzbacher, 1953)—and the tetracyclines are particularly effective in retarding the growth of the latter. Table 9.4 illustrates an experiment where small pieces of beef were irradiated with 10,000 rad or treated with 10 ppm oxytetracycline and then irradiated.

TABLE 9.4. *Effect of Gamma Irradiation (10,000 rad) Alone or in Combination with Oxytetracycline (10 ppm) on Bacterial Flora of Beef Muscle stored at 2°C* (Niven and Chesbro, 1956)

Treatment	Micro-organisms ($\times 10^3$/g meat) (days)			
	0	8	14	20
Control	90	700,000	4,000,000	—
Irradiated	0·5	100	60,000	800,000
Irradiated + antibiotic	0·05	1	60	2000

The complementary effect of irradiation and antibiotics against the bacteria is evident.

The problems for control by antibiotics in canned meats are very different from those in fresh meat. An antibiotic which is relatively heat stable (e.g. nisin, subtilin or tylosin) is needed and it must be especially effective against spore-forming bacteria (Barnes, 1957; Hawley, 1962). During prolonged storage the retention of nisin activity is enhanced by acid conditions and by short-time high-temperature heat treatments. For low acid foods, such as meat, the use of nisin and of similar antibiotics can only be considered in conjunction with sufficient heat to kill *Cl. Botulinum.*

Antibiotics might be usefully employed to control spoilage bacteria which are very heat resistant and which cannot otherwise be killed unless the product is given a heat treatment so excessive that its texture is damaged (Hansen and Riemann, 1958). In semi-preserved products, such as canned hams, mild heat treatment (or pasteurizing) will suffice to destroy any surviving faecal streptococci which would resist the antibiotics and would otherwise necessitate refrigerated storage for the product. The possibility of diminishing heat treatment, or curing salts, through the use of antibiotics could lead to some danger from *Cl. botulinum,* however, and antibiotics are, therefore, not permitted with semi-preserved meats (Hawley, 1962), although certain antibiotics are known to lower the heat resistance of spores of *Cl. botulinum* and *Cl. sporogenes* (Leblanc, Devlin and Stumbo, 1953).

Antibiotics have also been employed to permit the conditioning of meat (§§ 5.4.2 and 10.3.3.2) in a relatively short period at high temperature—both alone and in combination with pasteurizing doses (45,000 rad) of ionizing radiation (Wilson *et al.,* 1960).

9.3. CHEMICAL PRESERVATIVES

When hygienic principles were little practised, and less understood, chemical preservatives were not infrequently used in foods to offset what is now recognized as microbiologically dangerous action. Nevertheless, this remedy has drawbacks because chemical preservatives may be nonspecific protoplasmic poisons and as undesirable for the consumer as for the micro-organisms against which they are directed; moreover, their effect may be cumulative rather than immediate. The term was defined by the United Kingdom Preservatives Regulations of 1962 as follows:

> "Preservative" means any substance which is capable of inhibiting, retarding or arresting the process of fermentation, acidification or other deterioration of food or of masking any of the evidence of putrefaction; but does not include common salt (sodium chloride), lecithins, sugars or tocopherols; nicotinic acid or its amide; vinegar or acetic acid, lactic acid, ascorbic acid, citric acid, malic acid, phosphoric acid, pyrophosphoric acid or tartaric acid or the calcium, potassium or sodium salts of any of the acids specified in this subparagraph; glycerol, alcohol or potable spirits, isopropyl alcohol, propylene glycol, monoacetin, diacetin or triacetin; herbs or hop extract; spices or essential oils when used for flavouring purposes.

More recently, however, the addition of nicotinamide and ascorbic acid to meat, as colour preservatives, was prohibited. Formaldehyde, as such, is now prohibited, since it is demonstrably toxic (Wiley, 1908), but is permitted up to 5 ppm if extracted from wet strength wrapping materials.

Fresh meat, when in the intact carcase, is not usually severely contaminated except on the surface (cf. § 6.1). On the other hand, in preparing products containing comminuted or minced meats, there is every opportunity for massive bacterial contamination from the hands of operatives and from equipment; and this certainly occurred frequently in the past. It was in such a context that chemical preservatives were particularly employed in relation to meat.

Very few chemicals are now permitted as preservatives—and these only in minute specified quantities. Apart from nitrate, nitrite, sorbic acid and tetracyclines (which have already been considered in relation to curing and antibiotics), the United Kingdom Preservatives in Food Regulations 1962 lists only seven, namely sulphur dioxide, propionic acid, benzoic acid, methyl-*p*-hydroxy-benzoate, ethyl-*p*-hydroxy-benzoate, diphenyl, *o*-phenylphenol and copper carbonate. Of these seven only sulphur dioxide is permitted in meat preservation, up to 450 ppm being in sausage and sausage meat (Anon, 1972a). Its effect is antimicrobial; and at the permitted level it has no beneficial effect on meat colour, so that deception of the public on this basis is not possible (Kidney, 1967). Boric acid was also employed until relatively recently both in sausage meat and in curing; but its use in the United Kingdom was discontinued in the aforementioned Act of 1928. (This prohibition was temporarily suspended during the Second World War.)

Perhaps, under the general heading of chemical preservatives, carbon dioxide should be included (Callow, 1955a); also ozone (Kefford, 1948; Kaess, 1956), both of which have been used to discourage the growth of surface micro-organisms on beef carcases during prolonged storage at chill temperatures. Although ozone leaves no toxic residues in the meat, its use in the store can be dangerous for personnel. Moreover, it accelerates the oxidation of fat and is more effective against air-borne micro-organisms than against those on the meat. The latter destroys the gas (Kaess, 1956).

CHAPTER 10

THE EATING QUALITY OF MEAT

CONSIDERING the diversity and duration of the events which determine the nature of meat, it seems curious that the consumer's palate can only react to the commodity over a few minutes during mastication. No conscious sensation is derived from the process of digestion over the subsequent 10 hr or so when the amino acids, fatty acids, vitamins, minerals and other constituents are being liberated and absorbed into the body. Nevertheless, however fleeting, the organoleptic sensations may enhance or impair the efficacy of digestion by their reflex action on the production of gastric and intestinal juices—and thus the nutritive value of the food, as the work of Claude Bernard and Pavlov suggested in the nineteenth century and as most textbooks of physiology imply or testify. Indeed, there is evidence for the release of a substance by the brain itself which stimulates gastric contraction (Jefferson *et al.,* 1964).

Of the attributes of eating quality, colour, water-holding capacity and some of the odour of the meat are detected both before and after cooking and provide the consumer with a more prolonged sensation than do juiciness, texture, tenderness, taste and most of the odour which are detected on mastication. The attributes of eating quality will be considered in this chapter.

10.1. COLOUR

Since 1932, when Theorell crystallized the principal pigment of muscle and it was shown that myoglobin was not identical with the haemoglobin of the blood, it has been accepted that the colour of meat is not substantially due to haemoglobin unless bleeding has been faulty (§ 5.2.2). The appearance of the meat surface to the consumer depends, however, not only on the quantity of myoglobin present but also on the type of myoglobin molecule, on its chemical state and on the chemical and physical condition of other components in the meat. Each of these, in turn, is determined by a variety of factors.

10.1.1. *The Quantity and Chemical Nature of Myoglobin*

Factors determining the quantity of myoglobin were incidentally indicated in § 4.2. As one generalization, it is clear that a high level of muscular activity evokes the elaboration of more myoglobin—reflecting, in this respect, differences due to species, breed, sex, age, type of muscle and training. Thus, muscles of the hare have more myoglobin than those of the rabbit; those of racing thoroughbreds have more than those of draught horses; those of bulls have more than those of cows; and those of steers have more than those of calves. The constantly operating muscle of the diaphragm has more myoglobin than the occasionally and less intensively used l. dorsi; and free range animals have more muscle pigment than their stall-fed counterparts. Another kind of factor is the plane and nature of nutrition—a high plane, and a diet low in iron, both leading to low myoglobin concentrations (although by different mechanisms). The quantity-determining factor which is most difficult to understand is that causing the variability, occasionally encountered within a given muscle, when the myoglobin concentration may be several hundredfold different over distances of 1 cm.

Species differences in the myoglobin molecule have been observed. The hues of red oxymyoglobin and of brown metmyoglobin from beef and pork are not identical; but this subject has been little investigated. When freshly cut, the surface of pork l. dorsi forms oxymyoglobin at a faster rate than that of beef (Haas and Bratzler, 1965).

Most of the striking differences in the colour of meat surfaces arise from the chemical state of the myoglobin molecules. It is not appropriate to consider here details of the chemistry of the muscle pigment, which are available elsewhere (e.g. Lemberg and Legge, 1949); but brief comments are desirable. Some of the chemical states in which myoglobin may be encountered in meat are shown in Table 10.1. The myoglobin molecule consists of a haematin nucleus attached to a protein component of the globulin type: the molecular weight is about 17,000. The haematin portion comprises a ring of four pyrrole nuclei co-ordinated with a central iron atom. The iron may exist in both reduced and oxidized forms. In the ferrous form it can combine with gases such as oxygen and nitric oxide. The ability to combine with oxygen is lost when the globin portion of the molecule is denatured and the tendency for the iron to oxidize to the ferric form is then greatly increased; but union of the iron with nitric oxide is strengthened (Lemberg and Legge, 1949). Whilst, therefore, the oxidation of purplish-red myoglobin or of bright red oxymyoglobin to brown metmyoglobin is accelerated by any factors which cause denaturation of the globin (Brooks, 1929b, 1938; Watts, 1954) by the absence of reducing mechanisms and by low oxygen tension (cf. Fig. 7.3), these same circumstances enhance the stability of the red colour of cured meat, converting nitric oxide myoglobin into nitric oxide haemochromogen (Watts, 1954). In both of these pigments the iron is in the ferrous form, but nitrite will also react with metmyoglobin to form a red compound (Barnard, 1937)—metmyoglobin nitrite.

In the myoglobin, oxymyoglobin and metmyoglobin of fresh meat, or the nitric oxide myoglobin and metmyoglobin nitrite of cured meat, the haematin nucleus is intact and the protein is in a native form; but the colour and valency of the iron vary. On heating, as in cooking, the globin is denatured, but the haematin nucleus still remains intact as in the red globin haemochromogen, or more commonly brown globin haemichromogen and in red nitric oxide haemochromogen. It has been suggested that the colour complexes in cooked meat are denatured haemoproteins wherein the protein may be one or other of the several denatured proteins present, and not only globin (Ledward, 1971b). Irradiation of brown globin haemichromogen converts it to red globin haemochromogen (Tappel, 1957a). Denaturation of the globin and the reduction of the haematin nucleus occurs when myoglobin is exposed simultaneously to hydrogen sulphide and oxygen (forming green sulphymyoglobin) on the one hand, or to hydrogen peroxide and ascorbic acid (or other reducing agents) on the other (forming green choleglobin)—as caused by the growth of certain micro-organisms, or in tissue injury *in vivo*. Sulphmyoglobin formation is more likely to be observed in meat having an ultimate pH above 6 since, at lower pH values, bacteria capable of producing H_2S are unable to do so (Nicol, Shaw and Ledward, 1970; Shorthose, Harris and Bouton, 1972). If these conditions are intensified the porphyrin ring may be opened, although the iron remains, forming green verdohaem; and finally, on further or more intense exposure, the iron will be lost from the porphyrin, which will split from the protein moiety and open out, forming the chain of pyrroles characterizing yellow or colourless bile pigments. Excess of nitrite in cured meats can produce the crimson-red colour of metmyoglobin nitrite, and if the latter is treated with an even greater excess of nitrite and heated in acid conditions, green nitrihaemin is formed.

In fresh meat, before cooking, the most important chemical form is oxymyoglobin. Although it occurs on the surface only, this pigment is of major importance, since it represents the bright red colour desired by purchasers. In uncooked meat the cytochrome enzymes (§§ 4.2.1 and 5.3) are generally still capable of utilizing oxygen for a considerable period post-mortem. Although there is no oxygen in the depths of the meat, the gas can diffuse inwards for some distance from meat surfaces exposed to the air; and a point of balance is established between the rates of diffusion and of uptake by the cytochrome enzymes—and by myoglobin, in forming oxymyoglobin. The depth of penetration d is given by $d = \sqrt{2c_0 D/A_0}$, where c_0 is the pressure of oxygen on the surface and D and A, respectively, the coefficients of diffusion and consumption (Brooks, 1938). The bright red colour of oxyglobin will predominate—and be apparent to the observer—from the outside in to the point where the ratio oxymyoglobin: myoglobin is about 1 : 1, i.e. about 84 per cent of the total depth of oxygen penetration (Brooks, 1929b). Since different muscles have different inherent surviving respiratory activity, d will vary under a given set of conditions. Thus, after exposure of cut surfaces to the air for 1 hr at 0°C, the depth of the

TABLE 10.1. *Pigments found in Fresh, Cured or Cooked Meat*

Pigment	Mode of formation	State of iron	State of haematin nucleus	State of globin	Colour
1. Myoglobin	Reduction of metmyoglobin; de-oxygenation of oxymyoglobin	Fe^{++}	Intact	Native	Purplish-red
2. Oxymyoglobin	*Oxygenation* of myoglobin	Fe^{++} (or Fe^{+++}?)	Intact	Native	Bright red
3. Methmyoglobin	*Oxidation* of myoglobin, oxy-myoglobin	Fe^{+++}	Intact	Native	Brown
4. Nitric oxide myoglobin (nitrosomyoglobin)	Combination of myoglobin with nitric oxide	Fe^{++}	Intact	Native	Bright red (pink)
5. Nitric oxide metmyoglobin (nitrosometmyo-globin)	Combination of metmyoglobin with nitric oxide	Fe^{+++}	Intact	Native	Crimson
6. Metmyoglobin nitrite	Combination of metmyoglobin with excess *nitrite*	Fe^{+++}	Intact	Native	Reddish-brown
7. Globin myohaemo-chromogen	Effect of *heat*, denaturing agents on myoglobin, oxymyoglobin; irradiation of globin haemichromogen	Fe^{++}	Intact (usually bound to de-natured protein other than globin)	Denatured (usually detached)	Dull red
8. Globin myoheami-chromogen	Effect of *heat*, denaturing agents on myoglobin, oxymyoglobin, metmyoglobin, haemochrom-ogen	Fe^{+++}	Intact usually bound to de-natured protein other than globin)	Denatured (usually detached)	Brown (some-times greyish)

9. Nitric oxide myohaemochromogen	Effect of *heat*, denaturing agents on nitric oxide myoglobin	Fe^{++}	Intact	Denatured	Bright red (pink)
10. Sulphmyoglobin	Effect of H_2S and oxygen on myoglobin	Fe^{++}	Intact but one double bond saturated	Native	Green
11. Metsulphmyoglobin	Oxidation of sulphmyoglobin	Fe^{+++}	Intact but one double bond saturated	Native	Red
12. Choleglobin	Effect of hydrogen peroxide on myoglobin or oxymyoglobin; effect of ascorbic or other reducing agent on oxymyoglobin	Fe^{++} or Fe^{+++}	Intact but one double bond saturated	Native	Green
13. Nitrihaemin	Effect of large excess *nitrite* and *heat* on 5	Fe^{+++}	Intact but reduced	Absent	Green
14. Verdohaem	Effect of reagents as is 7–9 in excess	Fe^{+++}	Porphyrin ring opened	Absent	Green
15. Bile pigments	Effect of reagents as in 7–9 in large excess	Fe absent	Porphyrin ring destroyed chain of porphyrins	Absent	Yellow or colourless

oxymyoglobin layer was found to be 0·94 mm in horse psoas muscle in which respiratory activity is relatively high and 2·48 mm in horse l. dorsi in which respiratory activity is relatively low (Lawrie, 1953b). In bacon, where the respiratory enzymes are largely inactivated by the high salt concentration, the depth of penetration is about 4 mm (Brooks, 1938). Again, since the coefficient of diffusion decreases less than the respiratory activity for a given fall in temperature, the depth of the bright red layer of oxymyoglobin will be greater at 0°C than, for example, at 20°C (Brooks, 1929b, 1935; Urbain and Wilson, 1958)— hence the tendency for the colour of meat surfaces to become somewhat brighter when stored at lower temperatures.

As will be apparent from the above considerations, the principal pigment of cooked meats is brown globin haem*i*chromogen and, in the case of bacon, red nitric oxide haem*o*chromogen. Tappel (1957b), however, believes that a globin nicotinamide haemichromogen also contributes to the colour of cooked meat, but this has not been confirmed by quantum mechanical studies (Tarladgis, 1962). Brown pigmentation in cooked meats, unlike that in fresh, is normally a desirable attribute of meat quality. The temperature of cooking naturally affects the degree of conversion of the pigments. Thus, beef cooked to an internal temperature of 60°C has a bright red interior; that cooked to an internal temperature of 60–70°C has a pink interior; and that cooked to an internal temperature of 70–80°C higher is greyish brown (Jensen, 1949). Denaturation of myoglobin in meat is considerable at temperatures which cause negligible denaturation of the pigment in solution (Fig. 10.1; Bernofsky, Fox and Schweigert, 1959). Below 65°C, myoglobin denaturation, as measured by the percentage extractability of the pigment, may arise from enzymic action or coprecipitation rather than from the temperature. Myoglobin is one of the more heat-stable of the sarcoplasmic proteins. It is almost completely denaturated, however, between 80–85°C; and this has been made the basis of a test for determining whether or not meat has been heated to 90°C (Roberts, 1972). Meat so heated is unlikely to be a source of viable foot-and-mouth virus. It has been suggested that determination of the relative proportion of deamidated actin components may provide a measure of the severity of heat treatment sustained by cooked meat (King, 1978).

Other factors contribute to the brown colour of cooked meat, including the caramelization of carbohydrates and Maillard-type reactions between reducing sugars and amino groups. The latter is particularly marked in pork, where considerable production of reducing sugars occurs through amylolytic action post-mortem (Sharp, 1957, 1958) and largely determines the degree of browning in this meat, which has relatively little myoglobin (Pearson *et al.*, 1962).

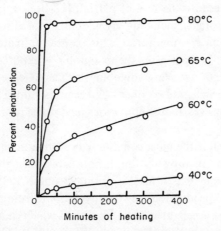

FIG 10.1 The effect of temperature on percentage denaturation of myoglobin from beef, as measured by decreased water-extractibility (Bernofsky *et al.*, 1959). (Courtesy Dr. J. B. Fox.)

10.1.2. *Discoloration*

If the ultimate pH of the meat is high, the surviving activity of the cytochrome enzymes will be greater (Lawrie, 1952b). Moreover, because the muscle proteins will be considerably above their iso-electric point, much of the water in the muscle will still be associated with them and the fibres will be tightly packed together, presenting a barrier to diffusion. As a result of these two factors, the layer of bright red oxymyoglobin becomes vanishingly small and the unpleasant, purplish-red colour of myoglobin itself will predominate to such an extent that the meat will appear dark (dark-cutting beef, "glazy" bacon). Furthermore, the high ultimate pH alters the absorption characteristics of the myoglobin, the meat surfaces becoming a darker red (Winkler, 1939). Such meat will also appear dark because its surface will not scatter light to the same extent as will the more "open" surface of meat of lower ultimate pH.

On the other hand, in the so-called white muscle condition in pigs (§§ 3.4.3 and 5.4.1) the meat is very pale. One reason is the relative absence of myoglobin: another is chemical change in the pigment. The latter occurs either because the rate of pH fall has been very fast (and the sarcoplasmic proteins, including myoglobin, exposed to low pH whilst post-mortem temperatures were still high) or the ultimate pH is very low (Brooks, 1930). In both cases the myoglobin is exposed to conditions causing its oxidation to metmyoglobin which has a low colour intensity. In addition, the structure is "open" and scatters light. The musculature of pigs reared in sweat-house conditions tends to be pale (Vetterlein and Kidney, 1965).

Metmyoglobin is the most commonly occurring undesirable pigment on meat surfaces: its brown colour is noticeable when about 60 per cent of the myoglobin exists in this form (Brooks, 1938). As already indicated, the production of metmyoglobin from myoglobin or oxymyoglobin is accelerated by all conditions which cause denaturation of the globin moiety (Brooks, 1929b; Watts, 1954). These include (as well as low pH) heat, salts and ultraviolet light. Prolonged storage, as is possible at chill temperatures, or shorter holding at higher temperatures, cause surface desiccation (§§ 7.1.1.1 and 9.1.1.2) thus increasing salt concentration and promoting the formation of metmyoglobin. Low temperatures delay metmyoglobin formation both directly and indirectly by suppressing the residual activity of the oxygen-utilizing enzymes.

The formation of metmyoglobin is maximal at about 4 mm oxygen pressure (cf. Fig. 7.3, p. 213: Brooks, 1935). The layer of brown metmyoglobin is thus formed a little below the meat surface (Brooks, 1935). On the other hand, oxidation of the pigment of cured meat, nitric oxide haemochromogen, is directly proportional to increasing oxygen tension (cf. §§ 8.3.2.2 and 8.3.3). It is thus not surprising that the rate of discoloration of cured meats increases directly with the pressure of oxygen under which they are packed; whereas that of fresh meat is inhibited by increasing oxygen pressure in the pack (Rickert *et al.*, 1957). Lamb has a higher residual oxygen demand than either beef or pork; and this may be related to its greater tendency to discolour when stored as fresh meat (Atkinson and Follet, 1971).

Metmyoglobin, once formed, can be reduced both anaerobically (Lawrie, 1952b) and aerobically by surviving enzymes of the cytochrome system and with nicotinamide adenine dinucleotide as coenzyme (Watts *et al.*, 1966). Oxygen uptake, and the concentration of this coenzyme, are highly correlated in beef and lamb (Atkinson and Follet, 1973). While there is a high negative correlation between *aerobic* reducing activity and metmyoglobin formation, however, there is little between the latter and metmyoglobin-reducing activity *anaerobically* (Ledward, 1972).

The mechanism is probably similar to that in red blood cells whereby any tendency for methaemoglobin to form is normally opposed by effective reducing systems involving flavoprotein enzymes (Gibson, 1948; Watts *et al.*, 1966). Because the bright red of oxymyoglobin is desirable, most prepackaged fresh meat is placed in an oxygen-permeable wrap; but after a few days, even at chill temperatures, some of the surface pigment begins to oxidize to metmyoglobin or to myochemichromogen, through incipient denaturation of the globin moiety. This prevents central packaging of fresh meat in oxygen-permeable wraps. If the meat is vacuum-packed, however, no oxygen can get in and the surviving activity of the cytochrome enzymes reduces the small amount of metmyoglobin which forms in these circumstances, replacing it by the purplish red of myoglobin (Dean and Ball, 1960). Vacuum-packed meats (e.g. in oxygen-*impermeable* shrinkable film) can be stored under chill conditions for some weeks. They can be allowed to reoxygenate before sale (thus restoring the bright-red colour of oxymyoglobin) when the film was removed. Centralized prepackaging of fresh meats has been established on such a basis. The cherry-red colour of the carbon monoxide derivative, which is more stable than oxymyoglobin, has been suggested as an alternative for prepacked meats. The colour stability of refrigerated meat will be retained for 15 days at 3°C by this method (Flain, 1964). Some success in retaining the bright-red colour of oxymyoglobin has attended the use of mixtures of carbon dioxide and oxygen as in-pack atmospheres. The carbon dioxide inhibits microbial growth (Taylor, 1971). The surfaces of bovine *psoas* and *gluteus medius* muscles tend to form metmyoglobin considerably faster than that of *l. dorsi* when exposed to air. Under oxygen, however, they resist discoloration for a comparable period at 4°C; although browning was retarded less at 7°C (MacDougall and Taylor, 1975).

Discoloration of both fresh and cured meats has become a serious problem with modern methods of prepackaging and display. Light of visible wavelength, which does not affect the pigment of fresh meat over 3 days, dissociates the nitric oxide from the cured meat pigment; and cured meats may be discoloured after only 1 hr exposure to visible light (Watts, 1954). Partially cooked cured products are especially susceptible. Incandescent, tungsten-filament and fluorescent lighting all cause the same degree of fading for a given time of exposure and light intensity. While ultraviolet light does not appear to have any greater effect than visible light on the fading of cured meats, it will cause brown discoloration in fresh meat—possibly through denaturation of the globin (Haurowitz, 1950). Freezing affords no protection against discoloration by light. There is evidence, for both beef and pork, that metmyoglobin formation occurs more rapidly in psoas muscles than in l. dorsi (Hood, 1971; Owen & Lawrie, 1975).

Attempts to avoid browning due to metmyoglobin formation, by incorporating ascorbic acid in meat products to reduce the oxidized pigment as soon as it forms (Bauernfeind, 1953)—and before extensive denaturation of the globin—or by the use of niacin (Coleman and Steffen, 1949), which is said to form a stable red pigment of myoglobin, have been made. The efficacy of ascorbic acid in this context has been utilized by pre-slaughter injections (D. E. Hood, personal communication). Whilst nicotinamide slows the rate of metmyoglobin formation, amounts as great as 60 mg/per cent are required; and nicotinic acid actually accelerates metmyoglobin formation (Kendrick and Watts, 1969). Both these expedients have recently been forbidden by legislation in the United Kingdom. That the brown pigment can be reduced again does not automatically mean that it will thereafter take up oxygen to form oxymyoglobin. The circumstances causing the pigment to oxidize may also have denatured the globin; and brown globin haem*i*chromogen, although it can be reduced to reddish globin haem*o*chromogen, cannot then form a co-ordination complex with oxygen. Meat of pH above 6 is considered unsuitable for holding in evacuated, gas-impermeable packs since bacterial production of H_2S leads to the formation of green sulphmyoglobin (Nicol *et al.*, 1970: Shorthose *et al.*, 1972).

Among other undesirable colours in meat reference may again be made to those discolorations caused by microbial growth (§§ 6.2) and to the excessive degree of unpleasant browning, accompanied by bitterness occurring in dehydrated meats (especially pork) during storage (§§ 8.1.3). Again, although the freezing of meat after the onset of rigor mortis is not detrimental to colour, there is considerable darkening of the lean and whitening of the fat observable in the fresh and cooked product when the meat has been blast frozen whilst post-mortem glycolysis is proceeding (Howard and Lawrie, 1956, 1957b). The nature of the colour change is unknown. Apart from browning of exposed surfaces through desiccation, increased time and temperature of holding post-mortem also tends to decrease the ability of freshly exposed surface to form oxymyoglobin (Bouton, Howard and Lawrie, 1957b).

Pink or green discolorations are occasionally encountered in the fat of cured meat. These are probably due to the metabolic products of halophilic bacteria (§ 6.2; Jensen, 1950). The fat of fresh meat from old dairy cows is sometimes distinctly yellow, due to the accumulation of carotenoid pigments in the tissue, and much of the present popular demand for young meat animals arises from the paleness of their intramuscular fat. Yellow or brownish discoloration of back fat in bacon has long been a problem. Three lipofuscin-like pigments have been isolated from discolored areas; but conditions responsible for their accelerated production have not yet been elucidated (Juhasz,

Berndorfer-Kraszner, Körmendy and Gabor, 1976). For meat products, such as sausages, the addition of porphyrins prepared from blood would give an attractive red colour at 100 ppm; and, being of natural origin, would not constitute an artificial contaminant (C. L. Walters, personal communication).

10.2. WATER-HOLDING CAPACITY AND JUICINESS

In that it effects the appearance of the meat before cooking, its behaviour during cooking and juiciness on mastication, the water-holding capacity of meat is an attribute of obvious importance. This is particularly so in comminuted meats such as sausages, where the structure of the tissue has been destroyed and it is no longer able to prevent the egress of fluid released from the proteins. Diminution of the *in vivo* water-holding capacity is manifested by exudation of fluid known as "weep" in uncooked meat which has not been frozen, as "drip" in thawed uncooked meat, and as "shrink" in cooked meats, where it is derived from both aqueous and fatty sources.

Not more than 5 per cent of the total water of muscle (i.e. about 4 per cent of the wet weight) is directly bound to hydrophilic groups on the proteins. This amount is scarcely altered by changes in the structure and charges of the latter (Hamm, 1960) although it is important in relation to processing, since its presence accelerates denaturation of proteins during dehydration and freezing (Greaves, 1960). Most of the observed changes in water-holding capacity involve alterations in the so-called "free" water, which is immobilized by the physical configuration of the proteins but is not bound to them. It is continuous with the so-called "loose" water which is expressed when the water-holding capacity drops. The stepwise release of water from meat by the application of different temperatures has shown that it is bound by the proteins in several layers, the water-holding forces decreasing with increasing distance from the protein (Hamm, 1960; Wierbicki, Tiede and Burrell, 1963). The n.m.r. spectra of water in muscle suggest that it exists in at least two *ordered* phases. These can also be distinguished by deuterium-exchange and vacuum-drying (Hazlewood, Nichols and Chamberlain,

1969). Heat denaturation of muscle proteins lessens the degree of this order.

10.2.1. *Uncooked Meat*

10.2.1.1. *Factors determining exudation*

The exudation of "weep" or "drip" will depend both on the quantity of fluid released from its association with the muscle proteins and on the extent to which, if released, it is permitted access to the exterior. Some considerations apply generally to all muscles. Thus, since post-mortem glycolysis in a typical muscle will normally proceed to an ultimate pH of about 5·5—and this is the iso-electric point of the principal proteins in muscle—some loss in water-holding capacity is an inevitable consequence of the death of the animal (§§ 5.3 and 5.4.1). The *extent* of post-mortem pH fall will, therefore, affect the waterholdiing capacity, and the higher the ultimate pH the less will be the diminution in water-holding capacity (Cook *et al.,* 1926; Empey, 1933). The sarcoplasmic proteins to which some of the water-holding capacity is due (Hamm, 1960, 1966) are especially affected by post-mortem pH fall (Scopes, 1964). Moreover, the loss of ATP and the consequent formation of actomyosin as muscles go into rigor mortis will cause loss of water-holding capacity at any pH (cf. § 4.2.3.). Fluid from the myofilaments is released, dilutes the sarcoplasm (Pearson *et al.,* 1974; Penny, 1977) and increases the extracellular space. This arises both because the water-holding capacity of actomyosin is less than that of the myosin and actin from which it forms and also because the lower ATP level initiates denaturation in those proteins whose integrity *in vivo* is particularly dependent on the provision of energy (§ 5.3).

The *rate* of post-mortem pH fall is also an important determinant of water-holding capacity (Lawrie, 1960; Penny, 1977). Denaturation of the sarcoplasmic proteins is worsened the faster the rate of pH fall (Scopes, 1964; Bendall and Wismer-Pedersen, 1962). A fast rate of pH fall (i.e. of ATP breakdown) will increase the tendency of the actomyosin to contract as it forms (Bendall, 1960) and thus express to the exterior fluid which has become dissociated from the proteins. When a fast rate of pH fall post-mortem is due to elevated temperatures (cf. § 4.2.2.) the enhanced loss of water-holding capacity observed is partly due to increased denaturation of the muscle proteins; and partly to enhanced movement of water into extracellular spaces (Penny, 1977).

Conditioning the meat (§ 5.4.1) increases its water-holding capacity (Cook *et al.*, 1926) and this at various environmental pH values (Fig. 10.2; Hamm, 1959). Although the pH of the meat itself may rise in these circumstances this does not account for the phenomenon (Hamm,

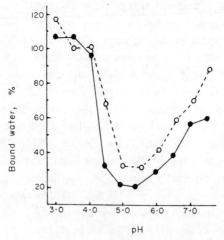

Fig. 10.2. The effect of conditioning on pH–hydration curve of beef muscle (Hamm, 1960). ● = 1 day post-mortem.   = 7 days post-mortem. (Courtesy Prof. R. Hamm.)

1960). The increase in the water-holding capacity is more likely to be caused by changes in the ion-protein relationships, there being a net increase in charge through absorption of K^+ ions and release of Ca^{++} ions (Arnold *et al.*, 1956).

Apart from these general effects, the water-holding capacity of meat is affected by several of the factors which cause differentiation in muscles, such as species, age and the muscular function (§ 4.3). It is found, for instance, that the water-holding capacity of pork is higher than that of beef (Körmendy, 1955; Schön and Stosiek, 1959b; Hamm, 1975). Again, although the age of the animal does not appear to be an influence with pork, it is with beef, calves having a greater water-holding capacity (Schön and Stosiek, 1959a). To some extent, these differences are a further reflection of differences in the rate and extent of pH fall (Figs. 4.4a, b), the ultimate pH in pork and veal tending to be higher than that in cattle (Lawrie, 1961; Lawrie *et al.,* 1963). Some of the differences between and within muscles in water-holding capacity (Taylor and Dant, 1971) can be similarly explained—but not all. Thus, the water *content* of different muscles in beef and pork varies (Tables 4.17a and 4.17b), but this could be due to pH differences (Lawrie *et al.,* 1963). On the other hand, both in beef and pork the l. dorsi has a lower water-holding capacity than the psoas (Hamm, 1960). This is so even when the rate and the extent of pH fall are identical (Howard *et al.,* 1960) suggesting that there are different types of protein present (Lockett *et al.,* 1962; cf. Table 4.20).

Muscles having a high content of intramuscular fat tend to have a high water-holding capacity (Saffle and Bratzler, 1959). The reasons for this effect—which is real enough—are unknown: possibly the intramuscular fat loosens up the microstructure, thus allowing more water to be entrained (Hamm, 1960). Within a given muscle, the water-holding capacity may vary appreciably, even when the ultimate pH is virtually constant (Fig. 10.3: Urbin, Zessin and Wilson, 1962).

All the factors affecting the water-holding capacity of muscle apply equally well to frozen and unfrozen meat. With frozen meat, however, removal of water from within the muscle cells during the process of freezing, as normally carried out commercially, provides an additional potential reservoir of fluid which appears as "drip" on thawing (§ 7.1.2.2) although it can be ameliorated by the same means as "weep" and can be largely avoided with very fast rates of freezing. These are not feasible commercially.

10.2.1.2. *Measures minimizing exudation*

In relation to sausage (and other comminuted meats), small retail cuts and, more recently, prepackaged cuts, there has, naturally, been much

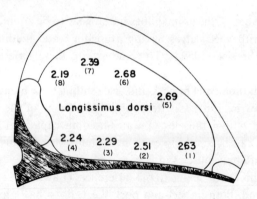

Fig. 10.3. Relative water-holding capacity within pork 1. dorsi muscle (Urbin *et al.*, 1962). (Courtesy Dr. M. C. Urbin.)

interest in means of diminishing "weep" or "drip". From the considerations above, it is clear that the use of meat having high ultimate pH, or in which post-mortem glycolysis (ATP breakdown) is slow, and rapid cooling of the carcase before the onset of rigor mortis will enhance water-holding capacity. Of course, if the temperature of the carcase is reduced *too* quickly during post-mortem glycolysis, cold shortening, with toughening and loss of water-holding capacity, will ensue (cf. § 5.4.1). Clearly the bulk of the portion of meat which is being considered, and the capacity of the refrigeration facility, will determine whether the effect on water-holding will be beneficial or deleterious. Again, the actual exudation will be less if the area of cut surface of meat is minimized, if it is cut along instead of across the grain, and, in the case of prepacked meat, if the wrapping film used is not shrunk too tightly on to the meat. With frozen meat it is desirable to use the fastest possible freezing rate *after* the onset of rigor mortis; but pre-rigor freezing is liable to cause the excessive "drip" of thaw rigor (§ 7.1.2.2). Pre-slaughter injections, designed to raise the ultimate pH (Howard and Lawrie, 1956; Penny, Voyle and Lawrie, 1963, 1964; Hatton, Lawrie, Ratcliff and Wayne, 1972), can lead to commercially significant decreases in exudation from fresh and preserved meat.

Sausage and comminuted meats are, on the one hand, more liable to exude fluid (even if the water-holding capacity of the proteins is intrinsically high) because the structure of the meat is destroyed in their preparation, thus removing its contribution to the physical retention of fluid. On the other hand, however, the nature of these products permits direct manipulation of the meat to enhance its water-holding capacity artificially. Before considering special effects, the behaviour of water itself as an additive should be noted. The ratio of water to meat affects the overall water-holding capacity of the mix. The latter, as measured by a centrifugal method (Sherman, 1961), is maximal when the ratio is about 2:1 (Table 10.2).

TABLE 10.2. *Influence of Water to Meat Ratio on Water Retention of Pork Muscle* (after Sherman, 1961)

Water: meat ratio	Per cent water retention at 0°C
No water added	−4·0
1:2	−1·0
1:1	−1·5
3:2	0·5
2:1	9·5
3:1	5·0
4:1	−5·0
5:1	−5·0
6:1	−6·0

The incorporation of the salts of strong acids, such as sodium chloride, in the comminuted meat mix is important in enhancing water-holding capacity (Gerrard, 1935) because of the salt-protein complex which is formed (Callow, 1927a) in such circumstances. The efficacy of different sodium salts and of different chlorides is shown in Table 10.3, for an ionic strength less than 0·4.

While the order for the sodium salts is the same at both high and low pH, that for the various cations is markedly different, the divalent species being less effective than the monovalent at relatively high pH, the converse tending to be true at relatively low pH.

The more strongly ions are bound by the protein the stronger will be the hydrating effect (Hamm, 1957). The effect of anions in shifting the

TABLE 10.3. *The Relative Effects of Various Sodium
Salts and Chlorides of Different Metals in Enhancing
the Water-holding Capacity of Muscle Homogenates:
Ionic Strength 0·4*
(Hamm, 1960)

pH	Order of efficacy
6·4 and 5·5	(a) *Sodium salts* $F^- < Cl^- < Br^- < CNS, I$
6·4	(b) *Chlorides* $Ca^{++} < Ba^{++} < Mg^{++} < K^+ < Na^+ < Li^+$
5·5	$K^+ < Na^+ < Mg^{++} < Ca^{++} < Li^+ < Ba^{++}$

iso-electric point to more acid values and in enhancing the water-holding capacity above the original iso-electric point was shown by Hamm in 1960. It has been presumed that the water-holding capacity of connective tissue proteins is similarly enhanced by ions.

At high ionic strength, salt has a dehydrating effect: hydration is at a maximum when the ionic strength is about 0·8–1·0. This corresponds to 5 and 8 per cent of sodium chloride for meat without, and with, 60 per cent added water, respectively (Callow, 1931; Hamm, 1957).

Certain salts of weak acids, in particular phosphates and polyphosphates, are also added to comminuted meats to enhance waterholding capacity, especially in continental-type sausages. Hamm and Grau (1958) found the following order of increasing efficacy of the sodium salts—monophosphate, cyclotriphosphate, diphosphate, tetraphosphate and triphosphate. The efficacy of triphosphate addition appears to depend upon its being enzymically broken down to diphosphate (Hamm, 1975). In agreement with the finding of Arnold *et al.* (1956) that increased hydratability in conditioned meat parallels loss of Ca^{++}, they suggested that the effect of such phosphates depended on their sequestering action on divalent cations, although this has been refuted (Sherman, 1961). Bendall (1954) concluded that the effects of most of these phosphates was largely one of ionic strength and pH; whereas that of pyrophosphate (in the presence of 1 per cent sodium chloride), which was much greater, was specific and due to the splitting of actomyosin

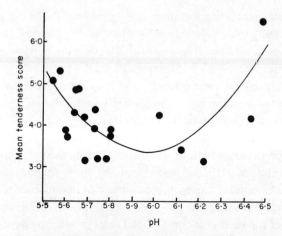

FIG. 10.4. Relationship between mean tenderness (as assessed by taste panel) and ultimate pH in beef muscle (after Bouton *et al.*, 1957).

into actin and myosin and to the formation by the latter of a sol, the effect reflecting that of ATP itself. This view was confirmed by Hellendoorn (1962).

The loss of water-holding capacity arising from the formation of actomyosin when the *in vivo* ATP level falls and rigor mortis ensues (§ 4.2.3), and the efficacy of pyrophosphate in improving it in minces, suggests that there would be some benefit in keeping the ATP high post-mortem. Unfortunately, no means of preventing rigor mortis by pre-slaughter treatment have been found, and the injection of pyrophosphate is fatal because of hypocalcaemia (Howard and Lawrie, 1957a). But comminuted meats permit manipulation to retain the high pre-rigor water-holding capacity of the myofibrillar proteins (Körmendy, 1955; Savic and Karan-Djurdjic, 1958). Successful procedures depend on there being a sufficiency of ATP remaining in the muscle. The addition of 2 per cent sodium chloride to pre-rigor meat appears to prevent the onset of rigor mortis and a fall in the water-holding capacity—although, strangely enough, it does not prevent the subsequent breakdown of ATP (Hamm, 1957). Indeed it is accelerated by the salt. Since sodium acetate has no such effect, Hamm believes that the binding of chloride ions is responsible. In practice, advantage can be taken of this effect by freezing comminuted pieces pre-rigor and subsequently thawing them in the presence of salt. In the absence of salt, the thawing of meat frozen pre-rigor causes excessive exudation (§ 7.1.2.2). The retention of water-holding capacity is even greater—and lasts much longer—if the pre-rigor meat is comminuted with salt *then* frozen (Hamm, 1966). This is because in the region of the freezing point (ca.—1°C) ATP breaks down faster in salted meat than unsalted. It is better therefore to salt pre-rigor meat before freezing than to add the salt during the preparation of the sausage emulsion (Honikel and Hamm, 1978). A similar enhancement of the water-holding capacity of sausage can be obtained if the salted meat is freeze-dried in the pre-rigor state (Honikel and Hamm, 1978).

Much of the success of comminuted meat production depends on the ability of the muscle proteins to hold fat as well as water. The factors determining the stability of sausage meat emulsions are thus important. A major function of salt in these products is to loosen the myofibrillar proteins and to increase their ability to emulsify fat, especially at pH values near their iso-electric point (Swift and Sulzbacher, 1963). There are limitations to the amount of fat which the protein–water gel can hold if the sausage is to maintain its structure during handling and processing. These limits are determined by a number of factors. Thus although mild warming of the emulsion in a chopper aids in releasing soluble proteins, temperatures above 22°C may cause the emulsion to break down (Wilson, 1960). Over-chopping increases the surface area of the fat particles to the extent that the water-protein phase is unable to hold them in the emulsified state. Over-mixing of the emulsion, particularly at temperatures from 18° to 22°C, may cause moisture and fat to separate. The addition of cooked rind, which contains partly-denatured collagen and elastin, enhances the water-holding ability of sausage meats to some extent (Heidtmann, 1959). During the heating of sausage mix, the coagulating network of proteins or filaments surrounds the melting fat particles which cannot therefore coalesce. The larger the meshes of the coagulated network, the less coalescence can occur and the greater the water-holding capacity (Hamm, 1975). Little is known about the role of the phase transitions of fats on the stability of emulsions.

Differential thermal analysis has been used to examine such phenomena with a view to achieving better emulsion control. It has been found that there are two primary ranges of melting in both beef and pork fats (Townsend *et al.*, 1968). The ranges are 3–14°C and 18–30°C for beef fats; and 8–14°C and 18–30°C for pork fats. The stability of emulsions above 18·5°C coincides with the onset of melting of the higher melting portion of the fats. The state of the proteins used is among the factors of importance. Thus, for example, the emulsifying capacity of beef semitendinosus muscle decreases from 30 min to 4 days post-mortem: thereafter, on storage at —4°C, it increases (Graner, Cahill and Ockerman, 1969).

Sugars, which are sometimes added to continental-type sausage meat, have no effect in enhancing water-holding although they have such an effect in intact muscular tissue (Hamm, 1960).

10.2.2. *Cooked Meat*

10.2.2.1. *Shrink on cooking*

The factors affecting loss of "weep" or "dry" from uncooked meat also apply to the water-holding capacity of cooked meat: relative differences are retained on heating (Bendall, 1946; Hamm and Deatherage, 1960). The losses due to the shrinkage on cooking, however, will be greater—to an extent determined by such extraneous circumstances as method, time and temperature of cooking—since the high temperatures involved will cause protein denaturation and a considerable lowering in water-holding capacity (Baker, 1942; Wierbicki *et al.*, 1954; Paul and Bratzler, 1955). Moreover, some of the shrink or juice on cooking will represent non-aqueous fluid, since the high temperatures will melt fat and tend to destroy the structures retaining it.

As an example of how the factors in § 10.2.1 are reflected in shrinkage and loss of juice on cooking, it may be mentioned that the induction of a high ultimate pH in muscle will diminish that particular portion of the cooking loss which is due to the exudation of moisture (Bouton *et al.*,

1957);† and the benefits of adding pyrophosphate to comminuted meats are retained on cooking (Bendall, 1954). On the other hand, a fast rate of pH fall will increase moisture loss in cooking. Thus, Sayre, Kiernat and Briskey (1964) found that where the pH of pork muscle at 40 min. post-mortem (pH_1) was lower than 5·9, cooking losses were about 40–50 per cent, whereas when the pH_1 was above 6·0, losses were only 20 per cent. Again, the effect of conditioning meat in enhancing water-holding capacity is to some extent reflected in diminished cooking losses; but this effect is not apparent with all joints (Bouton *et al.*, 1958).

Losses from good quality meat tend to be less *overall* than those from poor quality meat (Table 10.4). Although the former lose more fat

TABLE 10.4. *Percentage Cooking Losses from Good-
and Poor-quality Beef Joints*
(Bouton *et al.*, 1958)

Category of loss	Good grade		Poor grade	
	Sirloin roast	Topside roast	Sirloin roast	Topside roast
Total	28·9	41·3	41·7	48·3
Fat	17·8	1·4	4·8	−1·4[a]
Water	9·4	36·9	34·0	47·7
Residue	1·7	3·0	2·9	3·0

[a] Fat increment arises from that added to pan on cooking.

(which is expectable in view of their greater fat content) they lose less moisture, possibly because the structural changes caused by the presence of the fat enhance water-holding capacity (Saffle and Bratzler, 1959).

Table 10.4 also indicates the effect of the type of joint in determining cooking loss. In the sirloin, where there is considerable intramuscular fat the shrink is largely due to fat.

Chemical changes in meat proteins on subjection to dry heat up to

† The greater loss of moisture from meat of normal pH tends to cause more evaporative cooling; and under comparable conditions meat of high pH tends therefore to reach a rather greater internal temperature on cooking (Lewis, Brown and Heck, 1967).

80°C were indicated in §§ 8.1.1 and 8.2.2. There is a loss of free acidic groups and of water-holding capacity, and a rise of pH, as the temperature is increased from 0 to 80°C (Fig. 8.1).

There is also an increase in the buffering power of the meat in the region 5·0–7·0. Bendall (1946, 1947) attributed these effects to denaturation changes, particularly in the sarcoplasmic proteins. They were consistent with the fission of protein chains at labile linkages involving imidazole, —SH and —OH groups, followed by hydrogen bonding between carboxyl and amino groups.

However common the empirical observation that increasing temperature increases cooking loss, few controlled experiments have been carried out on this topic. Sanderson and Vail (1963) cooked beef muscles to constant internal temperatures of 60, 70 and 80°C and observed that, in these circumstances, the total cooking loss increased, only some of the increment, however, being due to loss of moisture (Table 10.5).

TABLE 10.5. *Effect of Internal Meat Temperature on Cooking Loss in Beef*

	Internal temperature of meat (°C)		
	60	70	80
Total cooking loss (% wet weight)	10·5	28·8	40·5
Moisture loss (% wet weight)	5·6	9·6	14·0

Meat cooked quickly to a given internal temperature has a lower cooking loss and is more juicy than that cooked slowly to the same temperature (Bramblett and Vail, 1964).

Although the conversion of collagen to gelatin at 100°C will tend to increase water-holding capacity (Hamm, 1960), this is offset by severe changes in the sarcoplasmic and myofibrillar proteins, for the overall water-holding capacity drops markedly as the temperature is raised between 80 and 100°C (Table 8.4).

These changes are sufficiently severe to make it relatively immaterial how long they are applied; on the other hand, with cooking temperatures below 70–80°C shrinkage increases with increasing time of cooking (Savic and Suvakov, 1963). Time–temperature curves of meat during cooking reveal a plateau at about 70°C suggesting that some chemical change is occurring at this point. It does not appear to be due to connective tissue breakdown (Lawrie and Portrey, 1967).

The quantity of juice obtained on heating increases further between 107° and 155°C (Tischer, Hurwicz and Zoellner, 1953). This probably reflects some of the protein breakdown, with destruction of amino acids, which occurs in such ranges of temperature (Beuk *et al.*, 1948). During roasting of the meat, coagulation of the proteins on the surface inhibits loss of fluid; and the more rapid the heating, the faster the formation of this layer and the lower the shrink (Andross, 1949). A similar explanation accounts for the lower shrink in meat cooked after immersion in boiling water rather than after slow raising of the temperature of initially cold water. Grilling and dielectric heating lower the loss of juice still further (Causey *et al.*, 1950).

10.2.2.2. *Juiciness*

The degree of shrinkage on cooking is directly correlated with loss of juiciness to the palate (Siemers and Hanning, 1953). Juiciness in cooked meat has two organoleptic components. The first is the impression of wetness during the first few chews and is produced by the rapid release of meat fluid; the second is one of sustained juiciness, largely due to the stimulatory effect of fat on salivation (Weir, 1960). This function of the latter explains why, for example, the meat of young animals gives an initial impression of juiciness but, due to the relative absence of fat, ultimately a dry sensation (Gaddis, Hankins and Hiner, 1950). Good quality meat is more juicy than that of poor quality, the difference being at least partly attributable to the higher content of intramuscular fat in the former (Gaddis *et al.,* 1950; Howard and Lawrie, 1956). An association between juiciness and intramuscular fat has been noted in comparing rib roasts from several groups of steers and bulls which had the same sire (Bryce-Jones, Houston and Harries, 1963): juiciness varied significantly between the groups.

There is some suggestion that juiciness reaches a mimimum when the pH level of the meat is about 6 (Howard and Lawrie, 1956); this possibly reflects the greater ability of the muscle proteins to bind water in this pH region; but, if this were the entire explanation, juiciness would be expected to decrease still further with even higher pH levels.

The process of freezing does not itself affect juiciness (Law and Vere-Jones, 1952; Brown, Bouton and Howard, 1954), there being no difference in this respect between meat which has been chilled or frozen and held for the same length of time. On the other hand, there is an effect of storage. Thus, beef held at —10°C for 20 weeks was much less juicy than corresponding beef held for a few days at 0°C (Howard and Lawrie, 1956). This effect is also apparent during conditioning, roasts and grills of beef being most juicy some 24 hr after slaughter and thereafter decreasing in juiciness in the following order: 3 days at 0°C, 2 days at 20°C, 14 days at 0°C (Bouton *et al.*, 1958).

Freeze drying, even when operated under optimum conditions, causes some loss in juiciness (Hamm and Deatherage, 1960); this can be offset to some extent by the induction of a high ultimate pH in the meat (Table 10.6).

The ranking order shows that juiciness was greatest in the fresh (frozen) meat of high ultimate pH, and somewhat less in corresponding dehydrated material; but both were considerably more juicy than the meat of low ultimate pH both before and after freeze drying.

10.3. TEXTURE AND TENDERNESS

10.3.1. *Definition and Measurement*

Of all the attributes of eating quality, texture and tenderness are presently rated most important by the average consumer and appear to be sought at the expense of flavour or colour. This notwithstanding it is most difficult to define what is meant by either term.

According to Hammond (1932a) texture, as seen by the eye, is a function of the size of the bundles of fibres into which the perimyseal septa of connective tissue divide the muscle longitudinally (§ 3.2.1).

TABLE 10.6. *The Sum of the Juiciness Ratings given by Eight Tasters for Control (Low Ultimate pH) and Adrenaline-treated (High Ultimate pH) Beef Before and After Freeze Drying* (Penny *et al.*, 1963)

Muscle	A. Control (low ultimate pH)		B. Adrenaline treated (high ultimate pH)	
	Fresh (frozen)	Dehy-drated	Fresh (frozen)	Dehy-drated
Semimembranosus	23	23	13	19
Biceps femoris	26	22	15	12
Psoas	23	25	12	16
L. dorsi (lumbar)	19	24	11	14
L. dorsi (thoracic)	26	25	10	20
Deep pectoral	25	24	10	19
Total	142	143	71	100

Coarse-grained muscles—in general those which have the greatest rate of post-natal growth—such as semimembranosus, have large bundles, fine-grained muscles (e.g. semitendinosus) have small bundles. The size of the bundles is determined not only by the numbers of fibres but also by the size of the latter. Coarseness of texture increases with age, but in muscles where the fibres are small it does not become quite so apparent as in those where they are large. In general, coarseness of texture is greater in the muscles of male animals, and in those of large frame; breed also has an effect (Hammond, 1932a).

The size of the fibre bundles is not the only factor determining coarseness, however. The *amount* of the perimysium round each bundle is important, the perimyseal layer being thick in coarse muscles (Ramsbottom, Strandine and Koonz, 1945). Since the elements defining texture are aspects of connective tissue, it might have been expected that there would have been a direct correlation between coarseness of grain and toughness after cooking. This is not so, however (Ramsbottom and

Strandine, 1948); yet there *is* an indirect correlation between muscle fibre diameter and tenderness (Hiner *et al.,* 1953). Such observations emphasize the complexity of texture and tenderness as attributes of eating quality.

The overall impression of tenderness to the palate includes texture and involves three aspects: firstly, the initial ease of penetration of the meat by the teeth; secondly, the ease with which the meat breaks into fragments; and thirdly, the amount of residue remaining after chewing (Weir, 1960).

There have been many attempts to devise objective physical and chemical methods of assessing tenderness which would compare with subjective assessments by taste panels. The difficulty of doing so is considerable. Thus physical methods have included the basis for measuring the force in shearing (Warner, 1928; Kramer, 1957; Winkler, 1939), penetrating (Tressler, Birdseye and Murray, 1932; Lowe, 1934), "biting" (Lehmann, 1907; Volodkevich, 1938), mincing (Miyada and Tappel, 1956), compressing (Sperring, Platt and Hiner, 1959) and stretching the meat (Wang *et al.,* 1956). Chemical methods have involved determination of connective tissue (Lowry, Gilligan and Katersky, 1941; Neuman and Logan, 1950) and enzymic digestion (Smorodintzev, 1934) amongst other criteria. The compression of meat through a small orifice (Sperring *et al.,* 1959) gives, on raw meat, an objective assessment closest to the tenderness ratings obtained by taste panel.

The degree of tenderness can be related to three categories of protein in muscle—those of connective tissue (collagen, elastin, reticulin, mucopolysaccharides of the matrix), of the myofibril (actin, myosin, tropomyosin) and of the sarcoplasm (sarcoplasmic proteins, sarcoplasmic reticulum). The importance of their relative contribution depends on circumstances such as the degree of contraction of the myofibrils, the type of muscle and the cooking temperature. Measurements of shear, compression and tensile force reflect changes in the myofibrillar structure. After the initial yield, applied forces reflect the state of the connective tissue. The latter may be determined by measuring adhesion values (Bouton, Harris and Shorthose, 1975).

10.3.2. *Pre-slaughter Factors*

Species is the most general factor affecting tenderness. To some extent this is a reflection of texture (§ 10.3.1). Thus the large size of cattle, in relation to sheep or pigs, is, generally, associated with a greater coarseness of their musculature (Hammond, 1932a). Although it has been the impression that pork contains little connective tissue compared with beef (Mitchell, Beadles and Kruger, 1927), Tables 4.17a and 4.17b show, respectively, that the hydroxyproline content of corresponding muscles of beef and pork vary from 350 to 1430 μg/g and from 420 to 2470 μg/g. Since hydroxyproline can be equated to connective tissue, this fact, and the discrepancy between the greater tenderness of veal and its high content of connective tissue in relation to beef, indicates that the type of connective tissue, as well as its quantity, is important.

Texture may also be implicated in breed differences in tenderness. The relatively greater tenderness of the meat from Aberdeen Angus cattle can be partly explained by their small size—this being reflected in fine grain (Hammond, 1963a). Nevertheless, other factors are involved, since dwarf beef was judged less tender than beef from normal-sized animals (Jacobson *et al.*, 1962) on the one hand, while the hypertrophic muscles of "doppelender" beef were at least as tender as those from normal animals (I. F. Penny, personal communication). The latter feature is also evident in cross-bred progeny. Thus, the toughness of the *semitendinosus* muscles of the offspring of 'doppelender' Aberdeen Angus bulls and Jersey cows was found to be less than in those where the sires were normal (Bouton, Ellis, Harris and Shorthose, 1976).

Carpenter *et al.* (1955) showed that the introduction of the Brahman breed deceased beef tenderness. More detailed data on the effect of breed are given in Table 10.7 (Palmer, 1963).

Even within a breed, however, tenderness is heritable to an extent of over 60 per cent (Cartwright, Butler and Cover, 1958), again indicating that texture is by no means its sole determinant. Different sires are associated with different degrees of tenderness (Bryce-Jones *et al.*, 1963); data in Table 10.8 indicate that such differences are covariant in different portions of the carcase.

TABLE 10.7. *The Relationship of Breed to Tenderness (Taste Panel)*

Breed	No. of cattle	Per cent cattle giving score of[a]				
		5–6	4–5	3–4	2–3	1–2
Angus	84	59	27	11	2	—
Brahman	196	9	27	40	21	3
Brangus	18	10	48	38	5	—
Devon	12	58	42	—	—	—
Hereford	48	40	48	11	2	—
Shorthorn	122	20	37	38	4	2

[a] Range 1–6: 1 being inedible, 6 excellent.

TABLE 10.8. *Influence of Sire on Mean Tenderness (Shear Force) of Beef Roasts from Groups[a] of Cattle[b]*

Sire group	7–8th rib	9–10th rib
1	5·8	6·1
2	6·1	6·2
3	7·4	6·8
4	7·6	7·6
5	9·4	7·3

[a] Increased force signifies less tenderness. [b] Six cattle in each group.

The connective tissue content of a given muscle may vary indeed between the individual pigs within a litter (Lawrie and Gatherum, 1964).

In general, increasing age connotates decreasing tenderness, although, as already mentioned, also a decrease in connective tissue content (Bate-Smith, 1948; Hiner and Hankins, 1950; and cf. Tables 4.12 and 4.16). This apparent contradiction may probably be explained by the fact that the connective tissue in young animals has a higher content of reticulin, and less cross-bonding, than collagen (Boucek *et al.*, 1961; Goll, Bray and Hoekstra, 1963). Typical data for beef animals at 18 and 30 months of age are given in Table 10.9.

The results of other workers are similar. Decrease of tenderness appears to be less marked with beef from animals older then 18 months,

TABLE 10.9. *Tenderness (Taste Panel) Rating*[a] *of Various Muscles from Beef Steers of Two Ages*
(after Simone, Carroll and Chichester, 1959)

Muscle	18 months	30 months
Adductor	4·67	3·85
Semimembranosus	3·91	3·35
L. dorsi (level 6–8th rib)	6·21	5·95
L. dorsi (level 9–11th rib)	6·16	5·57

[a] High signifies greater tenderness.

differences between 40 and 90-month-old animals being relatively small (Tuma, Henrickson and Moore, 1962). With increasing animal age, the proportion of salt and acid-soluble collagens decrease in bovine muscle; such differences have been demonstrated by starch gel electrophoresis. The extent of intra- and intermolecular cross-linking between the polypeptide chains of collagen concomitantly increases (Carmichael and Lawrie, 1967a, b; Bailey, 1968). Further reflections of the changing character of collagen with increasing animal age include a decreasing solubility on heating (19–24 per cent of total collagen is soluble in calves, 7–8 per cent in 2-year steers, and 2–3 per cent in old cows: Sharp, 1963–4; Hill, 1966) and decreasing susceptibility to attack by enzymes (Goll, Hoekstra and Bray, 1964); cf. Table 10.10.

TABLE 10.10. *Release of Soluble Proteins, Hydroxyproline and Ninhydrin-positive Material from the Connective Tissue of* Biceps femoris *of Beef by Collagenase after 12 hr Incubation*

Animal age, months	Sol. protein (μg/ml incubation medium)	Hydroxyproline	Ninhydrin-positive
1½	230·7 ±9·2	28·8 ±0·9	456 ±10
13—16	122·7 ±8·5	11·3 ±0·2	148 ± 7

In a comparison of the eating quality of bull and steer beef, using a series of entire and castrated twins, Bryce-Jones *et al.* (1963, 1964) found that steer meat was more tender, the difference being especially marked in 1. dorsi and semitendinosus muscles, and at the level of the 7–8th vertebrae.

Table 10.9 also indicates that there are distinct differences in tenderness between muscles. Intramuscular variability in tenderness was comprehensively studied in fifty beef muscles by Ramsbottom and Strandine (1948). For the raw muscles, the shear (i.e. the force required in 1b to shear a sample of $\frac{1}{2}$ in. diameter) ranged from 3·8 in the 1. dorsi to 20·0 in the cutaneous members, and in the cooked muscles from 7·1 in psoas major to 15·6 in sternocephalicus. In agreement with the latter data, the taste panel rated psoas major as most tender, whereas sternocephalicus was one of the toughest. The data for both beef and pork (Tables 4.17a and 4.17b) indicate that psoas major had least hydroxyproline of the muscles studied by Lawrie *et al.* (1963, 1964) although stroma nitrogen, representing insoluble protein of various origin, was higher in psoas than in 1. dorsi (Table 4.20). Lloyd and Hiner (1959) showed that muscles differed in their contents of (apparent) collagen and elastin and that there was a significant inverse correlation between the hydroxyproline of these alkali-insoluble protein fractions and tenderness (Table 10.11).

TABLE 10.11. *Hydroxyproline Content of Collagen and Elastion Fractions from Beef Muscles* (mg/100 g *Muscle*)

Muscle	Collagen hydroxyproline	Elastin hydroxyproline
Semitendinosus	84	3
L. dorsi	11	1
Psoas major	9	1

Differential extraction procedures, however, have not proved entirely satisfactory for determining the relative amounts of collagen and elastin in muscles. Hiner, Anderson and Fellers (1955) attempted to differentiate them by histological techniques. They concluded that, as assessed by size, distribution and frequency, elastin fibres were more numerous in muscles which were frequently in use (such as semi-membranosus and biceps femoris) than in those which were used less extensively (psoas major).

Tenderness within a given muscle may vary significantly (Bryce-Jones *et al.*, 1964). For example, there is a systematic decrease in tenderness in proceeding from the proximal to the distal end of beef semi-membranosus (Paul and Bratzler, 1955; Ginger and Weir, 1958). The tenderness of beef *Biceps femoris* increases from insertion to origin (Rogers, 1969), and lateral portions of pork 1. dorsi are more tender than medial portions (Urbin *et al.*, 1962). The other principal protein found in connective tissue is elastin. Its properties have been fully described by Partridge (1962). The molecule has a central core containing two unusual amino acids, desmosine and isodesmosine, which are derived from lysine.

Being most resistant to heat and thus to degradation on cooking, elastin would, at first sight, appear to constitute an important factor contributing to meat toughness. Fortunately the amount of elastin in most muscles, other than that associated with blood vessels, is very small. Nevertheless, notwithstanding its major concentration, the intractible nature of elastin cannot be entirely ignored in assessing meat texture, especially in those muscles where it appears to be more prevalent (e.g. semimembranosus). The mucoprotein of the ground substance, in which the fibres of collagen and elastin are embedded, is a minor constituent; its distribution parallels that of elastin (McIntosh, 1965).

It is probably justifiable to include the sarcoplasmic reticulum in the category of connective tissue. It surrounds individual myofibrils; and enhanced cohesion of myofibrils parallels "woodiness" in freeze-dried meat (Penny, Voyle and Lawrie, 1962), toughness in meat held aseptically at 37°C for 30 days (Sharp, 1963), and toughness in fish stored in ice (Love *et al.*, 1965).

Intramuscular fat (marbling) tends to dilute the connective tissue of elements in muscle in which it is deposited; and this may help explain the greater tenderness reported for beef from well-fed good-quality animals (Beard, 1924; Wanderstock and Miller, 1948).

10.3.3. *Post-slaughter Factors*

In general, the pre-slaughter factors which affect the tenderness do so by determining the amounts and distribution (texture) and the type of connective tissue. As we have seen, there is a common but not invariable indirect correlation between connective tissue and tenderness. Within a given muscle, however, where amounts and type of connective tissue are constant, there can be considerable differences in tenderness caused by post-slaughter circumstances. The most immediate of these is post-mortem glycolysis.

10.3.3.1. *Post-mortem glycolysis*

Marsh (1964) has indicated that there is a direct relationship between time before rigor mortis and tenderness *on cooking* and Locker (1960a) showed that for muscle not attached to the skeleton or otherwise held taut, the loss of tenderness during the onset of rigor mortis was directly related to the degree of shortening *at that time* (i.e. to the degree of interdigitation of actin and myosin filaments: Fig. 5.2). The degree of shortening, or of tension development, during the onset of rigor mortis in muscle which is free to shorten, is a direct function of temperature (Bendall, 1951; Marsh, 1954, 1962) down to about 14–19°C (Locker and Hagyard, 1963). If such isolated muscle is exposed to temperatures lower than about 14°C at this time, there is again an increasing tendency to shorten—it being as great at 2°C as at 40°C—and this is associated with decreased tenderness on cooking.

Although the marked shortening of muscle at high temperatures had long been known the cold-shortening phenomenon is a more recent factor. The cold-shortening/toughness relationship is by no means linear. On exposure of excised, pre-rigor muscle to temperatures which cause cold-shortening, the degree of toughness in the cooked meat increases as the degree of shortening increases from 20 to 40 per cent of the initial length; thereafter, as the degree of shortening increases to 60 per cent toughness once more decreases (Marsh and Leet, 1966). Shortening up to 40 per cent of initial length signifies a greater degree of interdigitation of actin and myosin, a greater measure of cross-bonding during the onset of rigor-mortis, and is reflected by a greater degree of toughness in the meat. Electron micrographs show that, in such muscles, the ends of the myosin filaments buckle against (or pierce) the Z-lines It is conceivable that the myosin filaments then link through the Z-line, leading to toughness (Dickinson, 1969; Voyle, 1969). It is suggested that, in shortened muscles, the myosin filaments fuse to form a continuum (Locker, 1976). Thus, whereas in cooking non-shortened muscle the myosin filaments would coagulate in discrete masses and myofibrils would break at the I band (from which myosin is absent), this weak point would not occur in shortened sarcomeres in general.

Voyle (1969) cautioned against accepting, too readily, the interdigitation of myosin and actin filaments as the sole explanation for toughness.† Indeed Bouton, Carroll, Harris and Shorthose (1973), whilst confirming that shear values are highly dependent on the degree of myofibrillar contraction in muscles of normal ultimate pH, also noted that adhesion values (which reflect the state of the intrafibrillar connective tissue) are significantly increased in contracted fibres. As an indication that collagen may make a more positive contribution to the degree of toughness in shortened muscle, Rowe (1974) found evidence for alterations in the perimyseal connective tissue which paralleled the degree of shortening of the sarcomeres. As the muscle contracted, the loose configuration of the collagen changed to a well defined lattice. In studying *raw* beef muscles, Rhodes and Dransfield (1974) found that the resistance to shear *increased* with extension above rest length. They explained this phenomenon by postulating that the cross-sectional area of stretched sarcomeres contained a relatively increased proportion of connective tissue.

It is important to note that, if muscle is cooked for four hours at 100°C (when connective tissue is destroyed), and whilst stretched to the point where there is no overlap of actin and myosin filaments, tensile strength remains at about two thirds of corresponding unstretched muscle

---

† Savell *et al.* (1977) demonstrated that markedly different tenderness ratings could be established in sarcomeres of a given length according to the degree of proteolytic enzyme activity which had taken place within them.

(Locker 1976). This clearly indicates that the gap filaments, which survive such treatment, may be a major factor determining the tensile strength of cooked muscle in normal circumstances.

It is of interest that the curves representing the inverse relationship between sarcomere length and toughness, whilst similar in shape, differ in the range of toughness values according to the connective tissue content of the muscle (J. R. Bendall, personal communication). The decrease in toughness observed in cooking muscles which have shortened beyond 40 per cent of their initial length may signify disruption or tearing of the structure (Marsh and Leet, 1966). Indeed electron micrographs have indicated that the phenomenon is probably due to the fracturing of certain sarcomeres by those which have severely shortened (Dickson, Marsh and Leet, 1970). Later studies (Marsh, Leet and Dickson, 1974) by electron microscope revealed that, with shortening greater than 50 per cent, a series of nodes developed in the fibre. These were regions of supercontraction: between them there was fracturing of the fibre which appeared sufficient to account for the decreased toughness. Similar considerations may apply to the tenderizing effect of high pressure (~ 100 MN^{-2}) on muscle, despite severe concomitant shortening (McFarlane, 1973).

If shortening of the muscle is *prevented* during the onset of rigor mortis as, for example, when the muscles are not excised but held rigid on the carcase, the temperature effect is not reflected by the degree of toughness in cooking. Nevertheless, even when held on the carcase, as in normal commercial practice, certain muscles still have a limited freedom to contract, and certain parts of muscles may shorten whilst other parts lengthen, thus causing local toughening even if the overall length is fixed (Marsh and Leet, 1966; Marsh, 1964; Marsh, Woodhams and Leet, 1968). (Clearly, it is not possible to cool the entirety of a large carcase to 15°C within a few moments of death when the *in vivo* temperature is about 37°C.) An interesting aspect of the limited shortening to which some muscles would be liable, even when held on the carcase, has been demonstrated (Herring, Cassens and Briskey, 1965). Thus, when beef carcases were suspended horizontally during post-mortem glycolysis, the sarcomere lengths in such muscles as psoas major and rectus femoris were greater—and toughness was less—than when carcases were suspended in a vertical position. Similar findings have been reported by Hostetler (1970). Suspension by the obturator foramen proved the most effective. Davey, Gilbert and Curson (1971) found that the tenderness of biceps femoris, semi-membranosus and l. dorsi (lumbar) was more than doubled by processing lamb carcases in a standing rather than a vertical position. The stretching which various muscles undergo in horizontally suspended carcases reduces that element of toughness due to contracted myofibrils and also to a minor degree, the adhesion of intrafibre connective tissue (Bouton, Fisher and Baxter, 1973).

It has been pointed out that cold-shortening is not likely to affect muscles deep in the carcase, as in the rump area of beef (L. Buchter, personal communication). Because of the initial high temperature in this region and its insulation, post-mortem glycolysis will be swift and will have proceeded to completion long before refrigeration can lower the temperature below 15°C. Indeed the speed of glycolysis in this region may lead to an exudative condition in beef, somewhat comparable to PSE in the pig. This can be avoided by removal of the meat from the hot carcase and swift cooling in air at 15°C.† Moreover, at this temperature and under these conditions there will be no "cold shortening" and, possibly because the shortening which tends to accompany the onset of rigor mortis when it occurs at body temperature will also be avoided, such meat may be even more tender than that left on the carcase (Schmidt *et al.,* 1970), and will have an enhanced water-holding capacity (Taylor and Dant, 1971). Thus, the bulk of the meat, in relation to the refrigeration capacity applied, will determine whether refrigeration during post-mortem glycolysis will enhance or detract from various aspects of meat quality (cf. § 10.2.1.2).

Locker and Hagyard (1963) failed to observe the cold-shortening effect in the psoas and l. dorsi muscles of rabbits (although these can be made to exhibit thaw rigor: cf. § 7.1.2.2). Bendall (personal com-

---

† It should be noted that the *rate* of heat removal is probably as important in causing "cold-shortening" as the cold temperature itself. Thus the high rate of cooling of excised muscles in a water bath could cause shortening and toughening even at 15°C (unpublished).

munication) found, however, that the soleus muscle of the rabbit *did* show the cold-shortening phenomenon. The latter is a so-called red muscle, resembling in this respect the beef muscles studied by the New Zealand workers, whereas the 1. dorsi of the rabbit is a so-called white muscle. In studying porcine muscles, Bendall (1975) confirmed that red muscles were susceptible to "cold-shortening", whereas those with less myoglobin were much less so. Similar considerations may explain the observation that the power developed in "cold-shortening" by bovine *sternomandibularis* muscles increases with animal age (Davey and Gilbert, 1975a) i.e. as they change to a "redder" type (Lawrie, 1952a).

Two mechanisms have been suggested for "cold-shortening". Cassens and Newbold (1967) believed that the sarcotubular system of pre-rigor muscle is stimulated to release calcium ions by the attainment of temperatures below about 15°C, whereby the contractile actomyosin ATP-ase is much enhanced (Newbold and Scopes, 1967). Indeed a 30-to 40-fold increase of the concentration of calcium ions in the vicinity of the myofibrils, as the temperature falls from 15 to 0°C, has been reported (Davey and Gilbert, 1974). It may be postulated that reabsorption of these ions could be more readily effected by a type of muscle wherein the sarcotubular system was relatively well developed; and Fawcett and Revel (1961) demonstrated that the system was more extensively elaborated in white muscles than in red. It would be expected, therefore, that the enhancement of actomyosin ATP-ase would be less easily suppressed in the latter and would more readily lead to marked interdigitation of myosin and actin filaments, i.e. shortening, as is observed.

Buege and Marsh (1975), however, showed that pre-rigor red muscles do not "cold-shorten" when cooled below 15°C if they are adequately supplied with oxygen. This resistance is annulled by reagents which uncouple the uptake of oxygen from resynthesis of ATP. They thus inferred that "cold-shortening" is due to the discharge of calcium ions from the muscle mitochondria under anaerobic conditions post-mortem and to failure by the sarcotubular system to reabsorb them effectively at low temperatures. Since red muscles contain a greater number of mitochondria than white (Paul and Sperling, 1952: Lawrie, 1952a), this feature could have significance in relation to the relative "cold-shortening" susceptibility of the two types of muscle.

There is clearly evidence for the involvement of both mechanisms.† The situation is not yet completely resolved, however, since porcine *l. dorsi,* although a white muscle, undergoes vigorous "cold-shortening" (Bendall, 1975).

At temperatures below the freezing point, damage to the sarcotubular system would be relatively severe in both red and white muscles; and its ability to recapture calcium ions adversely affected. If freezing had been sufficiently rapid after death to fix ATP concentrations at pre-rigor levels, this would be manifested as the phenomenon of "thaw-rigor" (unless thawing were extremely fast: cf. § 7.1.2.2.). It is found, in fact, that both red and white muscles are susceptible to the massive shortening of "thaw-rigor" (above). A comparison of the behaviour of red (semitendinosus) and white (psoas) muscles of the rabbit substantiates the view that "cold-shortening" and "thaw-rigor" both reflect abnormal post-mortem stimulation of the contractile actomyosin ATP-ase (Lawrie, 1968), whatever may be the precise mechanisms.

Shortening and toughening of muscles can be arrested, even if they are frozen pre-rigor, provided either that they are thawed on the carcase or, if they are excised, that they are slowly thawed at about —2°C, when the rigidity of the remaining ice will prevent shortening (Marsh, 1964; Marsh and Thompson, 1958) If pre-rigor frozen muscle is held for a month at —12°C, there is an even slower rate of ATP breakdown; but over this period it is sufficient to remove the prerequisite for "thaw-rigor" (Davey and Gilbert, 1976). The breakdown appears to be due to direct enzymic action; post-mortem glycolysis does not occur at this temperature (rapid thawing of such meat leads, of course, to the marked shortening of thaw-rigor).

The rate of post-mortem glycolysis has another effect on tenderness in addition to that on shortening during the onset of rigor mortis. Where

† Since the concentration of calcium-carrier protein in mitochondria is relatively very low in comparison with the calcium-binding mechanism in the sarcoplasmic reticulum, the involvement of mitochondrial Ca^{++} release in 'cold-shortening' seems likely to be a less significant mechanism than exchanges of Ca^{++} between the sarcoplasm and the sarcoplasmic reticulum (Graeser, 1977).

the rate of pH fall is inordinately fast, as in the white muscle condition in pigs (Bendall and Wismer-Pedersen, 1962), sarcoplasmic proteins are denatured and precipitate on to those of the myofibrils; and the latter may also be denatured to some extent, since they become less soluble in these circumstances. It has been shown that the ratio of insoluble myofibrillar protein to total protein in muscle is directly correlated with toughness (Hegarty, Bratzler and Pearson, 1963).

The *extent* of post-mortem glycolysis, apart from its rate, also has an effect on the tenderness of beef, pork and lamb (Howard and Lawrie, 1956; Lewis, Brown and Heck, 1962, Bouton, Carroll, Fisher, Harris and Shorthose, 1973). As the ultimate pH increases from 5·5 to 6·0, tenderness appears to decrease; at ultimate pH levels above 6, however, tenderness increases once again (Fig. 10.4). Both shear force and adhesion, as respective measures of the contributions of myofibrils and connective tissue to toughness, decrease as the ultimate pH rises (Bouton, Carroll, Harris and Shorthose, 1973). In the region of pH 6·8, tenderness becomes excessive and is associated with a jellylike consistency in the meat which lowers its overall acceptability (Bouton *et al.*, 1957). The exact tenderness/pH relationship varies between different muscles. Thus, in mutton, the pH of minimum tenderness was 5·64, 5·90 and 6·05 for biceps femoris, semitendinosus and 1. dorsi respectively (Bouton and Shorthose, 1969). If pre-rigor meat is heated quickly enough, so that the enzymes effecting post-mortem glycolysis are inactivated faster than the heat can accelerate their activity, a high pH will result. If it is of the order of 7 this would be expected to enhance tenderness (cf. Fig. 10.4) to a much greater extent than the shortening of the excised muscle would diminish it (even although such shortening during cooking is especially severe with rigor meat; Marsh, 1964). It has been shown, in fact, that the relative tenderness of pre-rigor cooked meat is directly related to the level of pH which has been attained at the moment of cooking (Miles and Lawrie, 1970). As indicated earlier, muscles which have shortened become less tender during subsequent conditioning (Davey, Kuttel and Gilbert, 1967). The enhanced tenderness is no doubt a reflection of the greater water content and water-holding capacity of the muscle proteins (§ 5.4.1) and of the consequent swollen nature of the muscle fibres at high pH. Some of the tenderness of pre-rigor meat can be similarly explained.

10.3.3.2. *Conditioning*

That the tenderness of beef† increases when it is conditioned (e.g. stored at chill temperatures for 10–14 days) has long been recognized (Lehmann, 1907); and, of course, such meat as venison is regularly aged for this pupose. The decrease in tenderness which is associated with the onset of rigor mortis (§ 10.3.3.1) is gradually reversed as the time of post-rigor conditioning increases. To reiterate the views in § 5.4.2, this is not due to the dissociation of the actomyosin formed during the onset of rigor mortis (Marsh, 1954), and the absence of any increase in end groups (Locker, 1906b) shows that the myofibrillar proteins are not apparently proteolysed in these circumstances. Moreover, the absence of soluble hydroxyproline-containing substances in meat, even after one year at 37°C, indicates there is no extensive proteolysis in connective tissue proteins (Sharp, 1959). Although there is no proteolysis of connective tissue proteins, certain cross-links in the collagen molecules are apparently broken, possibly due to the action of lysosomal enzymes (Etherington, 1971). A collagenolytic cathepsin, present in low concentrations in muscular tissue of the rat, has been shown to operate optimally at pH 3·5. At this pH (and 28°C) it cleaves the telopeptide region of insoluble collagen, liberating α-chains (Etherington, 1972). Its pH optimum would prevent its acting freely outside cells; but it may operate by some mechanism involving the local establishment of low pH environments. More subtle changes in these elements are not precluded, however, and, at any rate in the case of myofibrillar proteins, there is some suggestion that actin filaments may become dissociated from their attachments on the Z-line during conditioning (Davey, 1964); and also some suggestion that the network of the sarcoplasmic reticulum around the individual myofibrils may be disrupted at this time (Lawrie and Voyle, unpublished data). As already indicated (§ 5.4.1.), it may be that

† Pork and lamb are generally derived from animals which are too young for toughness to be a significant factor unless the meat has been processed.

the calcium-activated sarcoplasmic factor affects not the Z-line itself but the so-called gap filaments during ageing (Locker, 1976; Davey and Graafhuis, 1976; Locker, Daines, Carse and Leet, 1977). There is extensive proteolysis of the soluble sarcoplasmic proteins (Hoagland *et al.*, 1917); and, because of loss of calcium ions and the uptake of potassium ions, muscle proteins increase their water-holding capacity during conditioning (Arnold *et al.*, 1956).

Whatever the nature of the particular protein changes during conditioning, which are significant in relation to the increased tenderness, it is clear that muscles contain proteolytic enzymes (§ 5.4.2) which operate much more readily at 37°C than at 5°C (Sharp, 1963); and that, in general, higher temperatures of conditioning produce a given degree of tenderizing in a considerably shorter time than do lower temperatures. This effect has been studied by Bouton *et al.* (1958) and by Wilson *et al.* (1960). The former workers found that conditioning for 2 days at 20°C gave the same degree of tenderizing as 14 days at 0°C, and that the benefits of conditioning were more marked with beef of poor quality (cf. also Moran and Smith, 1929), which was initially tougher although the final degree of tenderness achieved was similar in beef of good and poor quality.

Wilson *et al.* (1960) employed antibiotics to control bacterial spoilage and were thus able to study temperatures as high as 49°C. Semimembranosus muscles from the rounds of beef carcasses which had been infused with oxytetracycline (to a concentration of 30–50 ppm) were employed. The muscles were prepared as $\frac{3}{4}$ in. steaks and vacuum sealed in plastic film. After appropriate conditioning periods at 2°C, 38°C, 43°C and 49°C, the meat was cooked and assessed for tenderness by a taste panel. Some of the results are given in Table 10.12.

As Table 10.12 shows, the tenderness score was increased by all conditioning procedures over that of controls. Moreover, the meat held for 2 days at 38°C, or for 1 day at 43° or 49°C, was more tender than that kept for 14 days at 2°C. The tenderness increment was particularly high in the meat held at 49°C, but the latter had a somewhat undesirable flavour. Conditioning at 38°C was difficult to control, even with the dose of ionizing radiation given to steaks at this temperature (in addition to the antibiotics) because of the greater risk of bacterial growth. The optimum time and temperature required to have the same degree of

TABLE 10.12. *Mean Tenderness Values For Beef Steaks conditioned in Various Ways* (after Wilson *et al.*, 1960)

Time and temperature of conditioning	Tenderness	
	Initial	Residual
Non-conditioned controls	5·2	5·2
14 days at 20°C	5·9	5·8
Non-conditioned controls[a]	5·3	5·5
2 days at 38°C	6·0	6·1
Non-conditioned controls	5·1	5·2
1 day at 43°C	6·3	6·2
Non-conditioned controls	5·2	5·4
1 day at 49°C	7·4	7·2

[a] Given 45,000 rad ionizing radiation.

tenderizing as that arising during 14 days at 0°C was 1 day at 43°C. If high temperature conditioning is applied, however, to increase immediately after slaughter, this can induce marked shortening of the muscles as they go into *rigor mortis* and consequent toughness, an adverse effect which has been observed in lamb carcases (Davey and Curson, 1971). When, however, muscles are restrained from shortening they are more tender if they undergo rigor mortis at 37°C than at 15°C (Locker and Daines, 1975), although changes in the bonds between myosin and the actin-tropomyosin-troponin complex have been cited as responsible (Locker and Daines, 1976) rather than alterations in the Z-lines or gap filaments (as above).†

At holding temperatures above 40°C the rate of conditioning decreases gradually up to 60°C. It then decreases sharply, ceasing altogether at 75°C (Davey and Gilbert, 1976b).‡

Wilson *et al.* (1960) also applied high-temperature conditioning to intact beef sides from animals which had been injected pre-slaughter with oxytetracycline. This work confirmed the earlier findings. About 0·5–1 ppm remained in the l. dorsi after 14 days at 2°C; and this appeared to be sufficient to control microbial growth. An interesting aspect of this study was the finding that, whereas the tenderness of l.

dorsi, semitendinosus and biceps femoris was greater after 14 days at 2°C than after 1 day at 43°C, the semimembranosus, as before, showed a greater increase in tenderness at the higher temperature of conditioning. This suggested that the latter might be more effective with intrinsically less tender muscles. Harris and McFarlane (1971) found that beef 1. dorsi muscle tenderized more rapidly than semimembranosus when aged at 0–1°C for up to 6 weeks (cf. § 5.4.1). This was true whether or not the muscles were stretched by hanging the carcases by the obturator foramen. Stretching was found to give a tenderizing effect equivalent to that obtained by ageing for 2 weeks at 0–1°C when using the conventional method of suspension.

10.3.3.3. *Cooking*

Whether cooking will cause an increase or a decrease in tenderness converting collagen to gelatin, it coagulates and tends to toughen the meat is raised, the time of the heating and the particular muscle being considered.

Whilst, in general, cooking makes connective tissue more tender by converting collagen to gelatin, it coagulated and tends to toughen the proteins of the myofibril. Both these effects depend on time and temperature, the former being more important for the softening of collagen and the latter more critical for myofibrillar toughening. Prolonged cooking times and relatively low temperatures are thus justified for meat which has much connective tissue and conversely

---

† Dutson (1977), however, attributed tenderness increments in such circumstances to the early operation of conditioning changes arising from enhanced proteolytic activity of lysosomal enzymes due to the high temperature-low pH combination; and, before the pH fell below 6, possibly also to enhanced CASF action.

‡ It is interesting to note the observations of Penny & Dransfield (1979) in this context. Although proteolysis of troponin T correlated with increasing tenderness in beef muscles when conditioning took place at temperatures between 3° and 15°C—and the rates of proteolysis increased with increasing temperature—the concomitant increase of tenderness was proportionately less at higher temperatures of ageing. This possibly reflects the involvement of protein denaturation as an additional factor in the latter circumstances; and recalls the observations of Sharp (1963) (§ 5.4.1.), who found that muscles stored at 37°C homogenized less readily than those stored at 0°C.

(Weir, 1960). The tenderizing effects of prolonged cooking is additional to that of ageing (conditioning) (Davey, Niederer and Graafhuis, 1976).

The degree of solubility of collagen increases with temperature. At about 60°C collagen shortens and is converted into a more soluble form (Bendall, 1946; Bear, 1952; Machlik and Draudt, 1963). The shrinkage temperature of collagen is fairly characteristic. Meat juices appear to play some part, however, in the effect (Giffee, Madison and Landmann, 1963) since the shrinkage temperature is 65°C, when collagen is heated in water (Winegarden *et al.*, 1952). The helical structure can be seen to unwind on heating for 10 minutes at 64°C (Anon, 1974b; Snowden and Weidemann, 1978). The percentage of collagen (beef) solubilized by heat increases gradually from about 60°C to 98°C. At the latter temperature conversion to gelatin is marked (cf. Table 10.13; Paul, 1975). Gelatin formation is swift with pressure cooking at 115–125°C (Bendall, 1946).

Partial reversion of the collagen to gelatin transformation explains the finding that, whereas meat cooked at 80°C is tougher when measured at 20°C than at 70°C, that cooked at 55°C shows no difference with the temperature of assessment (Ledward and Lawrie, 1975). Some of the discrepancies between objective assessment of meat tenderness at room temperature and subjective assessment by taste panel, using warm meat, may well be explained thereby.

In experiments with beef sternocephalicus muscle (Locker, Daines, Carse and Leet, 1977), in which the time of heating at 70°C was varied, it was found that when muscles were cooked beyond 40 minutes, myosin and actin denatured; but not collagen or gap filaments (cf. § 3.2.2.). The latter become stronger and more extensible. They even withstand heating for four hours at 100°C, when collagen is destroyed. In conditioned muscle, however, they appear to be attacked by the calcium-activated sarcoplasmic factor and then disintegrate on cooking (§ 5.4.1).

There is increased tenderness with increased solubilization of collagen in braising; but relatively little softening, despite increased collagen solubility, on roasting (Table 10.13).

The attainment of a given temperature by microwave energy is associated with less denaturation of the myofibrillar and sarcoplasmic

TABLE 10.13. *Effect of Temperature of Cooking on Shear Force and Collagen Solubilization in Various Beef Muscles,* (after Paul, 1975)

Muscle		Mean Internal Temperature (°C)			
		(a) Roasting			
		58°	67°	75°	82°
L. dorsi &	Shear Force (kg)	4·5	3·3	3·5	3·5
Triceps brachii	Collagen solubilized (%Total)	2·7	4·8	6·4	7·7
Semitendinosus	Shear Force (kg)	3·5	3·1	3·3	3·3
	Collagen Solubilized (%Total)	4·3	6·0	8·0	11·0
Biceps femoris	Shear Force (kg)	4·3	3·9	3·6	3·6
	Collagen Solubilized (%Total)	6·3	8·7	8·5	13·6
		(b) *Braising*			
		70°	98° (held 30 min)	98°	98° (held 90 min)
L. dorsi &	Shear Force (kg)	3·9	3·4	2·9	2·2
Triceps brachii	Collagen Solubilized (%Total)	3·7	11·3	21·5	44·9
Semitendinosus &	Shear Force (kg)	4·9	3·8	3·0	2·2
Biceps femoris	Collagen Solubilized (%Total)	4·9	10·2	23·3	52·0

proteins than when attained by conventional heating; but this can be attributed to the further progression of the same type of effects due to the increased time of cooking necessary with the latter process (Roberts and Lawrie, 1974). On the other hand, there is evidence that microwave heating preferentially increases the solubilization of collagen (McCrae and Paul, 1974).

These conflicting influences help to explain why different muscles react differently to cooking (cf. Table 10.13). Thus, beef 1. dorsi is tender and biceps femoris (which has about twice as much collagen) is tough when boiled to 61°C; but the converse holds when they are braised at

100°C (Cover and Hostetler, 1960). While 1. dorsi cooked at 60°C, 70° or 80°C showed no difference in shear force, there was a considerable decrease in the force required to shear semitendinosus and semi-membranosus when cooked at 70° and 80°C compared with 60°C (Sanderson and Vail, 1963); the latter two muscles having more connective tissue than 1. dorsi. Davey and Gilbert (1975 b, c), however, found that, with bovine sternomandibularis muscle at a given degree of shortening, the toughness when heated at 60°C was only half the value attained when heated at 80°C, although at the latter temperature the denatured collagen has a much reduced mechanical force compared to that of the native fibre. If the predominant collagen in a muscle has thermally-labile cross-links then heating will cause greater solubility and decreased shear values; whereas, if the collagen has heat-stable cross-links; increased tension and toughness will result on heating (Bailey and Sims, 1977). The relative contributions made by the collagens of the basement membrane, epimysium, perimysium and endomysium—and by the degree of heat-stable cross-linking in each—will influence the toughness of a given muscle when heated at constant sarcomere length.

Davey and Gilbert (1975b) showed that, for a given degree of shortening during the onset of rigor mortis, and a given cooking temperature, the meat of young beef animals was more tender than that of older ones. During the cooking of veal the collagen readily dissolves to set as a gel on cooling. On the other hand, using the same muscle and temperature, the collagen from older animals is insoluble and the meat tough. The highly cross-linked intramuscular collagen of the older animals binds the myofibrils together even when it is denatured, and generates greater tension during heat contraction (Bailey, 1974).

The effect of shortening during the onset of rigor mortis on subsequent toughness in cooked meat has been considered in detail above (§ 10.3.3.1). The shortening observed in these circumstances reflects the extent to which individual sarcomeres *contract,* i.e. the degree of interdigitation of actin and myosin filaments in each sarcomere. Cooking produces further, additional shortening by causing the sarcomeres to *shrink* overall. Such shrinkage of sarcomeres does not occur at temperatures up to 60°C but it does at 70°C (Giles,

1969). At the latter temperature the *M*-lines and *I*-bands become disrupted and changes are observed in the collagen fibres (which, at 70°C, are above their shrink temperature). Whereas with unshortened muscle, cooking shrinkage occurred along the fibres and precedes fluid discharge (transverse swelling accommodates entrapped fluid), such discharge occurs during the cooking of highly shortened muscle;and across the fibres. Cooking shortening at 80°C, of muscle which has not shortened during the onset of rigor mortis, contributes to toughening to the same degree as cold-shortening (Davey and Gilbert, 1975b, c).

However desirable from the point of view of increased tenderness, pressure cooking may be associated with detrimental changes in the biological value of the meat proteins. Thus, Beuk, Chornock and Rice (1948) showed that when pork was autoclaved at 112°C for 24 hr, 45 per cent of the cystine was destroyed. It appeared that the essential amino acids were unaffected; but this was as determined by acid hydrolysis of the meat. Enzymic digestion showed a lowered availability of several essential amino acids—tryptophan being especially affected. This would be reflected in their value during digestion. It should be emphasized, however, that no lowering of the nutritive value of meat would occur at temperatures below 100°C (Rice and Beuk, 1953); and the latter is substantially above the normal temperatures attained by meat during cooking.

10.3.3.4. *Processing*

Subsequent processing may alter meat tenderness. The effects of pre-rigor freezing have already been considered in relation to post-mortem glycolysis. Alterations of tenderness through freezing post-rigor meat are also known. Although the rates of freezing normally used in commerce have no effect in this respect, meat blast frozen at a rate sufficient to freeze the deepest portion of the carcase in 24 hr (§ 7.1.2.2) tends to be tougher on cooking than corresponding meat which has been chilled for the normal 2–3 days before freezing (Howard and Lawrie, 1956)—possibly because the latter has had what amounts to a short conditioning period (§§ 5.4 and 10.3.3.2). If, however, the rate of blast freezing is increased, so that the deepest part of the carcase freezes in only 18 hr, the meat is found to be as tender as corresponding meat frozen after 2–3 days chilling (Howard and Lawrie, 1957b). Since the absence of a chilling period in the former would again operate against tenderness, it must be presumed that this is more than offset by microstructural changes effected by the greater rate of freezing. Their nature is unknown for, although freezing makes post-rigor meat more tender when the rate is fast enough to cause intrafibrillar ice formation (Hiner, Madsen and Hankins, 1945; Hiner, 1951) such rates are virtually impossible with beef quarters. On the other hand, the necessary rates *could* occur in freezing steaks for prepackaged sale. An alternative or additional explanation of the toughening observed in the blast freezing of hot beef carcases could be the induction of "cold-shortening" (cf. § 10.3.3.1 above). The observed increase in tenderness with even faster blast freezing, could signify immobilization of the surface musculature by freezing before cold-shortening could occur.

In the accelerated freeze drying of meat, even under optimum operating conditions, the rehydrated product is somewhat less tender and more "woody" than fresh meat. This appears to be partly attributable to the effect of the plate temperature on the sarcoplasmic and myofibrillar proteins (§ 8.2.2) and it is largely obviated by the induction of a high ultimate pH. The latter, whilst producing excessive tenderness in fresh meat, restores a desirable degree of tenderness to the meat after accelerated freeze drying (Tables 8.10–8.12).

Ionizing radiation at sterilizing doses (about 5 Mrad) or above, causes changes in the meat proteins which increase tenderness (Coleby *et al.*, 1961). This is probably due to changes in the collagen molecule, for the shrink temperature of isolated collagen decreases from 61°C to 47°C with 5 Mrad and to 27°C with 40 Mrad (Bailey *et al.*, 1962).

10.3.4. *Artificial Tenderizing*

Attempts to make meat tender artificially are by no means new. They have included beating the meat, cutting it into small portions so that the strands of connective tissue were severed, marinading it with vinegar, wine or salt and enzymic tenderizing—inadvertently employed at least 500 years ago by the Mexican Indians when they wrapped meat in pawpaw leaves during cooking. In recent years such attempts have become more systematic.

Recognition that certain plants, fungi and bacteria produced non-toxic proteolytic enzymes (Balls, 1941; Hwang and Ivy, 1951) was followed by their incorporation into commercial meat tenderizers. These were first used as dips. As such, they were somewhat unsatisfactory since they over-tenderized the surface, producing a mushy texture (and sometimes unusual flavour), and, since they were unable to penetrate within the meat, left the interior unaffected. One method of overcoming this difficulty was to introduce the enzyme solution into the pieces of meat before cooking through fork holes (Hay, Harrison and Vail, 1953). Another was to pump the major blood vessels of the meat cuts post-mortem with enzyme-containing solution. A third was to rehydrate freeze-dried steaks in a solution containing proteolytic enzymes (Wang and Maynard, 1955). This ensured a much better distribution of the enzyme than did dipping or perfusion; but was still not ideal. Pre-slaughter injection of the live animal has proved to be the most effective method of introducing proteolytic enzymes into meat so that they penetrate uniformly into the furthest interstices of the tissue. This method was patented by Beuk *et al.* in 1959. A concentration of about 5 to 10 per cent of tenderizing enzyme is advocated; and the total quantity injected approximates to 0·5 mg/lb live weight, although it varies according to the enzyme employed. There is some suggestion that the more active muscles, which have more connective tissue, get more enzyme because they also have a greater vascularity. At enzyme levels suitable for tenderizing the muscles, the tongue, and organs such as liver may accumulate excessive quantities of enzyme and disintegrate on cooking. Animals are slaughtered 1–30 min after injection. In general, the injected enzymes do not harm the live animal. This is because the pH of the blood is considerably above their optimum pH, because they depend on —SH groups for activity and these are inoperative at *in vivo* oxygen tensions, and because they do not reach their optimum temperature of activity until, during cooking, the range 70–85°C is attained (Gottschall and Kies, 1942). Nevertheless, the oxygen supply is limited within the cartilage matrix, allowing *in vivo* enzymic activity. As a result the injection of papain (temporarily protected by oxidation against inactivation during its passage in the blood) is manifested in rabbits by a dropping of the ears (McCluskey and Thomas, 1958). Again, structural and histochemical changes have been detected in animal livers after injection of papain and ficin at doses of 200 mg/kg

TABLE 10.14. *Relative Potency of Preparations of Proteolytic Enzymes on Muscular Tissue* (after Wang *et al.*, 1957)

Enzyme preparation	Activity against		
	Acto-myosin	Collagen	Elastin
Bacterial and fungal			
Protease 15	+ + +	—	—
Rhozyme	+ +	—	—
Fungal amylase	+ + +	Trace	—
Hydralase D	+ + +	Trace	—
Plant			
Ficin (fig.)	+ + +	+ + +	+ + + +
Papain (pawpaw)	+ +	+	+ +
Bromelin (pineapple)	Trace	+ + +	+

body weight (Nestorov, Georgieva and Grosdanov, 1970). The toughness of lamb, induced by "cold-shortening" can be offset by pre-slaughter injections of papain at commercial dose levels (Rhodes and Dransfield, 1973).

There is significant breed effect. The introduction of Brahmain blood into cattle leads to a greater resistance to the tenderizing effects of papain (Huffman *et al.*, 1967).

Some of the enzymes which have been used in the tenderizing of meat are listed in Table 10.14.

It will be seen from Table 10.14 that the bacterial and fungal proteolytic enzymes act only on the proteins of the muscle fibre. They first digest the sarcolemma, causing disappearance of nuclei, then degrade the muscle fibre, eventually causing loss of cross-striations. The action of the proteolytic enzymes of plant origin is preferentially against connective tissue fibres. They first break up the mucopolysaccharide of the ground substance matrix, then progressively reduce the connective tissue fibres to an amorphous mass. It should be emphasized that these enzymes do not attack native collagen: they act upon the collagen as it is denatured by heat during cooking (Partridge, 1959). Elastin is not altered during conditioning or cooking and the activity of the proteolytic enzymes

TABLE 10.15. *Increasing Tenderness, and Decreasing Residue, through Enzymic Treatment of Beef*
(after Wang *et al.*, 1958)

Enzyme	Mean taste panel score		
	Concentration (%)	Tenderness	Residue
Fungal amylase	0	6·5	5·5
	0·045	7·4	5·4
Bromelin	0	6·5	5·5
	0·0003	7·6	4·5
Ficin A	0	6·2	6·1
	0·0003	7·9	5·9
Ficin B	0	5·8	5·8
Papain	0	5·5	5·6
	0·0003	7·0	4·6

against elastin fibres suggests the presence of an elastase (Wang *et al.*, 1958). Unlike the tenderizing changes during conditioning (§§ 5.4 and 10.3.3.2), the enzymes used in artificial tenderizing break down connective tissue proteins to soluble, hydroxyproline-containing molecules.

Some idea of the relative efficacy of these enzymes in tenderizing meat is given in Table 10.15. It will be noted that, in agreement with its lack of effect on connective tissue, the fungal enzyme has no effect on the residue as assessed by the taste panel after mastication.

As an alternative to the addition of proteolytic enzymes, meat might be artificially tenderized by stimulation of the muscle's own proteolytic (catheptic) activity. Induced vitamin E deficiency would enhance the activity of the lysosomal enzymes (Tappel *et al.*, 1962): their liberation from the containing cell particles may be increased by excess vitamin A.

As another alternative, the formation of the mucopolysaccharide of the ground substance matrix and of collagen could be suppressed by the administration of cortisone and through vitamin C deficiency respectively (Whitehouse and Lash, 1961; Stone and Meister, 1962).

Sodium chloride itself, and other salts, have a tenderizing action on meat which is not inconsiderable (Wang *et al.*, 1958; Kamstra and Saffle, 1959) and post-mortem perfusion of joints with salt solutions has been of some success in this context (Bouton and Howard, 1960). Some of these effects are due to an enhanced water-holding capacity—either direct, or, as in the case of phosphate, through a concomitant raising of the pH (Bendall, 1954). Even the injection of water enhances tenderness (Williams, 1964a). Experiments in Australia (Anon., 1971) showed that it was possible to tenderize both beef and mutton by subjecting the muscles from freshly slaughtered animals to very high pressures for short periods. Pressures of 100 MNm^{-2} applied for 2–4 min reduced the shear value (Warner-Bratzler) for various cuts by three to fourfold. Microscopic examination showed that such high pressures cause severe contraction and disorganization of the muscles. and McFarlane (1973) demonstrated that the application of/pre-rigor pressure (100 MNm^{-2}) at 30°C produced shortening of the muscles of the same order as that obtained in "cold-shortening", without the accompanying increase in toughness. Subsequently, it was found that combined pressure-heat treatments (150 MNm^{-2} at 60°C for 30 min.) effects a substantial decrease in shear force even in cold-shortened meat (Bouton, Ford, Harris, Macfarlane and O'Shea, 1977); and it was shown that it is the myofibrillar proteins which are primarily affected by the treatment (Bouton, Harris, Macfarlane and O'Shea, 1977). Adhesion values, which are believed to derive from connective tissue, are not affected. The imidazole groups of histidine appear to be implicated in the pressure solubilization effect (McFarlane and McKenzie, 1976).

10.4. ODOUR AND TASTE

10.4.1. *Definition and Nature*

Flavour is a complex sensation. It involves odour, taste, texture, temperature and pH. Of these, odour is the most important. Without it one or other of the four primary taste sensations—bitter, sweet, sour or saline—predominates. Odour and taste are most difficult to define objectively. It is true that, in recent years, gas chromatography has permitted precise measurement of the volatiles from foodstuffs; but this has not infrequently confused the issue. The compounds isolated have not always corresponded with recognized subjective odour responses. In considering the objective determination of taste, it is desirable to remember that, even with the primary sensation of bitterness, one person in three considers phenylthiocarbamide tasteless, although it is intensely bitter for two-thirds of the population (Blakeslee, 1932). Moreover, context is important. An agreeable odour in roast beef becomes nauseating when it emanates from a flower (*Iris foetidissima*: Moncrieff, 1951).

The evaluation of odour and taste still depends mainly on the taste panel. Variability between individuals in intensity and quality of response to a given stimulus, and in a given individual due to extraneous factors, makes the choosing of taste panel members, and the conditions of operation of the panel, matters of importance. The question has received considerable attention (Ehrenberg and Shewan, 1953; Peryam, 1958; Dawson, Bragdon and McManus, 1963). The operation of meat taste panels in particular has been investigated by Harries *et al.* (1963). It is not difficult to appreciate that there may well be genuine disagreement over the more subtle aspects of odour and taste.

The mechanisms by which human beings normally detect odour and taste will not be detailed here since full descriptions are available in physiological textbooks, but a few comments should be made. Response to odour occurs in the olfactory cells of the nasal surfaces and is conveyed from these to the brain for interpretation by the olfactory nerves. It is generally presumed that odoriferous substances react chemically with the olfactory nerve endings (Moncrieff, 1951). There appears to be a 1 : 1 relationship between the frequency of molecular vibration of the stimulating odoriferous compounds and the properties of the corresponding responses of the olfactory bulb (Wright, Hughes and Hendrix, 1967). In adult man, response to taste occurs in specialized cells on the tongue, the soft palate and the top of the gullet. As in the case of odour, it probably involves chemical reactions between the molecules concerned and the nerve endings in the taste cells—interpretation of the sensation again being made in the brain. Proteins have been isolated from the taste buds of cows and pigs, which form complexes with bitter and sweet substances directly in proportion to the actual bitter or sweet tastes of the latter (Dastoli, Lopiekes and Doig, 1968). While it has not been unequivocally shown how the dozen or so classes of responses (Bate-Smith, 1961) of the different olfactory cells are reflected morphologically, taste cells can be roughly localized, different areas of the tongue responding to the four primary sensations (bitter, sweet, sour and salt). There are also secondary taste reactions which can be described as metallic or alkaline (Moncrieff, 1951).

In ideal circumstances response to odour is about 10,000 times more sensitive than that to taste. Thus, while ethyl mercaptan can be detected in air at a concentration of 3×10^{-9} per cent, the sensation of bitterness, which is the most acute taste, is detectable from strychnine at a concentration in water of 4×10^{-5} per cent. Odour and taste in foodstuffs are important both aesthetically and physiologically for, if pleasant, they stimulate the secretion of digestive juices.

10.4.2. *Chemical Aspects*

The odour and taste of cooked meat arise from water or fat soluble precursors and by the liberation of volatile substances pre-existent in the meat. Of the very many volatiles which contribute to the aroma of cooked meat, pyrazines and several compounds containing sulphur or oxygen, play a significant part (Patterson, 1975). The volatiles from cooked lean meat include H_2S, ammonia, acetaldehyde, acetone and diacetyl; and there are traces of formic, acetic, propionic, butyric and isobutyric acids and of dimethylsulphide (Yueh and Strong, 1960). Water extracts of raw meat produce a meaty flavour on heating and such is already present in water extracts of cooked meat (Crocker, 1948; Kramlich and Pearson, 1958). The latter is stronger, however, suggesting that the interaction of the meat juices with the fibrillar elements during cooking makes a substantial contribution. Batzer *et al.* (1960) attempted to isolate from raw beef the precursors which eventually produce the distinctive odour and taste of the cooked commodity. Dialysis of a water-soluble extract of uncooked beef gave a

TABLE 10.16. *Amino Acids in Glycoprotein from Beef*

Amino acid	g/mol/equivalents
Serine	0·130
Glutamic acid	0·010
Glycine	0·025
Alanine	0·100
Isoleucine	0·016
Leucine	0·030
β-alanine	0·780

diffusate which produced an odour like that of broiled beef when heated with fat and the odour and taste of beef broth when heated in water. Further investigation (Batzer *et al.,* 1962) of the water-soluble dialysate showed that it contained, apart from other constituents, inosinic acid (or inosine and inorganic phosphate) and a glycoprotein, the carbohydrate portion of which is glucose, and having the relative amino acid composition shown in Table 10.16. When mixtures of some of these amino acids are added to glucose, inosine and inorganic phosphate, meaty-odours and tastes are produced on heating in fat or water. Gel permeation chromatography of extracts of raw beef yields a dozen fractions; half of these produce a recognizable boiled beef aroma on heating (Malbrouk, Jarboe and O'Conner, 1969). The two fractions giving the strongest odour represented nearly 80 per cent of the diffusate and contained methionine, cysteic acid and 2-deoxyribose.

Volatile products are derived from amino acids on pyrolysis. The products formed from dipeptides and dipeptide pairs depend on the *sequence* of amino acids. If this also applies to longer peptides it may explain why aromas derived by heating mixtures of single amino acids do not correspond exactly with those formed by heating meat extracts of similar composition (Merritt and Robertson, 1967). It has been claimed that the odour and taste of various meats can be produced artificially by heating a pentose or hexose monosaccharide with cysteine in excess water (Morton, Arkroyd and May, 1960). Pentose sugars (ribose, arabinose or xylose) are preferred since they give a flavour more like meat itself, whereas that produced when hexoses are involved is merely savoury. More full-bodied flavours are obtained by using, in addition to cysteine, one or more other amino acids such as glycine, glutamic acid, β-alanine, threonine, histidine, lysine, leucine, isoleucine, serine, or valine. Some of these correspond with the amino acids of the naturally occurring glycoprotein of beef (Table 10.16). Derivatives, or peptides, yielding these amino acids during the reaction are also effective. The use of ribose and cysteine alone gives a flavour akin to pork: if other amino acids, quantitatively equivalent to 1–3 times the weight of cysteine are used, a flavour like beef is obtained. Subsequently, it has become clear that the carbohydrate moiety may be an aliphatic aldehyde (e.g. acetaldehyde or isobutyraldehyde: May and Morton, 1961) or furan (May, 1961). Macy, Naumann and Bailey (1964) suggest that inosine has been implicated in meat flavour and browning because of its conversion to ribose. In 1967 Hoersch patented a synthetic meat flavour product by heating a mixture of sodium nitrite and seven amino acids to 120°C at pH 6.

It is of interest to recall that Japanese workers concluded that mononucleotides are substantially responsible for meat flavour. It appears to be essential that the purine moiety should be substituted with a hydroxyl group at position 6 and that the ribose be substituted with a phosphate group at position 5 (Kodama, 1913; Yoshida and Kageyama,

1956). As well as glutamic acid, inosine and hypoxanthine have been available as flavouring condiments in Japan. The traditionally accepted and scientifically demonstrated increase in the flavour of meat on ageing (Howe and Barbella, 1937; Harrison, 1948; Bouton *et al.*, 1958) may be related to the progressive nucleotide breakdown (§4.2.3) whereby ADP and AMP are respectively dephosphorylated and deaminated to inosinic acid (IMP), and the latter dephosphorylated to inosine or further split to ribose and hypoxanthine. The increase in concentration of hypoxanthine parallels the organoleptic change during conditioning (Howard, Lee and Webster, 1960). A marked increase in high molecular weight hydrocarbons, benzenoid compounds and pyrazines was detected after ageing of beef for thre weeks at 0–2°C (Coppock and McLeod, 1977). Changes in the free fatty acids during ageing no doubt contribute to the flavour alterations observed. Thus, the level of oleic acid in the intramuscular fat of *l. dorsi* has been observed to increase during 21 days storage of beef at 2°C (Hood and Allen, 1971).

Such findings suggest that the odour and taste of beef and pork can be artificially simulated, not only in the absence of purines and pyrimidines, but solely by water-soluble constituents. Hornstein and Crowe (1960, 1963), however, believe that species differences in taste and odour are determined by volatile fat soluble carbonyls which are characteristic and present in the meat before cooking. By lyophilizing a cold water extract of the *lean* from beef, pork and lamb, heating the resultant powder at 100°C and trapping the volatiles in liquid nitrogen, two fractions were obtained. The less volatile fraction has a meaty odour (Hornstein, Crowe and Sulzbacher, 1960) which is similar in the three species and has qualitatively the same infrared spectrum and the same profile when examined by gas chromatography (Hornstein and Crowe, 1960,1963). The gas chromatographic profile for the volatiles from lean whale meat had a component which was not present in other mammalian species (Hornstein, Crowe and Sulzbacher, 1963). This proved to be trimethylamine, however, which is exogeneous to the whale, being derived from bacterial degradation of the trimethylamine oxide of ingested krill (cf. Table 4.2 and Sharp and Marsh, 1953).

There are, of course, considerable differences between species in intramuscular fat (cf. Table 4.4, p. 95, and Dahl. 1958a); and, according to Hornstein and Crowe (1960, 1963), these are reflected in differences in volatiles produced from the heated fats and account for the differences in flavour of meat from the different species. This octanal, undecanal, hepta-2:4-dienal and nona-2:4-dienal are derived from heated pork fat, but not from beef fat, whilst few 2-enals or 2:4-dienals are produced from heated lamb fat. Nevertheless, the full aroma characteristic of species is not obtained if certain water-soluble components are absent (Wasserman and Spinelli, 1972). Species-specific flavours may be related to subtle differences in the amino acid and carbohydrate content of the adipose tissue (Wasserman and Spinelli, 1972).

For many years the water soluble flavour constituents of meat have been processed in the preparation of concentrated meat extracts. The non-volatile components in these are very similar to those present in the fresh meat (Wood and Bender, 1957; Bender, Wood and Palgrave, 1958). In each, there are appreciable quantities of salts, lactic acid, carnosine, creatine and hypoxanthine. The concentrates, which are subjected to prolonged heating, contain more creatine and are considerably darker–amino acids and sugars having reacted to form Maillard–type compounds. Additional volatile components in the concentrates include H_2S and isovaleraldehyde (Bender and Ballance, 1961).

10.4.3. *Variability in Odour and Taste*

Irrespective of the exact nature of meat odour and taste, and apart from species differences, they are affected by breed in sheep and cattle (Jacobson *et al.,* 1962). Some aspects of meat flavour are clearly inherited, since significant differences have been found between groups of beef animals having different sires but otherwise comparable (Bryce-Jones *et al.,* 1963).

Again, it is commonly accepted that older animals have more flavour than those which are young—as, for example, the distinctive taste of beef and and the insipid taste of veal testifies. Such age differences have been attributed to pigment content; but pure myoglobin gives only the metallic flavour of iron and it must be presumed that the concentration of some of the other constituents implicated above (§ 10.4.2) fluctuate in a similar way with age as myoglobin.

Differences between muscles are also well known—the tenderness of the psoas muscle being offset by its relative lack of flavour and the flavour of the diaphragm (skirt) being offset by its relative toughness. Scientific evaluation has fully substantiated such impressions. Thus beef 1. dorsi has apparently a better flavour than semitendinosus (Doty and Pierce, 1961; Howard and Lawrie, 1956).

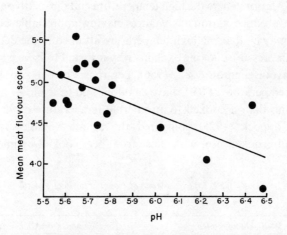

FIG. 10.5. Relationship between mean flavour (as determined by taste panel) and ultimate pH in beef muscle (after Bouton *et al.*, 1975).

Differences have been found in the precursors in different beef muscles (Mabrouk, Jerboe and O'Conner, 1969).

The biochemical condition of a given muscle is also a factor in determining flavour. In general, the higher the ultimate pH the lower is the flavour as determined by taste panel, possibly because the consequently swollen structure interferes with access to the palate of the substances concerned (cf. Fig. 10.5). A similar effect has been noted with cured meats. Thus bacon of relatively high ultimate pH appears less salty to the palate than that of low pH, even when the salt content is the same (Ingram, 1949a). Apart from this effect of high pH, however, substantial differences have been detected in the steam volatiles from normal lamb and beef (pH 5.5–5.8) and that having an ultimate pH above 6 (Park and Murray, 1975).

It will be clear that both the duration and temperature of cooking must influence the nature and intensity of odour and taste in meat. Since, except with pressure cooking, the interior of the pieces of meat which are being cooked cannot rise above 100°C until all the water has been driven off (Crocker, 1945), it will have relatively little flavour in comparison with the exterior, where the high temperature and the relative absence of moisture produce various substances having appreciable odour and taste. It may be that the high temperature attained in the depth of the meat with pressure cooking explains why it is said to have a somewhat better flavour (Fenton *et al.*, 1956). Leg roasts of lamb cooked to an interior temperature of 65°C have an odour and taste more characteristic of lamb than if cooked to an internal temperature of 75°C (Weir, 1960). Coppock (1975) compared the aroma volatiles from conventionally cooked beef with those from beef cooked by microwaves.

TABLE 10.17. *Effect of Mode of Cooking on Beef Volatiles*
(after Coppock, 1975)

Well-cooked, boiled	Underdone boiled or Microwave
High MW hydrocarbons	*Low MW hydrocarbons*
tetra–. penta–, hexa– and hepta–decanes	heptane, octane, decane, undecane, hept–1–ene, undec–4–ene
Benzenoids	*Pyrazines*
benzene, n–propylbenzene, toluene, *o*– and *p*–xylenes, ethylbenzaldehyde	dimethyl–. ethyl– and dimethylethyl–pyrazines
Furans	
2–ethyl– and 5–n–pentyl– furans	
Misc.	*Misc.*
3–methylbutanol, pyridine, 2–methylthiophen	acetone, methylbutanol

She found that, whereas the aroma of well-cooked, boiled beef was pleasant and spicy, and appeared to be predominantly associated with furans, pyridine, aldehydes and high molecular weight hydrocarbons, that of underdone boiled beef or microwave heated beef was relatively unpleasant and fatty and appeared to be predominantly associated with pyrazines, alcohols and hydrocarbons of low molecular weight (Table 10.17). To develop a similar degree of flavour intensity by microwaves as was present in well cooked, boiled beef required an hour's treatment; but this caused severe overheating.

Prolonged cooking, by causing marked breakdown of the meat proteins and the production of H_2S, is undesirable—though it may be necessary for tough meat (Weir, 1960). The odour and taste of beef roasts, cooked to an internal temperature of 82°C over 2 hr in an oven at 177°C, generally received a lower taste panel rating than grills from the same animal cooked to the same internal temperature over $\frac{1}{2}$ hr in an oven at 288°C (Howard, 1956; Howard and Lawrie, 1956; Bouton *et al.*, 1957, 1958). In canning, meat is subjected to high temperature for

TABLE 10.18 *Concentrations of Volatiles from Beef Canned to $F° = 10$ at Difference Temperatures* (p.p.b.)

	115°C	*121°C*	*131°C*
H_2S	6900	6400	4400
methylmercaptan	1400	1200	780
dimethylsulphide	810	770	530
2–methylpropanal	83	54	9
2–methylbutanal	79	43	30
2–ethylfuran	180	120	89

considerable periods determined by the product and intention; and there are concomitant changes in the concentrations of aroma components. Perrson and Von Sydow (1974) compared the effects of canning beef when processed to $F_0 = 10$ by three temperatures. The shorter heating time required at higher temperature decreased the concentrations of those compounds which could be related to the off-flavour in canned beef, i.e. aldehydes and sulphur-containing compounds (Table 10.18).

The addition of lysine or arginine to the beef before canning decreased the concentration of aldehydes and that of fumarate or malonate decreased the concentration of S-compounds. On storage of the canned beef over 12 months at 20°C the intensity of typical meat aroma decreased; but reheating at 121°C restored some of the original flavour attributes.

Attempts at extraneous enhancement of meat odour and taste have mainly been confined to cured meats and sausages, which frequently have added spices, condiments (including sodium glutamate), sugars, etc. (Gerrard, 1935; Wilson, 1960). Much of the flavour of bacon and of continental-type sausages depends on the metabolic activities of microorganisms whose growth is fostered by traditional manufacturing procedures (Tanner, 1944). To some degree this flavour is derived from the hydrolysis of fats and the breakdown of free fatty acids. The order in which the latter are attacked by the microorganisms depends on the microbial species which are present (Wahlroos and Niinivaara, 1969). In recent years systematic attempts have been made to introduce microorganisms deliberately in order to produce particular desired flavours. For instance, Niven, Deibel and Wilson (1958) have proposed the use of *Pediococcus cerevisiae* as a sausage starter culture; and McLean and Sulzbacher (1959) have demonstrated that the addition of a species of *Pseudomonas* to a meat curing brine significantly altered its flavour. In the future, it seems likely that very considerable advances will be made in the enhancement and control of meat odour and taste. This might be done by the addition to the comminuted product of controllable microorganisms capable of fostering flavour; or even by the pre-slaughter administration of desired, flavour-producing chemicals or microorganisms (e.g. *Thamnidium elegans*: Williams, 1946b).

10.4.4. *Undesirable Odour and Taste*

There is a gradual loss in flavour during storage and this may occur even in the frozen condition (Howard and Lawrie, 1956)—possibly due to the slow loss of highly volatile substances. In this connection it is interesting to note that a faint odour of diacetyl is not infrequently observed in frozen meat stores at $-10°C$. Such losses are unavoidable; but undesirable odour and taste may arise during the storage of meat because of microbial growth, chemical deterioration on the surface or tainting by extraneous agents.

Odours produced by micro-organisms growing on meat surfaces are not so objectionable as those due to the metabolic products of anaerobes (§ 6.2): they tend to be sour rather than putrid. The lipases of such micro-organisms will attack fat, splitting off fatty acids with more or less unpleasant consequences according to their nature (§ 7.1.1.2). The exact nature of the off-odours will, of course, depend on the types of micro-organisms growing, and these in turn will be determined by such factors as the temperature of storage and the nature of the product (fresh, cured, comminuted), as described in Chapter 6. Relatively high temperatures and the absence of oxygen will produce putrid off-odours through the breakdown of proteins, as in prepacked bacon stored at $20°C$ (Cavett, 1962), or in bone taint (§ 6.1.2.2)—in those deep-seated portions of the carcase which have not been cooled sufficiently quickly after death and where there is a reservoir of suitable micro-organisms in the lymph nodes (Nottingham, 1960). A species of *Proteus inconstans* has been isolated which produces "cabbage odour"—due to methane diol—in sliced, vacuum-packed bacon (Gardner and Patterson, 1975).

Free fatty acids, produced by microbial action or otherwise, will accelerate the development of oxidative rancidity. The latter will occur even at $-10°C$ during long storage. The conditions predisposing towards oxidative rancidity in intramuscular fat have been thoroughly investigated (Lea, 1939; Watts, 1954). Relatively little is known, however, concerning the compounds responsible for off-flavours which are produced by comparatively minor reactions, although they are principally carbonyls. Since there are over 200 different species of carbonyls present in such circumstances (Evans, 1961), it is not surprising that positive identification of the most troublesome members has proved difficult. Species differences in the development of off-odours and tastes arise from the different spectra of fatty acids produced by lipolysis, and of carbonyls produced during oxidative rancidity. The phospholipids of meat fats are the most unstable constituents and they may well play a major role in accelerating flavour deterioration (Younathan and Watts, 1960). The separated cephalin fractions of both beef and pork intramuscular fats produce fishy odours, but, during the oxidation of the corresponding unfractionated fats, their effect is less noticeable with pork (Hornstein, Crowe and Heimberg, 1961). The deliberate induction of a high ultimate pH has been shown to greatly retard the oxidation of fat in pork even at relatively elevated frozen storage temperature (cf. § 7.1.1.2). On the other hand, when formaldehyde–treated feed containing a high percentage of unsaturated fatty acids is fed to pigs, their fat is made even more unsaturated; and this is associated with an oily aroma (Ford, Park, Ratcliff and Murray, 1975). Such feeding to ruminants also leads to an enhanced tendency to undergo oxidative rancidity (although this can be controlled by permitted antioxidants). Moreover, the meat has a sweet aroma and flavour which some consumers find objectionable (Ford, Harris, McFarlane, Park and Shorthose, 1974).

When the flesh of certain pigs is heated, an unpleasant odour arises which is commonly referred to as boar odour—although it has been reported in the flesh of both sexes (Self, 1957). The agent responsible is fat soluble, but unsaponifiable (Craig, Pearson and Webb, 1962). Deatherage (1965) found that boar odour could be eliminated by implanting the animals with hexoestrol sometime before death. Using a combination of gas liquid chromatography and mass spectroscopy Patterson (1968a) has now identified the substance responsible as 5α-androst-16-ene-3-one. It is present in the flesh of most boars over 200 lb liveweight; but not in that of gilts or hogs. He suggests it is related to the corresponding alcohol, which is present in boar submaxillary gland (Patterson, 1968b). It is of interest to note that 44 per cent of men are unable to detect "boar odour" but only about 8 per cent of women cannot do so (Griffiths and Patterson, 1970). It has been shown that there is no effect of taint on eating quality until the level of androstenone rises above 1 μg/g (Patterson and Stinson, 1971). This signifies that about 50% of boars would yield satisfactory meat. Rhodes (1972) reported that when pork joints from 24 week old boar and gilt carcases were submitted to consumer panels (involving 400 households), there appeared to be no significant differences detected between their acceptibility. Since neither animal age nor weight is correlated with taint in the average boar of potential commercial value, a simple test to make an early detection of taint has been devised. This involves the heating of a sample of fat to about 375°C using an electrically operated soldering iron.

The food ingested by the animal is sometimes responsible for undesirable odours and tastes in the flesh. Beef fattened immediately before slaughter on crops with dieldrin may acquire a taint from this chemical, whilst animals grazing on pastures containing certain weeds (including pepper cress and ragweed) are unable to excrete indole and

TABLE 10.19. *Effect of Fodder Plants on Flavour of Meat from Sheep* (Anon. 1973)

Plant	Meat Flavour
Lucerne, white clover, sweet glycine	Sharp odour; objectionable when strong.
Perennial ryegrass, panic grass, kikuya grass	Strong meat odour/flavour (acceptable to some consumers)
Green oats	Strong meat flavour, pungent odour (acceptable to lamb consumers)
Rape	Sickly odour and flavour, undesirable to most.

skatole derived from the metabolism of tryptophan. This causes skatole taint (Empey and Montgomery, 1959) in the flesh. A number of off-flavours are detected in the meat of sheep when these graze certain pastures for some weeks before slaughter (Table 10.19). The effects are more noticeable at certain times of the year, at certain stages of growth of the plants and within certain soil conditions.

Under certain conditions of heating H_2S, liberated from the meat proteins, can react with mesityl oxide (derivable from the acetone in tin lacquers) to give various compounds, including 4-methyl-4-mercaptopenta-2-one, which produces a most offensive "catty" odour (Aylward, Coleman and Hausman, 1967). From time to time phenolic substances, used in dipping sheep, have been detected in the meat at time of consumption.

Meat, especially meat fat, which has been in refrigerated storage for a considerable time, as in shipment from the Southern Dominions to the United Kingdom may become unmarketable due to taints absorbed from extraneous sources such as diesel oil and fruits. Activated charcoal, placed in the cold store, will frequently reabsorb the taint from the meat (Macara, 1947).

The off-odours developed in meat stored above or below the freezing point are not a direct consequence of refrigeration; but other commercial processes may cause flavour changes e.g. dehydration, freeze dehydration and irradiation. Dehydrated and freeze dried meat is not only particularly susceptible to oxidative rancidity in the presence of oxygen but also, especially at high temperatures, to the development of mealy and paint-like odours. In the absence of oxygen bitter tastes develop because of Maillard-type reactions. Prophylactic procedures have been discussed in §§ 8.1.3 and 8.2.3. Irradiation causes both immediate and storage changes in the odour and taste of meat (§§ 9.1.2.1. and 9.1.2.2). The production of H_2S, mercaptans, carbonyls and aldehydes, especially in beef (Huber *et al.,* 1953), is largely responsible. In this context, within-package odour scavengers (Tausig and Drake, 1959), the addition of protective compounds such as ascorbic acid (Huber *et al.,* 1953) and irradiation at temperatures far below the freezing point (Hannan, 1955) have been used with some success. On storage, meat which has been sterilized by irradiation develops stale and bitter flavours. Some of these are due to surviving activity of the meat's proteolytic enzymes which produce free tyrosine from proteins.

CHAPTER 11

MEAT AND HUMAN NUTRITION

11.1. ESSENTIAL NUTRIENTS

Regarded nutritionally, meat is a very good source of essential amino acids; and, to a lesser extent, of certain minerals. Although vitamins and essential fatty acids are also present, meat is not usually relied upon for these components in a well-balanced diet. On the other hand an organ meat, such as liver, is a valuable source of vitamins A, B_1 and nicotinic acid. Even in respect of its accepted nutrient role, however, little is yet known about possible differences in the value of meat from different species, breeds and muscles. Moreover, since connective tissue proteins have a lower content of essential amino acids than those of contractile tissue, meat having a high percentage of collagen (or elastin) will also have a *relatively* lower intrinsic nutritive value. There is an inverse correlation between hydroxyproline and tryptophan in meat samples (Dahl, 1965); and less methionine in connective tissue (Bender and Zia, 1976). Although the rôle of muscular tissue is the same wherever it occurs, and consists predominantly of contractile proteins, the amino acid composition of which is said not to vary grossly between species (Crawford, 1968), the accessories of the contractile process are certainly not identical even between the muscles of a given species (cf. §4.3). There are differences in the contents of ancillary proteins, of free amino acids, of fatty acids and of various other substances; and in their character. These can be presumed not to be without nutritional significance, albeit subtle. It is well known of course that a muscle containing much connective tissue will provide meat which is relatively resistant to digestion and absorption, and that this will be worsened by faulty

367

cooking; but how important this may be in relation to the absorption of the nutrients of the meat has been little studied. Imposed on such gross differences of digestibility there may well be other factors in each muscle which affect its intrinsic nutritive value.

11.1.1. *Amino Acids*

The amino acid composition of the proteins of the principal types of meat is shown in Table 11.1. In respect of the essential amino acids, beef would appear to have a somewhat higher content of leucine, lysine and valine than pork or lamb; and a lower content of threonine. Despite the minor nature of these species differences, however, it should be pointed out that the meat represented in Table 11.1 is of random origin. It is certainly feasible that more significant differences may exist between

TABLE 11.1. *Amino-acid Composition in Fresh Meats*
(Schweigert and Payne, 1956)
(as % crude protein)

Amino acid	Category	Beef	Pork	Lamb
Isoleucine	Essential	5·1	4·9	4·8
Leucine	Essential	8·4	7·5	7·4
Lysine	Essential	8·4	7·8	7·6
Methionine	Essential	2·3	2·5	2·3
Cystine	Essential	1·4	1·3	1·3
Phenylalanine	Essential	4·0	4·1	3·9
Threonine	Essential	4·0	5·1	4·9
Tryptophan	Essential	1·1	1·4	1·3
Valine	Essential	5·7	5·0	5·0
Arginine	Essential for infants	6·6	6·4	6·9
Histidine	Essential for infants	2·9	3·2	2·7
Alanine	Non-essential	6·4	6·3	6·3
Aspartic acid	Non-essential	8·8	8·9	8·5
Glutamic acid	Non-essential	14·4	14·5	14·4
Glycine	Non-essential	7·1	6·1	6·7
Proline	Non-essential	5·4	4·6	4·8
Serine	Non-essential	3·8	4·0	3·9
Tyrosine	Non-essential	3·2	3·0	3·2

specific muscle locations; or that breed, and animal age, have important effects. It has been reported, for example, that the contents of arginine, valine, methionine, isoleucine and phenylalanine increase (relative to the concentrations of other amino acids) with increasing animal age (Gruhn, 1965).

Further, there is evidence that the content of certain essential amino acids may differ at different parts of the carcase. Some data on tryptophan and lysine in certain pork muscles are given in Table 11.2.

TABLE 11.2. *Tryptophan and Lysine in Pork Muscles*
(Hibbert and Lawrie, unpublished data)

Muscle	Tryptophan (mg/g)	Lysine (mg/g)
L. dorsi (4–6 lumbar)	0·015	0·089
L. dorsi (13–15 thoracic)	0·012	0·078
L. dorsi (8–12 thoracic)	0·018	0·061
Psoas	0·017	0·072
Semimembranosus	0·015	0·083
Rectus femoris	0·013	0·059
Supraspinatus	0·021	0·071

The amino acid content may be affected by processing (e.g. heat, ionizing radiation: §§ 7.2.2 and 9.1.1, above); but, unless processing conditions are both severe and prolonged, such destruction is minimal. Rather more important is the possibility that certain amino acids may become unavailable (Bender, 1966). Thus Dvorak and Vognarova (1965) found that after heating beef for 3 hr at a series of temperatures, 90 per cent of the available lysine was retained at 70°C and only 50 per cent at 160°C. There is a linear relationship between loss of available lysine in canned beef and the severity of the process (Ziemba and Mälkki, 1969). A 20 per cent fall in available tryptophan and methionine was observed in canned pork after only 40 min at temperatures above 70°C (Hibbert, 1973). Bender and Husaini (1976) found no loss in available methionine when beef was autoclaved for 1 hr at 115°C; but when it was processed in the presence of other food constituents, such as wheat flour and glucose, there was a loss in net protein utilization which could be related to a fall in available methionine. Amino acids can also become unavailable during the prolonged storage made possible by canning. Bender (1966) found that veal, canned in 1823, had a biological value of only 27 when examined in 1959, although analysis after acid hydrolysis indicated that there had been no destruction of amino acids, i.e. prolonged storage led to grossly reduced availability. On the other hand, over practical storage periods, he detected no diminution in biological value (after the initial loss caused by the process itself). Smoking and salting may also slightly diminish amino acid availability. Storage of freeze-dried meat for 1 year at 20°C, in air and with about 5 per cent available water, has been found to cause a loss of 50 per cent in available lysine, although this is unusual (Bender, 1966).

The exact way in which the individual human consumer will digest, absorb and utilize the amino acids of meat (or those of any other protein-containing food) cannot be presently predicted, although the existence of considerable variation, even amongst the majority, who are usually regarded as "normal", is proven (Williams, 1956). Some individuals differ in their metabolic response to protein-containing foods in a manner sufficiently marked as to be frankly "abnormal"; and in so far as meat is an important source of essential amino acids it is desirable to refer briefly to some major disturbances of protein metabolism (Carson, 1970). These include disorders of digestive enzymes (e.g. cystic fibrosis of the pancreas) and faulty mechanisms of intestinal amino acid transport (e.g. cystinuria, in which there is faulty absorption of cystine and dibasic amino acids; and Hartnup disease, where there is defective transport of neutral amino acids and malabsorption of tryptophan). In addition, there is a substantial number of genetically determined conditions in which the intermediary metabolism of one or several amino acids is defective. Finally, although cases of specific intolerance to meat proteins have not been reported, the latter are involved in certain abnormalities of general intolerance to protein foods (Kekomaki *et al.*, 1967).

11.1.2. *Minerals*

Mineral components in several meats are shown in Table 11.3 (after McCance and Widdowson, 1960). Of these, potassium is quantitatively the most important, followed by phosphorus: except in cured meat where sodium from the added salt predominates.

TABLE 11.3 *Mineral Content of Meat and Meat Products*
(after McCance and Widdowson, 1960)

Meat	Mineral (mg/100 g)					
	Na	K	Ca	Mg	Fe	P
Beef, steak (raw)	69	334	5·4	24·5	4·3	276
Beef, steak (grilled)	67	368	9·2	25·2	5·2	303
Mutton, chop (raw)	75	246	12·6	18·7	1·0	173
Mutton, chop (grilled)	102	305	17·8	22·8	2·4	206
Pork (raw)	45	400	4·3	26·1	1·4	223
Pork, chop (grilled)	59	258	8·3	14·9	2·4	178
Bacon (raw)	975	268	13·5	12·3	0·9	94
Bacon, back (fried)	2790	517	11·5	25·7	2·8	229
Liver, pig (raw)	85	319	5·1	23·3	13·0	372

Another general feature is the increase which occurs on cooking (which is mainly due to moisture loss). In respect of species differences the high content of iron in beef no doubt reflects the greater concentration of myoglobin in this species than that in mutton or pork. In general, meat is an important source of iron. Moreover, an additional nutritional attribute of meat is the fact that the iron it contains is in a highly available form; and enhances the uptake of iron from concomitantly eaten vegetable sources (Bender, 1975). The concentration of iron in liver is markedly higher than that in the muscular tissue of the three domestic meat species. It would appear that mutton contains more calcium than beef; but, of course, from the nutritional viewpoint, meat is not regarded as the principal source of this element.

11.1.3. *Vitamins*

The content of vitamins in various meats is shown in Table 11.4.

TABLE 11.4. *Vitamin Content of Various Raw Meats*
(after McCance and Widdowson, 1960)

Vitamin units/100 g raw flesh	Beef	Veal	Pork	Bacon	Mutton	Liver (Beef)
A (I.U.)	trace	trace	trace	trace	trace	20,000
B_1 (thiamin) (mg)	0·07	0·10	1·0	0·40	0·15	0·30
B_2 (riboflavin) (mg)	0·20	0·25	0·20	0·15	0·25	3·0
Nicotinic acid (mg)	5	7	5	1·5	5	13
Pantothenic acid (mg)	0·4	0·6	0·6	0·3	0·5	8
Biotin (μg)	3	5	4	7	3	100
Folic acid (μg)	10	5	3	0	3	300
B_6 (mg)	0·3	0·3	0·5	0·3	0·4	0·7
B_{12} (μg)	2	0	2	0	2	50
C (ascorbic acid) (mg)	0	0	0	0	0	30
D (I.U.)	trace	trace	trace	trace	trace	45

TABLE 11.5. *Comparison of Cooking Losses and Vitamin* B_1 *Retention
in Conventional and Microwave Cooking*

Sample	Cooking method	Internal temp. (°C)	Cooking losses: water and fat (% initial wt)	Vitamin B_1 retention in meat and dripping (% initial)
Beef	Conventional	62·5	18–20	81–86
	microwave	71	29–39	70–80
Pork	Conventional	85	34	80
	microwave	85	37	91
Beef loaves	Conventional	85	24	76
	microwave	85	27	80
Ham loaves	Conventional	85	18	91
	microwave	85	28	87

It is clear that the content of vitamin B_1 in pork (and even in bacon) is considerably higher than that in other meats; and that there is a relatively high concentration of folic acid in beef. On the other hand, an organ meat such as liver has a considerable content of a number of vitamins. Indeed, the concentration of vitamin A in the liver of polar bears has been associated with symptoms of hypervitaminosis in human consumers. Meat can be regarded as an important dietary source of vitamins B_1 and B_2; and in the United Kingdom meats provide about 40 per cent of the average nicotinic acid intake. The lability in processing of vitamin B_1, in particular, has been studied extensively. Some data, comparing conventional heating procedures with microwave heating, are given in Table 11.5 (Hallmark and van Duyne, 1961).

Despite shorter cooking times, losses were rather greater by the microwave procedure; but overall losses of vitamin B_1 were similar by both methods. The relative retention of vitamins B_1 and B_2 in several kinds of meat when cooked conventionally is shown in Table 11.6 (after Noble, 1965).

TABLE 11.6. *Retention of Vitamins* B_1 *and* B_2 *on Cooking*
(cuts of beef and veal cooked at 149°C: pork cooked at 175°C)

Type of meat	Time of cooking (min/lb)	% retention	
		B_1	B_2
Beef			
Short rib	30	25	58
Chuck	35	23	74
Round (roast)	27	40	73
Round (steak)	18	40	65
Veal			
Chops	—	38	73
Round (steak)	—	48	76
Pork	(Total time, min)		
Chops	50	44	64
Spare rib	120	26	72
Tenderloin	40	57	83

Vitamin B_1 is mainly lost from meat by leaching. Losses average about 15–40 per cent on boiling, 40–50 per cent on frying, 30–60 per cent on roasting and 50–70 per cent on canning (Harris and von Loesecke,

1960). Vitamins B_6, B_{12} and pantothenic acid have a similar order of lability to vitamin B_1. As distinct from the B vitamins, 90–100 per cent of vitamin A is retained after heating to internal temperatures as high as 80°C.

11.1.4. *Fatty Acids*

The unsaturated fatty acids, linoleic (C 18:2) linolenic (C 18:3) and arachidonic (C 20:4) appear to be essential. They are necessary constituents of cell walls, mitochondria and other intensely active metabolic sites. Whilst the body can produce oleic acid from saturated precursors, it cannot readily produce any of the above, unless one of them is available in the diet. In such sources as cereals and seeds, linoleic acid (in particular) is usually present at about 20 times the concentration found in meats. Differences in the component fatty acids are reflected in the iodine number of the fats. Those of plant origin have iodine values averaging about 120, whereas those of meat animals average about 60, that of pork being somewhat higher, and that of lamb somewhat lower, than the value for beef (cf. Tables 4.2 and 4.3). That there are differences between muscles within a given species in the concentrations of unsaturated fatty acids, and between different fractions within a single muscle, has already been indicated (§ 4.3.5).

In recent years the relative concentration of unsaturated fatty acids in meat and vegetable fats has been linked with another nutritional consideration. It has been suggested that a high ratio of unsaturated/saturated fatty acids in the diet is desirable as this may lower the individual's susceptibility to cardiovascular diseases, in general, and to coronary heart disease and cerebral vascular disease, in particular (Keys, Anderson and Grande, 1960). There is evidence that a diet which predominantly contains relatively saturated fats (such as those from meats) raises the level of cholesterol in the blood, thus enhancing the formation of intravascular fatty plaques and blood clots. It may predispose towards the development of anaerobic bowel microflora, such as *Bacteroides,* which convert cholic acid into desoxycholate, a carcinogen (Paterson, 1975).

To avoid possible health dangers from the consumption of the flesh of ruminants, a greater degree of unsaturation could be introduced into their fats. Normally the feeding of highly unsaturated vegetable fats to sheep and cattle with this intention would be invalidated because ingested fats would be reduced by the rumen bacteria. If, however, they are first treated with formaldehyde, they resist reduction and can raise the degree of unsaturation in the ruminant fat stores very considerably (Cook *et al.*, 1970). Again, selection for "doppelender" development in cattle, it has been suggested, would not only provide meat with greater efficiency but would also ensure that the fat was more highly unsaturated (Ashmore and Robinson, 1969).

There is as much evidence, however, to suggest that other factors, for example the intake of sucrose, may be responsible for cardiovascular diseases (Yudkin, 1964). Again, the incidence of such diseases is low in many countries where the intake of animal fats is high (e.g. among the Madai in East Africa: Yudkin, 1967). Elephants are vegetarian yet suffer severely from atherosclerotic conditions.

There is also evidence that polyunsaturated components of animal fats are essential for brain development, especially in the foetus (Crawford, 1975). When linoleic and linolenic acids are ingested, they are metabolized by animal liver to produce two families of long chain polyunsaturated fatty acids which are specific to animals. It is significant that brain cells contain these acids and not the parent linoleic and linolenic. Moreover the chain-elongation and desaturation of linoleic acid also gives rise to the prostaglandins which are important in controlling blood pressure and for other essential purposes. The lipids of free-living mammals such as the eland are predominantly polyunsaturated and phospholipid in nature whereas those of intensively reared animals are mainly saturated triglycerides. These facts suggest not that vegetables should be eaten and meat avoided, but that meat from wild or unimproved species should be preferentially sought (Crawford, 1975) (cf. § 1.3). In this context it is of interest to note that the concentration of C_{20} and C_{22} polyunsaturated fatty acids in whale muscle is about seven-fold greater than in that of domestic animals (Tveraaen, 1935)—a reflection of the lipid composition of the krill upon which this species subsists.

11.2. PREFABRICATED MEAT

The severe shortage of protein of high biological value in developing countries, and the high cost of meat in those which are more fortunate economically, has fostered great interest in the possibility of fabricating protein-rich foods from plant sources in a palatable form. Artificial meat-like products, which have controlled texture, flavour, colour and nutritive value (Sjostrom, 1963), have been marketed which can substitute directly for meat or can economically extend the bulk, and help the texture, of conventional meat products.

Among the vegetable proteins which have been exploited in this way are the glutens of wheat and the globulins of groundnut and soya bean. Protein isolated from the latter is of comparable biological value to that of meat, it is valuable in the manufacture of emulsion-type products (because of its power to emulsify, stabilize, texturize and hydrate comminuted meats) and it can be used as an ingredient of spun fibres. In most extraction procedures, defatted soya bean is heated with a slightly alkaline aqueous solution. The protein which dissolves is mechanically separated from residues and the major protein constituents precipitated by acid, forming a curd (which is subsequently neutralized by food-grade alkali). If an alkaline suspension of the soya protein curd is kept for some time at high pH, its capacity to aggregate as fibres is enhanced. The suspension is spun into an acid bath, when long filaments form. The native proteins of soya and of many other vegetables can also form a liquid homogenous suspension or mesophase (Tombs, 1972) with water and salt. The mesophase proteins can be extruded into water to form filaments. This procedure has the advantage that strong alkaline pH levels are not required. These prefabricated products combined with other food components, colouring and flavour, can be made up as simulated meats (Meyer, 1967), which are marketed as "meat steaks". Synthetic "ham", "beef", "pork" and "bacon" have been available in the U.S.A. since before 1960. Such are also made available as dehydrated meat "bits" for use in soups, stews, sausages and other comminuted foods for the general market, including institutional feeding (Coleman and Creswick, 1966). They may have a protein content as high as 30 per cent and have only 1 per cent of fat (none of it being of animal origin).

In frankfurter sausages the replacement of 4 per cent of meat protein with that from soya has been found to reduce the cost of the final product by 33 per cent; and the yield (based on the meat used) was increased by 40 per cent (Cook *et al.*, 1969).

Because of the intrinsic cheapness of proteins from vegetable and microbial origin and (depending on the source) the absence of nutritional disadvantages, there is bound to be a great increase in their use as substitutes for expensive proteins of animal origin. Clearly there is also an increasing possibility that the recommended levels of substitution could be exceeded; and a concomitant need to establish means of quantitatively determining the origin of proteins in food products (Food Standards Committee, 1975). Although serological methods can be employed to distinguish and quantify native proteins, processing (especially heating) renders them ineffective. It is still possible to use gel electrophoresis, in conjunction with disaggregating agents such as β-mercaptoethanol and urea, to assess the proteins' origin (Mattey, Parsons and Lawrie, 1970). Beyond a certain intensity of processing, however, such means of identification also become ineffective. On the other hand, if there were some component of meat which was robust to processing, which was characteristically present in myofibrillar proteins and which was absent from non-meat proteins, an accurate assessment of a product's lean meat content, could be made. 3-methylhistidine forms a standard component of myofibrillar proteins (Hardy *et al.*, 1970). Being an amino acid it survives even severe processing; and it appears to be absent from proteins of microbial or plant origin (Rangeley and Lawrie, 1976). The titre of 3-methylhistidine has been successfully employed, for example, to determine the content of meat protein in canned mixtures of beef and soya (Hibbert and Lawrie, 1972).

In view of the frequent drawbacks of low acceptability, absence of organoleptic quality and high cost in meat-like products prefabricated from vegetable or bacterial sources, it would seem highly desirable to reassess the potential for making edible foods from the substantial amounts of slaughterhouse protein which is currently wasted. Much of it is of high biological value and it would seem both economic and more rational nutritionally to investigate this possibility before relying too heavily on the unconventional. A considerable quantity of the protein from abattoirs which is now used as animal feed could be processed for direct inclusion in the human diet (Vickery, 1968). From the slaughter of New Zealand lambs alone it has been calculated that 11,000 tons of high-quality protein could be produced annually (Locker, 1968). This meat-based material would satisfy the protein requirements of 700,000 people. The upgrading of meat by-products would also assist, incidentally, in the control of environmental pollution. Meat protein concentrate of good nutritive value as human food can be economically produced (Levin, 1970) from slaughterhouse waste.

Native proteins can be recovered in good yield from bovine, ovine and porcine lungs, stomachs and blood plasma. Typical values for protein contents are given in Table 11.7.

TABLE 11.7. *Typical Protein Concentrations in Underutilised Tissues of Meat Animals*
(after Young and Lawrie, 1974)

Tissue	% Protein
Lung (bovine and ovine)	16–17
Lung (porcine)	14–15
Stomach (ovine)	12–14
Stomach (porcine)	14–15
Rumen (bovine)	10–13
Reticulum and Omasum (bovine)	9–10
Abomasum (bovine)	7–9
Blood plasma	7–8

Fibres containing 17–18 per cent protein, and simulating muscular tissue, can be spun from such sources. Those spun from stomachs and lung tend to have less mechanical strength than those from blood plasma; but since they have higher contents of isoleucine and methionine (which are deficient in the latter), both textural and nutritional benefits can be achieved by spinning fibres from mixed sources (Young and Lawrie, 1975; Swingler, Neale and Lawrie, 1978).

Since the proteins which can be readily extracted from stomachs and lungs are derived mainly from smooth muscle in these tissues, and since the latter closely resembles striated muscle in composition (§ 4.1.1), fibres from such sources would approximate closely to lean meat, notwithstanding their derivation from prohibited offal. They could thus pose both analytical and legislative problems.

Whilst the use of prefabricated meats from animal or vegetable sources in convenience foods, for special diets and as complementary feeding in underdeveloped areas, may be expected to increase steadily most authorities agree that they will not displace the demand for carcase meat in the foreseeable future. This is not only a question of eating quality. It reflects recognition that, notwithstanding their lower capacity for producing protein than vegetables or bacteria, meat animals represent the only economically feasible means of utilizing the protein in plant sources growing on poor ground. And it must be recognized that a great proportion of the world's land surface is only fit for grazing and not for cultivation. As Blaxter (1968) has emphasized, ruminants in particular can convert the fibrous portions of plants, which cannot be used directly for human food, into high-quality protein. The self-contained fermentation system of ruminants can produce desirable protein almost as efficiently as industrial fermentation plants can produce protein of a type which has yet to be established as organoleptically acceptable.

BIBLIOGRAPHY

ABRAHAM, E. P., CHAIN, E. B., FLETCHER, C. M., FLOREY, H. W., GARDNER, A. D. HEATLEY, N. G. and JENNINGS, M. A. (1941) *Lancet*, **ii,** 177.

ABRAHAMSON, H. (1949) *J. biol. Chem.* **178,** 179.

ACEVADO, I. and ROMAT, A. (1929) *Bol. Min. Agric., Buenos Aires* **28,** 221

ADACHI, R. R., SHEFFER, L. and SPECTOR, H. (1958) *Food Res.* **23,** 401.

ADAMS, J. M., JEPPESEN, P. G. N., SANGER, F. and BARRELL, B. G. (1969) *Nature, Lond.* **223,** 1009.

ADAMS, R. D., DENNY-BROWN, D. and PEARSON, C. M. (1962) *Diseases of Muscle: A Study in Pathology,* 2nd ed., Henry Kimpton, London.

ADDIS, P. B. (1969) *Proc. 22nd Ann. Recip. Meat Conf., Pomona, Calif.,* p. 151.

AITKEN, A., CASEY, J. C., PENNY, I. F. and VOYLE, C. A. (1962) *J. Sci. Fd. Agric.* **13,** 439.

AKERS, J. M. (1969) *Food Manuf.* **44,** No. 1, 22.

ALLEN, D. M. (1974) *Proc. 27th Ann. Recip. Meat Conf.,* Nat. Livestock and Meat Bd., Chicago, p. 56.

ALLEN, L. M. and PATTERSON, D. S. R. (1971) in *2nd Symposium Condition and Meat Quality in Pigs* (Animal Res. Inst.: Zeist), p. 90.

ALLEN, E. (1968) *Proc. 21st Ann. Recip. Meat Conf., Athens, Georgia,* p. 306.

ALLEN, E., BRAY, R. W. and CASSENS, R. G. (1967) *J. Food Sci.* **32,** 26.

ALLEN, E., CASSENS, R. G. and BRAY, R. W. (1967) *J. Anim. Sci.* **26,** 36.

ALLEN, W. M., HERBERT, C. N. and SMITH, L. P. (1974) *Vet. Rec.* **94,** 212.

ANDERSON, A. W. (1955) *Munic. Engng.* **40,** 1119.

ANDERSON, A. W., NORDEN, H. C., CAIN, R. F., PARRISH, G. and DUGGAN, D. (1956) *Food Tech.* **10,** 575.

ANDO, N. and NAGATA, Y. (1970) *Proc. 16th Meeting European Meat Res. Workers, Varna,* p. 859.

ANDREWS, F. N., BEESON, W. M. and JOHNSON, F. D. (1954) *J. Anim. Sci.* **13,** 99.

ANDROSS, M. (1949) *Brit. J. Nutr.* **3,** 396.

ANON. (1938) *C.S.I.R.O., Aust., Sect. Food Pres. Circ.,* No. 2, p. 72.

ANON. (1944) *U.S. Dept. Agric. Circ.,* No. 706.

ANON. (1950) *The Australian Environment,* 2nd ed., C.S.I.R.O., Melbourne.

ANON. (1955) *Wld. Hlth. Org. Tech. Rept. Ser.,* No. 99.

ANON. (1957a) *Beretn. Akad. tek. Videns., Kbh.,* No. 27.

ANON. (1957b) Meat Hygiene, *FAO Agric. Studies,* No. 34.

ANON. (1961) *Analyst* **86,** 557.

ANON. (1962) *A.R.C. and M.R.C. Report of the Joint Committee on Antibiotics in Animal Feeding,* H.M.S.O., London.

ANON. (1963) *Analyst* **88,** 422.

ANON. (1967) *Joint Survey of Pesticide Residues in Foodstuffs Sold in England and Wales (Assoc. of Public Analysts)*, p. 22.
ANON. (1968) *Ann, Rept. Australian Meat Bd.*, p. 117.
ANON. (1971) *2nd Symposium Condition and Meat Quality in Pigs*. Animal Res. Inst. Zeist.
ANON. (1972a) Food Additives and Contaminants Committee, *Report on the Review of the Preservatives in Food Regulations, 1962* H.M.S.O., London.
ANON. (1972b) *Ann. Rept. C.S.I.R.O.*, Meat Res. Lab. pp. 18, 34.
ANON. (1973a) *Production Year Book*, F.A.O., Rome, **27**.
ANON. (1973b) *Meat Res. in C.S.I.R.O.*, p. 2.
ANON. (1974a) *Meat Res. Inst. Ann. Rept. 1972–73*, p. 11.
ANON. (1974b) *Meat Res. in C.S.I.R.O.*, p. 9.
ANSON, M. L. and MIRSKY, A. E. (1932–33) *J. gen. Physiol.* **16**, 59.
ANTHONY, W. B. (1969) Animal Management Conf., Syracuse, N.Y.
APPERT, N. (1810) *The Art of Preserving Animal and Vegetable Substances for Many Years*, Patris & Cie, Paris.
ARAKAWA, N., GOLL, D. E. and TEMPLE, J. (1970) *J. Fd. Sci.* **35**, 703.
ARNOLD, N., WIERBICKI, E. and DEATHERAGE, F. E. (1956) *Food Tech.* **10**, 245.
ASHMORE, C. R. and ROBINSON, D. W. (1969) *Proc. Soc. exptl. Biol. Med.* **132**, 548.
ASSMAN, H., BIELENSTEIN, H., HOBBS, H. and JEDELOH, B. (1933) *Deutsch. med. Wchn.* **59**, 122.
ATKINSON, J. L. and FOLLET, M. J. (1971) *Proc. 17th Meeting European Meat Res. Workers, Bristol*, p. 685.
ATKINSON, J. L. and FOLLET, M. J. (1973) *J. Fd. Technol.* **8**, 51.
AWAD, A., POWRIE, W. D. and FENNEMA, O. (1968) *J. Food Sci.* **33**, 227.
AYLWARD, F., COLEMAN, G. and HAISMAN, D. R. (1967) *Chem. Ind.* 1563.

BACH, L. M. N. (1948) *Proc. Soc. exp. Biol. Med.* **67**, 268.
BADAWAY, A. M., CAMBPELL, R. M., CUTHBERTSON, D. P., and FELL, B. L. (1957) *Nature, Lond.* **180**, 756.
BAGGER, S. V. (1926) *J. Path. Bact.* **29**, 225.
BAILEY, A. J. (1968) *Nature, Lond.* **160**, 447.
BAILEY, A. J. (1974) *Path. Biol.* **22**, 675.
BAILEY, A. J., BENDALL, J. R. and RHODES, D. N. (1962) *Intl. J. appl. Radn. Isotopes* **13**, 131.
BAILEY, A. J., PEACH, C. M. and FOWLER, L. J. (1970) *Biochem. J.* **117**, 819.
BAILEY, A. J. and ROBINS, S. P. (1973a) In *Biology of the Fibroblast*, (Eds. E. Kulonen and J. PIKKARAINEN), Acad. Press, N.Y., p. 385.
BAILEY, A. J. and ROBINS, S. P. (1973b) *Matrix Biol.* **1**, 130.
BAILEY, A. J. and ROBBINS, S. P. (1976) *Sci. Prog.*, Oxf., **63**, 421.
BAILEY, A. J. and SIMS, T. J. (1977) *J. Sci. Fd. Agric.* **28**, 565.
BAILEY, C. and COX, R. P. (1976) *The Chilling of Beef Carcases*, Inst. Refrig. London.
BAILEY, C., JAMES, S.T., KITCHELL, A.G. and HUDSON, W. R. (1974) *J. Sc. Fd. Agric.* **25**, 81.
BAILEY, K. (1946) *Nature, Lond.* **157**, 368.

BAILEY, K. (1954) *The Proteins*, vol. II Part B (Eds. H. NEURATH and K. BAILEY), p. 951, Academic Press, New York.

BAILEY, M. E. and KIM, M. K. (1974) *Proc. 20th Meeting Europ. Meat Res. Workers*, Dublin, p. 35.

BAIN, N., HODGINS, W. and SHEWAN, J. M. (1958) *2nd Intl. Symp. Fd. Microbiol. Camb.* (Ed. B. P. EDDY), p. 1, London, H.M.S.O.

BAIRD, D. M., NALBANDOV, A. V. and NORTON, H. W. (1952) *J. Anim. Sci.* **11,** 292.

BAKER, L. C. (1942) *Chem. Ind.* **41,** 458.

BAKER, M. L., BLUNN, C. T. and PLUM, M. (1951) *J. Hered.* **42,** 141.

BALDWIN, E. (1967) *Dynamic Aspects of Biochemistry*, 5th ed., Cambridge Univ. Press.

BALL, C. O. (1938) *Food Res.* **3,** 13.

BALL C. O. (1959) *Food Tech.* **13,** 193.

BALLS, A. K. (1938) *Ice and Cold Storage* **41,** 85.

BALLS, A. K. (1941) *U.S. Dept. Agric. Circ.*, No. 631.

BANFIELD, F. H. and CALLOW, E. H. (1934) *Ann. Rept. Fd. Invest. Bd., Lond.*, p. 72.

BANFIELD, F. H. and CALLOW, E. H. (1935) *J. Soc. chem. Ind.* **54,** 413T.

BARBER, R. S., BRAUDE, R. and MITCHELL, K. G. (1955) *J. agric. Sci.*, **46,** 97.

BARDSLEY, A. J. and TAYLOR, A. McM. (1962) *B.F.M.I.R.A. Res. Repts.*, No. 99.

BARLOW, J. and KITCHELL, A. G. (1966) *J. appl. Bact.* **29,** 185.

BARNARD, R. D. (1937) *J. biol. Chem.* **120,** 177.

BARNES, E. M. (1956) *Food Manuf.* **31,** 508.

BARNES, E. M. (1957) *J. Roy. Soc. Health* **77,** 446.

BARNES, E. M. (1958) *Brit. vet. J.* **144,** 333.

BARNES, M. J., CONSTABLE, B. J. and KODICEK, E. (1969) *Biochem. J.* **113,** 387.

BARNES, E. M. and INGRAM, M. (1956) *J. appl. Bact.* **19,** 117.

BARNES, E. M. and KAMPELMACHER, E. H. (1966) *Proc. 1st Intl. Congr. Indust. Aliment. Agricol., Abidjan*, p. 1093.

BARNES, R. H., LUNDBERG, W. O., HANSON, H. T. and BURN, G. O. (1943) *J. biol. Chem.* **149,** 313.

BARRETT, A. J. (1977) In *Proteinases in Hammalian Cells and Tissues,* (Ed. A. J. BARRETT) p. 1, North Holland Publish. Co. Amsterdam.

BARRON, E. S. G. and DICKMAN, S. (1949) *J. gen. Physiol.* **32,** 595.

BARRON, E. S. G. and LYMAN, C. M. (1938) *J. biol. Chem.* **123,** 229.

BATE-SMITH, E. C. (1937a) *Ann. rept. Fd. Invest. Bd., Lond.*, p. 15.

BATE-SMITH, E. C. (1937b) *Proc. Roy. Soc.* **B 124,** 136.

BATE-SMITH, E. C. (1938) *J. Physiol.* **92,** 336.

BATE-SMITH, E. C. (1948) *J. Soc. chem. Ind.* **67,** 83.

BATE-SMITH, E. C. (1957) *J. Linn. Soc. (Bot.)* **55,** 669.

BATE-SMITH, E. C. (1961) *New Scientist* **11,** 329.

BATE-SMITH, E. C. and BENDALL, J. R. (1947) *J. Physiol.* **106,** 177.

BATE-SMITH, E. C. and BENDALL, J. R. (1949) *J. Physiol.* **110,** 47.

BATZER, O. F. and DOTY, D. M. (1955) *J. Agric. Food Chem.* **3,** 64.

BATZER, O. F., SANTORO, A. T. and LANDMANN, W. A. (1962) *J. Agric. Food Chem.* **10,** 94.

BATZER, O. F., SANTORO, A. T., TAN, M. C., LANDMANN, W. A. and SCHWEIGERT, B. S. (1960) *J. Agric. Food Chem.* **8,** 498.

BATZER, O. F., SLIWINSKI, R. A., CHANG, L., PIH, K., FOX, J. B. Jr., DOTY, D. M., PEARSON, A. M. and SPOONER, M. R. (1959) *Food Tech.* **13**, 501.

BATZER, O. F., SRIBNEY, M., DOTY, D. M. and SCHWEIGERT, B. S. (1959) *J. Agric. Food Chem.* **5**, 700.

BAUERNFEIND, J. C. (1953) *Adv. Fd. Res.* **4**, 359.

BEAR, R. S. (1952) *Adv. Prot. Chem.* 7, 69.

BEARD, F. J. (1924) cited by WANDERSTOCK, J. F. and MILLER, J. I. (1948) *Food Res.* **13**, 291.

BEATTIE, W. A. (1956) *A Survey of the Beef Cattle Industry of Australia,* Bulletin No. 278, C.S.I.R.O., Melbourne.

BEATTY, C. H. and BOCEK, R. M. (1970) in *The Physiology and Biochemistry of Muscle as a Food,* vol. II, p. 155 (Eds. E. J. BRISKEY, R. G. CASSENS and B. B. MARSH), Univ. Wisconsin Press.

BEECHER, G. R., KASTENSCHMIDT, L. L., CASSENS, R. G., HOEKSTRA, W. G. and BRISKEY, E. J. (1968) *J. Food. Sci.* **33**, 84.

BENDALL, J. R. (1946) *J. Soc. chem. Ind.* **65**, 226.

BENDALL, J. R. (1947) *Proc. Roy. Soc.* **B 134,** 272.

BENDALL, J. R. (1951) *J. Physiol.* **114,** 71.

BENDALL, J. R. (1954) *J. Sci. Fd. Agric.* **5,** 468.

BENDALL, J. R. (1960) *The Structure and Function of Muscle,* vol. 3 (Ed. G. H. BOURNE), p. 227, Academic Press, New York.

BENDALL, J. R. (1962) *Recent Advances in Food Science,* vol 1, p. 58, Butterworths, London.

BENDALL, J. R. (1963) *Proc. Meat Tenderness Symp.,* p. 33, Campbell Soup Co., Camden, N.J.

BENDALL, J. R. (1966) *J. Sci. Fd. Agric.* **17,** 334.

BENDALL, J. R. (1967) *J. Sci. Fd. Agric.* **18,** 553.

BENDALL, J. R. (1969) *Muscles, Molecules and Movement,* p. 22, Heinemann Educ. Books Ltd., London.

BENDALL, J. R. (1975) *J. Sci. Fd. Agric.* **26,** 55.

BENDALL, J. R. (1978) *Meat Sci,* **2,** 91.

BENDALL, J. R. and DAVEY, C. L. (1957) *Biochim. Biophys. Acta,* **26,** 93.

BENDALL, J. R., HALLUND, O. and WISMER-PEDERSEN, J. (1963) *J. Food. Sci.* **28,** 156.

BENDALL, J. R. and LAWRIE, R. A. (1962) *J. comp. Path.* **72,** 118.

BENDALL, J. R. and LAWRIE, R. A. (1964) *Amin. Breed Abs.* **32,** 1.

BENDALL, J. R. and MARSH, B. B. (1951) *Proc. 8th Int. Congr. Refrig., Lond.,* p. 351.

BENDALL, J. R. and WISMER-PEDERSEN, J. (1962) *J. Food Sci.* **27,** 144.

BENDER, A. E. (1966) *J. Food Technol.* **1,** 261.

BENDER, A. E. (1975) In *Meat* (Eds. D. J. A. COLE and R. A. LAWRIE) Butterworth, London. p. 433.

BENDER, A. E. and BALLANCE, P. E. (1961) *J. Sci. Fd. Agric.* **12,** 683.

BENDER, A. E. and HUSAINI (1976) *J. Fd. Technol.* **11,** 499.

BENDER, A. E. and ZIA, M. (1976) *J. Fd. Technol.* **II,** 495.

BENDER, A. E., WOOD, T. and PALGRAVE, J. A. (1958) *J. Sci. Fd. Agric.* **9,** 812.

BENNETT, H. S. (1960) *The Structure and Function of Muscle,* vol. 1 (Ed. G. H. BOURNE), p. 137, Academic Press, New York.

BERG, R. T. and BUTTERFIELD, R. M. (1975) In *Meat* (Eds. D. J. A. COLE and R. A. LAWRIE) Butterworth, London, p. 19.

BERGMANN, A. (1847) *Göttnger, Studien* 1, 595, cited by N. C. WRIGHT (1954) *loc.· cit.*

BERMAN, M. (1961) *J. Food Sci.* 26, 422.

BERNARD, C. (1877) *Leçons sur la Diabète et le Glycogénèse animale*, p. 426, Baillière, Paris.

BERNOFSKY, C., FOX, J. B. Jr. and SCHWEIGERT, B. S. (1959) *Food Res.* 24, 339.

BERNOTHY, J. M. (1963) *Nature, Lond.* 200, 86.

BETTS, A. O. (1961) *Vet. Rec.* 73, 1349.

BEUK, J. F., CHORNOCK, F. W. and RICE, E. E. (1948) *J. biol. Chem.* 175, 291.

BEUK, J. F., CHORNOCK, F. W. and RICE, E. E. (1949) *J. biol. Chem.* 180, 1243.

BUEK, J. F., SAVICH, A. L., GOESER, P. A. and HOGAN, J. M. (1959) U.S. Pat. No. 2,903,362.

BIGALKE, R. C. (1964) *New Scientist* 14, 141.

BING, R. (1902) *Virchows Arch. path. Anat.* 170, 171, cited by ADAMS *et al.* (1962).

BIÖRCK, G. (1949) *Acta med. scand.* 133, Sup. 226.

BJERRE, J. (1956) *The Last Cannibals,* Michael Joseph, London.

BLAKESLEE, A. F. (1932) *Proc. Nat. Acad. Sci., U.S.A.* 18, 120.

BLANCHAER, M. and VAN WIJHE, M. (1962) *Nature, Lond.* 193, 877.

BLAXTER, K. L. (1962) *Vits. Hormones* 20, 633.

BLAXTER, K. L. ((1968) *Science J.* 4, 53.

BLAXTER, K. L. (1971–72) *Scot. Agric.* 51, 225.

BLAXTER K. L. and McGILL, R. F. (1955) *Vet. Rev.* 1, 91.

BLAXTER, K. L. and WOOD, W. A. (1952) *Brit. J. Nutr.* 6. 144.

BLOMQUIST, S. M. (1957) *Food Manuf.* 32, 227.

BLOMQUIST, S. M. (1958) *Food Manuf.* 33, 491.

BLOMQUIST, S. M. (1959) *Food Manuf.* 34, 21.

BOARDMAN, N. K. and ADAIR, G. S. (1956) *Nature, Lond.* 170, 679.

BOCEK, R. M., BASINGER, G. M. and BEATTY, C. H. (1966) *Amer. J. Physiol.* 210, 1108.

BODWELL, C. E. and McLAIN, P. E. (1971) In *The Science of Meat and Meat Products* (2nd Ed.) (Eds. J. F. PRICE and B. S. SCHWEIGERT), W. H. Freeman, San Francisco, p. 78.

BOREK, E. and WAELSCH, H. (1951) *J. biol. Chem.* 190, 191.

BORTON, R. J., BRATZLER, L. J. and PRICE, J. F. (1970) *J. Fd. Sci.* 35, 783.

BOUCEK, R. J., NOBLE, and N. L. MARKS, A. (1961) *J. Gerontol.* 5, 150.

BOULEY, M. (1874) *C. R. Acad. Sci. Fr.* 79, 739.

BOUTON, P. E., BROWN, A. D. and HOWARD, A. (1954) *C.S.I.R.O. Food Pres. Quart.* 14, 62.

BOUTON. P. E., FISHER, A. L. HARRIS, P. V. and BAXTER, R. I. (1973) *J. Fd. Technol.* 8, 39.

BOUTON, P. E., FORD, A. L., HARRIS, P. V., MACFARLANE, J. J. and O'SHEA, J. M. (1977) *J. Fd. Sci.* 42, 132.

BOUTON, P. E., HARRIS, P. V., MACFARLANE, J. J. and O'SHEA, J. M. (1977) *Meat Sci.* 1, 307.

BOUTON, P. E., HARRIS, P. V. and SHORTHOSE, W. R. (1975) *J. Text. Stud.* 6, 297.

BOUTON, P. E., HARRIS, P. E., SHORTHOSE, W. R. and ELLIS, R. W. (1978) *Meat Sci.* 2, 161.

BOUTON, P. E., HARRIS, P. V., SHORTHOSE, W. R. and SMITH, M. G. (1974) *J. Fd.Techol.* **9,** 31.

BOUTON, P. E., CARROL, Γ. D., FISHER, A. L. HARRIS, P. V. and SHORTHOSE, W. R. (1973) *J. Fd. Sci.* **38,** 816.

BOUTON, P. E., CARROL, F. D., HARRIS, P. V. and SHORTHOSE, W. R. (1973) *J. Fd. Sci.* **38,** 401.

BOUTON, P. E., ELLIS, R. W., HARRIS, P. V. and SHORTHOSE, W. R. (1976) *Meat Res. C.S.I.R.O.,* 42.

BOULTON, P. E. and HOWARD, A. (1956) *C.S.I.R.O. Food Pres. Quart.* **16,** 50.

BOUTON, P. E. and HOWARD, A. (1960) *Proc. 6th Meeting European Meat Res. Workers, Utrecht.* Pap. No. 24

BOUTON, P. E., HOWARD, A. and LAWRIE, R. A. (1957) *Spec. Rept. Fd. Invest. Bd., Lond.,* No. 66.

BOUTON, P. E., HOWARD, A. and LAWRIE, R. A. (1958) *Spec. Rept. Fd. Invest. Bd., Lond.,* No. 67.

BOUTON, P. E. and SHORTHOSE, W. R. (1969) *Proc. 15th Meeting European Meat Res. Workers. Helsinki,* p. 78.

BOVARD, K. P. and HAZEL, L. N. (1963) *J. Anim. Sci.* **22,** 188.

BOWES, J. H., ELLIOT, R. G. and MOSS, J. A. (1957) *J. Soc. Leather Trades' Chemists* **41,** 249.

BRADEN, A. W. H., SOUTHCOTT, W. H. and MOULE, G. R. (1964) *Aust. J. agric. Res.* **15,** 142.

BRAMBLETT, V. D., HOSTETLER, R. L., VAIL, G. E. and DRAUDT, H. N. (1959) *Food Tech.* **13,** 707.

BRAMBLETT, V. D. and VAIL, G. E. (1964) *Food Tech.* **18,** 123.

BRASCH, A. and HUBER, W. (1947) *Science* **105,** 112.

BRAUDE, R. (1950) *Brit. J. Nutr.* **4,** 138.

BRAUDE, R. (1967) *Proc. C.I.C.R.A. Conf., Dublin,* p. 21.

BRIGELOW, W. D. and ESTY, J. R. (1920) *J. infect. Dis.* **27,** 602.

BRISKEY, E. J. (1964) *Adv. Food Res.* **13,** 90.

BRISKEY, E. J. (1969) in *Recent Points of View on the Condition and Meat Quality of Pigs for Slaughter,* p. 41 (Eds. W. SYBESMA, P. G. VAN DER WALS and P. WALSTRON), Res. Inst. Animal Husbandary, Zeist.

BRISKEY, E. J. and WISMER-PEDERSEN, J. (1961) *J. Food Sci.* **26,** 297.

BRISSEY, G. E. (1952) U.S. Pat. No. 2,596,067.

BROCKMANN, M. C. (1969) *Proc. 15th Meeting European Meat Res. Workers, Helsinki,* p. 468.

BROCKMANN, M. C. (1970) *Food Technol.,* Champaign, **24,** 896.

BRODY, S. (1927) *Mo. agric. Expt. Sta. Res. Bull.,* Nos. 97, 98, 101, 104.

BROOKS, J. (1929a) *Ann. Rept. Fd. Invest. Bd. Lond.,* p. 29.

BROOKS, J. (1929b) *Biochem. J.* **23,** 1391.

BROOKS, J. (1930) *Biochem. J.* **24,** 1379.

BROOKS, J. (1931) *Ann. Rept. Fd. Invest. Bd., Lond.,* p. 36.

BROOKS, J. (1933) *J. Soc, chem. Ind.* **52,** 17T.

BROOKS, J. (1935) *Proc. Roy. Soc.* **B 118,** 560.

BROOKS, J. (1937) *Proc. Roy. Soc.* **B 123,** 368.
BROOKS, J. (1938) *Food Res.* **3,** 75.
BROOKS, J., HAINES, R. B., MORAN, T. and PACE, J. (1940) *Spec. Rept. Fd. Invest. Bd., London.,* No. 49.
BROWN, A. D., COOTE, G. G. and MEANEY, M. F. (1957) *J. appl. Bact.* **20,** 75.
BROWN, R. H., BLASER, R. E. and FONTENOT, J. P. (1963) *J. Anim. Sci.* **22,** 1038.
BRUMBY, P. J. (1959) *N.Z.J agric. Res.* **2,** 683.
BRYCE-JONES, K. (1962) *Inst. Meat Bull.,* April, p. 2.
BRYCE-JONES, K. (1969) *Inst. Meat Bull.* No. 65, p. 3.
BRYCE-JONES, K., HOUSTON, T. W. and HARRIES, J. M. (1963) *J. Sci. Fd. Agric.* **14,** 637.
BRYCE-JONES, K., HOUSTON, T. W. and HARRIES, J. M. (1964) *J. Sci. Fd. Agric.* **16,** 790.
BRYNKO, C. and SMITHIES, W. R. (1956) *Food in Canada* **16** (10), 26.
BUEGGE, D. R. and MARSH, B. B. (1975) *Biochem. biophys. Res. Commun.* **65,** 478.
BURLEIGH, I. G. (1974) *Biol. Rev.* **49,** 267.
BURN, C. G. amd BURKET, L. W. (1938) *Arch. Path.* **25,** 643.
BURRIS, M. J., BOGARD, R., OLIVER, A. W., McKEY, A. O. and OLDFIELD, J. E. (1954) *Ore. Agric. Expt. Sta. Tech. Bull.,* No. 31.
BURTON, V. L. (1949) *J. Am. Chem. Soc.* **71,** 4117.
BUSCH, W. A., STROMER, M. H. GOLL, D. E. and SUZUKI, A. (1972) *J. cell Biol.* **52,** 167.
BUSCH, W. A., GOLL, D. E. and PARRISH, F. C., Jr. (1972) *J. Fd. Sci.* **37,** 289.
BUTTERFIELD, R. M. and BERG, R. T. (1966) *Aust. vet. Sci.* 7, 389.
BYWATERS, E. G. L. (1944) *J. Am. med. Ass.* **124,** 1103.

CAIN, R. F., ANGLEMIER, A. F., SATHER, L. A. BAUTISTA, F. R. and THOMPSON, R. H. (1958) *Food Res.* **23,** 603.
CALLOW, E. H. (1925–26) *Ann. Rept. Fd. Invest. Bd., Lond.,* p. 17.
CALLOW, E. H. (1927a) *Ann. Rept. Fd. Invest. Bd., London.,* p. 17.
CALLOW, E. H. (1927b) *Analyst* **52,** 391.
CALLOW, E. H. (1930) *Ann. Rept. Fd. Invest. Bd., Lond.,* p. 71.
CALLOW, E. H. (1931) *Ann. Rept. Fd. Invest. Bd., Lond.,* p. 134.
CALLOW, E. H. (1932) *Ann. Rept. Fd. Invest. Bd., Lond.,* p. 97.
CALLOW, E. H. (1933) *Ann. Rept. Fd. Invest. Bd., Lond.,* p. 100.
CALLOW, E. H. (1934) *Food Invest. Bd., Lond., Leafl.* No. 5.
CALLOW, E. H. (1935) *Ann. Rept. Fd. Invest. Bd., Lond.,* p. 57.
CALLOW, E. H. (1936) *Ann. Rept. Fd. Invest. Bd., Lond.,* pp. 75, 81.
CALLOW, E. H. (1937) *Ann. Rept. Fd. Invest. Bd., Lond.,* pp. 34, 49.
CALLOW, E. H. (1938a) Transit Shrinkage in Fasting Pigs, *Bacon Development Board Bull.,* No. 3, London.
CALLOW, E. H. (1938b) *Ann. Rept. Fd. Invest. Bd., Lond.,* p. 54.
CALLOW, E. H. (1939) *Ann. Rept. Fd. Invest. Bd., Lond.,* p. 29.
CALLOW, E. H. (1947) *J. agric. Sci.* **37,** 113.

CALLOW, E. H. (1948) *J. agric. Sci.* **38,** 174.

CALLOW, E. H. (1954) *Ann. Rept. Fd. Invest. Bd., Lond.,* p. 28.

CALLOW, E. H. (1955a) *Inst. Meat Bull.,* March, p. 2.

CALLOW, E. H. (1955b) *Ann. Rept. Fd. Invest. Bd., Lond.,* p. 16

CALLOW, E. H. (1956) *J. Sci. Fd. Agric.* **7,** 173.

CALLOW, E. H. (1958) *J. agric. Sci.* **51,** 361.

CALLOW, E. H. (1961) *J. agric. Sci.* **56,** 265.

CALLOW, E. H. (1962) *J. agric. Sci.* **58,** 295.

CALLOW, E. H. and BOAZ, T. G. (1937) *Ann. Rept. Fd. Invest. Bd., Lond.,* p. 51.

CALLOW, E. H. and INGRAM, M. (1955) *Food* **24,** 52.

CALLOW, E. H. and SEARLE, R. L. (1956) *J. agric. Sci.* **48,** 61.

CAMERON, H. S., GREGORY, P. W. and HUGHES, E. H. (1943) *J. vet. Res.* **4,** 387.

CANONICO, P. G. and BIRD, J. W. G. (1970) *J. cell. Biol.* **45,** 321.

CARBEN, F., FUCHS, F. and KNAPPEIS, G. G. (1965) *J. cell. Biol.* **27,** 35.

CARMICHAEL, D. J. and LAWRIE, R. A. (1967a) *J. Food Technol.* **2,** 299.

CARMICHAEL, D. J. and LAWRIE, R. A. (1967b) *J. Food Technol.* **2,** 313.

CARPENTER, J. W., PALMER, A. Z., KIRK, W. G. PEACOCK, F. M. and KOGER, M. (1955) *J. Anim. Sci.* **14,** 1228.

CARSE, W. A. (1973) *J. Fd. Technol.* **8,** 163.

CARSE, W. A. and LOCKER, R. H. (1974) *J. Sci. Fd. Agric.* **25,** 1529.

CARSON, N. (1970) in *Proteins as Human Food* (Ed. R. A. LAWRIE), Butterworths, London, p. 458.

CARSTEN, M. E. (1968) *Biochemistry* **7,** 960.

CARTWRIGHT, T. C., BUTLER, O. D. and COVER, S. (1958) *Proc. 10th Res. Conf., Amer. Meat Inst. Found.,* p. 75.

CASSENS, R. G. (1970) in *The Physiology and Biochemistry of Muscle as a Food,* vol. II (Eds. E. J. BRISKEY, R. G. CASSENS and B. B. MARSH), Univ. Wisconsin Press, Madison, p. 679.

CASSENS, R. G., COOPER, C. C. and BRISKEY, E. J. (1969) *Acta neuropath. (Berl.)* **12,** 300.

CASSENS, R. G. and NEWBOLD, R. P. (1966) *J. Sci. Fd. Agric.* **17,** 254.

CASSENS, R. G. and NEWBOLD, R. P. (1967) *J. Food Sci.* **32,** 269.

CASTELLANI, A. G. and NIVEN, C. F. JR. (1955) *Appl. Microbiol.* **3,** 154.

CAUSEY, M., HAUSRATH, M. E., RAMSTAD, P. E. and PENTON, F. (1950) *Food Res.* **15,** 237, 249, 256.

CAVETT, J. J. (1962) *J. appl. Bact.* **25,** 282.

CHAMBERS, R. and HALE, H. P. (1932) *Proc. Roy. Soc.* **B 110,** 336.

CHAMPAGNAT, A. (1966) 7th Intl. Congr. Nutrition, Hamburg.

CHAMPION, A., PARSONS, A. L. and LAWRIE, R. A. (1970) *J. Sci. Fd. Agric.* **21,** 7.

CHAPPEL, J. B. and PERRY, S. V. (1953) *Biochem. J.* **55,** 586.

CHARLES, L. M. T. and NICOL, T. (1961) *Nature, Lond.* **192,** 565.

CHEAH, K. S. (1971) *Fed. Eu. Biochem. Soc. Letters,* **19,** 105.

CHEAH, K. S. (1973) *J. Sci. Fd. Agric.* **24,** 51.

CHEAH, K. S. (1976) *J. Fd. Technol.* **11,** 181.

CHEAH, K. S. and CHEAH, A. M. (1976) *J. Sci. Fd. Agric.* **27,** 1137.

CHRISTIAN, J. H. B. and SCOTT, W. J. (1953) *Aust. J. biol. Sci.* **6,** 565.

CHRYSTALL, B. B. and DEVINE, C. E. (1976–77) *Ann. Res. Rept.*, Meat Ind. Res. Inst. N.Z. Inc., p. 32.

CHRYSTALL, B. B. and DEVINE, C. E. (1978) *Meat Sci.* **2**, 49.

CLAUSEN, H. (1965) *Wld., Rev. Anim. Prod.* **1**, 28.

CLAYTON, W. (1932) *Food Manuf.* **7**, 109.

CLELAND, K. W. and SLATER, E. C. (1953) *Biochem. J.* **53**, 547.

COHEN, B. and CLARK, W. M. (1919) *J. Bact.* **4**, 409.

COLE, H. A. and PERRY, S. V. (1975) *Biochem. J.* **119**, 525.

COLDITZ, P. J. and KELLAWAY, R. C. (1972) *Aust. J. agric. Res.* **23**, 717.

COLEBY, B. (1959) *Intl. J. appl. Radn. Isotopes* **6**, 71.

COLEBY, B., INGRAM, M., RHODES, D. N. and SHEPHERD, H. J. (1962) *J. Sci. Fd. Agric.* **13**, 628.

COLEBY, B., INGRAM, M. and SHEPHERD, H. J. (1961) *J. Sci. Fd. Agric.* **12**, 417.

COLEMAN, H. M. and STEFFEN, H. H. (1949) U.S. Pat. 2,491,646.

COLEMAN, R. and CRESWICK, N. (1966) U.S. Pat. No. 3,253,931.

COOK, C. F. and LANGSWORTH, R. F. (1966) *J. Food Sci.* **31**, 497.

COOK, C. F., MAYER, E. W., CATSIMPOULAS, N. and SIPOS, E. F. (1969) *Proc. 15th Meeting European Meat Res. Workers, Helsinki*, p. 381.

COOK, G. A., LOVE, E. F. G., VICKERY, J. R. and YOUNG, W. G. (1926) *Aust. J. exp. Biol. med. Sci.* **3**, 15.

COOK, J. W. (1933) *Proc. Roy. Soc.* **B 113**, 277.

COOK, J. W. (1934) *Nature, Lond.* **134**, 758.

COOK, L. J. SCOTT, T. W., FERGUSON, K. A. and MCDONALD, I. (1970), *Nature, Lond.* **228**, 178.

COPPOCK, B. (1975) Ph.D. Dissertation, Univ. London.

COPPOCK, B. M. and MACLEOD, G. (1977) *J. Sci. Fd. Agric.* **28**, 206.

CORI, C. F. (1956) *Enzymes: Units of Biological Structure and Function* (Ed. O. H. GAEBLER), p. 573, Academic Press, New York.

CORI, C. F. and CORI, G. T. (1928) *J. biol Chem.* **79**, 309.

CORI, G. T. (1957) *Mod Probl. Paediat.* 344.

COSMOS, E. (1966) *Develop. Biol.* **13**, 163.

COSNETT, K. S., HOGAN, D. J., LAW, N. H. and MARSH, B.B. (1956) *J. Sci. Fd. Agric.* **7**, 546.

COVER, S. and HOSTETLER, R. L. (1960) *Texas Agric. Expt. Sta. Bull.*, No. 947.

CRAIG, H. B., PEARSON, A. M. and WEBB, N. B. (1962) *Food Res.* **27**, 29.

CRAWFORD, M. A. (1968) *Proc. Nutr. Soc.* **27**, 163.

CRAWFORD, M. A. (1975) In *Meat* (Eds. D. J. A. COLE and R. A. LAWRIE), Butterworth, London, p. 451.

CRAWFORD, M. A., GALE, M. M., WOODFORD, M. H. and CASPED, N. M. (1970) *Intl. J. Biochem.* **1**, 295.

CRICHTON, D. B. (1972) *J. Physiol.* **226**, 68.

CRICK, F. H. C., BARNETT, L., BRENNER, S. and WATTS-TOBIN, R. J. (1961) *Nature, Lond.* **192**, 1227.

CRITCHELL, J. T. and RAYMOND, J. (1912) *A History of the Frozen Meat Trade*, 2nd ed., Constable & Co. Ltd., London.

CROCKER, E. C. (1945) *Flavor*, McGraw-Hill, New York.

CROCKER, E. C. (1948) *Food Res.* **13**, 179.
CROMBACH, J. J. M. L., DE ROVER, W. and DE GROOTE, B. (1956) *Proc. 3rd Intl. Congr. Anim. Prod., Cambridge,* sect. III, p. 80.
CRUFT, P. G. (1957) *Meat Hygiene,* F.A.O. Agric. Series, No. 34, p. 147.
CUFF, P. W. W., MADDOCK, H. M., SPUR, V. C. and CATRON, D. V. (1951) *Iowa State Coll. Sci. J.* **25**, 575.
CUMMINS, P. and PERRY, S. V. (1973) *Biochem. J.* **133**, 765.
CUTHBERTSON, A. and POMEROY, R. W. (1962) *J. Agric. Sci.* **59**, 207, 215.
CUTHBERTSON, A. and POMEROY, R. W. (1970) *Anim. Prod.* **12**, 37.
CUTTING, C. L. and BANNERMAN, A. (1951) *Fd. Invest. Bd., Lond., Leafl.,* No. 14.
CUTTING, C. L. and MALTON, R. (1971) *Meat Res. Inst.,* Memo No. 2.
CURLEY, A., SEDLAK, V. A., GIRLING, E. F., HAWK, R. E., BARTHEL, W. F., PIERCE, T. E. and LIKOSKY, W. A. (1971) *Science,* **172**, 65.
CZOK, R. and BÜCHER, TH. (1960) *Adv. Prot. Chem.* **15**, 315.

DAHL, O. (1958a) *Svensk kem. Tidskrift.* **70**, 43.
DAHL, O. (1958b) *J. Refrig.* **1**, 170.
DAHL, O. (1965) *J. Sci. Fd. Agric.* **16**, 619.
DAINTON, F. S. (1948) *Rep. Progr. Chem.* **45**, 5.
DAINTY, R. H., SHAW, B. G., de BOER, K. A. and SCHEPS, E. S. J. (1975) *J. appl. Bact.* **139**, 73.
DALE, W. M. and DAVIES, J. V. (1951) *Biochem, J.* **48**, 129.
DASTOLI, F. R., LOPIEKES, D. V. and DOIG, A. R. (1968) *Nature, Lond.* **218**, 884.
DAVEY, C. L. (1960) *Arch. Biochem. Biophys.* **89**, 303.
DAVEY, C. L. (1961) *Arch. Biochem. Biophys.* **95**, 296.
DAVEY, C. L. (1964) *Ann. Rept. Meat Ind. Res. Inst.,* N.Z., p. 17.
DAVEY, C. L. and CURSON, P. (1971) *Meat Ind. Res. Inst.,* N.Z., Rept. No. 215.
DAVEY, C. L. and GILBERT, K. V. (1967) *J. Food Technol.* **2**, 57.
DAVEY, C. L., and GILBERT, K. V. (1969) *J. Food Sci.* **34**, 69.
DAVEY, C. L., GILBERT, K. V., and CURSON, P. (1971) *Ann. Rept. Meat Ind. Res. Inst.,* N.Z., p. 39.
DAVEY, C. L., and GRAAFHUIS, (1976a) *Experentia,* **32**, 32.
DAVEY, C. L., and GRAAFHUIS, A. E. (1976b) *J. Sci. Fd. Agric.* **27**, 301.
DAVEY, C. L., and GILBERT, K. V. (1974) *J. Fd. Technol.* **9**. 51.
DAVEY, C. L., and GILBERT, K. V. (1975a) *J. Sci. Fd. Agric.* **26**, 755.
DAVEY, C. L., and GILBERT, K. V., (1975b) *J. Fd. Technol.* **10**, 333.
DAVEY, C. L., and GILBERT, K. V. (1975c) *J. Sci. Fd. Agric.* **26**, 953.
DAVEY, C. L., and GILBERT, K. V. (1976a) *J. Sci. Fd. Agric.* **27**, 1085.
DAVEY, C. L., and GILBERT, K. V. (1976b) *J. Sci. Fd. Agric.* **27**, 244.
DAVEY, C. L., NIEDERER, A. F. and GRAAFHUIS, A. E. (1976) *J. Sci. Fd. Agric.* **27**, 251.
DAVEY, C. L., KUTTEL, H. and GILBERT, K. V. (1967) *J. Food Technol.* **2**, 53.
DAVEY, C. L., (1970) *Ann. Rept. Meat Ind. Res. Inst.,* N.Z., p. 26.
DAVEY, C. L., and DICKSON, M. R. (1970) *J. Food Sci.* **35**, 56.

DAVIDSON, H. R. (1953) *The Production and Marketing of Pigs,* 2nd ed., Longmans, London.
DAVIES, R. E. (1963) *Nature, Lond.* **199,** 1068.
DAWSON, E. H., BRAGDON, J. L. and MCMANUS, S. (1963) *Food Tech.* **17,** Nos. 9, 45, 51; Nos, 10, 39, 43.
DEAN, R. W. and BALL, C. O. (1960) *Food Tech.* **14,** 222, 271.
DEATHERAGE, F. E. (1955) *1st Intl. Conf. on Antibiotics in Agriculture, Washington,* Nat. Acad. Sci., Nat. Res. Counc. Publ. No. 397, p. 211.
DEATHERAGE, F. E. (1957) U.S. Pat. No. 2,786,768.
DEATHERAGE, F. E. (1965) *Proc. 1st Intl. Congr. Food Sci. Tech.* **2,** 65.
DEATHERAGE, F. E. and FUJIMAKI, M. (1964) *J. Food Sci.* **29,** 316.
DE DUVE, C. (1959a) *Subcellular Particles,* p. 128, Ronald Press, New York.
DE DUVE, C. (1959b) *Exp. Cell. Res.,* Suppl. **7,** 169.
DE DUVE, C. and BEAUFAY, H. (1959) *Biochem. J.* **73,** 610.
DEIBEL, R. H. and NIVEN, C. F., JR. (1959) *Appl. Microbiol.* **7,** 138.
DENNY-BROWN, D. (1929) *Proc. Roy. Soc.* **B 104,** 371.
DENNY-BROWN, D. (1961) *Neuromuscular Disorders* **38,** 147.
DESOUBRY, M. A. and PORCHER, M. C. M. C. (1985) *C. R. Soc. Biol., Paris* **47,** 101.
DESROISER, N. W. (1959) *The Technology of Food Preservation,* AVI Publishing Co., Westport, Conn.
DICKINSON, A. G., HANCOCK, J. L., HOVELL, J. R. and TAYLER, ST. C. S. (1962) *Amin. Prod.* **4,** 64.
DICKINSON, M. R. (1969) *Ann. Rept. Meat Ind. Res. Inst., N.Z.,* p. 17.
DICKSON, M. R., MARSH, B. B. and LEET, N. G. (1970) *Ann. Rept. Meat Ind. Res. Inst., N.Z.,* p. 31.
DIEHL, J. F. (1966) *Proc. 2nd Intl. Congr. Fd. Sci. Tech., Warsaw,* C.3.9.
DICKSON, M. and WEBB, E. C. (1958) *Enzymes,* p. 152, Longmans, London.
DOLMAN, C. E. (1957) *Meat Hygiene, F.A.O. Agric. Series,* No. 34, p. 11.
DOTY, D. M. (1960) *The Science of Meat and Meat Products,* Amer. Meat Inst. Found., p. 288, Einhold Publishing Co., New York.
DOTY, D. M. and PIERCE, J. C. (1961) *U.S. Dept. Agric. Tech. Bull.,* No. 1231.
DOTY, D. M. and WACHTER, J. P. (1955) *J. Agric. Food Chem.* **3,** 61.
DOWBEN, R. M. and ZUCKERMAN, L. (1963) *Nature, Lond.* **197,** 400.
DOZIER, C. C. (1924) *J. Infect. Dis.* **35,** 134.
DRAKE, M. P., GERNON, G. D. and KRAUS, F. J. (1961) *J. Food Sci.* **26,** 156.
DREYFUS, J. C., SCHAPIRA, G. and SCHAPIRA, F. (1954) *J. clin. Invest.* **33,** 794.
DRUMMOND, J. C. and MACARA, T. (1938) *Chem. Ind.,* p. 828.
DUBE, G., BRAMBLETT, V. D., JUDGE, M. D. and HARRINGTON, R. B. (1972) *J. Fd. Sci.* **37,** 13.
DUBOWITZ, V. (1963) *Nature, Lond.* **197,** 1215.
DUBOWITZ, V. (1966) *Nature, Lond.* **211,** 884.
DUBOWITZ, V. and PEARSE, A. S. E. (1961) *J. path. Bact.* **81,** 365.
DUESBERG, J. (1909) *Arch. Zellforsch. mikr. Anat.* **4,** 602, cited by ADAMS, DENNY-BROWN and PEARSON (1962), *loc. cit.*
DUFF, J. T., WRIGHT, G. G. and YANNSKY, A. (1956) *J. Bact.* **72,** 455.

DUGAN, L. R. (1957) *Amer. Meat Inst. Found. Circ.,* No. 36.
DUGAN, L. R. and LANDIS, P. W. (1956) *J. Amer. Oil Chem. Soc.* **33,** 152.
DUNCAN, W. R H and GARTON, C. A. (1967) *J. Sci. Fd. Agric.* **18,** 99.
DUNKER, C. F., BERMAN, M., SNIDER, G. G. and TUBIASH, II. S. (1953) *Food Tech.* **7,** 288
DUNKER, C. F. and HANKINS, O. G. (1955) *Food Tech.* **7,** 505.
DUNKER, C. F., HANKINS, O. G. and BENNETT, O. L. (1945) *Food Res.* **10,** 445.
DUTSON, T. (1976) *Proc. 29th Ann. Recip. Meat Conf.,* Provo, Utah, p. 336.
DUTSON, T. (1977) *Proc. Ann. Recip. Meat Conf.,* p. 79.
DUTSON, T. and LAWRIE, R. A. (1974) *J. Fd. Technol.* **9.** 43.
DVORAK, Z. and VOGNAROVA, I. (1965) *J. Sci. Fd. Agric.* **16,** 305.
DYETT, E. J. (1969) *Proc. 15th Meeting European Meat Res. Workers, Helsinki,* p. 509.

EARLE, R. L. and FLEMING, A. K. (1967) *J. Food Technol.* **21,** 79.
EBASHI, S. and EBASHI, F. (1964) *Jap. J. Biochem.* **55,** 604.
EBASHI, S. and ENDO, M. (1968) *Prog. Biophys. molec. Biol.* **18,** 125.
EDDY, B. P. (1958) *The Microbiology of Fish and Meat Curing Brines,* p. 87, H.M.S.O., London.
EDDY, B. P., GATHERUM, D. P. and KITCHELL, A. G. (1960) *J. Sci. Fd. Agric.* **11,** 727.
EDDY, B. P. and INGRAM, M. (1956) *J. appl. Bact.* **19,** 62.
EDDY, B. P. and INGRAM, M. (1965) *Proc. 1st Intl. Congr. Food Sci. Tech. 2,* 405.
EDDY, B. P. and KITCHELL, A. G. (1959) *J. appl. Bact.* **22,** 57.
EDDY, B. P. and KITCHELL, A. G. (1961) *J. Sci. Fd. Agric.* **12,** 146.
EHRENBERG, A. S. C. and SHEWAN, J. M. (1953) *J. Sci. Fd. Agric.* **10,** 482.
EISEN, A. Z., BAUER, E. A. and JEFFREY, J. H. (1971) *Proc. natl. Acad. Sci. U.S.A.* **68,** 248.
ELLIOT, G. F. (1968) *J. theoret. Biol.* **21,** 71.
ELTON, C. (1927) *Animal Ecology,* Sidgwick & Johnson, London.
EMERSON, C., BRADY, D. E. and TUCKER, L. N. (1955) *Univ. Missouri Coll. Agric. Res. Bull.,* No. 470.
EMERY, A. E. H. (1964) *Nature, Lond.* **201,** 1044.
EMMENS, C. W. (1959) *Progress in the Physiology of Farm Animals,* vol. 3 (Ed. J. HAMMOND), p. 1047, Butterworths, London.
EMMENS, C. W. and BLACKSHAW, A. W. (1956) *Physiol. Rev.* **36,** 2.
EMPEY, W. A. (1933) *J. Soc. chem. Ind.* **52,** 230 T.
EMPEY, W. A. and MONTGOMERY, W. A. (1959) *C.S.I.R.O. Food Pres. Quart.* **19,** 30.
EMPEY, W. A. and SCOTT, W. J. (1939) *C.S.I.R.O. Bull.,* No. 126.
EMPEY, W. A. and VICKERY, J. R. (1933) *J. Coun. sci. industr. Res. Aust.* **6,** 233.
ENGEL, W. K. (1963) *Nature, Lond.* **200,** 588.
ENGELHARDT, V. A. (1946) *Adv. Enzymol.* 6, 147.
ERDÖS, T. (1943) *Stud. Inst. med. Chem. Univ. Szeged* **3,** 51.
ETHERINGTON, D. J. (1971) *Proc. 17th Meeting Meat Res. Insts.,* Bristol, p. 632.
ETHERINGTON, D. J. (1972) *Biochem. J.* **127,** 685.
ETHERINGTON, D. J. (1973) *Eur. J. Biochem.* **32,** 126.
ETHERINGTON, D. J. (1974) *Biochem.* **137,** 547.
EVANS, C. D. (1961) *Proc. Flavour Chem. Symp.,* p. 123, Campbell Soup Co., Camden, N.J.

FAWCETT, D. N. and REVELL, J. P. (1961) *J. biophys. biochem. Cytol.* **10**, Suppl., p. 89.
FEARSON, W. R. and FOSTER, D. L. (1922) *Biochem. J.* **16**, 564.
FELL, H. B. and DINGLE, J. T. (1963) *Biochem. J.* **87**, 403.
FENTON, F., FLIGHT, I. T., ROBSON, D. S., BEAMER, K. C. and HOW, I. S. (1956) *Cornell Univ. agric. Expt. Sta., Ithaca, N.Y. Mem.*, No. 341.
FERNAND, V. S. V. (1949) Ph.D. Thesis, Univ. London.
FICKER, M. (1905) *Arch. Hyg., Berl.* **54**, 354.
FIDDLER, W., DOERR, R. C., ERTEL, J. R. and WASSERMAN, A. E. (1971) *J.O.A.C.* **54**, 1160.
FIDDLER, W., DOERR, R. C. and WASSERMAN, A. E. (1970) *Agric. Food Chem.* **18**, 310.
FINDLAY, J. D. (1950) *Bull. Hannah Dairy Res. Inst.*, No. 9.
FINDLAY, J. D. and BEAKLEY, W. R. (1954) *Progr. in the Physiology of Farm Animals* (Ed. J. HAMMOND), vol. 1, p. 252, Butterworths Scientific Publications, London.
FINN, D. B. (1932) *Proc. Roy. Soc.* **B 111**, 396.
FIRMAN, M. C., BACHMANN, H. J., HEYRICH, F. J. and HOPPER, P. F. (1959) *Food Tech.* **13**, 529.
FISCHER, R. G., BLAIR, J. M. and PETERSEN, M. S. (1954) *The Quality and Stability of Canned Meats,* Q.M. Food and Container Inst., Nat. Res. Coun., Washington.
FLAIN, R. (1964) *Food Tech.* **18**, 753.
FLEMING, A. (1929) *Brit. J. exp. Path.* **10**, 226.
FLEMING, A. K. (1969) *J. Food Technol.* **4**, 199.
FLUX, D. S., MUMFORD, R. E. and BARCLAY, P. C. (1961) *N.Z. J. agric Res.* **4**, 328.
FOLEY, C. W., HEIDENREICH, C. J. and LASLEY, J. F. (1960) *J. Hered.* **51**, 278.
FOLLET, M. J. (1974) Ph.D. Dissertation, Univ. Nottingham.
FOLLET, M. J. NORMAN, G. A. and RATCLIFF, P. W. (1974) *J. Fd. Technol.* **9**. 509.
FOOD STANDARDS COMMITTEE (1975) *Report on Novel Proteins,* H.M.S.O., London.
FORD, A. L., HARRIS, P. V., McFARLAND, J. J., PARK, R. J. and SHORTHOSE, N. R. (1974) *C.S.I.R.O. Meat Res.* Rept. No. 2/74.
FORD, A. L. PARK, R. J., RATCLIFF, D. and MURRAY, K. E. (1975) *Meat Res. in C.S.I.R.O.* p. 21.
FOSTER, W. W. and JASON, A. C. (1954) U.K. Pat. Applic. No. 24,329/54.
FOSTER, W. W. and SIMPSON, T. H. (1961) *J. Sci. Food Agric.* **12**, 363.
FOX, J. B., JR. (1962) *Proc. 14th Res. Conf., Amer. Meat Inst. Found. Chicago,* p. 93.
FOX, J. B., JR., STREHLER, T., BERNOFSKY, C. and SCHWEIGERT, B. S. (1958) *J. Agric. Food Chem.* **6**, 692.
FOX, J. B., JR. and THOMSON, J. S. (1963) *Biochem.* **2**, 465.
FREARSON, N. and PERRY, S. V. (1975) *Biochem. J.* **151**, 99.
FREARSON, N., SOLERO, R. J. and PERRY, S. V. (1976) *Nature, Lond.* **264**, 801.
FRICKE, H. (1938) *Cold Spr. Harb. Symp. quant. Biol.* **6**. 134.
FURMINGER, I. G. S. (1964) *Nature, Lond.* **202**, 1332.

GADDIS, A. M., HANKINS, O. G. and HINER, R. L. (1950) *Food Tech.* **4**, 498.
GALE, E. F. (1947) *The Chemical Activities of Bacteria,* Univ. Tut. Press, London.
GALTON, M. M., LOWERY, W. D. and HARDY, A. V. (1954) *J. infect. Dis.* **95**, 236.

GAMMON, D. L., KEMP, J. D., EDNEY, J. M. and VARNEY, W. Y. (1968) *J. Food Sci.* **33,** 417.
GARDNER, G. A., CARSON, A. W. and PATTON, J. (1967) *J. appl. Bact.* **30,** 321.
GARDNER, G. A. and PATTERSON, R. L. S. (1975) *J. appl. Bact.* **39,** 263.
GARDNER, G. A. and PATTON, J. (1969) *Proc. 15th Meeting European Meat Res. Workers.* *Helsinki,* p. 176.
GARNER, F. H. (1944) *The Cattle of Britain,* Longmans, London.
GARTON, G. A., DUNCAN, W. R. H. and MCEWAN, E. H. (1971) *Canad. J. Zool.* **49,** 1159.
GARVEN, H. S. D. (1925) *Brain* **48,** 380.
GAUNT, R. A., BIRNIE, J. H. and EVERSOLE, W. J. (1949) *Physiol. Rev.* **29,** 281.
GAUTHIER, G. F. (1969) *Zellforsch.* **95,** 462.
GEORGE, J. C. and NAIK, R. M. (1958) *Nature, Lond.* **181,** 782.
GEORGE, J. C. and SCARIA, K. S. (1958) *Nature, Lond.* **181,** 783.
GERGELY, J. (1970) in *The Physiology and Biochemistry of Muscle as a Food,* vol. II (Eds. E. J. BRISKEY, R. G. CASSENS and B. B. MARSH), Univ. Wisconsin Press, Madison, p. 349.
GERGELY, J., PRAGEY, D., SCHOLTZ, A. F., SEIDEL, J. C., SRÉTER, F. A. and THOMPSON, M. M. (1965) in *Molecular Biology of Muscular Contraction,* p. 145, Igaku Shoin Ltd., Tokyo.
GERRARD, F. (1935) *Sausage and Small Goods Manufacture,* 1st ed., Leonard Hill, London.
GERRARD, F. (1951) *Meat Technology,* 2nd ed., Leonard Hill, London.
GERSHMAN, L. C., STRACHER, A. and DREIZEN, P. (1969) *J. biol. Chem.* **244,** 2726.
GIBBONS, N. E. (1958) *The Microbiology of Fish and Meat Curing Brines* (Ed. B. P. EDDY), p. 69, H.M.S.O., London.
GIBBONS, N. E. and ROSE, D. (1950) *Canad. J. Res.* **28,** 438.
GIBSON, Q. H. (1948) *Biochem. J.* **42,** 13.
GIFFEE, J. W., MADISON, H. L. and LANDMANN, W. A. (1963) *Proc. 9th Meeting European Meat Res. Workers,* Paper No. 28.
GILBERT, K. V. and DAVEY, C. L. (1976) *N.Z. J. agric. Res.* **19,** 1.
GILES, B. G. (1969) *Proc. 15th Meeting European Meat Res. Workers, Helsinki,* p. 289.
GILL, C. O., PENNEY, N. and NOTTINGHAM, P. M. (1976) *Appl. envir. Microbiol.* **31,** 465.
GILLESPIE, C. A., SIMPSON, D. R. and EDGERTON, V. R. (1970) *J. Histochem. Cytochem.* **18,** 552.
GINDLIN, I., FRID, N. and YAKEVLEV, N. (1958) *Bull. Inst. Froid. Annexe,* 1958–2, p. 153.
GINGER, B. and WEIR, C. E. (1958) *Food Res.* **23,** 662.
GINGER, I. D., LEWIS, U. J. and SCHWEIGERT, B. S. (1955) *J. Agric. Food Chem.* **3,** 156.
GINSBERG, A., REID, M., GRIEVE, J. M. and OGONOWSKI, K. (1958) *Vet. Rec.* **70,** 700.
GOLDBERG, H. S. (1962) *Antibiotics in Agriculture* (Ed. M. WOODBINE), p. 289, Butterworths, London.
GOLDBERG, H. S., WEISER, H. H. and DEATHERAGE, F. E. (1953) *Food Tech.* **7,** 165.
GOLDSCHMIDT, V. M. (1922) *Naturwiss.* **10,** 918; *Chem. Abs.* **17,** 3664.
GOLDSCHMIDT, V. M. (1923) *Videnskorps. Skrift.,* Mat-Nat. Kl. No. 23; *Chem. Abs.* **17,** 3665.
GOLDSPINK, G. (1962a) *Comp. Biochem. Physiol.* **7,** 157.
GOLDSPINK, G. (1962b) *Proc. Roy. Irish Acad.* **62B,** 135.
GOLDSPINK, G. (1962c) Ph.D Thesis, Univ. of Dublin.

GOLDSPINK, G. (1970) in *The Physiology and Biochemistry of Muscle as a Food*, vol II, p. 521 (Eds. E. J. BRISKEY, R. G. CASSENS and B. B. MARSH) Univ. Wisconsin Press, Madison.

GOLDSPINK, G. and MCLOUGHLIN, J. V. (1964) *Irish J. agric. Res.* **3,** 9.

GOLL, D. E., BRAY, R. W. and HOEKSTRA, W. G. (1963) *J. Food Sci.* **28,** 503.

GOLL, D. E. (1968) *Proc. 21st Ann. Recip. Meat Conf., Athens, Georgia*, p. 16.

GOLL, D. E. (1970) in *The Physiology and Biochemistry of Muscle as a Food*, vol. II, p. 255 (Eds. E. J. BRISKEY, R. G. CASSENS and B. B. MARSH), Univ. Wisconsin Press, Madison.

GOLL, D. E. STROMER, M. H., ROBSON, R. M., TEMPLE, J., EASON, B.A. and BUSCH, W. H. (1974) *J. Anim. Sci.* **33,** 963.

GORDON, R. A. and MURRELL, W. G. (1967) *C.S.I.R.O. Food Pres. Quart.* **27,** 6.

GOTTSCHALL, R. A. and KIES, M. W. (1942) *Food. Res.* **7,** 373.

GOULD, M. K. and RAWLINSON, W. A. (1959) *Biochem. J.* **73,** 41.

GOULD, S. E., GOMBERG, H. J. and BETHALL, F. H. (1953) *Amer. J. publ. Hlth.* **43,** 1550.

GRAESER, M. L. (1974) *Proc. 27th Ann. Recip Meat Conf.* Meat Livestock and Meat Bd., Chicago, p. 337.

GRAHAM, A. and HUSBAND, P. M. (1976) *Meat Res. C.S.I.R.O.*, p. 10.

GRAESER, M. L., CASSENS, R. G., HOEKSTRA, W. G., BRISKEY, E. J., SCHMIDT, G. R., CARR, S. D. and GALLOWAY, D. E. (1969b) *J. Anim. Sci.* **28,** 589.

GRANER, M., CAHILL, V. R. and OCKERMAN, H. (1969) *Food Technol.* **23,** 94.

GRAU, F. and SMITH, M. G. (1974) *J. appl. Bact.* **137,** 111.

GRAU, R. (1952) *Fleischwirts.* **4,** 83.

GRAU, R. and FRIESS-SCHULTHEISS, A. *Fleischwirts.* **14,** 207.

GRAU, R. and HAMM, R. (1952) *Fleischwirts.* **4,** 295.

GRAESER, M. L. (1977) *Proc. Ann. Recip. Meat Conf.* p. 149.

GREASER, M. L., CASSENS, R. G., HOEKSTRA, W. G. and BRISKEY, E. J. (1969a) *J. Food Sci.* **34,** 633.

GREAVES, R. I. N. (1960) *recent Research in Freezing and Drying* (Eds. A. S. PARKES and A. U. SMITH), p. 203, Blackwell, Oxford.

GREEN, F. and BRONLEE, L. E. (1965) *Aust. vet. J.* **41,** 321.

GREENBAUM, A. L. and YOUNG, F. G. (1953) *J. Endocrin.* **9,** 127.

GREENBERG, L. A., LESTER, D. and HAGGARD, H. W. (1943) *J. biol. Chem.* **151,** 665.

GREENBERG, R. A. (1972) *Proc. Meat Ind. Res. Conf.* A.M.I.F., Chicago, p. 25.

GREENBERG, R. A. (1975) *Proc. Meat Ind. Res. Conf.* A.M.I.F., Chicago, p. 71.

GREENE, H. (1956) in RUSSELL, F. C. and DUNCAN, D. L. (1956) *loc. cit.*

GREGORY, K. E. and DICKERSON, G. E. (1952) *Mo. Agric. Exp. Sta. Res. Bull.*, No. 493.

GREGORY, P. W. and CASTLE, W. E. (1931) *J. exp. Zool.* **59,** 199.

GREVER, A. B. G. (1955) *Ann. Inst. Pasteur, Lille* **7,** 24.

GRIFFITHS, E., VICKERY, J. R. and HOLMES, N. E. (1932) *Spec. Rept. Fd. Invest. Bd., Lond.*, No. 41.

GRIFFITHS, N. M. and PATTERSON, R. L. S. (1970) *J. Sci. Food Agric.* **21,** 4.

GRONINGER, H. S., TAPPEL, A. L. and KNAPP, F. W. (1956) *Food Res.* **21,** 555.

GROSS, J. (1958) *J. exp. Med.* **107,** 265.

GROSS, J. (1961) *Sci. Amer.* May, p. 120.
GROSS, J. (1970) In *Chemistry and Molecular Biology of the Intracellular Matrix* (Ed. E. A. BALEZS), Vol. 3, p. 1623. Acad. Press, N.Y.
GRUHN, H. (1965) *Sond. Nahrung,* **9,** 325.
GULBRANDSEN, L. F. (1935) *Amer. J. Hyg.* **22,** 257.
GUSTAVSEN, K. H. (1956) *The Chemistry and Reactivity of Collagen,* p. 174, Academic Press, New York.

HAAS, M. C. and BRATZLER, L. J. (1965) *J. Food Sci.* **30,** 64.
HADLOK, R. (1969) *Proc. 15th Meeting European Meat Res. Workers, Helsinki,* p. 149.
HAFEZ, E. S. E. (1961) *Cornell Vet.* **51,** 299.
HAGAN, H. F. (1954) *Proc. 6th Res. Conf., Amer. Meat Res. Inst. Found., Chicago,* p. 59.
HAGYARD, C. J., and HAND, R. J. (1976–77) *Ann. Res. Rept.,* Meat Ind. Res. Inst. N.Z. Inc., p. 31.
HAINES, R. B. (1931) *J. Soc. chem. Ind.* **50,** 223T.
HAINES, R. B. (1933) *J. Soc. chem. Ind.* **52,** 13T.
HAINES, R. B. (1934) *J. Hyg., Camb.* **34,** 277.
HAINES, R. B. (1937) *Spec. Rept. Food Invest. Bd., Lond.,* No. 45.
HAINES, R. B. and SMITH, E. C. (1933) *Spec. Rept. Food Invest. Bd., Lond.,* No. 43.
HALL, G. O. (1950) U.S. Pat. No. 2513094.
HALLECK, F. E., BALL, C. O. and STIER, E. F. (1958) *Food Tech.* **12,** 197, 654.
HALLMARK, E. L. and VAN DUYNE, F. U. (1961) *J. Amer. diet. Ass.* **45,** 139.
HALLUND, O. and BENDALL, J. R. (1965) *J. Food Sci.* **30,** 296.
HALVORSON, H. O. (1955) *Ann. Inst. Pasteur, Lille* **7,** 53.
HAMDY, M. K., MAY, K. N. and POWERS, J. J. (1961) *Proc. Soc. exp. Biol. Med.* **108,** 185.
HAMILTON, R. G. and RICHERT, S. H. (1976) *C.S.I.R.O. Div. Fd. Res,* Meat Res. Lab., Pap. No. 12.
HAMM, R. (1953) *Deut. Lebensm. Rundschau* **49,** 153.
HAMM, R. (1955) *Fleischwirts.* **7.** 196.
HAMM, R. (1957) *Z. Lebensmitt. Untersuch.* **106,** 281.
HAMM, R. (1959) *Z. Lebensmitt. Untersuch.* **110,** 95, 227.
HAMM, R. (1960) *Adv. Fd. Res.* **10,** 356.
HAMM, R. (1966) *Fleischwirts.* **18,** 856.
HAMM, R. (1975) In *Meat* (Eds. D. J. A. COLE and R. A. LAWRIE), Butterworth, London, p. 321.
HAMM, R. and DEATHERAGE, F. E. (1960a) *Food Res.* **25,** 387.
HAMM, R. and DEATHERAGE, F. E. (1960b) *Food Res.* **25,** 573.
HAMM, R. and GRAU, R. (1958) *Z. Lebensmitt. Untersuch.* **108,** 280.
HAMM, R. and KORMENDY, L. (1966) *Fleischwirts.* **46,** 615.
HAMM, R. and HOFMANN, K. (1965) *Nature, Lond.* **207,** 1269.
HAMMOND, J. (1932a) *Growth and Development of Mutton Qualities in the Sheep,* Oliver & Boyd, London.
HAMMOND, J. (1932b) *J. Roy. agric. Soc.* **93,** 131.
HAMMOND, J. (1933–4) *Pig Breeders' Annual,* p. 28, Nat. Pig Breeders' Assoc., London.
HAMMOND, J. (1936) *Festschrift. Prof. Duerst Berne.*

HAMMOND, J. (1940) *Farm Animals: Their Breeding, Growth and Inheritance,* 1st ed., Edward Arnold, London.

HAMMOND, J. (1944) *Proc. Nutr. Soc.* **2,** 8.

HAMMOND, J. (1949) *Brit. J. Nutr.* **3,** 79.

HAMMOND, J. (1963a) Personal communication.

HAMMOND, J. (1963b) *Meat Trades J.* **190,** 439.

HAMMOND, J. (1957) *Outlook in Agriculture* **1,** 230.

HAMMOND, J., JR. and BATTACHANYHA, P. (1944) *J. agric. Sci.* **34,** 1.

HAMMOND, J., JR., HAMMOND, J. and PARKES, A. S. ((1942) *J. agric. Sci.* **32,** 308.

HAMOIR, G. and LASZT, L. (1962) *Biochim. biophys. Acta.* **59,** 365.

HANKINS, O. G. SULZBACHER, W. L., KAUFFMAN, W. R. and MAYO, M. E. (1950) *Food Tech.* **4,** 33.

HANNAN, R. S. (1955) *Spec. Rept. Fd. Invest. Bd., Lond.,* No. 61.

HANSEN, D. and RIEMANN, H. (1958) *Slagteriernes Forskningsinstitut,* Denmark, No. 84.

HANSEN, N. H. (1960) *Slagteriernes Forskningsinstitut,* Denmark, No. 28.

HANSON, J. and HUXLEY, H. E. (1953) *Nature, Lond.* **172,** 530.

HANSON, J. and HUXLEY, H. E. (1955) *Symp. Soc. exp. Biol.* **9,** 228.

HANSON, J. and LOWEY, J. (1963) *J. mol. Biol.* **6,** 46..

HANSON, S. W. F. (1961) *The Accelerated Freeze-drying (AFD) Method of Food Preservation,* H.M.S.O., London.

HARDY, W. V., DOWNING, H. E., REYNOLDS, W. M. and LUTHER, H. G. (1953–4) *Antibiotics Annual,* p. 372, Medical Encyclopaedia Inc., New York.

HARDY, M. F., HARRIS, C. J., PERNY, S. V. and STONE, D. (1970) *Biochem. J.* **120,** 643.

HARDY, W. B. (1927) *J. gen. Physiol.* **8.** 641.

HARRIS, J. M., BRYCE-JONES, K., HOUSTON, T. W. and ROBERTSON, J. (1963) *J. Sci. Fd. Agric.* **14,** 501.

HARRIES, J. M., HUBBARD, A. W., ALDER, F. E., KAY, M. and WILLIAMS, D. R. (1968)*Brit. J. Nutr.* **22,** 21.

HARRINGTON, G. (1962) *Outlook in Agriculture* **3,** 180.

HARRIS, G. W., REED, M. and FAWCETT, C. P. (1966) *Brit. med. Bull.* **22,** 266.

HARRIS, P. V. and McFARLANE, J. J. (1971) *Proc. 17th Meeting Res. Inst.,* Bristol, p. 102.

HARRIS, R. E. and VON LOESECKE, H. (1960) *Nutritional Evaluation of Food Processing,* Wiley, New York.

HARRISON, D. L. (1948) *Iowa Sta. Coll. J. Sci.* **23,** 36.

HARRISON, W. C. (1967) *Health Phys.* **13,** 383.

HATTON, M. W. C., LAWRIE, R. A., RATCLIFF, P. W. and WAYNE, N. (1972) *J. Fd. Technol.* **7,** 443.

HAUGHEY, D. P. and MARER, J. M. (1971) *J. Fd. Technol.* **6,** 119.

HAUROWITZ, F. (1950) *Chemistry and Biology of Proteins,* Academic Press, New York.

HAWLEY, H. B. (1962) *Antibiotics in Agriculture* (Ed. M. WOODBINE), p. 272, Butterworths, London.

HAY, P. H., HARRISON, D. L. and VAIL, G. E. (1953) *Food. Tech* **7,** 217.

HAZLEWOOD, C. F., NICHOLS, B. L. and CHAMBERLAIN, N. F. (1969) *Nature, Lond.* **222,** 747.

HEAD, J. F. and PERRY, S. V. (1974) *Biochem. J.* **137,** 145.

HEAD, J. F., WEEKS, R. A. and PERRY, S. V. (1977) *Biochem. J.* **161**, 465.

HEADIN, P. A., KURTZ, G. W. and KOCH, R. B. (1961) *J. Food Sci.* **26**, 112, 212.

HEGARTY, G. R , HRATZLER, L. J. and PEARSON, A. M (1963) *J. Food Sci.* **28**, 525.

HEIDENHAIN, M. (1913) *Arch. mikr. Anat.* **83**, 427.

HEIDENRICH, C. J., GARWOOD, V. A. and HARRINGTON, R. B. (1964) *J. Anim. Sci.* **23**, 496.

HEIDTMANN, R. (1959) *Fleischwirts.* **11**, 199.

HELANDER, E. (1957) *Acta physiol. scand.*, Suppl. **41**, 141.

HELANDER, E. (1958) *Nature, Lond.* **182**, 1035.

HELANDER, E. (1959) *Acta morph. neer-scand.* **22**, 230.

HELLENDOORN, E. W. (1962) *Food Tech.* **16**, 119.

HENDERSON, D. W., GOLL, D. E. and STROMER, M. H. (1970) *Amer. J. Anat.* **128**, 117.

HENRICKSON, R. L., BRADY, D. E., GEHRKE, C. W. and BROOKS, R. F. (1955) *Food Tech.* **9**, 290.

HENRICKSON, R. L., PARR, A. F., CAGLE, E. D., ARGANOSA, F. C. and JOHNSON, R. G. (1969) *Proc. 15th Meeting European Meat Res. Workers, Helsinki,* p. 23.

HENRY, M., ROMANI, J. D. and JOUBERT, L. (1958) *Rev. Path. gén Physiol clin.* **696**, 355.

HERRING, H. K. (1968) *Proc. 21st Ann. Recip. Meat Conf., Athens, Georgia,* p. 47.

HERRING, H. K., CASSENS, R. G. and BRISKEY, E. J. (1965) *J. Food Sci.* **30**, 1049.

HERSCHDOERFER, S. M. and DYETT, E. J. (1959) *5th Meeting European Meat Res. Workers, Paris,* Paper No. 27.

HERTER, M. and WILSDORF, G. (1914) *Deut. Landwirtschafts-Gesellschaft,* Heft 270, Berlin.

HERZ, K. O. and CHANG, S. S. (1970) *Adv. Food Res.* **18**, 2.

HESS, E. (1928) *J. Bact.* **15**, 33.

HEYWOOD, S. M. (1970) in *The Physiology and Biochemistry of Muscle as a Food,* vol. II, p. 13 (Eds. E. J. BRISKEY, R. G. CASSENS and B. B. MARSH), Madison, Univ. Wisconsin Press.

HEYWOOD, S. M. and RICH, A. (1968) *Proc. Nat. Acad. Sci., U.S.A.* **59**, 590.

HIBBERT, I. (1973) Ph.D. Dissertation, Univ. Nottingham.

HIBBERT, I. and LAWRIE, R. A. (1972) *J. Fd. Technol.* **7**, 326.

HICKS, E. W., SCOTT, W. J. and VICKERY, J. R. (1956) *Food Pres. Quart.* **16**, 72.

HILL, A. V. (1930) *Proc. Roy. Soc.* **B 106**, 477.

HILL, H. J. and HUGHES, C. E. (1959) *Armour's Analysis* **8**, 1.

HIMWICH, H. E. (1955) *Sci. Amer.* **195**, 74.

HINER, R. L. (1951) *Proc. 2nd Res. Conf., Amer. Meat. Inst. Found.,* p. 92.

HINER, R. L., ANDERSON, E. E. and FELLERS, C. R. (1955) *Food Tech.* **9**, 80.

HINER, R. L., GADDIS, A. M. and HANKINS, O. G. (1951) *Food Tech.* **5**, 223.

HINER, R. L. and HANKINS, O. G. (1950) *J. Anim. Sci.* **9**, 347.

HINER, R. L., HANKINS, O. G., SLOANE, H. S., FELLERS, C. R. and ANDERSON, E. E. (1953) *Food Res.* **18**, 364.

HINER, R. L., MADSEN, L. L. and HANKINS, O. G. (1945) *Food Res.* **10**, 312.

HOAGLAND, R., MCBRYDE, C. N. and POWICK, W. C. (1917) *U.S. Dept. Agric. Bull.,* No. 433.

HOBBS, B. C. (1955) *Ann. Inst. Pasteur, Lille* **7**, 190.

HOBBS, B. C. (1960) *6th Meeting European Meat Res. Workers, Utrecht,* Paper No. 32.

HOERSCH, T. M. (1967) U.S. Pat. No. 3, 316,099.
HOET, J. P. and MARKS, H. P. (1926) *Proc. Roy. Soc.* **B 100,** 72.
HOFLUND, S., HOLMBERG, J. and SELLMAN, G. (1956) *Cornell Vet.* **46,** 51.
HOLLENBECK, C. M. and MARINELLI, L. J. (1963) *Proc. 15th Res. Conf., Amer. Meat Inst. Found., Chicago,* p. 67.
HOLLIS, F., KAPLOW, M. KLOSE, R. and HALIK, J. (1968) *Tech. Rept. 62–26 FL.* U.S. Army, Natick.
HOLMES, A. W. (1960) Uniliver, U.K. Pat. No. 848,014.
HOLTFRETER, J. (1934) *Archiv. f. Entwicklungsmechanik* **132,** 307, cited by J. NEEDHAM (1942) *loc. cit.*
HOLTZER, H., MARSHALL, J. M., JR and FINOK, H. (1957) *J. biophys. biochem. Cytol.* **3,** 705.
HONIKEL, K. O. and HAMM, R. (1978) *Meat Sci.* **2.**
HOOD, D. E. (1971) *Proc. 17th Meeting European Meat Res. Workers, Bristol,* p. 677.
HOOD, R. L. and ALLEN, E. (1971) *J. Fd. Sci.* **36,** 786.
HORNSEY, H. C. (1959) *J. Sci. Fd. Agric.* **10,** 114.
HORNSTEIN, I., CROWE, P. F. and HEIMBERG, M. J. (1961) *Foods Res.* **26,** 581.
HORNSTEIN, I., CROWE, P. F. and HINER, R. L. (1968) *J. Food Sci.* **32,** 650.
HORNSTEIN, I., CROWE, P. F. and SULZBACHER, W. L. (1960) *J. Agric. Food Chem.* **8,** 65.
HORNSTEIN, I., CROWE, P. F. and SULZBACHER, W. L. (1963) *Nature, Lond.* **199,** 1252.
HOSTETLER, R. L. (1970) *Proc. 16th Meeting European Meat Res. Workers, Varna,* p. 100.
HOUGHAM, D. and WATTS, B. M. (1958) *Food Tech.* **12,** 681.
HOUTHIUS, M. J. J. (1957) Meat Hygiene, *F.A.O. Agricultural Series,* No. 34, p. 111.
HOWARD, A. (1956) *C.S.I.R.O. Food Pres. Quart.* **16,** 26.
HOWARD, A, and LAWRIE, R. A. (1956) *Spec. Rept. Fd. Invest. Bd., Lond.,* No. 63.
HOWARD, A. and LAWRIE, R. A. (1957a) *Spec. Rept. Fd. Invest. Bd., Lond.,* No. 65.
HOWARD, A. and LAWRIE, R. A. (1957b) *Spec. Rept. Fd. Invest. Bd., Lond.,* No. 64.
HOWARD, A., LAWRIE, R. A. and LEE, C. A. (1960) *Spec. Rept. Fd. Invest. Bd., Lond.,* No. 68.
HOWARD, A., LEE, C. A. and WEBSTER, H. L. (1960) *C.S.I.R.O. Div. Food Pres. Tech. Paper,* No. 21.
HOWARD, A. J. (1949) *Canning Technology,* J. and A. Churchill, London.
HOWE, P. E. and BARBELLA, N. G. (1937) *Food Res.* **2,** 197.
HUBER, W., BRASCH, A. and WALY, A. (1953) *Food Tech.* **7,** 109.
HUFFMAN, D. L., PALMER, A. Z., CARPENTER, J. W., HARGROVE, D. D. and KOGER, M. (1967) *J. Anim. Sci.* **26,** 290.
HUNT, S. and MATHESON, N. (1958) *Nature, Lond.* **181,** 472.
HUXLEY, H. E. (1960) *The Cell* (Ed. J. BRACHET and A. E. MIRSKY), vol. 4, p. 365, Academic Press, New York.
HUXLEY, H. E. (1963) *J. mol. Biol.* **7.** 281.
HUXLEY, H. E. (1969) *Science* **164,** 1356.
HUXLEY, H. E. (1971) *Proc. Roy. Soc.* **B. 178,** 131.
HUXLEY, H. E. and HANSON, J. (1957) *Biochim. biophys. Acta.* **23,** 229, 250.
HUXLEY, H. E. and HANSON, J. (1960) *The Structure and Function of Muscle* (Ed. G. H. BOURNE), vol. 1, p. 183, Academic Press, New York.

HWANG, K. and IVY, A. C. (1951) *Ann. N.Y. Acad. Sci.* **54**, 143.

INGRAM, D. L. (1974) In *Heat Loss from Animals and Man* (Eds. J. L. MONTEITH & I. H. MOUNT), p. 233, Butterworth, London.
INGRAM. G. C. (1971) *Ann. Rept. A.R.C. Meat Res. Inst., 1970–71*, p. 71.
INGRAM, M. (1948) *Ann. Inst. Pasteur, Lille* **75**, 139.
INGRAM, M. (1969a) *J. Soc. chem. Ind.* **68**, 356.
INGRAM, M. (1949b) *Food Manuf.* **24**, 292.
INGRAM, M. (1952) *J. Hyg. Camb.* **50**, 165.
INGRAM, M. (1958) *The Chemistry and Biology of Yeasts*, p. 603, Academic Press, New York.
INGRAM, M. (1959) *Intl. J. appl. Radn. Isotopes* **6**, 105.
INGRAM, M. (1960) *J. appl. Bact.* **23**, 206.
INGRAM, M. (1962) *J. appl. Bact.* **25**, 259.
INGRAM, M., HAWTHORNE, J. R. and GATHERUM, D. P. (1947) *Food Manuf.* **10**, 457, 506, 543.
INGRAM, M. and HOBBS, B. C. (1954) *J. Roy. sanit. Inst.* **74**, 12.
INGRAM, M. and RHODES, D. N. (1962) *Food Manuf.* **37**, 318.
IRVING, J. (1956) *J. appl. Physiol.* **9**, 414.
IRVING, L. (1951) *Fed. Proc.* **10**, 543.
ISKANDARYAN, A. K. (1958) *Proc. 4th Meeting European Meat Research Workers, Camb.,* Paper No. 25.

JACOBSON, M. WELLER, M. GALGON, M. W. and RUPNOW, E. H. (1962) *Factors in the Flavour and Tenderness of Lamb, Beef and Pork,* Washington Agric. Exp. Sta.
JAKOBSSON, B. and BERGTSSON, N. E. (1969) *Proc. 15th Meeting European Meat Res. Workers, Helsinki,* p. 482.
JANICKI, M. A., KOLACZYK, S. and KORTZ, J. (1963) *Proc. 9th Meeting European Meat Res. Workers, Budapest,* Paper No. 2.
JANSEN, M. M. (1966) *Acta vet. Scand.* **7**, 394.
JASPER, T. W. (1958) *Bull. Int. Froid. Annexe* 1958–2, p. 475.
JEFFERSON, N. C. ARAI, T., GEISEL, T. and NECHELES, H. (1964) *Science*, **144**, 58.
JENSEN, L. B. (1945) *Microbiology of Meats,* 2nd ed., Garrard Press, Champaign, Ill.
JENSEN, L. B. (1949) *Meat and Meat Foods,* p. 47, Ronald Press, New York.
JENSEN, L. B. and HESS, W. R. (1941) *Food Res.* **6**, 273.
JOCSIMOVIC, J. (1969) *J. Sci. agric. Res., Beograd* **22**, 109.
JOHNS, A. T., MANAGAN, J. L. and REID, C. S. W. (1957) *NZ. vet. J.* **5**, 115.
JOHNSON, D. W. and PALMER, L. S. (1939) *J. agric. Res.* **58**, 929.
JOHNSON, P. and PERRY, S. V. (1970) *Biochem. J.* **119**, 293.
JOHNSON, T. H. and BANCROFT, M. J. (1918) *Proc. Roy. Soc., Queensland,* **30**, 219.
JØRGENSEN, T. W. (1963) *Proc. 9th Meeting European Meat Research Workers, Budapest,* Paper No. 3.
JOUBERT, D. H. (1956) *J. agric. Sci.* **47**, 59.

JUDGE, M. D. and STOB, M. (1963) *J. Anim. Sci.* **22**, 1059.

JUHÁSZ, A., BERNDORFER-KRASZNER, E., KÖRMENDY, L. and GABOR, T. (1976) *Acta Aliment.* **5**, 23.

JUL, M. (1957) *Food Manuf.* **32**, 259.

JUL, M., NEILSON, H. and PETERSEN, H. (1958) *Fleischwirts.* **10**, 840.

KAESS, G. (1956) *Aust. J. appl. Sci.* **7**, 242.

KAESS, G. and WEIDEMANN, J. F. (1961) *Food Tech.* **15**, 129.

KAESS, G. and WEIDEMANN, J. F. (1962) *Food Tech.* **16**, 125.

KAESS, G. and WEIDEMANN, J. F. (1963) *Proc. 9th Meeting European Meat Res. Workers, Budapest,* Paper No. 58.

KAESS, G. and WEIDEMANN, J. F. (1973) *J. Fd. Technol.* **8**, 59.

KAMSTRA, L. D. and SAFFLE, R. L. (1959) *Food Tech.* **13**, No, 11, 652.

KASSAI, D. and KÁRPÁTI, GY. (1963) *Proc. 9th Meeting European Meat Res. Workers, Budapest,* Paper No. 59.

KASTENSCHMIDT, L. L. (1970) in *The Physiology and Biochemistry of Muscle as a Food,* vol. II, p. 735 (Eds. E. J. BRISKEY, R. G. CASSENS and B. B. MARSH), Univ. Wisconsin Press, Madison.

KAUFFMAN, R. G., CARPENTER, Z. L., BRAY, R. W. and HOEKSTRA, W. G. (1964) *J. Food Sci.* **29**, 65.

KAY, C. M. and PABST, H. F. (1962) *J. biol. Chem.* **237**, 727.

KAY, M. and HOUSEMAN, R. (1975) In *Meat* (Eds. D. J. A. COLE & R. A. LAWRIE), Butterworth, London, p. 85.

KEFFORD, J. F. (1948) *J. Coun. sci. industr. Res. Aust.* **21**, 116.

KELLER, H. and HEIDTMANN, H. H. (1955) *Fleischwirts.* **7**, 502.

KEKOMAKI, M. VISAKORPI, J. K., PERHEENTUPA, J. and SAXEN, L. (1967) *Acta paediat. Scand.* **56**, 617.

KEMPE, L. L. (1955) *Appl. Microbiol.* **3**, 346.

KENDRICK, J. L. and WATTS, B. M. (1969) *J. Food Sci.* **34**, 292.

KEYS, A., ANDERSON, J. T. and GANDE, F. (1960) *J. Nutr.* **70**, 257.

KIDNEY, A. J. (1967) *Proc. 13th Meeting European Meat Res. Workers, Rotterdam,* Paper No. A 7.

KIDWELL, J. F. (1952) *J. Hered.* **43**, 157.

KING, N. L. R. (1978) *Meat Sci.* **2**. 313.

KITCHELL, A. G. (1958) *2nd Intl. Symp. Fd. Microbiol., Camb.* (Ed. B. P. EDDY), p. 191, H.M.S.O., London.

KITCHELL, A. G. (1959) *Proc. 10th Intl. Congr. Refrig., Copenhagen* **3**, 65.

KITCHELL, A. G. (1967) *Inst. Meat Bull.,* Jan., p. 7.

KITCHELL, A. G. (1971) *Proc. 17th Meeting Meat Res. Inst., Bristol,* p. 194.

KITCHELL, A. G. and INGRAM, M. (1956) *Ann. Inst. Pasteur, Lille* **8**, 121.

KITCHELL, A. G. and INGRAM, M. (1963) *Food Process. Packag.* **32**, 3.

KIVIRIKKO, K. I. (1963) *Nature, Lond.* **197**, 385.

KJ ØLBERG, O., MANNERS, D. J. and LAWRIE, R. A. (1963) *Biochem. J.* **87**, 351.

KLICKA, M. W. (1969) *Proc. Sympos. Feeding the Military Man,* U.S. Army, Natick, p. 63.

KNAPPEIS, G. G. and CARLSEN F. (1968) *J. cell Biol.* **38**, 202.
KNIGHT, B. C. J. G. and FILDES, P. (1930) *Biochem. J.* **24**, 1496.
KOCHAKIAN, C. D. and TILLOTSON, C. (1957) *J. Endocrin.* **60**, 607.
KODAMA, S. (1913) *J. Tokyo Chem. Soc.* **34**, 751.
KOEPPE, S. (1954) *Rev. de conserve* **9**, 83.
KOHLBRUGGE, J. H. F. (1901) *Zbl. Bakt.* **I**, Abt. **29**, 571, cited by R. B. HAINES (1937) *loc. cit.*
KOLEDIN, I. G. (1963) *Proc. 9th Meeting European Meat Res. Workers, Budapest,* Paper No. 6.
KÖRMENDY, L. (1955) *Élelmezési Ipar.***8**, 172.
KÖRMENDY, L. and GANTNER, G. Y. (1958) *Proc. 5th Meeting European Meat Res. Workers, Cambridge,* Paper No. 21.
KORNER, A. (1963) *Biochem, J.* **89**, 14p.
KOTERA, A., YOKOYAMA, M., YAMAGUCHI, M. and MIYAZAWA, Y. (1969) *Biopolymers* **7**, 99.
KRAFT, A. A. and AYRES, J. C. (1952) *Food Tech.* **6**, 8.
KRAMER, A. (1957) *Food Eng.* **29**, 57.
KRAMER, H. and LITTLE, K. (1955) *Nature and Structure of Collagen* (Ed. J. T. RANDALL), p. 33, Butterworths, London.
KRAMLICH, W. E. and PEARSON, A. M. (1958) *Food Res.* **23**, 567.
KRYLOVA, N. N., BAZAROVA, K. I. and KAZNETSNOVA, V. V. (1962) *Proc. 8th Meeting European Meat Res. Workers, Moscow,* Paper No. 38.
KUNKEL, H. O. (1961) *Biochemical and Fundamental Physiological Bases for Genetically Variable Growth of Animals,* College Station, Texas Agric. Exp. Sta.
KUPRIANOFF, J. (1956) *Proc. Int. Inst. Refrig.* **53**, 129.
KURICHARA, K. and WOOL, I. G. (1968) *Nature, Lond.* **219**, 721.
KYLE, R. (1972) *Meat Production in Africa: the Case for a New Domestic Species,* Univ. Press, Bristol.

LAAKKONEN, E., WELLINGTON, G. H. and SHERBON, J. W. (1970) *J. Fd. Sci.* **35**, 175, 178.
LAING, J. A. (1959) *Progress in the Physiology of Farm Animals (* Ed. J. HAMMOND), vol. 3, p. 760, Butterworths, London.
LAMMING, G. E. (1956) *Rep. Sch. Agric.,* p. 66, Univ. Nottingham.
LAMPREY, H. F. (1963) *J. E. Afr. Wildl.* **1**, 63.
LANDMANN, W. A. (1963) *Proc. Meat Tenderness Sympos.,* p. 87, Campbell Soup Co., Camden, New Jersey.
LAPSHIN, I. (1962) *Proc. 8th Meeting European Meat Res. Workers, Moscow,* Paper No. 39.
LAW, N. H. and VERE-JONES, N. W. (1955) *D.S.I.R., N.Z., Bull.,* No. 118.
LAWRIE, R. A. (1950) *J. agric. Sci.* **40**, 356.
LAWRIE, R. A. (1952a) *Nature, Lond.* **170**, 122.
LAWRIE, R. A. (1952b) Ph.D. Dissertation, Univ. Cambridge.
LAWRIE, R. A. (1953a) *Biochem. J.* **55**, 298.
LAWRIE, R. A. (1953b) *Biochem. J.* **55**, 305.

LAWRIE, R. A. (1953c) *J. Physiol.* **121**, 275.
LAWRIE, R. A. (1955) *Biochim. biophys. Acta.* **17**, 282.
LAWRIE, R. A. (1958) *J. Sci. Fd. Agric.* **9**, 721.
LAWRIE, R. A. (1959) *J. Refrig.* **2**, 87.
LAWRIE, R. A. (1960) *Brit. J. Nutr.* **14**, 255.
LAWRIE, R. A. (1960) *J. comp. Path.* **70**, 273.
LAWRIE, R. A. (1961) *Brit. J. Nutr.* **15**, 453.
LAWRIE, R. A. (1966) in *Physiology and Biochemistry of Muscle as a Food*, p. 137 (Eds. E. J. BRISKEY, R. G. CASSENS and J. C. TRAUTMAN), Univ. Wisconsin Press, Madison.
LAWRIE, R. A. (1968) *J. Food Technol.* **3**, 203.
LAWRIE, R. A. (1975) In Meat (Eds. D. J. A. COLE and R. A. LAWRIE), Butterworth, London, p. 249.
LAWRIE, R. A. and GATHERUM, D. P. (1962) *J. agric. Sci.* **58**, 97.
LAWRIE, R. A. and GATHERUM, D. P. (1964) *J. agric. Sci.* **62**, 381.
LAWRIE, R. A., GATHERUM, D. P. and HALE, H. P. (1958) *Nature, Lond.* **182**, 807.
LAWRIE, R. A., MANNERS, D. J. and WRIGHT, A. (1959) *Biochem. J.* **73**, 485.
LAWRIE, R. A., PENNY, I. F., SCOPES, R. K. and VOYLE, C. A. (1963) *Nature, Lond.* **200**, 673.
LAWRIE, R. A. and POMEROY, R. W. (1963) *J. agric. Sci.* **61**, 409.
LAWRIE, R. A., POMEROY, R. W. and CUTHBERTSON, A. (1963) *J. agric. Sci.* **60**, 195.
LAWRIE, R. A., POMEROY, R. W. and WILLIAMS, D. R. (1964) *J. agric. Sci.* **62**, 89.
LAWRIE, R. A. and PORTREY, E. (1967) *Ann. Rept. Sch. Agric., Univ. Nottingham*, p. 135.
LAWRIE, R. A., SHARP, J. G., BENDALL, J. R. and COLEBY, B. (1961) *J. Sci. Fd. Agric.* **12**, 742.
LAWRIE, R. A. and VOYLE, C. A. (1962) *Ann. Rep. Low. Temp. Res. Sta.*, p. 16.
LEA, C. H. (1931) *J. Soc. chem. Ind.* **50**, 215 T.
LEA, C. H. (1937) *J. Soc. chem. Ind.* **56**, 376 T.
LEA, C. H. (1938) *Spec. Rept. Fd. Invest. Bd., Lond.*, No. 46.
LEA, C. H. (1939) *Rancidity in Edible Fats*, Chemical Publishing Co., New York.
LEA, C. H. (1943) *J. Soc. chem. Ind.* **62**, 200.
LEA, C. H. (1959) *Intl. J. appl. Radn. Isotopes* **6**, 86.
LEA, C. H. (1962) *Recent Advances in Food Research* (Eds. J. HAWTHORN and J. M. LEITCH), vol. 1, p. 83, Butterworths, London.
LEA, C. H., HAINES, R. B. and COULSON, C. A. (1936) *Proc. Roy. Soc.* **B 120**, 47.
LEA, C. H., HAINES, R. B. and COULSON, C. A. (1937) *Proc. Roy. Soc.* **B 123**, 1.
LEA, C. H. and HANNAN, R. S. (1950) *Nature, Lond.* **65**, 438.
LEA, C. H. and HANNAN, R. S. (1952) *Food Science* (Eds. T. N. MORRIS and E. C. BATE-SMITH), p. 228, Cambridge Univ. Press.
LEA, C. H., McFARLANE, J. J. and PARR, L. J. (1960) *J. Sci. Fd. Agric.* **11**, 690.
LEA, C. H., SWOBODA, P. A. T. and GATHERUM, D. P. (1969) *J. Sci. Fd. Agric.* **74**, 279.
LEACH, T. M. (1971) *Proc. 17th Meeting Meat Res. Inst.*, Bristol, p. 161.
LEBLANC, F. R., DEVLIN, K. A. and STUMBO, D. R. (1953) *Food Tech.* **7**, 181.
LEDGER, H. P. (1959) *Nature, Lond.* **184**, 1405.
LEDWARD, D. A. (1971a) *J. Fd. Sci.* **36**, 138.
LEDWARD, D. A. (1971b) *J. Fd. Sci.* **36**, 883.

LEDWARD, D. A. (1972) *J. Fd. Sci.* **37**, 634.

LEDWARD, D. A. CHIZZOLINI, R. and LAWRIE. R. A. (1975) *J. Fd. Technol.* **10**, 349.

LEDWARD, D. A. and LAWRIE, R. A. (1975) *J. Sci. Fd Agric.* **26**, 691.

LEE, C. A. and WEBSTER, H. L. (1963) *C.S.I.R.O. Div. Food Pres. Tech. Paper*, No. 30.

LEET, N. G., DEVINE, C. E. and GAVEY, A. B. (1977) *Meat Sci.* **1**, 229.

LEHMANN, K. B. (1904) *Z. Biol.* **45**, 324.

LEHMANN, K. B. (1907) *Arch. Hyg.* **63**, 134.

LEHMANN, B. T. and WATTS, B. M. (1951) *J. Am. Oil Chemists' Soc.* **28**, 475.

LEIGHTON, G. R. and DOUGLAS, L. M. (1910) *The Meat Industry and Meat Inspection*, vol. II, Educational Book Co., London.

LEISTNER, L. (1960) *Proc. 12th Res. Conf.*, p. 17, Amer. Meat Inst. Found., Chicago.

LEMBERG, R. and LEGGE, J. W. (1949) *Haematin Compounds and Bile Pigments*, Interscience, London.

LEMBERG, R. and LEGGE, J. W. (1950) *Ann. Rev. Biochem.* **19**, 431.

LEVIN, E. (1970) *Food Technol.* **24**, 19.

LEVINE, R. and GOLDSTEIN, M. S. (1955) *Rec. Progr. Hormone Res.* **11**, 343.

LEWIS, P. K., JR., BROWN, C. J, and HECK, M. C. (1962) *J. Anim, Sci.* **21**, 196.

LEWIS, P. K., JR., BROWN, C. J. and HECK, M. J. (1967) *Food Tech.* **21**, 75A.

LIJINSKY, W. and EPSTEIN, S. S. (1970) *Nature, Lond.* **225**, 21.

LINDBERG, P. and ORSTADIUS, K. (1961) *Acta vet. scand.* **2**, 1.

LINEWEAVER, H., ANDERSON, J. D. and HANSON, H. L. (1952) *Food Tech.* **6**, 1.

LINEWEAVER, H. and HOOVER, S. R. (1941) *J. biol. Chem.* **137**, 325.

LISTER, D. (1969) in *Recent Points of View on the Condition and Meat Quality of Pigs for Slaughter*, p. 123 (Ed. W. SYBESMA, P. G. VAN DER WALS and P. WALSTRON), Res. Inst. Animal Husbandry, Zeist.

LOBLEY, G. E., PERRY, S. V. and STONE, D. (1971) *Nature, Lond.* **231**, 317.

LOCKER, R. H. (1956) *Biochim. biophys. Acta* **20**, 514.

LOCKER, R. H. (1960a) *Food Res.* **25**, 304.

LOCKER, R. H. (1960b) *J. Sci. Fd. Agric.* **11**, 520.

LOCKER, R. H. (1968) *Proc. 10th Meat Ind. Res. Conf., Hamilton, N.Z.*, p. 3.

LOCKER, R. H. (1973) *J. Fd. Technol.* **8**, 71.

LOCKER, R. H. (1976) *Proc. 18th Meat Res. Conf., Rotorua*, p. 1.

LOCKER, R. H. and DAINES, G. J. (1975) *J. Sci. Fd. Agric.* **26**, 1721.

LOCKER, R. H. and DAINES, G. J. (1976) *J. Sci. Agric.* **27**, 244.

LOCKER, R. H., DAVEY, C. L., NOTTINGHAM, P. M., HAUGHEY, D. P. and LAW, W. H. (1975) *Adv. Fd. Res.* **21**, 158.

LOCKER, R. H., DAINES, G. J., CARSE, W. A. and LEET, N. G. (1977) *Meat Sci.* **1**, 87.

LOCKER, R. H. and HAGYARD, C. J. [1963] *J. Sci. Food Agric.* **14**, 787.

LOCKER, R. H. and HAGYARD, C. J. (1968) *Arch. Biochem. Biophys.* **127**, 370.

LOCKER, R. H. and LEET, N. G. (1975) *J. Ultrastruct. Res.* **52**, 64.

LOCKETT, C., SWIFT, C. E. and SULZBACHER, W. L. (1962) *J. Food Sci.* **27**, 36.

LODGE, G. A. (1970) in *Proteins as Human Food*, p. 141 (Ed. R. A. LAWRIE), Butterworths, London.

LÖRINCZ, F. and BIRO, G. (1963) *Acta Morph., Budapest* **12**, 15.

LOVE, R. M. (1955) *J. Sci. Fd. Agric.* **6**, 30.

LOVE, R. M. (1956) *Nature, Lond.* **178,** 198.

LOVE, R. M. (1958) *J. Sci. Fd. Agric.* **9,** 257, 262.

LOVE, R. M. and ELERIAN, M. K. (1963) *Proc. 11th Intl. Congr. Refris.,* Munich, p. 887.

LOVE, R. M. and HARALDSSON, S. B. (1961) *J. Sci. Fd. Agric.* **12,** 442.

LOWE, B. (1934) M.Sc. Thesis, Univ. Chicago.

LOWEY, S. (1968) *Symposium on Fibrous Proteins,* Butterworth, London, p. 124.

LOWEY, S., SLAYTER, H. S., WEEDS, A. G. and BAKER, H. (1969) *J. molec. Biol.* **42,** 1.

LOWRY, O. H., GILLIGAN, D. R. and KATERSKY, E. M. (1941) *J. biol. Chem.* **139,** 795.

LOYD, E. J. and HINER, R. L. (1959) *J. Agric. Food. Chem.* **7,** 860.

LUDVIGSEN, L. (1954) *Beretn. Forsøgslab. Kbh.,* No. 272.

LUDVIGSEN, J. (1957) *Acta endocrin., Copenhagen* **26,** 406.

LUSHBOUGH, C. H. and URBIN, M. C. (1963) *J. Nutr.* **81,** 99.

LUYERINK, J. H. and VAN BAAL, J. P. W. (1969) *Proc. 15th Meeting European Meat Res. Workers, Helsinki,* p. 41.

LUYET, B. J. (1961) *Proc. Symp. Low Temperature Biology,* p. 63, Campbell Soup Co., Camden, N. J.

LUYET, B. J. (1962) *Freeze-drying of Foods,* p. 194, Nat. Res. Counc., Nat. Acad. Sci., Washington, D.C.

LUYET, B. J., RAPATZ, G. L. and GEHENIO, P. M. (1965) *Biodynamica.* **9,** 283.

LYNCH, G. P., OLTJEN, R. R., THORNTON, J. W. and HINER, R. L. (1966) *J. Anim. Sci.* **25,** 1133.

MACARA, T. J. R. (1947) *Mod. Refrig.* **50,** 63.

McARDLE, B. (1956) *Brit. med. Bull.* **12,** 226.

McBRIDE, G. (1963) *Animal Behaviour* **11,** 53.

McBRYDE, C. N. (1911) *J. agric. Sci.* **33,** 761.

McCANCE, R. A. and WIDDOWSON, E. M. (1946) *The Chemical Composition of Food,* H.M.S.O., London.

McCANCE, R. A. and WIDDOWSON, E. M. (1959) *J. Physiol.* **147,** 124.

McCANCE, R. A. and WIDDOWSON, E. M. (1960) M.R.C. *Spec. Rept.* No. 297, H.M.S.O., London.

McCONNELL, P. (1902) *The Elements of Agricultural Geology,* Lockwood, London.

McCRAE, S. E. and PAUL, P. C. (1974) *J. Fd. Sci.* **39,** 18.

McDONALD, I. W. (1968) *Aust. vet. J.* **44,** 145.

McDONALD, M. A. and SLEN, S. B. (1959) *Canad. J. Anim. Sci.* **39,** 202.

MacDOUGALL, D. B. and TAYLOR, A. A. (1975) *J. Fd. Technol.* **10,** 339.

McELHINNEY, J., HANSON, A. O., BECKER, R. A., DUFFIELD, R. B. and DIVEN, B. C. (1949) *Phys. Rev.* **75,** 542.

MACFADYEN, A. and ROWLAND, S. (1900) *Proc. Roy. Soc.* **B 66,** 488.

MACFARLANE, J. J. (1973) *J. Fd. Sci.* **38,** 294.

MACFARLANE, J. J. and MACKENZIE, I. J. (1976) *J. Fd. Sci.* **41,** 1442.

MACHLIK, S. M. and DRAUDT, H. N. (1963) *J. Food Sci.* **28,** 711.

McINTOSH, E. N. (1965) *J. Food Sci.* **30,** 986.

McKELLAR, J. C. (1960) *Vet. Rec.* **72**, 507.

McLAIN, P. E., CREED, G. J., WILLEY, E. R. and HORNSTEIN, I. (1970) *J. Food Sci.* **35**, 258.

McLAIN, P. E., PEARSON, A. M., BRUNNER, J. R. and CREVASSE, G. A. (1969) *J. Food Sci.*, **34**, 115.

McLAREN, A, and MICHIE, D. (1960) *Nature, Lond.* **187**, 363.

McLEAN, R. A. and SULZBACHER, W. L. (1953) *J. Bact.* **65**, 428.

McLEAN, R. A. and SULZBACHER, W. L. (1959) *Appl. Microbiol.* **7**, 81.

MACLENNAN, D. and WONG, P. T. S. (1971) *Proc. Nat. Acad. Sci., U.S.A.* **68**, 1231.

McLEOD, K., GILBERT, K. V., WYBORN, R., WENHAM, L. M., DAVEY, C. L. and LOCKER, R. H. (1973) *J. Fd. Technol.* **8**, 71.

McLUSKEY, R. T. and THOMAS, L. (1958) *J. exp. Med.* **108**, 371.

McMAHAN, J. R., DOWNING, H. E., OTTKE, R. C., LUTHER, H. G. and WRENSHALL C. L. (1955–6) *Antibiotics Annual*, p. 727.

McMEEKAN, C. P. (1940) *J. agric. Sci.* **30**, 276, 287.

McMEEKAN, C. P. (1941) *J. agric. Sci.* **31**, 1.

MABROUK, A. F., JARBOE, J. K. and O'CONNER, E. M. (1969) *J. Agric. Fd. Chem.* **17**, 5.

MACY, R. L., NAUMANN, H. D. and BAILEY, M. E. (1964) *J. Food Sci.* **29**, 136.

MADSEN, J. (1942) *Beretn. Vet. Landbohøjskoles Slagterilaboratorium*, Kbh., No. 11.

MAILLET, M. (1955) *Ann. Inst. Pasteur, Lille* **7**, 9.

MAJOR, R. and WATTS, B. M. (1948) *J. Nutr.* **35**, 103.

MALTON, R. (1971) *Proc. 17th Meeting European Meat Res. Workers, Bristol*, p. 486.

MARKAKIS, P. C., GOLDBLITH, S. A. and PROCTOR, B. E. (1951) *Nucleonics* **9**, 71.

MARKS, E. P. and REINECKE, J. P. (1964) *Science* **143**, 961.

MARSH, B. B. (1952a) *Biochim. biophys. Acta.* **9**, 247.

MARSH, B. B. (1952b) *Biochim. biophys. Acta.* **9**, 127.

MARSH, B. B. (1954) *J. Sci. Fd. Agric.* **5**, 70.

MARSH, B. B. (1962) *4th Meat Industry Res. Conf., Hamilton*, Meat Industry Res. Inst. N.Z. Inc. Publ, No. 55, p. 32.

MARSH, B. B. (1964) *Ann. Rept. Meat Ind. Res. Inst., N.Z.*, p. 16.

MARSH, B. B. and LEET, N. G. (1966) *J. Food Sci.* **31**, 450.

MARSH, B. B., LEET, N. G. and DICKSON, M. R. (1974) *J. Fd. Technol.* **9**, 141.

MARSH, B. B. and THOMPSON, J. T. (1958) *J. Sci. Fd. Agric.* **9**, 417.

MARSH, B. B., WOODHAMS, P. M. and LEET, N. G. (1968) *J. Food Sci.* **33**, 12.

MARSHALL, J. M., HOLTZER, H., FRICK, H. and PEPE, F. (1959) *Exp. Cell. Res.*, suppl. 7, p. 219.

MARTIN, G. R., BYERS, P. H. and PIEZ, K. A. (1975) *Adv. Enzymol.* **42**, 167.

MARTIN, S., BATZER, O. F., LANDMANN, W. A. and SCHWEIGERT, B. S. ((1962) *J. Agric. Food Chem.* **10**, 91.

MARTIN, W. M. (1948) *Food Ind.* **20**, 832.

MARUYAMA, K. (1970) in *Physiology and Biochemistry of Muscle as a Food*, vol. II (Eds. E. J. BRISKEY, R. G. CASSENS and B. B. MARSH), Univ. Wisconsin Press, Madison, p. 373.

MARUYAMA, K., MATSUBARA, S., NATORI, R., NONOMURA, Y., KIMURA, S., OHASHI, K., MURAKAMI, F., HANDA, S. and EGUCHI, G. (1977) *J. Biochem.*, Tokyo, **82**, 317.

MASON, I. L. (1951) *Tech. Bull. Commonwealth Bureau Animal Breeding and Genetics*, No. 8.

406   *Bibliography*

MATHESON, N. A. (1962) *Rec. Adv. Food Sci.* (Eds. J. HAWTHORN and J. M. LEITCH), vol. 2, p. 51, Butterworths, London.
MATTEY, M., PARSONS, A. L. and LAWRIE, R. A. (1970) *J. Fd. Technol.* **5,** 41.
MAURER, F. (1894) *Gegensbaurs Jb.* **21,** 473, cited by PICKEN (1960) *loc. cit.*
MAY, C. G. (1961) U.K. Pat. No. 858,333.
MAY, C. G. and MORTON, I. D. (1961) U.K. Pat. No. 858,660.
MEDREK, T. F. and BARNES, E. M. (1962) *J. appl. Bact.* **25,** 159.
MELROSE, D. R. and GRACEY, W. (1975) In *Meat* (Eds. D. J. A. COLE & R. A. LAWRIE), Butterworth, London, p. 109.
MENZ, L. and LUYET, B. (1961) *Biodynamica* **8,** 261.
MERRITT, C., JR., BRESNICK, S. R., BAZINET, M. L., WALSH, J. T. and ANGELINI, P. (1959) *J. Agric. Food. Chem.* **7,** 784.
MERRITT, C. JR. and ROBERTSON, D. H. (1967) *J. Gas Chrom.* **5,** 96.
MERYMAN, H. T. (1956) *Science* **124,** 515.
MEYER, E. W. (1967) *Proc. Intl. Conf. Soybean Protein Foods,* U.S.D.A. Pubn. ARS-7-35, p. 142.
VON MICKWITZ, G. and LEACH, T. M. (1977) *Review of Preslaughter Stunning in E.C.,* C.E.C. Inform. Agnc. No. 30.
MIDDLEHURST, J., PARKER, N. S. and COFFEY, M. F. (1969) *C.S.I.R.O. Food Pres. Quart.* **29,** 21.
MILER, K. (1963) *Proc. 9th Meeting European Meat Res. Workers, Budapest,* Paper No. 44.
MILES, C. L. and LAWRIE, R. A. (1970) *J. Fd. Technol.* **5,** 325.
MILLER, R. L. and UDENFRIEND, S. (1970) *Arch. Biochem. Biophys.* **139,** 104.
MILLIKAN, G. A. (1939) *Physiol. Rev.* **19,** 503.
MILLS, F. and URBIN, M. C. (1960) *The Science of Meat and Meat Products* (Ed. Amer. Meat Inst. Found.), p. 373, Reinhold Publishing Co., New York.
MITCHELL, H. H., BEADLES, J. R. and KRUGER, J. H. (1927) *J. biol. Chem.* **73,** 767.
MITCHELL, H. H. and HAMILTON, J. S. (1933) *J. agric. Res.* **46,** 917.
MITCHELL, H. H., HAMILTON, J. S. and HAINES, W. T. (1928) *J. Nutr.* **1,** 165.
MIYADA, D. S. and TAPPEL, A. L. (1956) *Food Tech.* **10,** 142.
MOHR, V. and BENDALL, J. R. (1969) *Nature, Lond.* **223,** 404.
MONCRIEFF, R. W. (1951) *The Chemical Senses,* 2nd ed., Leonard Hill, London.
MORAN, T. (1930) *Proc. Roy. Soc.* **B 107,** 182.
MORAN, T. (1932) *J. Soc. chem. Ind.* **51,** 16T, 20 T.
MORAN, T. (1937) *Proc. Roy. Soc.* **B 105,** 177.
MORAN, T. and SMITH, E. C. (1929) *Spec. Rept. Fd. Invest. Bd., Lond.,* No. 36.
MOORE, V. J., LOCKER, R..H. and DAINES, C. J. (1976–77) *Ann. Res. Rept., Meat Ind. Res. Inst. N.Z. Inc.* p. 38.
MORGAN, B. (1957) *Food Process.* **18,** 24.
MORGAN, M., PERRY, S. V. and OTTAWAY, J. (1976) *Biochem. J.* **157,** 687.
MORLEY, M. J. (1966) *J. Fd. Technol.* **1,** 303.
MORPURGO, B. (1897), cited by DENNY-BROWN (1961) *Arch. path. Anat.* **150,** 522.
MORTON, I. D., ARKROYD, P. and MAY, C. G. (1960) U.K. Pat. No. 836,694.
MOSSEL, D. A. A. (1955) *Ann. Inst. Pasteur, Lille* **7,** 171.

MOSSEL, D. A. A., DIJKMANN, K. E. and SNŸDERS, J. M. A. (1975) In *Meat* (Eds. D. J. A. COLE & R. A. LAWRIE), Butterworth, London, p. 223.
MÜLLER, E. A. (1957) *J. Amer. Physiol. ment. Rehabilitation* **11**, 41.

NEEDHAM, D. M. (1926) *Physiol. Rev.* **6**. 1.
NEEDHAM, D. M. (1960) *The Structure and Function of Muscle* (Ed. G. H. BOURNE). vol. 2, p. 55, Academic Press, New York.
NEEDHAM, J. (1931) *Chemical Embryology*, p. 1577, Cambridge Univ. Press.
NEEDHAM, J. (1942) *Biochemistry and Morphogenesis*, Cambridge Univ. Press.
NESTOROV, N., GEORGIEVA, R. and GROSDANOV, A. (1970) *Proc. 16th Meeting European Meat Res. Workers, Varna*, p. 771.
NEUMANN, R. E. and LOGAN, M. A. (1950) *J. biol. Chem.* **184**, 299.
NEUVY, A. and VISSAC, B. (1962) *Contribution à l'étude du phénomène culard*, Union NationalE des Livres Généalogiques, Paris.
NEWBOLD, R. P. and SCOPES, R. K. (1967) *Biochem. J.* **105**, 127.
NICOL, D., SHAW, M. K. and LEDWARD, D. A. (1970) *Appl. Microbiol.* **19**, 937.
NEWBOLD, R. P. and TUMA, R. K. (1976) *Meat, Res. C.S.I.R.O.* p. 37.
NICOL, T. and WARE, C. C. (1960) *Nature*, Lond. **185**, 42.
NICOL, T., MCKELVIE, P. and DRUCE, C. G. (1961) *Nature, Lond.* **190**, 418.
NIELL, J. M. and HASTINGS, A. B. (1925) *J. biol. Chem.* **63**, 479.
NIVEN, C. F., JR. (1951) *Amer. Meat Inst. Found. Circ.*, No. 2.
NIVEN, C. F., JR. (1958) *Ann. Rev. Microbiol.* **12**, 507.
NIVEN, C. F., JR. (1963) *Int. J. appl. Radn. Isotopes* **14**, 26.
NIVEN, C. F., JR. and CHESBRO, W. R. (1956) *Proc. 8th Res. Conf., Amer. Meat Inst. Found., Chicago*, p. 47.
NIVEN, C. F., JR. DEIBEL, R. H. and WILSON, G. D. (1958) *Amer. Meat Inst. Found. Circ.*, No. 41.
NIVEN, C. F., JR. and EVANS, J. B. (1957) *J. Bact.* **73**, 758.
NOBLE, I. (1965) *J. Amer. diet. Ass.* **47**, 205.
NOTTINGHAM, P. M. (1960) *J. Sci. Fd. Agric.* **11**, 436.
NOTTINGHAM, P. M. (1963) Hygiene in Meat Works, *Meat Ind. Res. Inst. N.Z. Inc. Publ.*, No. 72.
NOTTINGHAM, P. M., PENNEY, N. and HARRISON, J. C. L. (1973) *N.Z. J. agric. Res.* **17**, 79.
NOTTINGHAM, P. M. and URSELMANN, A. J. (1961) *N.Z. J. agric. Res.* **4**, 449.

OBANU, Z. A., LEDWARD, D. A. and LAWRIE, R. A. (1975) *J. Fd. Technol.* **10**, 667.
OGILVY, W. S. and AYRES, J. C. (1951) *Food Tech.* **5**, 97.
OGLE, C. and MILLS, C. A. (1933) *Amer. J. Physiol.* **103**, 606.
OPIE, L. H. and NEWSHOLME, E. H. (1967) *Biochem. J.* **103**, 391.
OWEN, J. E. and LAWRIE, R. A. (1975) *J. Fd. Technol.* **10**, 169.
OWEN, J. E., LAWRIE, R. A. and HARDY, B. (1975) *J. Sci. Fd. Agric.* **26**, 31.

408 Bibliography

PAGE, S. (1968) *Brit. med. Bull.* **24**, No. 2, 170.

PÁLLSON, H. (1939) *J. agric. Sci.* **29**, 544.

PÁLLSON, H. (1940) *J. agric. Sci.* **30**, 1.

PÁLLSON, H. (1955) *Progress in the Physiology of Farm Animals* (Ed. J. HAMMOND), vol. 2, p. 430, Butterworths, London.

PÁLLSON, H. and VERGÉS, J. B. (1952) *J. agric. Sci.* **42**, 1.

PALMER, A. Z. (1963) *Proc. Meat Tenderness Symp.*, p. 161, Campbell Soup Co., Camden, N.J.

PALMER, A. Z., BRADY, D. E., NAUMANN, H. D. and TUCKER, L. N. (1955) *Food Tech.* **7**, 90.

PARAKKAL, P. F. (1969) *J. cell Biol.* **41**, 345.

PARK, R. J. and MINSON, D. J. (1972) *J. Agric. Sci.* **79**, 473.

PARK, R. J. and MURRAY, K. E. (1975) *Meat Res. in C.S.I.R.O.* p. 22.

PARKER, C. J. JR. and BERGER, C. K. (1963) *Biochim. biophys. Acta* **74**, 730.

PARRY, D. A. (1970) In *Proteins as Human Food* (Ed. R. A. LAWRIE), Butterworth, London, p. 365.

PARSONS, A. L., PARSONS, J. L., BLANSHARD, J. M. V. and LAWRIE, R. A. (1969) *Biochem. J.* **112**, 673.

PARTRIDGE, S. M. (1959) *Ann. Rept. Low Temp. Res. Sta., Cambridge*, p. 19.

PARTRIDGE, S. M. (1962) *Adv. Prot. Chem.* **17**, 227.

PARTRIDGE, S. M. and DAVIS, H. F. (1955) *Biochem. J.* **61**, 21.

PASSBACH, F. L., JR., MULLINS, A. M., WIPF, V. K. and PAUL, B. A. (1969) *Proc. 15th Meeting European Meat Res. Workers, Helsinki*, p. 64.

PATERSON, J. L. (1975) *In Meat* (Eds. D. J. A. COLE & R. A. LAWRIE), Butterworth, London, p. 471.

PATTERSON, R. L. S. (1968a) *J. Sci. Fd. Agric.* **19**, 31.

PATTERSON, R. L. S. (1968b) *J. Sci. Fd. Agric.* **19**, 434.

PATTERSON, R. L. S. (1975) In *Meat* (Eds. D. J. A. COLE & R. A. LAWRIE), Butterworth, London, p. 359.

PATTERSON, R. L. S. and MOTTRAM, D. S. (1974) *J. Sci. Fd. Agric.* **25**, 1419.

PATTERSON, R. L. S. and STENSON, C. G. (1971) *Proc. 17th Meeting Meat Res. Inst.* Bristol, p. 148.

PAUL, P. and BRATZLER, L. J. (1955) *Food Res.* **20**, 626.

PAUL, M. H. and SPERLING, E. (1951) unpublished observations, cited by D. E. GREEN (1951) *Biol. Rev.* **26**, 445.

PAUL, M. H. and SPERLING, E. (1952) *Proc. Soc. exp. Biol. Med.* **79**, 352.

PAUL, P. C. (1975) In *Meat* (Eds. D. J. A. COLE & R. A. LAWRIE), Butterworth, London, p. 403.

PAVEY, R. L. (1972) *Contract 17–70–C–001*, U.S. Army, Nattick.

PEARSE, A. S. (1939) *Animal Ecology*, 2nd ed., McGraw-Hill, New York.

PEARSON, A. M., HARRINGTON, G., WEST, R. G. and SPOONER, M. (1962) *J. Food Sci.* **27**, 177.

PEARSON, A. M., WEST, R. G. and LEUCKE, R. W. (1959) *Food Res.* **24**, 515.

PEARSON, R. T., DUFF, I. D., DERBYSHIRE, W. and BLANSHARD, J. M. V. (1974) *Biochim. biophys. Acta* **362**, 188.

PENNY, I. F. (1960a) *Food Process. Packag.* **29**, 363.

PENNY, I. F. (1960b) *Chem. Ind.* **11**, 288.

PENNY, I. F. (1967) *Biochem. J.* **104**, 609.

PENNY, I. F. (1968) *J. Sci. Fd. Agric.* **19**, 578.

PENNY, I. F. (1969) *J. Fd. Technol.* **4**, 269.

PENNY, I. F. (1972) *J. Sci. Fd. Agric.* **23**, 403.

PENNY, I. F. (1974) *J. Sci. Fd. Agric.* **25**, 1273.

PENNY, I. F. (1977) *J. Sci. Fd. Agric.* **28**, 329.

PENNY, I. F. and DRANSFIELD, E. (1979) *Meat Sci. 3*. In press.

PENNY, I. F. and FERGUSON-PRICE, R. (1979) *Meat Sci. 3*. In press.

PENNY, I. F. and LAWRIE, R. A. (1964) unpublished data.

PENNY, I. F., VOYLE, C. A. and DRANSFIELD, E. (1974) *J. Sci. Fd. Agric.* **25**, 703.

PENNY, I. F., VOYLE, C. A. and LAWRIE, R. A. (1963) *J. Sci. Fd. Agric.* **14**, 535.

PENNY, I. F., VOYLE, C. A. and LAWRIE, R. A. (1964) *J. Sci. Fd. Agric.* **15**, 559.

PERIGO, J. A., WHITING, E. and BOSHFORD, T. E. (1967) *J. Fd. Technol.* **2**, 377.

PERNOTTY, J. M. (1963) *Nature, Lond.* **200**, 86.

PERRIÉ, W. T. and PERRY, S. V. (1970) *Biochem. J.* **119**, 31.

PERRON, R. B. and WRIGHT, B. A. (1950) *Nature, Lond.* **166**, 863.

PERRSON, T. and VAN SYDOW, E. (1974) *J. Fd. Sci.* **39**, 406.

PERRY, S. V. (1974) *Biochem. Soc. Sympos.* **39**, 115.

PERRY, S. V., COLE, H. A., MORGAN, M., MOIR, A. J. G. and PIRES, E. (1975) *Abs. 9th Febs, Meet* **31**, 163.

PERRY, T. W., BEESON, W. M., ANDREWS, F. N. and STOTS, M. (1955) *J. Anim. Sci.* **14**, 329.

PERUTZ, M. F. (1962) *Proteins and Nucleic Acids: Structure and Function*, Elsevier, London.

PERYAM, D. R. (1958) *Food Tech.* **12**, 231.

PETERS, R. A. (1957) *Adv. Enzymol.* **18**, 113.

PETERSEN, A. C. and GUNDERSON, N. F. (1960) *Food Tech.* **14**, 413.

PHILLIPS, G. O. (1954) *Nature, Lond.* **172**, 1044.

PICKEN, L. (1960) *The Organization of Cells*, Clarendon Press, Oxford.

PIEZ, K. A. (1965) *Biochemistry*, N.Y. **4**, 2590.

PIEZ, K. A. (1968) *Ann. Rev. Biochem.* **26**, 305.

POMEROY, R. W. (1941) *J. agric. Sci.* **31**, 50.

POMEROY, R. W. (1960) *J. agric. Sci.* **54**, 57.

POMEROY, R. W. (1971) *Ann. Rept. A.R.C. Meat Res. Inst., 1970–71*, p. 26.

POMEROY, R. W. and WILLIAMS, D. (1962) *Anim.Prod.* **4**, 302.

PORTER, K. (1961) The Sarcoplasmic Reticulum, Supplement, *J. biophys. biochem. Cyt.* **10**, 219, Rockefeller Inst. Press, New York.

PORZIO, M. A., PEARSON, A. M. and CORNFORTH, D. P. (1979) *Meat Sci. 3*. In press.

PRATER, A. R. and COOTE, G. G. (1962) *C.S.I.R.O. Div. Food Pres. Tech. Paper*, No. 28.

PRATT, G. B. and EKLUND, O. F. (1954) *Quick Frozen Foods* **16**, 50.

PRESTON, T. R. (1962) *Antibiotics in Agriculture* (Ed. M. WOODBINE), p. 214, Butterworths, London.

PRESTON, T. R., WHITELAW, F. G., AITKEN, J. N., McDIARMID, A. and CHARLESTON, E. B. (1963) *Anim. Prod.* **5**, 47.

PUTNAM, F. W. (1953) *The Proteins,* vol. 1, Part B (Eds. H. NEURATH and K. BAILEY), p. 808, Academic Press, New York.

RADOUCO-THOMAS, C., LATASTE-DOROLLE, C., ZENDER, R., BUSSET, R., MEYER, H. M. and MOUTON, R. F. (1959) *Food Res.* **24**, 453.

RALSTON, A. T. and DYER, I. A. (1959) *J. Anim. Sci.* **18**, 1181.

RANDALL, C. J. and BRATZLER, L. J. (1970) *J. Fd. Sci.* **35**, 245, 248.

RANDALL, C. J. and MACRAE, H. F. (1967) *J. Fd. Sci.,* **32**, 182.

RANGELEY, W. R. and LAWRIE, R. A. (1976) *J. Fd. Technol.* **11**, 143.

RANGELEY, W. R. D. and LAWRIE, R. A. (1977) *J. Fd. Sci. Technol.* **12**, 9.

RAMSBOTTOM, J. M. (1971) In *The Science of Meat and Meat Products* (2nd Ed.), (Eds. J. F. PRICE & B. S. SCHWEIGERT), W. H. FREEMAN, San Francisco, p. 513.

RAMSBOTTOM, J. M. and KOONZ, G. H. (1939) *Food Res.* **4**, 425.

RAMSBOTTOM, J. M. and STRANDINE, E. J. (1948) *Food Res.* **13**, 315.

RAMSBOTTOM, J. M. and STRANDINE, E. J. (1949) *J. Anim. Sci.* **8**, 398.

RAYMOND, J. M., STRANDINE, E. J. and KOONZ, G. H. (1945) *Food Res.* **10**, 497.

RAYMOND, J. (1929) *The Frozen and Chilled Meat Trade,* vol. 2, p. 28, Gresham Publishing Co., London.

REED, R., HOUSTON, T. W. and TODD, P. M. (1966) *Nature, Lond.* **211**, 534.

REGIER, L. W. and TAPPEL, A. L. (1956) *Food Res.* **21**, 630.

RESSLER, C. (1962) *J. biol. Chem.* **237**, 733.

RHODES, D. N. (1966) *J. Sci. Fd. Agric.* **17**, 180.

RHODES, D. N. (1972) *J. Sci. Fd. Agric.* **23**, 1483.

RHODES, D. N. and DRANSFIELD, E. (1973) *J. Sci. Fd. Agric.* **24**, 1583.

RHODES, D. N. and DRANSFIELD, E. (1974) *J. Sci. Fd. Agric.* **25**, 1163.

RHODES, D. N. and SHEPHERD, H. J. (1966) *J. Sci. Fd. Agric.* **17**, 287.

RICE, E. E. and BEUK, J. F. (1953) *Adv. Food. Res.* **4**, 233.

RICE, E. E., BEUK, J. F., KAUFFMAN, F. L., SCHULTZ, H. W. and ROBINSON, H. E. (1944) *Foods Res.* **9**, 491.

RICHARDSON, W. D. and SCHERUBEL, E. (1909) *J. ind. eng. Chem.* **1**, 95.

RICKENBACKER, J. R. (1959) *Farmers Cooperative Services,* U.S. Dept. Agric. Service Dept., No. 42.

RICKERT, J., BRESSLER, L., BALL, C. O. and STIER, E. F. (1957) *Food Tech.* **11**, 625.

RITCHEY, S. J., COVER, S. and HOSTETLER, R. L. (1963) *Food Tech.* **17**, 76.

ROBERTS, P. C. B. and LAWRIE, R. A. (1974) *J. Fd. Technol.* **9**, 345.

ROBERTS, T. A. (1971) *Ann. Rept. Meat Res. Inst., Bristol,* p. 42.

ROBERTS, T. A. and INGRAM, M. (1976) *Proc. 2nd. intl. Sympos. Nitrite Meat Prod.,* Zeist, p. 29, Pudoc, Wageningen.

ROBERTS, W. K. and SELL, J. L. (1963) *J. Anim. Sci.* **22**, 1081.

ROBERTSON, J. D. (1957) *J. Physiol.* **140**, 58.

ROBINS, S. P. and BAILEY, A. J. (1972) *Biochem. biophys. Res. Commun.* **48**, 76.

ROBINS, S. P., SHIMOKOMAKI, M. and BAILEY, A. J. (1973) *Biochem. J.* **131**, 771.

ROBINSON, D. (1939) *Science* **90**, 276.

ROBINSON, M. E. (1924) *Biochem. J.* **18**, 255.

ROBINSON, R. H. M., INGRAM, M., CASE, R. A. M. and BENSTEAD, J. G. (1953) *Spec. Rept. Fd. Invest. Bd., Lond.,* No. 59.

ROBINSON, T. J. (1951) *J. agric Sci* **41,** 16.

ROBSON, R. M., GOLL, D. E. ARAKAWA, N. and STROMER, M. M. (1970) *Biochim. biophys. Acta* **200,** 296.

ROBSON, R. M., TUBATABAI, L. B., DAYTON, W. R., ZEECE, M. G., GOLL, D. E. and STROMER, M. H. 1974) *Proc. 27th Ann. Recip. Meat Conf.* (Nat. Livestock & Meat Bd.: Chicago), p. 199.

ROJERS, P. J. (1969) *Proc. 22nd Ann. Recip. Meat Confce., Pomona, Calif.,* p. 166.

ROLFE, E. J. (1958) *Fundamental Aspects of the Dehydration of Foodstuffs,* p. 211, Society of Chemical Industry, London.

ROMANUL, F. C. A. (1964) *Nature, Lond,* **201,** 307.

ROMANUL, F. C. A. and VAN DER MEULEN, J. P. (1967) *Acta neurol.* **17,** 387.

RONGEY, E. H., KAHLENBERG, O. J. and NAUMANN, H. D. (1959) *Food Tech.* **13,** 640.

RONZONI, E., WALD, S. M., BERG, L. and RAMSEY, R. (1958) *Neurology* **8,** 359.

ROSS COCKRILL, W. (1975) In *Meat* (Eds. D. J. A. COLE & R. A. LAWRIE), Butterworth, London, p. 507.

ROWE, R. W. D. (1974) *J. Fd. Technol.* **9,** 501.

RUBASHKINA, S. S. (1953) *Coll. Works All-Union Res. Inst. Meat Industry, U.S.S.R.* **5,** 91.

RUBENSTEIN, H. S. and SOLOMON, M. L. (1941) *Endocrin.* **28,** 229.

RUMEN, N. M. (1959) *Acta chem. scand.* **13,** 1542.

RUSSELL, F. C. and DUNCAN, D. L. (1956) *Minerals in Pasture: Deficiencies and Excess in Relation to Animal Health,* 2nd ed., Commonwealth Bureau of Animal Nutrition. Tech. Comm., No. 15, Commonwealth Agricultural Bureaux, Slough.

SAFFLE, R. L. and BRATZLER, L. J. (1959) *Food Tech.* **13,** 236.

SAIR, L. and COOK, W. H. (1938) *Can. J. Res.* **D 16,** 255.

SAIR, R. A., LISTER, D., MOODY, W. G., CASSENS, R. G., HOEKSTRA, W. G. and BRISKEY, E. J. (1970) *Amer. J. Physiol.* **218,** 108.

SANDERSON, M. and VAIL, G. E. (1963) *J. Food Sci.* **28,** 590.

SANGER, F. (1945) *Biochem. J.* **39,** 507.

SATORIOUS, M. J. and CHILD, A. M. (1938) *Food Res.* **3,** 619.

SAVAGE, W. G. (1918) *J. Hyg. Camb.* **17,** 34.

SAVARY, P. and DESNUELLE, P. (1959) *Biochim. biophys. Acta* **31,** 26.

SAVELL, J. W., DUTSON, T., CARPENTER, Z. L. and HOSTETLER, R. L. (1977). *J. Fd. Sci.,* In press.

SAVIC, I. and KARAN-DJURDJIC, S. (1958) *Proc. 4th Meeting European Meat Res. Workers, Cambridge,* Paper No. 36.

SAVIC, I. and SUVAKOV, M. (1963) *Proc. 9th Meeting European Meat Res. Workers, Budapest,* Paper No. 49.

SAYRE, R. N., BRISKEY, E. J. and HOEKSTRA, W. G. (1963a) *Proc. Soc. exp. Biol. Med.* **122,** 223.

SAYRE, R. N., BRISKEY, E. J. and HOEKSTRA, W. G. (1963b) *J. Food sci.* **28,** 292.

SAYRE, R. N. BRISKEY, E. J. and HOEKSTRA, W. G. (1963c) *J. Anim. Sci.,* **22,** 1012.

SAYRE, R. N., KIERNAT, B. and BRISKEY, E. J. (1964) *J. Food Sci.* **29,** 175.

SCARBOROUGH, D. A. and WATTS, B. M. (1949) *Food Tech.* **3**, 152.

SCHAUB, M. C. and PERRY, S. V. (1969) *Biochem. J.* **115**, 993.

SCHAUB, M. C., PERRY, S. V. and HÄCKER, W. (1972) *Biochem. J.* **126**, 237.

SCHILLER, S. P. (1966) *Ann. Rev. Physiol.* **28**, 137.

SCHMIDT, C. F. (1961) *Rept. Europ. Meeting. Microbiol. Irrad. Foods,* Append. II, F.A.O., Rome.

SCHMIDT, C. F., LECHOWICH, R. V. and FOLINAZZO, J. F. (1961) *J. Food Sci.* **26**, 626.

SCHMIDT, G. R. and GILBERT, K. V. (1970) *J. Fd. Technol.* **5**, 331.

SCHMIDT, G. R., GILBERT, K. V., DAVEY, C. L., NOTTINGHAM, P. M. and DE LAMBERT, M. (1970) *Ann. Rept. Meat Ind. Res. Inst.,* No. 2, p. 28.

SCHMIDT, G. R., ZUIDAN, L. and SYBESMA, W. (1971) in *2nd Symposium Condition and Meat Quality in Pigs* (Animal Res. Inst.: Zeist), p. 245.

SCHOENHEIMER, R. (1942) *The Dynamic State of Body Constituents,* Harvard Univ. Press, Cambridge, Mass.

SCHÖN, L. and STOSIEK, M. (1958a) *Fleischwirts.* **10**, 550.

SCHÖN, L. and STOSIEK, M. (1958b) *Fleischwirts.* **10**, 769.

SCHWARTZ, K. (1962) *Vits. Hormones* **20**, 463.

SCHWEIGERT, B. S. (1959) *Int. J. appl. Radn. Isotopes* **6**, 76.

SCHWEIGERT, B. S., MCINTIRE, J. M. and ELVEHJEM, C. A. (1944) *J. Nutr.* **27**, 419.

SCHWEIGERT, B. S. and PAYNE, B. J. (1956) *Amer. Meat Inst. Bull.* No. 30.

SCOPES, R. K. (1964) *Biochem. J.* **91**, 201.

SCOPES, R. K. (1966) *Biochem. J.* **98**, 193.

SCOPES, R. K. (1970) in *The Physiology and Biochemistry of Muscle as a Food,* vol. II, p. 471 (Eds. E. J. BRISKEY, R. G. CASSENS and B. B. MARSH), Univ. Wisconsin Press: Madison.

SCOPES, R. K. (1974) *Biochem. J.* **142**, 79.

SCOPES, R. K. and LAWRIE, R. A. (1963) *Nature, Lond.* **197**, 1202.

SCOPES, R. K. and NEWBOLD, R. P. (1968) *Biochem. J.* **109**, 197.

SCOTT, W. J. (1936) *J. Coun. Sci. Ind. Res. Aust.* **9**, 177.

SCOTT, W. J. (1953) *Aust. J. biol. Sci.* **6**, 549.

SCOTT, W. J. (1957) *Adv. Food Res.* **7**, 84.

SCOTT, W. J. and VICKERY, J. R. (1939) *C.S.I.R.O. Bull.,* No. 129.

SEARCY, D. J., HARRISON, D. L. and ANDERSON, L. L. (1969) *J. Food Sci.* **34**, 486.

SEAWARD, M. R. D., CROSS, T. and UNSWORTH, B. A. (1976) *Nature, Lond.* **261**, 407.

SEIFTER, S. and GALLOP, P. M. (1966) In *The Proteins: Composition, Structure and Function* (2nd Ed.), (Ed. H. Neurath), Acad. Press, New York, p. 155.

SELF, H. L. (1957) *Proc. 9th Res. Conf., Amer. Meat Inst. Found.,* p. 53.

SELYE, H. (1936) *Nature, Lond.* **138**, 32.

SELYE, H. (1944) *Canad. Med. Ass. J.* **50**, 426.

SELYE, H. (1946) *J. clin. Endocrin.* **6**, 117.

SELYE, H. (1950) *The Physiology and Pathology of Exposure to Stress,* Acta Inc., Montreal.

SHACKLADY, C. A. (1970) in *Proteins as Human Food,* p. 317 (Ed. R. A. LAWRIE), Butterworths, London.

SHARP, J. G. (1953) *Spec. Rept. Fd. Invest. Bd., Lond.,* No. 57.

SHARP J. G. (1957) *J. Sci. Fd. Agric.* **8**, 14, 21.

SHARP, J. G. (1958) *Ann. Rept. Fd. Invest. Bd., Lond.,* p. 7.

SHARP, J. G. (1959) *Proc. 5th Meeting European Meat Res. Workers, Paris,* Paper No. 17.

SHARP, J. G. (1963) *J. Sci. Fd. Agric.* 14, 468

SHARP, J. G. (1964) *Proc. 1st Intl. Congr. Food Sci. Tech., Lond.*

SHARP, J. G. and MARSH, B. B. (1953) *Spec. Rept. Fd. Invest. Bd., Lond.,* No. 58.

SHARP, J. G. and ROLFE, E. J, (1958) *Fundamental Aspects of the Dehydration of Foodstuffs,* p. 197, Society of Chemical Industry, London.

SHAW, C., STITT, J. M. and COWAN, S. T. (1951) *J. gen. Physiol.* 5, 1010.

SHAW, F. D. (1973) *Meat Res. in C.S.I.R.O.* p. 16.

SHAW, F. D., HARRIS, P. V., BOUTON, P. E., WEST, R. R. and TURNER, R. H. (1976) *Meat Res. in C.S.I.R.O.,* p. 7.

SHAW, M. G. (1977) *J. med. Microbiol.* 10, 29.

SHAW, M. K. (1963) *9th Meeting European Meat Res. Workers, Budapest,* Paper No. 61.

SHAY, B. J. and EGAN, A. F. (1976) *Meat Res. in C.S.I.R.O.,* p. 29.

SHEA, K. G. (1958) *Food Tech.* 12, 6.

SHERMAN, J. D. and DAMESHEK, W. (1963) *Nature, Lond.* 197, 469.

SHERMAN, P. (1961) *Food Tech.* 15, 79.

SHERMAN, W. C., HALE, W. H., REYNOLDS, W. M. and LUTHER, H. G. (1957) *J. Anim. Sci.* 16, 1020.

SHERMAN, W. C., HALE, W. H., REYNOLDS, W. M. and LUTHER, H. G. (1959) *J. Anim. Sci.* 18, 198.

SHESTAKOV, S. D. (1962) *Proc. 8th European Meeting Res. Workers, Moscow,* Paper No. 18.

SHIKAMA, K. (1963) *Sci. Rept. Tohoku Univ.* 22, 91.

SHIMOKOMAKI, M., ELSDEN, D. F. and BAILEY, A. J. (1972) *J. Fd. Sci.* 37, 892.

SHORLAND, F. B. (1953) *J. Sci. Fd. Agric.* 4, 497.

SHORTHOSE, W. R., HARRIS, P. V. and BOUTON, P. E. (1972) *Proc. Soc. Anim. Prod.* 9, 387.

SHRIMPTON, D. H. and BARNES, E. M. (1960) *Chem. Ind.* 1492.

SIEMERS, L. L. and HANNING, F. (1953) *Food. Res.* 18, 113.

SIMONE, H., CARROLL, F. and CHICHESTER, C. O. (1959) *Food Tech.* 13, 337.

SINGH, O. H., HENNEMAN, H. A. and REINEKE, E. P. (1956) *J. Anim. Sci.* 15, 624.

SISSONS, S. and GROSSMAN, J. D. (1953) *The Anatomy of Domestic Animals,* Saunders, London.

SJOSTRÖN, L. B. (1963) *Food Tech.* 17, 266.

SLIWINSKI, R. A., MARGOLIS, R., PIH, K. LANDMANN, W. A. and DOTY, D. M. (1961) *Amer. Meat Inst. Found. Bull.,* No. 45.

SMITH, A. U. (1958) *Biol. Rev.* 33, 197.

SMITH D. S. (1966) *Prog. Biophys. molec. Biol.* 16, 107.

SMITH, E. C. (1929) *Proc. Roy. Soc.* **B** 105, 198.

SMITH, E. L., PARKER, L. F. J. and FANTES, K. H. (1948) *Biochem. J.* 43, proc. xxx.

SMITH, G. C., PIKE, M. I. and CARPENTER, Z. L. (1974) *J. Fd. Sci.* 39, 1145.

SMITH, M. G. (1973) *Meat Res. in C.S.I.R.O.,* p, 21.

SMITH, M. G. and GRAHAM, A. (1978) *Meat Sci.* 2 (In press).

SMORODINTZEV, I. A. (1934) *Z. Lebensmitt. Untersuch.* 67, 429.

SNOKE, J. E. and NEURATH, H. (1950) *J. biol. Chem.* 187, 527.

SNOWDEN, L. McK. and WEIDEMANN, J. F. (1978) *Meat Sci.* **2,** 1.

SOLOV'EV, V. I. (1952) *Myasnaya Industriya, U.S.S.R.* **23,** 43.

SOLOV'EV, V. I. and KARPA, I. N. (1967) *Proc. 13th Meeting European Meat Res. Workers, Rotterdam.* Paper No. D 11.

SOMLYO, A. P., DEVINE, C. E., SOMLYO, A. V. and NORTH, R. V. (1973) *Proc. Roy. Soc.* **B, 262,** 333.

SPENCER, R. (1971) *Proc. 17th Meeting Europ. Meat Res. Inst.,* Bristol, p. 161.

SPERRING, D. D., PLATT, W. T. and HINER, R. L. (1959) *Food Tech.* **13,** 155.

SRÉTER, F. A. (1964) *Fed. Proc.* **23,** 930.

STEINBERG, M. P., WINTER, J. D. and HUSTRALID, A. (1949) *Food Tech.* **3,** 367.

STENBOCK-FERMOR, COUNT (1915) *Anthr.* **26,** 298.

STOLL, N. R. (1947) *J. Parasit.* **33,** 1.

STONE, N. and MEISTER, A. (1962) *Nature, Lond.* **194,** 555.

STRANDBERG, K., PARRISH, F. C., GOLL. D. E. and JOSEPHSON, S. A. (1973) *J. Fd. Sci.* **38,** 69.

STRAUB, F. B. (1942) *Stud. Inst. med. chem. Univ. Szeged* **2,** 3.

STRENSTRÖM, W. and LOHMANN, A. (1928) *J. biol. Chem.* **79,** 673.

STROTHER, J. W. (1975) In *Meat* (Eds. D. J. A. COLE & R. A. LAWRIE), Butterworth, London, p. 183.

SULZBACHER, W. L. (1952) *Food Tech.* **6,** 341.

SULZBACHER, W. L. and GADDIS, A. M. (1968) in *The Freezing Preservation of Foods,* 4th ed., vol. 2, 159, AVI: Westpoint, Conn.

SULZBACHER, W. L. and McLEAN, R. A. (1951) *Food Tech. Champaign.* **5,** 7.

SUTHERLAND, E. W. and ROBINSON, G. A. (1966) *Pharmacol. Rev.* **18** (1), 145.

SVEDBERG, T. and BROHULT, S. (1939) *Nature, Lond.* **143,** 938.

SWIFT, C. E. and SULZBACHER, W. L. (1963) *Food Tech.* **17,** 106.

SWINGLER, G. R., NEALE, R. J. and LAWRIE, R. A. (1978) *Meat Sci.* **2,** 31.

SZENT-GYÖRGI, A. G. (1953) *Arch. Biochem.* **60,** 180.

TALLON, H. H., MOORE, S. and STEIN, W. H. (1954) *J. biol. Chem.* **211,** 927.

TAMM, W. (1930) *Z. ges. Kält.,* Beih. R. 3, H. 4, cited by J. KUPRIANOFF (1956).

TANNER, F. B. (1944) *The Microbiology of Foods,* 2nd ed., Garrard Press, Champaign, III.

TAPPEL, A. L. (1952) *Food Res.* **17,** 550.

TAPPEL, A. L. (1956) *Food Res.* **21,** 195.

TAPPEL, A. L. (1957a) *Food Res.* **22,** 408.

TAPPEL, A. L. (1957b) *Food Res.* **22,** 404.

TAPPEL, A. L., ZALKIN, H., CALDWELL, K. A., DESAI, I. D. and SHIBKO, S. (1962) *Arch. Biochem. Biophys.* **96,** 340.

TARLADGIS, B. G. (1962) *J. Sci. Fd. Agric.* **13,** 481.

TARR, H. L. A., SOUTHCOTT, B. H. and BISSETT, H. M. (1952) *Food tech.* **6,** 363.

TAUSIG, F. and DRAKE, M. P. (1959) *Food Res.* **24,** 224.

TAYLER, C. R. (1968) *Nature, Lond.* **219,** 181.

TAYLER, C. R. (1969) *Sci. Amer.* **220,** 86.

TAYLER, E. L. and PARFITT, J. W. (1959) *Intl. J. appl. Radn. Isotopes* **6,** 194.

TAYLOR, A. A. (1971) *Proc. 17th Meeting European Meat Res. Workers, Bristol,* p. 662.

TAYLOR, A. A. and DANT, S. J. (1971) *J. Food Technol,* **6,** 131.

TAYLOR, A. McM. (1958) *Food Manuf.* **33,** 286.

TAYLOR, A McM (1963) *Inst, Meat Bull.,* July, p. 4.

TERRELL, R. N., SUESS, G. G. and BRAY, R. W. (1969) *J. Anim. Sci.* **28,** 449, 454.

THEORELL, H. (1932) *Biochem. Z.* **252,** 1.

THOMAS, J., ELSDEN, D. J. and PARTRIDGE, S. M. (1963) *Nature, Lond.* **200,** 651.

THOMAS, L. (1956) *J. exp. Med.* **104,** 245.

THOMPSON, J. S., FOX, J. B., JR. and LANDMANN, W. A. (1962) *Food Tech.* **16,** 131.

THORNLEY, M. J. (1963) *J. appl. Bact.* **26,** 334.

THORNLEY, M. J., INGRAM, M. and BARNES, E. M. (1960) *J. appl. Bact.* **23,** 487.

THORNTON, H. (1949) *Textbook of Meat Inspection,* Baillière, Tindall & Cox, London.

THORNTON, R. A. and ROSS, D. J. (1959) *N.Z.J. agric. Res.* **2,** 1002.

TILGNER, D. J. (1958) *Fleischwirts.* **8,** 741.

TILGNER, D. J., MILER, K., PROMINSKI, J. and DARNOWSKI, G. (1962) *Tech. mesa. Beograd,* Paper No. 1, 12.

TISCHER, R. G., HURWICZ, H. and ZOELLNER, J. A. (1953) *Food Res.* **18,** 539.

TOLMACHOFF, I. P. (1929) *Trans. Amer. phil. Soc.* **23,** Part 1.

TOMBS, M. P. (1972) *British Patent* **1,** 265, 661.

TOPEL, D. G. (1969) in *Points of View on the Condition and Meat Quality of Pigs for Slaughter,* p. 91 (Eds. W. SYBESMA, P. G. VAN DER WALS and P. WALSTRON), Res. Inst. Animal Husbandry, Zeist.

TOPEL, D. G., MARKEL, R. A. and WISMER-PEDERSEN, J. (1967) *J. Anim. Sci.* **26,** 311.

TOWER, S. S. (1937) *J. comp. Neurol.* **67,** 241.

TOWER, S. S. (1939) *Physiol. Rev.* **19,** 1.

TOWNSEND, W. E. and BRATZLER, L. J. (1958) *Food Tech.* **12,** 663.

TOWNSEND, W. E., WITANAEUR, L. P., RELOFF, J. A. and SWIFT, C. E. (1968) *Food Tech. Champaign,* **22,** 71.

TRESSLER, D. K., BIRSEYE, C. and MURRAY, W. T. (1932) *Ind. Eng. Chem.* **24,** 242.

TRESSLER, D. K. and EVERS, C. F. (1947) *The Freezing Preservation of Foods,* AVI Publishing Co., New York.

TULLOH, N. M. (1964) *Aust. J. agric. Res.* **15,** 333.

TULLOH, N. M. and ROMBERG, B. (1963) *Nature, Lond.* **200,** 438.

TUMA, H. L., HENRICKSON, R. L., STEPHENS, D. F. and MOORE, R. (1962) *J. Anim. Sci.* **21,** 848.

TURKKI, P. R. and CAMPBELL, A. M. (1967) *J. Food. Sci.* **32,** 151.

TURMAN, E. J. and ANDREWS, F. N. (1955) *J. Anim. Sci.* **14,** 7.

TVERAAEN, T. (1935) *Hvalràd Skr.* No. 11, p. 5.

UDENFRIEND, S., SHORE, P. A., BOGDANSKI, D. F., WASSBACH, H. and BRODIE, B. B. (1957) *Rec. Prgr. Hormone Res.* **13,** 1.

UMENO, S. and NOBATA, R. (1938) *J. Jap. Soc. vet. Sci.* **17,** 87.

URBAIN, W. M. and JENSEN L. B. (1940) *Food Res.* **5,** 593.

URBIN. M. C. and WILSON, G. D. (1958) *Proc. 10th Res. Conf., Amer. Meat Inst. Found.,* p. 13.

URBIN, M. C., ZESSIN, D. A. and WILSON, G. D. (1962) *J. Anim. Sci.* **21,** 9.

416   *Bibliography*

VALIN, C. (1968) *J. Fd. Technol.* **3**, 171.
VALIN, C. (1970) *Ann. Biol. Anim. Bioch. Biophys.* **10**, 317.
VALLYATHAN, N. V., GRINYAR, I. and GEORGE, J. C. (1970) *Can. J. Zool.* **48**, 377.
VANICHENI, S., HAUGHHEY, D. P. and NOTTINGHAM, P. M. (1972) *J. Fd. Technol.* **7**, 259.
VENUGOPAL, B. and BAILEY, M. E. (1978) *Meat Sci.* **2**, 227.
VERATTI, E. (1902) *Mem. reale Inst. Lombardo* **19**, 87.
VETTERLAIN, R. and KIDNAY, A. J, (1965) *Proc. 11th Meeting Meat Res. Workers, Belgrade.*
VICKERY, J. R. (1932) *Spec. Rept. Fd. Invest. Bd., Lond.* No. 42.
VICKERY, J. R. (1953) *J. Aust. Inst. agric. Sci.* **19**, 222.
VICKERY, J. R. (1968) *Meat Ind. Bull., Aust.* Jan., p. 31.
VICKERY, J. R. (1977) *C.S.I.R.O. Div. Fd. Res. Tech. Pap. No. 42.*
VIGNOS, P. J. and LEFKOWITZ, M. (1959) *J. clin. Invest.* **38**, 873.
VILLEE, C. A. (1960) *Developing Cell Systems and their Control* (Ed. D. RUDNICK), p. 93, Ronald Press, New York.
VOLEKNER, H. H. and CASSON, J. L. (1951) *J. Anim. Sci.* **10**, 1065.
VOLODKEVITCH, N. N. (1938) *Food Res.* 3, 221.
VOYLE, C. A. (1969) *J. Fd. Technol.* **4**, 275.
VOYLE, C. A. and LAWRIE, R. A. (1964) *J. Roy. microsc. Soc.* **81**, 173.

WAHLROOS, Ö. and NIINIVAARA, F. P. (1969) *Proc. 15th Meeting European Meat Res. Workers, Helsinki,* p. 226.
WALLACE, L. R. (1945) *J. Physiol.* **104**, 33.
WALLACE, L, R. (1948) *J. agric. Sci.* **38**, 93.
WALLS, E. W. (1960) *The Structure and Function of Muscle* (Ed. G. H. BOURNE), vol. 1, p. 21, Academic Press, New York.
WALTERS, C. L. (1973) *Proc. Inst. Fd. Sci. Technol.* **6**, 106.
WALTERS, C. L., CASSELDEN, R. J. and TAYLOR, A. McM. (1967) *Biochim. biophys. Acta* **143**, 310.
WALTERS, C. L. and TAYLOR, A. McM. (1963) *Food Tech.* **17**, 119.
WALTERS, C. L. and TAYLOR, A. McM. (1964) *Biochim. biophys. Acta* **86**, 448.
WALTERS, C. L. and TAYLOR, A. McM. (1965) *Biochim. biophys. Acta* **96**, 522.
WANG, H., ANDREWS, F., RASCH, E., DOTY, D. M. and KRAYBILL, H. R. (1953) *Food Res.* **18**, 351.
WANG, H., AUERBACH, E., BATES, V., ANDREWS, F., DOTY, D. M. and KRAYBILL, H. R. (1954a) *Food Res.* **19**, 154.
WANG, H., AUERBACH, E., BATES, V., ANDREWS, F., DOTY, D. M. and KRAYBILL, H. R. (1954b) *Food Res.* **19**, 543.
WANG, H., DOTY, D. M., BEARD, F. J., PIERCE, J. C. and HANKINS, O. G. (1956) *J. Anim. Sci.* **15**, 97.
WANG, H. and MAYNARD, N. (1955) *Food Res.* **20**, 587.
WANG, H., WEIR, C. E., BIRKNER, M. and GINGER, B. (1957) *Proc. 9th Res. Conf., Amer. Meat Inst. Found.,* p. 65.
WANG, H., WEIR, C. E., BIRKNER, M. and GINGER, B. (1958) *Food Res.* **23**, 423.

WARNER, K. F. (1928) *Proc. Amer. Soc. Anim. Prod.*, p. 114.

WARREN, S. (1943) *Arch. Path.* **35**, 347.

WARRINGTON, R. (1974) *Vet Bull.* **44**, 617.

WASSERMAN, A. E. (1966) *J. Food Sci.* **31**, 1005.

WASSERMAN, A. and SPINELLI, A. M. (1972) *J. agric. Food Chem.* **20**, 171.

WATSON, J. D. and CRICK, F. H. C (1953) *Nature, Lond.* **171**, 737, 964.

WATTS, B. M. (1954) *Adv. Food Res.* **5**, 1.

WATTS, B. M., KENDRICK, J., ZIPSTER, M., HUTCHINS, B. and SALEH, (1966) *J. Food. Sci.* **31**, 855.

WATTS, B. M. and LEHMANN, B. T. (1952a) *Food Res.* **17**, 100.

WATTS, B. M. and LEHMANN, B. T. (1952b) *Food Tech.* **6**, 194.

WEBER, A., HERZ, R. and REISS, I. (1963) *J. gen. Physiol.* **46**, 679.

WEBER, H. H. and MEYER, K. (1933) *Biochem. Z.* **266**, 137.

WEBSTER, A. J. F. (1974) In *Heat Loss from Animals and Man* (Eds. J. L. MONTEITH & L. E. MOUNT), p. 205, Butterworth, London.

WEBSTER, A. J. F. (1976) In *Principles of Cattle Production* (Eds. H. SWAN & W. H. BROSTER), p. 103, Butterworth, London.

WEBSTER, A. J. F. and YOUNG, B. A. (1970) *Univ. Alberta Feeders Day Rept. No. 49*, p. 34, Univ. Alberta, Edmonton.

WEBSTER, H. L. (1953) *Nature, Lond.* **172**, 453.

WEINSTOCK, I. M., GOLDRICH, A. D. and MILHORAT, A. T. (1956) *Proc. Soc. exp. Biol. Med.* **91**, 302.

WEIR, C. E. (1960) *The Science of Meat and Meat Products* (Ed. Amer. Meat Inst. Found.), p. 212, Reinhold Publishing Co., New York.

WEISER, H. H., KUNKLE, L. E. and DEATHERAGE, F. E. (1954) *Appl. Microbiol.* **2**, 88.

WEISS, J. (1952) *Nature, Lond.* **169**, 460.

WEISS, J. (1953) *Ciba Found. Colloq. Endocrin.* **7**, 142.

WEST, R. G., PEARSON, A. M. and McARDLE, F. J. (1961) *J. Food Sci.* **26**, 79.

WEST, W. T. and MASON, K. E. (1958) *Amer. J. Anat.* **102**, 323.

WHITEHAIR, L. A., BRAY, R. W., WECKEL, K. G., EVANS, G. W. and HEILIGMAN, F. (1964) *Food Tech.* **18**, 114.

WHITEHEAD, W. L., GOODMAN, C. and BREGER, I. A. (1951) *J. Chim. Phys.* **48**, 184.

WHITEHOUSE, M. W. and LASH, J. W. (1961) *Nature, Lond.* **189**, 37.

WHITMANN, H. G. (1961) *Proc. 5th Intl. Congr. Biochem., Moscow*, Symp. No. 1, Pergamon Press, Oxford.

WIDDOWSON, E. M. (1970) in *The Physiology and Biochemistry of Muscle as a Food*, vol. II, p. 511 (Eds. E. J. BRISKEY, R. G. CASSENS and B. B. MARSH), Univ. Wisconsin Press, Madison.

WIDDOWSON, E. M., DICKERSON, J. W. T. and McCANCE, R. A. (1960) *Brit. J. Nutr.* **14**, 457.

WIERBICKI, E. and DEATHERAGE, F. E. (1958) *J. Agric. Food Chem.* **6**, 387.

WIERBICKI, E., KUNKLE, L. E., CAHILL, V. R. and DEATHERAGE, F. E. (1954) *Food Tech.* **8**, 506.

WIERBICKI, E., KUNKLE, L. E., CAHILL, V. R. and DEATHERAGE, F. E. (1956) *Food. Tech.* **10**, 80.

WIERBICKI, E., TIEDE, M. G. and BURRELL, R. C. (1963) *Fleischwirts.* **15,** 404.
WILDE, W. S. and SHEPPARD, C. W. (1955) *Proc. Soc. exp. Biol. Med.* **88,** 249.
WILEY, H. (1908) *U.S. Dept. Agric., Washington, D.C., Bur. Chem. Bull.,* No. 84.
WILKINSON, J. M., PERRY, S. V., COLE, H. A. and TRAYER, I. P. (1972) *Biochem. J.* **127,** 215.
WILLIAMS, B. E. (1964a) Canad. Pat. No. 683,929.
WILLIAMS, B. E. (1964b) U.S. Pat. No. 3, 128,191.
WILLIAMS, E. J. (1968) in *Quality Control in the Food Industry,* vol. II, p. 252 (Ed. S. M. HERSCHDOERFER), Acad. Press, London.
WILLIAMS, J. D., ANSELL, B. M., REIFFEL, L. and KARK, R. M. (1957) *Lancet* **ii,** 464.
WILLIAMS, R. J. (1956) *Biochemical Individuality,* John Wiley, New York.
WILSON, G. D. (1960) *The Science of Meat and Meat Products* (Ed. Amer. Meat Inst. Found.) pp. 328, 349, Reinhold Publishing Co., New York.
WILSON, G. D. (1961) *Proc. 13th Res. Conf., Amer. Meat Inst. Found. Chicago,* p. 113.
WILSON, G. D., BRAY, R. W. and PHILLIPS, P. H. (1954) *J. Anim. Sci.* **13,** 826.
WILSON, G. D., BROWN, P. D., CHESBRO, W. R., GINGER, B. and WEIR, C. E. (1960) *Food Tech.* **14,** 143, 186.
WILSON, G. S. and MILES, A. A. (1955) *Topley and Wilson's Principles of Bacteriology and Immunity,* 4th ed., vol. 1, p. 977, Edward Arnold, London.
WINDRUM, G. M., KENT, P. W. and EASTOE, J. E. (1955) *Brit. J. exp. Path.* **36,** 49.
WINEGARDEN, M. E., LOWE, B., KASTELLIC, J., KLINE, E. A., PLAGGE, A. R. and SHEARER, P. S. (1952) *Food Res.* **17,** 172.
WINKLER, C. A. (1939) *Canad. J. Res.* **D. 17,** 8.
WISMER-PEDERSEN, J. (1959a) *Food Res.* **24,** 711.
WISMER-PEDERSEN, J. (1959b) *Acta agric. scand.* **9,** 69, 91.
WISMER-PEDERSEN, J. (1960) *Food Res.* **25,** 789.
WISMER-PEDERSEN, J. (1969a), *Proc. 15th Meeting Meat Res. Workers, Helsinki,* p. 454.
WISMER-PEDERSEN, J. (1969b) in *Recent Points of View on the Condition and Meat Quality of Pigs for Slaughter* (Eds. W. SYBESMA, P. G. VAN DER WALS and P. WALSTRON), Res. Inst. Animal Husbandry, Zeist.
WISTREICH, H. E., MORSE, R. E. and KENYON, L. J. (1959) *Food Tech.* **13,** 441.
WOESSNER, J. F., Jr. and BREWER, T. H. (1963) *Biochem. J.* **89,** 75.
WOOD, J. D., GREGORY, N. G., HALL, G. M. and LISTER, D. (1977) *Brit. J. Nutr.* **37,** 167.
WOOD, T. and BENDER, A. E. (1957) *Biochem. J.* **57,** 366.
WOOD, J. D. and LISTER, D. (1973) *J. Sci. Fd. Agric.* **24,** 1449.
WOOD, J. M. and EVANS, G. G. (1973) *Proc. Inst. Fd. Sci. Technol.* **6,** 111.
WRENSHALL, C. L. (1959) *Antibiotics: their Chemistry and Non-medical Uses* (Ed. H. S. GOLDBERG), p. 549, D. van Nostrand, New York.
WRIGHT, N. C. (1954) *Progress in the Physiology of Farm Animals* (Ed. J. HAMMOND), vol. 1, p. 191, Butterworths, London.
WRIGHT, N. C. (1960) *Hunger: Can it be averted?* (Ed. E. J. RUSSELL and N. C. WRIGHT), p. 1, Brit. Ass. Adv. Sci., London.
WRIGHT, R. H., HUGHES, J. R. and HENDRIX, D. E. (1967) *Nature, Lond.* **216,** 404.
WYCKOFF, R. W. G. (1930a) *J. exp. Med.* **51,** 921.
WYCKOFF, R. W. G. (1930b) *J. exp. Med.* **52,** 435.

YEATES, N. T. M. (1949) *J. agric. Sci.* **39**, 1.
YESAIR, J. (1930) *Canning Tr.* **52**, 112.
YOSHIDA, T. and KAGEYAMA, H. (1956) Jap. Pat. No. 732
YOUNATHAN, M. T. and WATTS, B. M. (1960) *Food Res.* **25**, 538.
YOUNG, R. H. and LAWRIE, R. A. (1974) *J. Fd. Technol.* **9**, 69.
YOUNG, R. H. and LAWRIE, R. A. (1975) *J. Fd. Technol.* **10**, 453.
YUDKIN, J. (1964) *Proc. Nutr. Soc.* **23**, 149.
YUDKIN, J. (1967) *Am. J. clin. Bact.* **20**, 108.
YUEH, M. H. and STRONG, F. M. (1960) *J. Agric. Food Chem.* **8**, 491.

ZAKULA, R. (1969) *Proc. 15th Meeting European Meat Res. Workers, Helsinki,* p. 157.
ZEBE, E. (1961) *Ergeb. Biol.* **24**, 247.
ZENDER, R., LATASTE-DOROLLE, C., COLLET, R. A., ROWINSKI, P. and MOUTON, R. F. (1958) *Food Res.* **23**, 305.
ZENKER, F. A. (1860) *Virchows Arch. path. Anat.* **18**, 561.
ZEUNER, F. E. (1963) *A History of Domesticated Animals,* Hutchinson, London.
ZIEMBA, Z. and MÄLKKI, Y. (1969) *Proc. 15th Meeting Meat Res. Workers, Helsinki,* p. 461.
ZINNERMANN, B. K., TIMPL. R., and KUHN, Z. (1973) *Eur. J. Biochem.* **35**, 216.

INDEX